YAZOO

SOUTHERN CLASSICS SERIES

John G. Sproat, General Editor

YAZOO;

OR,

ON THE PICKET LINE OF FREEDOM IN THE SOUTH

A PERSONAL NARRATIVE

Albert T. Morgan

with a new introduction by Joseph Logsdon

University of South Carolina Press
Published in cooperation with the Institute for
Southern Studies and the South Caroliniana Society
of the University of South Carolina.

© 2000 University of South Carolina

Published in Columbia, South Carolina, by the
University of South Carolina Press

Manufactured in the United States of America

04   03   02   01   00   5   4   3   2   1

Library of Congress Cataloging-in-Publication Data

Morgan, A. T. (Albert Talmon)
    Yazoo, or, On the picket line of freedom in the South : a
personal narrative/Albert T. Morgan ; with a new introduction
by Joseph Logsdon.
        p.   cm.—(Southern classics series)
    "Published in cooperation with the Institute for Southern
Studies and the South Caroliniana Society of the University of
South Carolina."
    Includes bibliographical references (p.).
    ISBN 1–57003–359–5 (pbk. : alk. paper)
    1. Reconstruction—Mississippi.   2. Mississippi—Social
conditions.   3. Mississippi—Politics and government—
1865–1950.   4. Yazoo County (Miss.)—Social conditions.
5. Yazoo County (Miss.)—Politics and government.
6. Freedmen—Mississippi—Yazoo County—Social conditions.
7. Yazoo County (Miss.)—Race relations.   8. Morgan, A.T.
(Albert Talmon)   9. Politicians—Mississippi—Yazoo County—
Biography.   I. Title: On the picket line of freedom in the
South.   II. University of South Carolina. Institute for
Southern Studies.   III. South Caroliniana Society.   IV. Title.
V. Series.
F341 .M84   2000
976.2'49—dc21   00–033790

CONTENTS

*Roman-numeral chapter headings skip from XL to L in the original
edition; original headings are retained in the Southern Classics
edition.

ILLUSTRATIONS

GENERAL EDITOR'S PREFACE

Yazoo is grass-roots history at its best. Few accounts of Reconstruction match it as a firsthand record of the trials and tribulations the freedmen faced in interacting with their former masters. It is also the absorbing story of one man's work on behalf of simple justice, made all the more poignant by a new and appreciative introductory essay. The book revives the reputation of Albert T. Morgan as a pioneer in the struggle to achieve racial harmony; the essay is a testament to the late Joe Logsdon's dedication as a historian and human being to the same goal.

Southern Classics returns to general circulation books of importance dealing with the history and culture of the American South. Sponsored by the Institute for Southern Studies and the South Caroliniana Society of the University of South Carolina, the series is advised by a board of distinguished scholars who suggest titles and editors of individual volumes to the general editor and help establish priorities in publication.

Chronological age alone does not determine a title's designation as a Southern Classic. The criteria also include significance in contributing to a broad understanding of the region, timeliness in relation to events and moments of peculiar interest to the American South, usefulness in the classroom, and suitability for inclusion in personal and institutional collections on the region.

JOHN G. SPROAT
General Editor

INTRODUCTION

The world moves, though Yazoo may remain a
dead sea. History has changed the meaning of
fame. Formerly it was a report, now it is a
judgment.

Albert T. Morgan, *Yazoo; or, On
the Picket Line of Freedom in the South*

In 1884, Albert T. Morgan, a disillusioned, almost anony-
mous pension clerk, wrote those words.[1] They probably
had little meaning in his own time, penned as they were
at the end of a self-published book whose subject the
nation's leaders had long since chosen to forget. The last
chapter ended with a forthright defense of his 1870 interracial marriage in Yazoo County, Mississippi—almost a
disjointed afterword, for the author did not write his
lengthy account to justify that marriage. Rather, he
wished to carve an epitaph for the defenders of democracy who lay buried in the graveyards of Yazoo County.
But his marriage, as well as the outlook that led to it—
and, to be sure, from it—separated him from most Americans not only of his day but of many years afterward. He
knew it. He realized that he could speak only to some
generation yet unborn.

Albert Talmon Morgan was a carpetbagger—or so his
critics and most American historians once labeled him.
But he was also a man before his time, sublimely confident that he was right, and he left us with an account

that has stood the test of time. Most accounts of Reconstruction in Mississippi to that time had justified Morgan's enemies, virtually ignoring his memoirs and paying scant attention to a rejoinder by John R. Lynch, one of Morgan's black compatriots in that state. More recent scholars, paying fresh attention to the Reconstruction years, have affirmed both Lynch's 1913 memoirs, *Facts of Reconstruction,* and Morgan's earlier account.[2]

It is easy to see why. Morgan's memoirs, it is now clear, provide a rare glimpse of Reconstruction at the grassroots level. Few black Southerners or their radical white allies left behind detailed accounts of their struggles in the South during that era. Fewer still left any personal records that spanned the full decade of postwar turmoil. And none spoke with such candor about interracial sex, perhaps the touchstone of American racist behavior, in that era as in our own. As a detailed account of local politics, especially within a black belt county of the deep South during Reconstruction, *Yazoo; or, On the Picket Line of Freedom* is without peer in historical literature.

Although Morgan participated in statewide politics as a prominent Republican leader, first as a delegate to the constitutional convention of 1868 and later as a member of the Mississippi Senate, he decided to relate little of those activities or of the leading statewide figures he came to know, such as J. L. Alcorn, Blanche K. Bruce, James Z. George, Adelbert Ames, John R. Lynch, or L. Q. C. Lamar. Instead he provided a sustained, revealing narrative about the social and political dynamics of Reconstruction on the plantations, in the local courthouse, out on the deserted roads and byways, and even in the bedrooms of leading planters and politicians. He concentrated on events in Yazoo, a black belt county far away from Washington, D.C., isolated even from the state capital and generally unreported in the legislative journals and major daily newspapers of the time. He did not focus on the formula-

tion of legislation or policy but rather revealed their imple-
mentation and the resistance they provoked in the local
arena of nineteenth-century life. Although his memoirs
are partisan observations, they provide as well unusual
insight into the Reconstruction story.

In some respects, Morgan had much in common with
his white contemporaries who, like him, cast their lot in
the post–Civil War South. He had served courageously in
the war as a Union officer. He was ambitious—on the
make, actually. And he reflected the abolitionist influence
and egalitarian mind-set of the Republican Midwest,
especially in the areas of New England settlement. But
in other respects, Morgan stood apart from his peers by
virtue of his 1870 marriage to a radical, self-willed,
northern black schoolteacher named Carolyn Victoria
Highgate, with whom he raised several children in Mississippi during Reconstruction.[3] Coming at the height of
his political activities, the marriage forced him to raise
questions and seek answers as few other Americans did
in that era.

Where did such a man come from, and what forces in
his time produced such an outlook? He was born in Wisconsin in 1842 to parents who had migrated to Wisconsin
from New York in 1845. Both parents, George and
Eleanor Morgan, had been born in New Hampshire and
raised their children as devout Baptists and abolitionists.
As a sign of that training, both Albert and his older
brother had enrolled at Oberlin College, a hotbed of abolitionism, before the outbreak of the Civil War. Composed
of twelve children, the family lived on a modest farm and
helped run a mercantile business near Fox Lake. All of
the children attended the local public schools. The parents also practiced what they preached. During the Civil
War, they joined a Freedmen's Aid Society to raise funds
for the general welfare and education of slaves emancipated by the Union army.[4]

XX   INTRODUCTION

Morgan and his older brother, Charles, came to Mississippi for economic rather than political reasons, investing their hard-earned family capital in rebuilding the war-torn economy of the state. If anything, his parents discouraged them from going south and recommended that their sons emulate their own westward trek for opportunity and social mobility. But the young men's experience during the war as Union soldiers had given them a glimpse of the fertile lands of the American South and the greater potential for economic success. With this pattern, they followed in the path of many other Union veterans who tried to become farmers and planters in the great Mississippi Valley. In fact, by 1867, more than a dozen other Union veterans had joined them in Yazoo County.[5] Not by their own choosing, they eventually became deeply involved in Reconstruction politics.

Morgan described his experience as being "on the picket line of freedom in the South"—in part a soldier's phrase about the outposts of an army near the enemy's lines, but more fully the phrase of a severely wounded veteran of Gettysburg and other campaigns who embraced the ultimate implications of what the Civil War meant to those it had freed from chattel slavery. The line he chose to defend cut across what he called "the old stubble ground of slavery." Morgan wrote to explain the difficulties that he and his compatriots faced in Mississippi and why they failed. Racial prejudice obviously was at the core of their failure. But Morgan learned to probe more than the obvious. His own profound experience made him dismiss the usual excuses or explanations for the failure of Reconstruction—corruption, high taxes, Republican vindictiveness—especially as they applied to the place where he had cast his lot. In Yazoo County and Mississippi generally, there had been little corruption, no dramatic rise in taxation, no vengeful violence by former slaves, and virtually no exclusion of native whites from political life and influence. Yet his adopted county and state witnessed some of the most reactionary violence of the era. Indeed, Yazoo was where former slaveholders initiated the outrageous terror of the Mississippi Plan, testing the will of the nation to defend the Constitution and finding it wanting.

Why, then, did the experiment in interracial democracy fail? Morgan zeroed in on the activities of the slaveholding elite of Mississippi and particularly Yazoo County. This was the group that orchestrated the reaction. Whereas they manipulated the racial prejudice of others, they, Morgan learned, were not especially prejudiced against color. Their appreciation for beautiful black women could be seen on the faces of the racially mixed population. They could cooperate politically with black men, even proud, angry black men, when such tactics served their purposes. What Morgan found was an elite single-mindedly motivated by rational self-interest, especially in terms of their own power, the maintenance of which, they believed, depended ultimately on supporting "the superiority of all white men at whatever cost."[6]

A glance at Yazoo County as it was before the war sustains Morgan's description and helps explain both his eventual defeat and the downfall of interracial democracy after 1865.

I

Antebellum Yazoo County engulfed a marvelously fertile cotton-producing basin that made it one of the most dynamic centers of the Old South on the eve of the Civil War. It was one of Mississippi's largest and wealthiest counties. Lying in the rich bottom lands of the Yazoo River, it had experienced extremely rapid expansion in the decade before the Civil War. It rose from the eighteenth-largest county of the state in 1850 to eighth place, with 22,373 inhabitants, in 1860. That year, it had more farm acreage and of greater total value than any county in the state and outstripped all others in Mississippi's chief product: King Cotton. From the tiny settlement at Yazoo City, the county's only urban community, more than 64,000 bales wended down the Yazoo River to Vicksburg, on to New Orleans, and ultimately to the textile mills of the world.[7]

Large feudal racial baronies dominated Yazoo plantation society. In 1860, almost three-fourths of its population, precisely 16,716 African Americans, were slaves. Only four other counties in the state contained more humans in bondage. In fact, every black person in the county was enslaved; not a single one of Mississippi's meager and declining free black population (733 people, the lowest in the South) lived in Yazoo. At the other end of the spectrum, those who controlled the mass of these African American slaves came from a small proportion of the white families in the county. Less than 40 percent of the adult white men were slaveholders, or just 10 percent of the total adult male population. And among these slaveholders, a mere one-third—13 percent of adult white men or just 3 percent of the total adult male population—controlled 60 percent of the total population under a harsh system of chattel slavery. Probably few communities in history ever witnessed such oligarchic and despotic control.[8]

The distribution of slaves closely paralleled the distribution of wealth in real estate. Not a single black man owned property, and more than half of the white adult men were likewise propertyless. Together, these propertyless men constituted 87 percent of the adult male population.[9] Indeed, the elite who owned most of the land and slaves did not exceed 15 percent of the adult white male population, a proportion that shrinks to a mere 5 percent if slaves are included in the total adult male population.[10]

Despite such elite control of wealth, most white residents were directly involved in the exploitation of slave labor. Of the 1,611 white men over 20, more than half (845) were either slaveholders or overseers. This proportion would be even higher if slave renters and the older sons of slaveholders and overseers could be accurately factored into the adult male population directly involved in the operations of slavery. Only 315 white men listed in the census as laborers can be safely excluded from those directly involved in the exploitation of black labor, and they usually held temporary, plantation-related jobs. Some worked directly on the plantations in various skilled and unskilled positions, and others lived in Yazoo City, which served primarily as a depot for the incoming and outgoing goods of the surrounding plantations. Even in this small community (940 whites; 525 blacks), more than 90 of its 340 white adult men were either slaveholders or overseers.[11]

The economic dominance of the large slaveholding elite (those with twenty or more slaves) clearly translated into local political power. Their power, moreover, survived the sweeping democratic reforms that Mississippi leaders instituted in their state constitution of 1832. The reforms, predominantly universal manhood suffrage, ushered in an apparent democratic order only for the whites who made up one-quarter of the Yazoo population in 1860. Had Jacksonian democracy been extended to the underlying black population at that time, the complexion of the antebellum electorate in both Yazoo County and the state as a whole would have been dramatically different, as Figure 1 shows. In less than a decade, such a revolution would take place in Mississippi.[12]

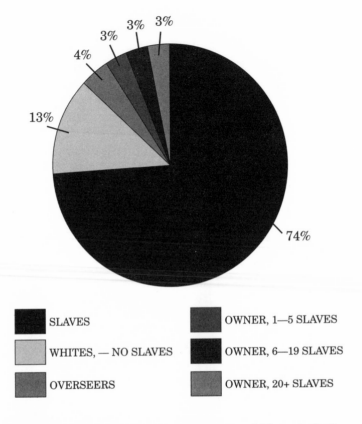

Fig. 1 What the Yazoo County electorate would have looked like in 1860 had Jacksonian Democracy been color-blind

Theoretically, after 1832, Yazoo's small cadre of large slaveholders should no longer have been able to dominate the county's politics. Among other reforms, the new state constitution counted only the white population in establishing electoral districts. More important, it removed property or educational qualifications for voting or office-holding. Such a rule augured considerable impact because more than half of the adult white men in Mississippi were both illiterate and propertyless. Henceforth, almost every important public office, including all judicial positions, would be chosen by ballot.[13]

The Mississippi Constitution of 1832 also thoroughly reorganized local government, reducing the control of the justice of peace, an office inherited from old colonial patterns on the southern seaboard. In the reorganized framework, four judicial bodies made decisions within the counties: the circuit court, the probate court, the board of police, and the justices of the peace. The circuit court had jurisdiction over several counties but held regular sessions in each. One judge handled all cases for his multicounty district with a clerk assigned to record the deliberation and decisions in each county. Both posts were filled by election for four-year terms. This court had jurisdiction over all but civil cases worth less than fifty dollars. Those minor cases were all that remained under the jurisdiction of the justices of the peace, the number of which varied within each county. Yazoo had ten. Each justice had a constable to carry out his orders. Both the justice and the constable were elected for two-year terms. The probate court had jurisdiction within the county over all matters of wills, the protection of minors' legal rights, and all persons mentally incapable of taking care of their legal affairs. A judge and a clerk, each elected for two years, handled this court's affairs.

Clearly the most important body within each county was the board of police, which consisted of five members elected for two-year terms. This body directed the building and maintenance of roads, bridges, and ferries within the county; set local taxes; issued licenses for businesses; supervised the care of funds for education and the infirm poor; controlled local elections; established slave patrols; and reserved broad police powers over affairs within the county. It also nominated twenty property owners for the grand jury, fifteen of whom were chosen by the circuit court, to determine all indictments within the county. The clerk of the probate court took charge of the police board's records.

To carry out the orders of the board of police, the constitution established several county executive offices: a sheriff, a tax collector, an assessor, a coroner, a county treasurer, a surveyor, and a ranger. All were elected for two-year terms. The sheriff was the key officer of local government, enforcing all the enactments of the local judicial bodies and the state legislature. He could also be—and usually was—the tax collector. The latter office provided his chief source of income, primarily a guaranteed percentage of all state and local taxes, in addition to the fees for various other duties of his office that were regulated by law.

The assessor determined the valuation of all property for tax purposes and drew up a list of all freeholders, from which jurors were selected. His salary was a flat 5 percent of all taxes collected. The coroner checked the cause of all undetermined deaths in the county and filled any vacancy in the office of the sheriff until a special election could be called by the board of police. The treasurer supervised the collection and disbursement of all county funds, receiving as his salary 3 percent of fees of moneys collected. The surveyor, for a stipulated schedule of fees, made all legal measurements of property, while the ranger took charge of all stray animals and livestock within the county.

In addition, the county staff included various appointed officials, such as deputy sheriffs and assessors, as well as commissioners of the infirm poor and of public education, plus a host of temporary clerks at election time. The only other elected officials in the county filled the several posts in the municipal government of Yazoo City, which had very limited jurisdiction and authority.[14]

Although approximately thirty elected officials served county government, primary political power and responsibility rested in the hands of the board of police and the sheriff who carried out its orders, and both institutions remained firmly in the hands of Yazoo's political elite. The Jacksonian constitutional reforms of 1832 had little impact on the hold that this tiny group maintained on local political power. It is important to remember also that the authority of the large slaveholders over the mass of the population remained personal and private, outside the channels of local government. Slaveholders held almost absolute control over their slaves, for only the most serious of crimes brought slaves into local courts. This state of private law certainly reduced the costs of local government, but it also compounded the tyranny and autocracy in Yazoo County.

Although smaller slaveholders almost always held the minor elected offices, these men could carry out their duties only with the sanctions of the board of police. Indeed, they could not even assume their posts without the approval of the largest local property owners. Each elected official had to secure a sizable bond before taking office to ensure good behavior. These bonds varied from $20,000 for the sheriff (plus a sum double the amount of the preceding year's taxes if he served in the dual capacity of tax collector) to $500 for the lowly ranger. By law, persons failing to obtain the necessary bond before taking the oath of office had to vacate the position. If at any time during their tenure the sureties wished to withdraw the bond, officeholders had to find new financial backers or step down from office. Stiff state fines penalized anyone who tried to hold office without an adequate bond. Bonding may well have been designed to ensure honest handling of public funds, but it also served to place officeholders, especially key county officials, at the will of their wealthy sponsors.[15]

Several police board members served consecutive terms, but partisanship apparently caused frequent changes. These turnovers, however, had little effect on the economic status of the thirteen men who served on the board of police from 1853 to 1861. All were slaveholders, with average holdings of more than 40 slaves, ranging from a low of 10 to a high of 131. The value of their real estate averaged $33,894, from a low of $4,260 to a high of $80,000. The total of their property holdings, primarily slaves and land, averaged $84,724, from a low of $22,191 to a high of $201,110. There were a few wealthier men in the county, to be sure, but not many. All but two members of the board of police belonged to the elite class that comprised the top 10 percent of the white adult men.[16]

The decisions of these men showed little benevolence for the black or white poor. Public services were minimal. Yazoo authorities never levied taxes for local schools, which the state constitution had made the sole jurisdiction of the counties. Only the federally mandated income from certain public lands found its way to education, but even most of those funds ended up squandered or diverted to private purposes. Most schools were private academies for the county's elite. Justice and relief of the infirm poor also remained the prerogative of the ruling oligarchy. The board of police set expenditures for these purposes and selected the men who supervised their operation. Almost all of the commissioners for education and the poor, as well as the grand jurors who brought all criminal indictments inside the county, were men in the image of the members of the board of police. No black residents, of course, and few if any but wealthy white gentry filled those posts.[17]

This pattern of tight-fisted oligarchy did not show any change until the Civil War dislocated normal affairs. As that crisis approached in Yazoo County, the leaders opened a vigorous debate about their response. The record shows no fundamental debate about slavery or the political framework of the county. Instead, its leaders argued over the best strategy to protect the institution of slavery on which their social status and political power depended.

In the antebellum period, Yazoo had been one of Mississippi's Whig strongholds. Its presidential nod had gone to the nominee of the Whig Party or its successor American (Know-Nothing) Party in every election since 1840 except one, in 1852. In 1860, the white leadership was sharply divided and aroused. More than 90 percent of the eligible electorate turned out to cast 739 votes for John Bell (a former Whig) and 688 for the Democrat, John C. Breckinridge. A token four votes went to the only Northerner on the Mississippi ballot, Stephen A. Douglas. If black men could have voted, Lincoln surely would have been the resounding victor in Mississippi and particularly in Yazoo, but the Republican won nary a vote in the state. After the shock of Lincoln's national success, Yazoo's leaders sent their largest slaveholder, Henry Vaughn, to the secessionist convention of 1861. G. B. Wilkinson, another large slaveholder and a lawyer, accompanied him. Both voted against all delay or compromise measures and finally declared their county for secession.[18]

II

Local government in Yazoo County maintained surprising continuity during the Civil War. All eleven members of the board of police who served during the war were slaveholders. Only one broke the pattern of unusually great wealth. Serving three consecutive terms, he was an older man, in his sixties, born in Pennsylvania. His presence made a noticeable but not startling alteration in the averages of wealth and slaveholding for the wartime membership of the board.[19] Because large slaveholders held the other four positions on the board, their hegemony continued.

The slight decline in slaveholding averages for the two wartime boards elected in 1862 and 1864 had little to do with the changing whims or ideology of the voters, because at least three members left public service for the officer corps of the Confederate army. Their places were taken by men who were too old to fight and were also, as it happened, smaller slaveholders. The wealth of these replacements lowered the averages of land and slaveholding on the wartime boards. [20]

That any slaveholders remained to serve in local government is the more remarkable, because an amazing proportion of Yazoo's white male adults entered the army, especially after the conscription acts of 1862. If one former officer's figures are correct (and Morgan's estimate affirms that judgment), a staggering 85 to 90 percent of the eligible white men listed in the 1860 census served in the war.[21]

If the war had little impact on the power structure of Yazoo County, it nonetheless changed the agenda and activities of local government. The board of police quickly responded to the mobilization of military forces, providing $200 to the county's first volunteer company, which was raised by S. M. Phillips and stationed at the critical coastal defenses of Pensacola, Florida. The board refused to take the rasher action advocated by more zealous citizens who petitioned it to turn all its funds over to the county's volunteers. But the board raised its bounty to

$300 per company and, in July 1861, appropriated a much larger sum of $3,000 to supply the county's five companies with winter clothing, indicating its recognition of a protracted struggle. By the end of November, almost $5,000 had been allocated for military expenditures.[22]

Wartime pressures also led the local authorities to clamp down even more tightly on the black masses of the county. In 1861, a sweeping set of orders reorganized and strengthened the normal system of slave patrols. The Mississippi legislature gave counties a free hand to deal with any subversives, especially free black residents. The county boards could either issue special permits for free black Mississippians to remain in their locales or, after March 1861, arbitrarily sell them into slavery. Yazoo did not have to face the dilemma because it had no free black residents. Ironically, the Civil War brought the county its first free black person, when a Confederate officer who was also a large slaveholder obtained passage of a special state statute that permitted him to manumit his valet, David Woolridge ("Cottonridge" in Morgan's narrative) for "fidelity" and "gallantry" in the first battle at Bull Run. Despite the absence of a so-called free black problem, the board demonstrated its fear as well as its willingness to use the harsh state laws when it seized a free black outsider, Joe Coleman, and sold him into slavery. This hysteria manifested itself again in July 1861, when eighty-five property owners in one county district petitioned the board to supply them with double-barreled shotguns so that they could protect themselves against "insurrection or invasion by enemies within or without." The board turned down that request but then issued an order for a hasty canvass of available guns in the county. It also helped raise detachments of older men and younger boys to assist regular army companies stationed in the area to guard against internal threats.[23]

The chief financial burden for the county's government was not for armament but for social welfare, the largest appropriation of which was for dependents of Confederate soldiers. For this purpose, the board had to double taxes. Only an appropriation at the end of 1861 by the state legislature saved the board from collecting its own tax. The board quickly selected a five-man commission of large slaveholders to dispense the state welfare fund. Within the next five months, the new commissioners distributed almost $6,000 to destitute families of volunteers. The next three months required $5,000 more. By October 1862, the board of police had to restore its original tax hike to make up for the swelling demands that state funds could not meet. County expenditures for this purpose continued until the spring of 1863 at the rate of more than $1,000 a month. It is easy to see why taxes mushroomed during the war to levels well beyond the antebellum period or the succeeding reconstruction years.[24]

Military hostilities did not interrupt local government in Mississippi until the spring of 1863, when a flotilla of ironclads moved up the Yazoo River as part of the overall Union force tightening its grip on the Confederate stronghold at Vicksburg. A committee of local civilian officials negotiated with Union officers for protection of property and gained permission to continue their own police force in Yazoo City. Not until July 1863 was real damage done, when a more powerful armada moved up the river after the fall of Vicksburg and retreating Confederate forces destroyed a fleet of twenty-three private steamboats worth more than $800,000 to keep them from falling into enemy hands. When Confederates also torpedoed a Union ironclad, the invaders seized 2,000 bales of cotton and 800 head of mules, demolished a small ship yard, and took 300 prisoners before they pulled back to the Mississippi River. Only occasional Union gunboat forays for cotton followed this major expedition until the spring of 1864, when Federal armies left the county and surrounding region in the wake of the Union army's final campaigns against the Atlantic coastal fortresses of the Confederate government.[25]

During the year of military operations in the area, from May 1863 to May 1864, local government ceased to operate regularly in Yazoo County. Few officials apparently resigned their posts or fled far from the area. Elections in the fall of 1862 ensured continuity of elected leaders from January 1863 to January 1865. The office-holders simply drew back into the vacuum left by the withdrawal of Union armies. Draft exemptions for local officials had apparently secured a reliable cadre during the war. They carefully guarded and maintained local records. As soon as Federal forces threatened the area, the board of police ordered the sheriff to secret those records away. The board's foresight proved wise, because a company of Union soldiers burned down the county courthouse in May 1864, just before the general evacuation.[26]

If the year-long military rampage failed to disrupt the structure and workings of Yazoo's local government, the incursion of Union troops thoroughly shattered social and economic life in the county. Two planting seasons were lost, and the black laboring force was scattered. Planters forced part of the servile population to accompany them into the relative safety of the Alabama black belt near Selma; Confederate military commanders conscripted a second portion as a labor force for their armies; and a third part fled to Union lines to join the Union army, scout for the invaders, or work lands for Northern lessees along the safer confines of the Mississippi River, which was still patrolled by Union gunboats.[27]

In the summer of 1864, the former rulers of Yazoo County began to reassemble the pieces of their shattered domain. Poor whites were among the first to feel the brunt of the oligarchs' restored authority. Elected in 1861 as Circuit Judge for Yazoo and neighboring counties, Robert S. Hudson took charge. Angered by the "filthy, base, disloyal, deserting, stealing, murdering population" that had left the hill country of central Mississippi to raise crops on the abandoned river bottoms, he had at least ten men arrested and four executed for "treason and other crimes." In some neighboring counties of his circuit, Hudson complained that armed "deserters" ran candidates for police boards in the fall elections of 1864. But no such threat apparently faced the resolute rulers of Yazoo. Three prewar slaveholders were restored to power on the Yazoo board. Although meetings were irregular, the board managed to pay outstanding bills and salaries, authorize road repairs, collect old taxes, set new rates for 1864, rent temporary county offices, appoint grand jurors and commissioners, bring its old records out of hiding, and still show a treasury balance of more than $10,000. By war's end in April 1865, it was fully reorganized and meeting regularly. Returning federal commanders, however, had different ideas. They disbanded the state legislature on May 18 and, four days later, seized state records. A tiny garrison of black troops in Yazoo City ensured that county officials also ceased operations.[28]

III

The interruption of local government at the end of the war was brief and incomplete. The oldest form of local Mississippi authority remained, as justices of the peace continued to wield power and planters ran their plantations virtually unchecked. Within a month of the disbandment of the legislature, moreover, President Andrew Johnson made William Sharkey provisional governor of Mississippi, and Sharkey in turn issued a proclamation on July 1 restoring all county officials who had been hold-

ing office on May 22. He also directed the sheriffs to hold
elections of delegates to a state constitutional convention
on August 14. He simply made the former Confederate
authorities take the President's generous amnesty oath
pledging future loyalty to the Union.[29]

The mind and attitude of Yazoo's leaders were probably well represented by their delegates, both former Whig
slaveholding lawyers: J. H. Wilson and Robert S. Hudson, the latter the county's stern Civil War circuit judge.
They voted as a unit in the touchy debates that followed
in the constitutional convention. Although both claimed
to have been hesitant about secession, neither showed
any moderation in planning the restoration of state
authority and postwar policy. Wilson seldom spoke out
during the deliberations, but Hudson led the convention's
recalcitrant rebel forces.

Constantly voted down by the majority of delegates
and slapped back in debate by leaders who had already
visited with Andrew Johnson, Hudson was adamant
about maintaining the old order. He asked for a committee to petition the President to release from prison both
Jefferson Davis and Charles E. Clark, Mississippi's
wartime governor. On the matter of meeting Andrew
Johnson's demand that the state constitutional convention decree the end of slavery, Hudson voted with a stubborn minority of delegates who insisted that Lincoln's
Emancipation Proclamation lacked legal effect and that
the abolition clause then being inserted into their state
constitution had resulted from force alone. Hudson also
introduced the most popular of the recalcitrants'
motions—a declaration abolishing slavery in Mississippi,
conditioned by a proviso insisting that such action would
not rule out federal compensation and that Congress
should admit the state's representatives to its next session and allow the state complete autonomy in restoring
local government.

Hudson was particularly insistent about the immediate restoration of local government. He pointed to a case of the federal army's interference with the provisional authorities in Yazoo County and pleaded with his fellow delegates not to leave even a temporary vacuum of power at the county level to tempt the occupying military authorities to assert their power over civilians. To achieve that end, Hudson proposed that the convention call for no new elections for either state judicial positions or any local offices but rather confirm the men already chosen for those posts during the fall of 1864, the last months of the Confederacy. When a more cautious delegate pointed out that even Sharkey's temporary reinstatement of those officials had brought severe criticism in the North, Hudson exploded: "It is not a political question; it is one that certainly does not concern the North." Hudson's reactionary stance may not have dominated the outcome of the more moderate convention majority, but his zealousness and gadfly influence eventually gave the body a frightful reputation in the eyes of Northern public opinion. Before the conclusion of the convention's deliberations, he managed to extract authority from the convention managers that eventually jeopardized Andrew Johnson's more cautious policy to restore home rule and white supremacy. Indeed, it was the rashness of bitter-enders like Hudson that helped mobilize opposition among Northern Republicans.

Hudson had earlier demonstrated his heavy hand in restoring "order" in Yazoo County during the last months of the war. He urged the convention now to follow his example by giving county authorities temporary power to hang anyone for "grand larceny, robbery, rape, arson, and burglary" until the new legislature assembled. Cooler heads again prevailed. But apparently to mollify the recalcitrant forces that had won few victories in the convention, the managers appointed Hudson to fill a vacancy on a committee that the convention had charged to make special recommendations to the next legislature to regulate black Mississippians. That appointment may have been the chief slip by the convention's careful managers.[30]

Hudson won election to chair the important committee. Its recommendations, reported to the legislature in October, clearly reflected his reactionary vision of social order. Embarrassed moderates published the introduction to his report but refused to publish the text of his recommendations. Instead, the legislative leaders sent his work to a special joint committee to finish the task of shaping the legal status of the state's black residents. To steel the resolve of the legislators against expected criticism of their work, Hudson's printed peroration once again flouted Northern opinion, insisting that "while some of the proposed legislation may seem rigid and stringent to the sickly humanitarians, they can never disturb, retard or embarrass the good and true, useful and faithful of either race. . . ." Unhappy Mississippians, black or white, were advised to leave the state.[31]

The judge had no reason to worry about the legislature's resolve. However much it may have modified Hudson's recommendations, it enacted one of the most severe Black Codes produced by any of the provisional legislatures called into session during the fall of 1865 at the conclusion of the various state constitutional conventions. The Mississippi code prohibited its black citizens from owning farmland or guns, renting land, or testifying in court against whites. To force African Americans to labor for white planters, the legislature placed so-called black minors under the control of their former owners and compelled every adult to sign a contract for employment. Had Yazoo's leadership had its way, all of Mississippi's black residents would have been made the legal wards of agents selected for them by the local police boards. Although worried moderates in the legislature defeated that measure, the final version of the Black

Code was harsh enough to anger moderate Northern observers into issuing calls for the President to either halt or seriously alter his plans for Reconstruction.

Hudson's outlook undoubtedly reflected his experience and personal interests in Yazoo County. In fact, he made his state of mind clear in a letter to President Andrew Johnson, in which he pictured the freed slaves of Yazoo "in idleness and utter demoralization." If allowed any freedom, he asserted, black laborers would run off to Freedmen's Bureau agents who had been stationed in Mississippi to assist the freed population in their adjustments to free labor and civil society. In truth, Hudson admitted that the Freedmen's Bureau agents seldom interfered and usually sent the black laborers back to their former plantations with little redress, but the flights, he complained, disrupted planters' routines and caused inefficiencies on the plantations. He added that he was just "boarding" his own former chattels.[32]

Actually, local officials had almost complete control of the area by November 1865. The army had pulled the few black troops back to Vicksburg, and the single Freedmen's Bureau agent who remained in Yazoo City could only write unheeded dispatches of desperation to his commanders. His letters provide a vivid picture of affairs in the county, especially those that contain moving affidavits by black workers.

One such deposition by freedman Robert James underscored the plight of black residents in Yazoo with the restoration of traditional authority. Struggling with his former master, who was intent on beating him with a stick, James described how he bit the planter's finger, then wrested the stick from him and threw it away. The white man threatened to have his former slave killed, warning him that the planters "had their own law now and Provost Marshals has nothing to do with it now. . . . [T]hey could do as they pleased with their darkeys."[33]

A deposition from one "Nellie" documented the oppression in Yazoo as planters took advantage of the new Black Code. Nellie's former master, James Anderson, had recently forced her husband to flee for refusing to sign an annual labor contract. Anderson then seized her children and threatened to see her "in hell" if she dared filed a complaint. If her husband returned, he warned her, "he would kill him or hire someone to do it."[34]

Alarmed and bewildered by the mounting violence, Freedman's Bureau agent Charles W. Clarke begged headquarters for guidance. Although he hoped his superiors would at least curtail the new state laws, their reply confirmed his worst fears. The bureau challenged only the prohibition against black farmers leasing land and let all other provisions of the laws stand. Moreover, Clarke soon learned that his services were no longer needed in Yazoo, as the bureau suspended operations there and sent no replacement agent until spring 1867. Local authorities had a free hand in maintaining "order" in the county.[35]

Except for some labor contracts, little evidence exists in Yazoo public records that county officials played much of a part in shackling laborers to yearly contracts, but planters used local government in other ways to bolster their individual and collective power. Evidence abounds in the minutes of the probate court of seizures of black children of the kind that had made Nellie risk her life to report to the Freedmen's Bureau. The wartime judge of that court, Robert Mayes (who later became a leader of the Ku Klux Klan and appeared in Morgan's account as "Syam"), had won reelection in the October elections of 1865. He spent most of his time on the reestablished court during December apprenticing "orphaned minors" until their adulthood to former masters, actions that were ill-disguised devices to reenslave them. Not only the affidavit of Nellie, but subsequent legal suits of black parents for the restoration of their children also testify to this legal kidnapping by the old planters. The probate court in Yazoo placed at least 250 black minors under the complete control of their former masters. Many freedmen ran away, leading the court to issue warrants for their arrest. The practice did not end until the imposition of military government under congressional Reconstruction in April 1867.[36]

For almost two years after the end of the Civil War, local authorities operated in Yazoo with little if any outside interference. The slate of country officials chosen in October 1865 demonstrated little or no break with the past. Two former nonslaveholders joined the board: one had been an antebellum lawyer in Yazoo City who had served as an officer in the Confederate army; the other had no record of military service. Neither offered any dissent to the board's majority of former slaveholders. Almost all the remaining reappointed holdovers from 1864 gained reelection, and the board of police once again chose the various appointed officials almost exclusively from the ranks of antebellum slaveholders.[37]

It was during this period of restored Confederate authority in the autumn of 1865 that Albert T. Morgan came to Yazoo County. He paid little attention, it seems, to the political reorganization of local government. One of the men who, a decade later, would plot his murder wondered many years afterward about Morgan's "acumen in selecting Yazoo county for his activities."[38]

Although Morgan's political tragedy may be rooted in his political inexperience, it was never the product of his illusions. Rather, it stemmed more from his stubborn courage and the formidability of the foes he faced. Better knowledge of the county's rigid social and political structure might have kept him from going to Yazoo in 1865, but that understanding, when it finally came, could not scare him away. It only served to drive him toward economic disaster and political defeat.

At first, Morgan and his brother were welcomed warmly by the local elite in Yazoo. Major James J. B. White (who appears as "Colonel Black" in the memoirs) eagerly leased land to the two brothers and tried to show them how to ingratiate themselves with their neighbors. But the relationship that the newcomers developed with their black workers soon led to estrangement from the former slaveholders. Morgan recalled that the growing displeasure of the restored oligarchy led to his social exclusion by 1866. Snubs he could ignore. Other encounters were more punishing, such as when some planters—with the cooperation of local officials—seized his property in August 1867 and ruined his farm and lumbering business. One of his partners fled, but Morgan and his brother stayed and decided to orchestrate some changes in Yazoo County.

Like his black neighbors, Morgan quickly found that the federal military authorities appointed to guide the reconstruction of Mississippi offered little assistance or security. The new Freedmen's Bureau agent may have been well meaning, but he was almost as powerless as his predecessor in 1865. He wrote lengthy reports about attacks against local unionists, northern migrants, and black laborers, but received virtually no assistance from military headquarters. The infrequent dispatch of federal troops to the area brought scant relief. Indeed, the military commander put them at the disposal of local officials to break up meetings of the freedmen and their few Yankee allies or to force laborers to complete local harvests.[39]

The Military Reconstruction Acts of 1867 awarded the vote to all adult black males for the first time and directed the five Union generals, now in charge of civil affairs, to call new state constitutional conventions in their districts. Although subordinate to the new federal military authority, local officials in Yazoo seldom experienced any interference in their deliberations or actions. The mayor of Yazoo City lost his position, but all other local officials continued in their posts until 1869. As a result, black voters who attempted to register as voters under the 1867 federal mandates faced economic intimidation and outright violence.

For a moment it appeared that real change might yet take place when the new electorate in Yazoo (2,816 black voters, 1,014 white voters) managed to choose three beleaguered dissidents to represent them in the new constitutional convention elected in 1868: Albert T. Morgan; an African American blacksmith named William Leonard; and the former Freedmen's Bureau agent, Charles W. Clarke, who had taken up farming in Yazoo after his discharge from the army in the fall of 1865.[40]

But Mississippi's white establishment turned back this initial challenge in the June 1868 ratification election. The three lost narrowly in Yazoo County, where conservative white leaders had failed to stage a boycott of the ratification election in order to keep the required majority of voters from endorsing the new constitution, but won elsewhere in Mississippi. The proscriptions against former Confederate officeholders that Morgan and other radicals had drawn up in the convention proved too great a departure and caused disunion in the ranks of black voters. Intimidation, force, and violence also helped lower the black voting turnout for the constitution and the Republican ticket.[41]

IV

As it happened, the obstinacy of Mississippi whites only temporarily delayed the state's reconstruction. Elected president in 1868, Ulysses S. Grant appointed a resolute commanding general, Adelbert Ames, to oversee the process of bringing the state back into the Union. Put under military authority following the defeat of the radical constitution, Mississippi now faced a more vigorous style of administrative supervision. Black voters registered in even greater numbers than before, and an impatient Congress ordered the removal of all civilian officeholders in the state. To fill the vacancies, Ames moved swiftly to appoint over 2,000 men who could swear to the ironclad oath that they had given no assistance or encouragement to the Confederacy. In October 1869, a now well-protected black majority electorate secured passage of the constitution, stripped of the Confederate officeholding proscriptions, and elected a full slate of new state and local officials who reflected the expanded democratic order.[42]

The new constitution made few changes in the framework of local government in Mississippi. The local courts received the most substantial overhaul. Judges were appointed rather than elected, and the probate court disappeared in favor of chancery courts, which took over the whole range of equity litigation on the county level. The constitution also extended the jurisdiction of the justices of the peace to cases that amounted to less than $150. Other structural changes in local government were minor. The new measures merged the offices of coroner and ranger and changed the name of the board of police to the board of supervisors. Most important, the constitution issued a strong mandate to counties to develop a system of public education. Otherwise local government on paper differed little from that fashioned by the constitution of 1832.[43]

Nonetheless, a revolution had taken place. Local government finally began to reflect the makeup and wishes of its vast black majority. Few of the large exslaveholders won any significant positions, and in the next two elections, black candidates gained an increasing share of local offices, including a majority of the board of supervisors (the renamed board of police) in 1873, when Morgan was also elected county sheriff.

Few counties in Mississippi would elect as many significant black officials.[44] But the new local officials in Yazoo, under Morgan's aegis, achieved more than just a turnover in the county's officeholders. In 1869, the county was without a free public school building, a public courthouse, or a decent facility for prisoners, the insane, or the infirm poor. Roads and bridges were in terrible condition, and the county treasury had little but outstanding debts. By 1875, new roads and bridges had been built, a handsome courthouse and jail had been erected, the poor farm had been repaired and reorganized, and, most dramatically, over one hundred free school buildings had been constructed and opened throughout the county for blacks and whites. All this innovation was accomplished with only a slight increase in taxes; indeed, taxes were actually being reduced by 1875. By any standard, Yazoo was one of the best run counties in Mississippi and the entire South. The black poor were also witnessing significant economic improvement, even in the face of the national depression that began in 1873. Over 300 of the former propertyless black laborers owned farm land, with a few owning as many as 2,000 acres. A revolution was underway in Yazoo that was as extensive as could be found anywhere in the rural South during Reconstruction.

Despite the sudden changes, Morgan found that not all white residents opposed what was happening. In fact, a substantial minority of white voters joined his coalition, including even a few former large slaveholders. According to Morgan's estimates, the resolute, reactionary elite drew continuing support from only one-third of the poor, illiterate white class that made up about half of the white population. Moreover, only a handful of the recalcitrants were willing to risk their personal safety by turning to violent resistance as long as the federal government threatened some sort of sanctions. But the assurance of that ultimate enforcement was the linchpin of Morgan's revolution.

By 1875, democracy had reached its zenith in the county. As Morgan relates in great detail, the spectacular victory was short-lived. Rejected three times in their appeals to black voters, Yazoo's former Confederate rulers finally turned to organized violence in the fall elections of 1875, spearheading a systematic program of terror that spread across the state and overthrew Republican control. Morgan barely escaped with his life, and many of his less fortunate compatriots were murdered. President Grant, Union generals, and the Congress ignored their pleas for help.[45] The new powers in Yazoo County announced that 4,007 men had voted for the Democrats and only 7 for the Republicans, a blatant lie. Not a single black voter, they insisted, deviated from the Democratic cause.[46]

The new slate of officials in the county represented a clean sweep by the old regime. All five members of the board of supervisors were former slaveholders, and three were antebellum members of that body. Another prewar slaveholding member of the board of police was sent to the state legislature as a representative, joined by two other exslaveholders, one of whom was the infamous postwar architect of the Black Codes, Robert S. Hudson.

The county's nonslaveholders or postwar white newcomers who played key roles in the 1875 violent coup d'état against the Republicans shared little of the victors' spoils. When some of them later tried to gain office by forming an interracial independents' movement in 1879, planters murdered them in broad daylight on the streets of Yazoo City. Government returned to the hands of the antebellum oligarchy and their families, who ironically now enjoyed even greater power in state and national affairs, because the county's black majority was now counted as five-fifths of a person for the purposes of representation. The few remaining dissidents in the county adjusted to the change. Even a few of the prominent Northern white Republican officeholders managed to withdraw silently from politics, marry Southern women, and prosper.[47]

Morgan had always recognized that the only hope for countering the resourcefulness and the constant appeals to racial caste of the former ruling elite lay in the *"steady, unswerving power from without."*[48] Some of his associates—black and white—thought that they could bargain and compromise with the old elite. Morgan's own brother took that line and failed in a neighboring county, as Morgan had predicted. One of the most courageous black leaders in the county, William Henderson Foote, followed a similar strategy after 1875 but was eventually murdered. Others felt that they could match the terror of the old elite using organized armed force under state militia authority. Morgan's brave black compatriot, Charles Caldwell, insisted on such tactics in 1875, but he was also hunted down and brutally assassinated.[49]

After he fled to Washington, Morgan tried to rally Congress and other Northern Republican leaders. Although he helped secure a congressional inquiry of the Mississippi coup d'état, he found that national Republican leaders had abandoned the experiment of bringing democracy to the American South. When, in 1876, Democratic leaders in the last three Republican states—Florida, Louisiana, and South Carolina—adopted the Mississippi Plan of organized terror to intimidate black voters, the contested presidential election of 1876 produced a "corrupt bargain" that gave those states to the Democrats in exchange for continued Republican control of the presidency under Rutherford B. Hayes, who pledged to end all federal enforcement of the Reconstruction laws.

V

Albert T. Morgan refused to compromise his beliefs in 1875, in 1876, or in 1884 when he wrote this remarkable book about grassroots Reconstruction in the deep South. He remained adamantly opposed to white supremacy for the rest of his life. But fidelity to principle could not shield his subsequent career from a series of frustrations and personal failures. Shortly after his narrow escape from Mississippi, he took up residence in Frederick Douglass's townhouse in the nation's capital. With the support of Washington's black community and through the efforts of Mississippi's black senator Blanche K. Bruce, he received a minor appointment to the U.S. Pension Office. Although he used his new base to speak out about the collapse of democracy and civil rights in the post–Reconstruction South, he rarely gained the ear of national Republican leaders and even had to pay a printer to have his memoirs published in 1884. His efforts affirmed his enduring commitment to his youthful ideals, to be sure, but no longer did they influence national leaders or even reach a significant audience.

After Grover Cleveland won the presidency for the Democratic party in 1884, conservative Mississippi Democrats made a special effort to ensure the permanency of Morgan's removal from federal service.[50] Thereafter Morgan drifted westward, first taking his family to Kansas, where many black Southerners had fled in the Exoduster Movement following the overthrow of Reconstruction. When the economic crisis of the 1890s struck, he succumbed again to the lure of the frontier and went off to the silver mines of Colorado. This time he left his wife and children in Topeka, promising to call for them when he found success in the wilds of the Colorado mountains. But success never came. After their youngest son died in 1894, his wife Carrie went on the road with their remaining son, Bert, to manage the stage careers of her four attractive daughters. Ashamed of his economic failures, Morgan occasionally visited his family but never permanently regrouped with them again.

This was not wholly his choice, for he had become an embarrassment to his family. After his daughters decided it was easier to pass into the white community, his frank and open acknowledgment of his interracial marriage threatened their futures. Thereafter, their lives were plagued by tragedy. After one daughter died in 1898, the musical act the children created broke up, and they scattered to seek lives in the white world. Although Albert managed to live a relatively respectable life as a white-collar railroad employee in Indiana, three of his daughters suffered broken marriages, and two of them—after their African American ancestry was revealed publicly—ended their lives as inmates of insane asylums. His youngest daughter Nina Lillian, who took the pen name Angela, gained some fame as a writer in the 1920s, but only after carefully covering up all traces of her Mississippi birth and the true identity of her parents. Later, she and her mother sought refuge in England from the racism that had plagued their lives. Morgan's only bequest to his increasingly embittered wife was the meager Civil War pension that had sustained him since the 1890s.[51]

Despite these ordeals—or perhaps because of them—Morgan held firmly to his principles and integrity. In fact, he reformed his critique of American life and extended his vision beyond the nation's boundaries. In 1896 he rejected the Republican Party and flirted with Populism, though the racism of William Jennings Bryan ultimately left him with no meaningful political alternative at the turn of the century.

By that time, his old faith in nineteenth-century Republican idealism had evolved to embrace socialist convictions. Morgan now condemned not only the "mobocratic champions of 'white supremacy'" in the South, but also the "trusts" of corporate and financial capitalism across the nation. Both, he insisted, oppressed American labor, black and white, and blunted the exercise of democratic government. His hope had grown faint for American leadership. To him, Theodore Roosevelt and other Progressive politicians offered no meaningful reform.

Morgan hoped someday to see a peaceful, worldwide application of Christian ideals and democratic socialist principles, but he feared inevitable bloodshed stemming from the "Socialism of Carl [sic] Marx." As it entered the twentieth century, the United States offered him little basis for hope. The nation's deep-seated racism and imperialistic greed, he believed, had twisted democracy at home and thrust the country's leadership outward in a worldwide contest with the European powers that was "backed by a demand for the supremacy of the white race in all of the world's affairs."[52]

In 1912, Morgan looked back over his career with a mixture of detached humor and utter cynicism. He mocked himself as "the happiest man on the top o'Earth—not excepting J. Pierpont, J. D., King George or any son-of-gun for whom we fought, an bled an—lived to die for, all those blessed years."[53] Morgan's convictions were the product of an unusual American idealism—an uncompromising insistence that "no man is fit to govern another." Such resolve allowed him to maintain his vision of a democratic nation from the cauldron of Reconstruction until his dying day. It would serve any reader well to understand his experience and appreciate his determined vision for an interracial democracy in the United States.

Caution is certainly advisable. Vernon L. Wharton, an early revisionist historian of the African American experience in Mississippi during Reconstruction—a white Southerner who shared Morgan's vision and paid his own price within his professional guild—properly warned, just before his own death, of trying to find heroic figures in the Reconstruction story:

> There can be no doubt that there were some people of heroic quality among carpetbaggers, scalawags, and Negroes who fought the "battle for democracy" in the South; but most were little known men who died on the line of battle. The records of survivors generally show either a successful leap into the white Democracy or a shoddy and pathetic struggle for very small messes of Republican political pottage.[54]

Morgan always rejected any saintly accolades for himself, reserving such awards for the black men who died on "the old stubbleground of slavery." But he deserves to survive the grave as one of those teachers who, as he predicted at the end of this book, would "appear to instruct all in the language and justice of truth." The warnings about shortcomings are probably better reserved for those of us who read his memoirs. He penned his own words of caution, and they deserve to be highlighted before we begin his remarkable story:

> Let the incredulous reader withhold his smile or scorn until in the course of this history, we shall have dug down to Elisha's bones. Then, if he be a lover of his country, of justice and of liberty, let him accompany the spirit of the immortal Lincoln from

the dedication ceremonies at Gettysburg to that Yazoo grave-yard, and there again resolve, "that government of the people, by the people and for the people shall not perish from the earth."[55]

NOTES

1. Albert T. Morgan, *Yazoo; or, on the Picket Line of Freedom in the South* (Washington, D.C., 1884), 511–12.

2. John R. Lynch, *The Facts of Reconstruction* (New York, 1913). For early accounts of Reconstruction in Mississippi and Yazoo County, see James W. Garner, *Reconstruction in Mississippi* (New York: Macmillan, 1901); John S. McNeily, "War and Reconstruction in Mississippi, 1863–1890," *Publications of the Mississippi Historical Society, Centenary Series* 2 (1918), 165–535; Robert Bowman, "Reconstruction in Yazoo County," *Publications of the Mississippi Historical Society* 7 (1903), 115–130; and Elizabeth Caldwell, "Reconstruction in Yazoo County, Mississippi," unpublished master's thesis (University of North Carolina, 1931). Revisionist accounts include Vernon L. Wharton, *The Negro in Mississippi* (Chapel Hill: University of North Carolina Press, 1947); David Overy, *Wisconsin Carpetbaggers in Dixie* (Madison: State Historical Society of Wisconsin, 1961); and Richard N. Current, *Three Carpetbagger Governors* (Baton Rouge: Louisiana State University Press, 1967) and *Those Terrible Carpetbaggers: A Reinterpretation* (New York: Oxford University Press, 1988).

3. For a revealing portrait of Carolyn Highgate, her mother, and her sister, Edmonia, who all served as teachers for southern freedpeople during the Civil War and Reconstruction, see Dorothy Sterling, ed., *We Are Your Sisters: Black Women in the Nineteenth Century* (New York: Norton, 1984), 440–43. The Highgate family had lived in Albany and Syracuse, where the father, a barber, not only sent his children to the public schools but made sure that his daughters graduated from Syracuse University. The father died before the war, and an older brother died fighting at Petersburg. Extensive correspondence describing the mother and daughter as teachers in the South can be

found in the American Missionary Association Papers at the Amistad Research Center, Tulane University.

4. U.S. Bureau of the Census, manuscript census for Dodge County, Wisconsin, 1860. See also *Fox Lake Gazette,* May 25 and October 5, 1864.

5. Lawrence N. Powell, *New Masters: Northern Planters During the Civil War and Reconstruction* (New Haven, Conn.: Yale University Press, 1980).

6. Morgan, *Yazoo,* 448.

7. U.S. Bureau of the Census, *Eighth Census of the United States, 1860, Population,* 272; *Agriculture,* 84–85.

8. The information is derived from two sources: Yazoo County, Mississippi, manuscript minutes of the Board of Police, 1854–1860 (hereafter cited as "Minutes of the Board of Police"); and U.S. Bureau of the Census, manuscript census for Yazoo County, 1860 (hereafter cited as "MS Yazoo Census").

9. MS Yazoo Census. The combined holdings of real estate and personal property (primarily slaves) alter the percentages of domination only slightly. Because many slaveholders, merchants, and skilled workers rented their real estate, ownership of land by itself may be an inaccurate measure of wealth in Yazoo County.

10. Ibid.

11. Ibid.

12. Ibid.

13. Mississippi, *Constitution of 1832,* article 5, section 13–23.

14. Ibid. See also Mississippi, *The Revised Code of the Statute Laws of the State of Mississippi* (Jackson, Miss., 1857), chapters 3, 4, 6, 7, 13, 60, 61, 69.

15. Mississippi, *Revised Code* (1857), chapters 3, 6, 58, 69. For an appraisal of the composition and operation of state and local government throughout the lower Mississippi during the 1850s, see Ralph A. Wooster, *The People in Power* (Knoxville, Tenn.: University of Tennessee Press, 1969). By ignoring black residents as part of the population, the impact of bonding requirements, and the breakdown of population and voting in individual counties, Wooster found more so-called democracy than this analysis. He did note, however, the disproportionate

share of power that large slaveholders held in both rich black belt counties and state government. See pages 38, 58, 101.

16. Minutes of the Board of Police, MS Yazoo Census.

17. Ibid.

18. Percy Rainwater, *Mississippi, Storm Center of Secession, 1856–1861* (Baton Rouge, La.: Louisiana State University Press, 1938), 15, 199; Mississippi, *Journal of the State Convention* (Jackson, Miss., 1861), 14–16; MS Yazoo Census.

19. This member, Samuel Dilly, was succeeded in office after the war by the first nonslaveholder on the board, W. W. Lumbley. Their particular district, Beat 1, had the lowest slaveholding average in the period from 1853 to 1865. It was located on the fringe of the bottom lands, where smaller farmers were concentrated.

20. The average size of slaveholdings even rose slightly to 44, ranging from 1 for the elderly Pennsylvania transplant to 131 for the largest slaveholding member. The value of real estate dropped to $30,612 from the antebellum average of $33,894, and total property holdings also declined from $84,724 to $79,916. Minutes of the Board of Police, MS Yazoo Census.

21. Robert Bowman, "Yazoo County in the Civil War," *Publications of the Mississippi Historical Society* 7 (1903), 58–60.

22. Ibid; Minutes of the Board of Police, vol. 1(A): 274, 285, 290, 294, 313.

23. Ibid, vol. 1(A): 257, 294, 295, 318, 347. See also Mississippi, *Laws of Mississippi, 1861–62*, p. 238.

24. Ibid, vol. 1(A): 314, 328, 342, 359.

25. *Official Records of the Union and Confederate Navies in the War of the Rebellion,* Series 1, vol. 25: 9–10, 282–293

26. Minutes of the Board of Police, vol. 1(A): 366; Bowman, "Yazoo County in the Civil War," 69.

27. Bowman, "Yazoo County in the Civil War," 65; *Official Records of the Union and Confederate Navies . . . ,* series 1, vol. 25: 280, 282.

28. Minutes of the Board of Police, vol. 1(A): 366, 369, 371, 376, 378; Garner, 59–61; James W. Silver, ed., "The Breakdown of Morale in Central Mississippi in 1864: Letters of Judge Robert S. Hudson," *Journal of Mississippi History* 16 (1954), 106, 116–117.

29. Garner, *Reconstruction in Mississippi,* 96–100. For a

copy of Sharkey's July 1 proclamation, see Mississippi, *Journal of the Proceedings and Debates in the Constitutional Convention of the State of Mississippi* (Jackson, Miss., 1865), 4–7.

30. Garner, 24–25, 39, 53–78, 164–178, 195–196, 260, 277.

31. Mississippi, *Journal of the Senate* (1865), 13–17, 18–21, appendix.

32. Robert S. Hudson to Andrew Johnson, November 2, 1865, Andrew Johnson Papers, Library of Congress.

33. Charles Clarke to J. W. Weber, November 20, 1865, box 10, Freedmen's Bureau Records, 1865–68, Records Group 105, National Archives.

34. Ibid.

35. Charles Clarke to J. W. Weber, November 30, 1865, with an endorsement of Weber to Clarke, December 5, 1865, box 405, Freedmen's Bureau Records, 1865–68, Records Group 105, National Archives.

36. Yazoo County, Mississippi, manuscript minutes of the Probate Court, vol. 1: 97–450 *passim.*

37. Minutes of the Board of Police; MS Yazoo Census.

38. E. H. Anderson, "A Memoir of Reconstruction in Yazoo City," *Journal of Mississippi History* 4 (1942), 192.

39. D. H. White to A. W. Preston, April 23, 24, 1867; Allen P. Higgins to A. W. Preston, June 30, July 31, 1867; Allen P. Higgins to James Sunderland, September 23, 25, October 31, 1867; D. H. White to M. Barber, November 15, 30, December 12, 1867, all in vol. 324, Freedmen's Bureau Records. See also Daniel Hitchcock to D. Jones, September 21, 1867 (copy); Dr. Franklin to General Ord, September 25, 1867, in Letters Received, 1867, Bureau of Civil Affairs, Fourth Military District, Records Group 98, National Archives.

40. "Final Report on Registration," received September 13, 1867, Bureau of Civil Affairs, Fourth Military District, Record Group 104: box 1, National Archives; Mississippi, *Journal of the Proceedings in the Constitutional Convention,* 1868 (Jackson, Miss., 1871), 20. Vernon L. Wharton fails to include Leonard among the African American delegates in the convention; Wharton, *The Negro in Mississippi,* 147–148.

41. On the 1868 ratification election, see Lawrence N. Powell, "Correcting for Fraud: The Mississippi Ratification Election

of 1868," *Journal of Southern History* 75 (November 1989), 633–58.

42. Garner, *Reconstruction in Mississippi,* 230–46.

43. Mississippi, *Constitution of 1868–1869,* articles 5, 6, 8; *Revised Code of 1871,* chapters 3, 8–11, 22, 39, 53; *Mississippi Laws, 1873 (Called Session),* 15–17.

44. See appendix, table 5. A comparison of black officeholders in other counties can be found in Wharton, *The Negro in Mississippi,* 167–72.

45. Current, *Those Terrible Carpetbaggers,* 322–23.

46. This election was examined in great detail by a Congressional investigation in 1876; U.S. Senate, *Mississippi in 1875: Report of the Select Committee to Inquire into the Mississippi Election of 1875* . . . 44th Congress, 1st Session, Report No. 527, 2 vols. For the testimony about Yazoo County, see vol. 2, 164–1785.

47. U.S. Bureau of the Census, manuscript census for Yazoo County, 1880. See also appendix, table 7.

48. Morgan, *Yazoo,* 323. Emphasis in the original.

49. Herbert Aptheker, "Mississippi Reconstruction and the Negro Leader, Charles Caldwell," *Science and Society* 11 (Fall 1947), 369–71.

50. Frank E. Smith, *The Yazoo* (New York: Rinehart, 1954), 166.

51. Affidavit, Albert T. Morgan Jr., May 10, 1923; A. T. Morgan to A. T. Morgan Jr., March 15, 1920; E. L. Howard to Commissioner of Pensions, October 27, 1923; Questionnaire, April 30, 1915, all in the manuscript Civil War Pension Records, Claim C 160702, National Archives. In various compendia of writers in the United States, Angela Morgan claimed northern birth and parents with different names. Neither her poetry nor her novels give any indication of her mixed racial background or family history. See the Angela Morgan Papers, Bentley Historical Library, University of Michigan. For one of her fabricated autobiographies that includes a disguised but admiring rendering of her father's idealism, see Angela Morgan, "Imprisoned Splendor," in William L. Stidger, *The Human Side of Greatness* (New York: Harper & Brothers, 1935), 208–211. See also her obituary in the *New York Times,* January 25, 1957.

52. Albert T. Morgan, *On Our Way to the Orient or Mr. Bryan, Don't You Know?* (Denver, Colo., n.p., 1909), 21, 47–48, 71, 73.

53. A. T. Morgan to J. L. Davenport, December 25, 1912, in the MS Civil War Pension Records, Claim C 160702, National Archives.

54. Vernon L. Wharton, "Reconstruction," in *Writing Southern History,* edited by Arthur S. Link and Rembert W. Patrick (Baton Rouge, La.: Louisiana State University Press, 1965), 314–315.

55. Morgan, *Yazoo,* 202.

YAZOO

TO THE MEMORY

OF THOSE MEN AND WOMEN

WHO HAVE DIED ON SLAVERY'S STUBBLE-GROUND

IN THE WAR FOR SELF-

PRESERVATION.

PREFACE TO THE 1884 EDITION

And they cast the man into the sepulchre of Elisha; and when the man was let down he revived and stood upon his feet.

In these pages the reader will find faithfully set out a simple and truthful narrative of the principal incidents and events in the public and private life of the author during his residence in Yazoo County, Mississippi, together with occasional pictures* illustrative of the social condition of the people of that State. The characters are real persons, whose true names are given only in cases where it was found impossible to disguise their identity. The conversations quoted, of course, are not verbatim. They are, nevertheless, strictly within the line of truth.

Both in gathering the material and preparing for the public, the author has encountered certain obstacles which many never will be able adequately to appreciate, because it will be impossible for them to stand in his place. Nothing is asked or expected, however, more than an honest judgment upon his motive and his work.

*The illustrations from the first edition are not included in the Southern Classics edition.

YAZOO;

OR,

ON THE PICKET LINE OF FREEDOM.

CHAPTER I.

THE WAR IS OVER—SOUTHWARD HO!—A WONDERFUL COUNTRY.

CHARLES and I were strangers in Mississippi. Although born in New York, we were raised in Wisconsin on a farm of what, in that State, is called "openings" and prairie land. Therefore we knew something about farming. I had had some experience in my father's store and wheat warehouse. Perfectly familiar with the crops and the soils of Wisconsin, we knew nothing about those of the Mississippi lowlands, and until we went South with the Union armies neither of us had seen a cotton boll. During the last two years of the war many Union soldiers, tempted by the large returns on the capital invested in cultivating cotton, remained behind when their commands returned home to be mustered out, and engaged in that business.

Charles' service had been in the army which occupied the cotton territory, and it was what he had seen, as well as the information that he had gained from these Yankee planters during his three years with the armies of Thomas and Sherman, that tempted him, when the last armed rebel had surrendered, to seek a permanent home in the far South.

To me, brother Charles always seemed possessed of a wonderful power of self-control. He never lost his head. My affection for him was only less than my love for father, and I know that his love for me was very great. I had an abiding faith in him; in his clear head, sound judgment and good heart. Therefore, he did not have to persuade me to accompany him. I was only too glad of his offer to take me along as an equal partner with himself.

Father only said: " Boys, you'll rue the day."

Mother—they are both dead now—" Children, I don't feel exactly right about it."

But we were both of age, and had wills of our own. Of course we went.

It was early autumn when we landed at Vicksburg, 1865. Nearly every steamer from above brought large quantities of freight and many prospectors like ourselves. The town was astir with young life, and new vigor everywhere manifested itself. New stores and new residences were building, the levees were being repaired, and, though the works of the two armies had been dismantled, they had not yet been leveled down.

The caves in which the citizens had taken refuge during the siege and the point where Pemberton met Grant and arranged the terms of surrender were objects of great interest to all strangers. The hotels were full; they overflowed, and we had been obliged to seek accommodation in a private family, known to our agent to be highly respectable, but so reduced in circumstances by the war that they were willing to accept such means of gaining a livelihood.

Several days were spent in "doing" the town and surrounding country. Thus we became acquainted with several old and new settlers, and with the general business and commercial interests of the place.

Land agents were numerous. Each one had lengthy lists of "plantations for sale," and "plantations for rent." These varied in size from a hundred to ten thousand acres. Nearly all were amply described, their varied attractions set forth with great apparent exactness, and owners or agents were always only too glad to show their premises to whomsoever might come along.

We had spent about a month examining such as we could hope, from the description of them in the hands of the agent, might meet our requirements, without success, when one day Mrs.——, the only other guest of our hostess, received a letter from a "dear old friend" of hers, living "up the Yazoo," at Yazoo City, announcing that she had been "utterly ruined by the war"—all her slaves had run off with the first Yankee troops that came into that section.

This was true of most of her neighbors. She had not been able to educate her daughters as she had hoped. Indeed, they did not know how they were to live, unless it could be made off "Tokeba." How to do that was the question now confronting her. Her husband was not suited to the task of organizing a new force for the plantation under the "free system," and if he were, where was the money coming from? It could not be borrowed on the plantation for security. It was not to be had of any one in that region; for they all were as good as bankrupt. She had racked her brain for weeks, ay, months, for some way out of the dilemma.

For a time she had hoped that the terms granted by the "Yankee General Sherman to General Johnston" might be interpreted as fairly indicative of the purposes of their "conquerors" toward "the South." But not only had there been no serious resistance, anywhere, to the annullment of Sherman's "generous terms," the assassination of "Abe Lincoln" had apparently given the Yankees a pretext for still more radical measures, which she believed would be certain to follow, than even the "Bureau for the Freedmen,"* and she had come to the conclusion there was no use "trying to hold out any longer."

* Bureau Refugees, Freedmen and Abandoned Lands.

The negroes were free, and the sooner the fact was recognized by them the better. They might talk if they pleased, but she was going to look out for herself and her children. If she could find some "suitable Northern gentleman of means" to take it, she would lease Tokeba. It might seem like vandalism almost to the merely sentimental, but she had passed that stage. It was purely a question of bread. Would not Mrs. —— look around and see if she could not find some one among the "new-comers," of whom there were a great many, as she had been told, with the "requisite capital for so large a place as Tokeba?"

This Mrs. —— was a relict of one of the best-known families of the South. Her husband had held high places in the councils of the nation. He was dead now. Her only son had been killed while aiding in the defense of Richmond. Her only daughter had entered a convent. She herself was a Catholic—a lady of rare accomplishments, and her afflictions had ennobled her.

She went directly to Charles with the letter. So anxious was she to "serve" her "old friend" she read the whole of it to us both, that we might "know something of her character," she said.

She knew the place well; had spent some of the happiest moments of her life there as the guest of her correspondent, and she felt certain we should be delighted with it and with the family of her friend, about all of whom she had many pleasant things to say. We had been under the same roof for only a little over a month; had met each other at the table, in the parlor, and had mingled with the family and their guests in their homes, but beyond this, Mrs. —— knew no more of us than of any other travelers who might come along, yet she frankly avowed that she already knew us well enough to justify her in commending us to her "dear old friend" as the very persons she would choose for herself to become the new masters of the "dear old home place." The upshot of it all was that the next day, armed with a letter from Mrs.—— to her old friend, "Mrs. Charlotte Black, Yazoo City, Miss.,"

Charles took the Yazoo River packet, bound for that town, while I remained to take a steamboat the day following for a point about two hundred miles up the Mississippi River, where I was to examine a plantation which our agent had recommended to us.

I landed there in the night. The only shelter I could find was a plain board shanty with two rooms, occupied by a freedman and his wife. He was absent in New Orleans for supplies. After great persuasion I succeeded in getting shelter and a "bed" on the floor before the high fire-place.

On returning next day from my visit to the plantation, I observed there were a good many men in and about an old barn-like structure some distance back from the river bank. A shed at the landing, this structure, and my shelter were the only buildings I could see. My landlady told me they were holding "co't" there that day.

She had already spread a table for fifteen or twenty guests, who soon after began to gather around it. I thought they returned my salutations gruffly, and that they appeared curious about me. At each end of the table was a large bottle of whisky, which was offered to me, but I declined, saying I never drank anything.

This resulted in a request, which was more like a demand, for my name. One who appeared to be the leader, asked me where I came from, and what my business there was. This I frankly made known to them, and then the "late war" became the only topic of conversation. Finally, the spokesman announced that "no Yankee radical could ever come into that county, make a crop and get away with it," and the crowd joined in abusive personal epithets.

It occurred to me that I ought to get away from them; but how ? There was no boat, nor would there be until the following morning, perhaps not then. I resolved to try and shame them. So rising, I said I had indeed been in the Federal army, and had never yet been ashamed of the fact. I was there for the purpose of engaging in a legitimate business

enterprise, as I had a right to do, and concluded by saying,
that if they really possessed any of that "chivalry" they
claimed as peculiar to the Southern character, they would
not have treated an utter stranger as they had done me.
Then I left the table, and passed into the only other room
in the building. A thin board partition divided me from
them, and, although their talk was in a much lower key than
before, I could hear most of it.

When they had finished their meal, the leader, whom they
called Major, came in, apologized to me and quite warmly
urged me to " accept the hospitalities of my home, sir, such
as it is," etc., assuring me of his " personal protection," and
concluded with a hint that he might, after all, determine to
lease his own plantation, or, we might find one in his neighborhood that would suit me.

It was " agreed" that he should send his " boy," with the
Major's " own saddle horse," for me in the morning, and we
separated; he for his home, while I took the steamer, which
happened to be on time early next morning, for Vicksburg.

The fact is, after they had all gone I had a brief consultation with my landlady, and concluded that would be the
safer course for me. For, while so much of their talk as I
had been able to hear was about me, she assured me their
plan was to decoy me to the country, where they would be
in waiting, and hang me to a tree by the roadside. During
the presence of her guests this woman had been in full
sympathy with them, so far as I could see. But no sooner
were we alone than she manifested great concern for my
safety.

I related this experience to different Southern men, whom I
saw on my return to Vicksburg, and each one declared they
were " some irresponsible, worthless fellows " who had, probably, never been in the Confederate army, and I ought
not to heed anything they said or did.

Nevertheless they were in attendance at court, some of
them as jurymen. Nearly all wore the Confederate gray, and
carried pistols.

Two days afterward Charles returned. He took occasion to see Mrs. —— at once, and inform her that he had rented Tokeba for three years, subject to my approval.

She was "perfectly delighted."

That evening Charles and I sat up until after midnight talking over the matter. He gave me a detailed account of his trip, beginning with incidents of the journey to Yazoo City, in the course of which he had met several Northern men *en route* to different points on the Yazoo River, and with a purpose similar to his own.

He had also met and conversed with several citizens of Yazoo City returning from Vicksburg with supplies for their plantations or stores.

All seemed to vie with each other in expressions of welcome to him, on learning the object of his visit. As to Tokeba, it offered greater advantages for the development of our plans than he had seen anywhere else, and he gave me a minute description of it.

Formerly, if for nothing else than to tease him, it had been a sort of habit with me to oppose all manner of criticisms to his premises or conclusions.

On this occasion I began by relating my experience with Major —— and his friends. He indignantly replied that I ought not to class the " denizens of such a region " with "a civilized community like Yazoo," and reminded me that there was neither city nor town of any importance nearer than a hundred miles, if· so near ; that it was an "out of the way place, anyway," where the "influences of civilization " had " doubtless been excluded since the war began," while Yazoo City, on the contrary, was " quite a commercial centre." Then, unfolding his map, he proceeded to trace out the numerous advantages possessed by Yazoo City geographically, from a commercial point of view, with results that astonished me.

We had already been able to form pretty accurate notions of the fertility of the region, but my mind had not taken it all in before. Under the light shed upon it by my brother, I was now able to see that the intersection of the great "slopes" from the South and East, with those from the North and West, near the confluence of the Missouri, Mississippi and Ohio rivers, formed the geographical centre of a territory equal in area to the whole of Europe; leaving out Russia, Norway and Sweden; that debouching from this centre, the Mississippi River was the only water outlet for that vast region, and drained nineteen States of our Union; fully one and a quarter million square miles; that the average width of this river from Cape Girardeau to the Gulf of Mexico was more than three thousand feet, and that it flowed for a distance of more than twelve hundred miles, through a deposit of alluvium sufficient in area and capacity of productiveness to feed and clothe the populations of the United States, Great Britain and Ireland, France, Italy, and Spain; that the Yazoo, one of the "feeders" of this central channel, drained fifteen thousand square miles; that Yazoo City was situated at the base of the range of tertiary hills which bound this alluvial region along its whole extent on the east, was one hundred and twelve miles from Vicksburg, on the Yazoo River; and that the Great Northern Railroad, running from New Orleans and connecting with Louisville, passed through the county on the east of the town only twenty-six miles away! Prior to coming South, to give me the benefit of a comparison, we had, upon my brother's motion, taken a trip through Missouri into Kansas, as far as we could go by rail. Not far beyond Sedalia we spent three days, prospecting upon the prairie lands of that region. While there, we learned that a tract of ten thousand acres, belonging to a rebel general, who had expatriated himself upon the surrender of Lee, was for sale, and could be had for ten dollars per acre. We rode over portions of this tract. It was rich prairie loam, with some stretches of oak, and the railroad ran through the centre of it.

Charles was strongly tempted to stop there. But anxious

to know more of the " wonderful " soils of the Mississippi
bottoms, after going on into Kansas, we concluded to postpone purchase until after we had made a close personal in-
spection of the cotton territory.

For some months the influential newspapers North had contained glowing descriptions of parts of the South, and editorials
encouraging immigration into that region. The former cry, "Go
West, young man," had undergone just enough variation by
the substitution of " South " for " West," to effect a change,
already quite apparent, in the purposes of those of the North
who were seeking new homes, and as Charles touched this
point, he grew eloquent indeed.

In his view he saw such a tide of thrifty emigrants and
others with capital setting southward, as within twenty-five
years would make the two million people of the Mississippi
lowlands twenty millions, and in a century a hundred millions.
" Thanks to the overthrow of slavery," my brother exclaimed; " these great natural advantages can no longer be
hidden from the home-seekers of the world."

In his opinion we were fortunate beyond measure in having
presented to us an opportunity to precede, if we could not
lead, this vast host, in the work of laying the foundations of
this new empire by building canals, railroads, and other facilities for its development.

One of the first of his plans, after our three years of planting, embraced the constructing of a railroad from Yazoo City
east, connecting with the Great Northern at some convenient point, so as to give the inhabitants of the Yazoo Delta
a competing line of transportation for their commerce.
Situated as Yazoo City was there was nothing in the way
of its becoming a great commercial centre.

As to the people, nothing could exceed their desire for
" oblivion of the past," and for a recognition by " Northern
gentlemen " and " capitalists " of the natural advantages of
their town and section for the profitable investment of their
money, their labor, and their brains.

At last, and as a clincher, my brother related how the price
at first demanded was ten dollars an acre for the open or
ploughed lands, being the same as that asked by other owners.
But as our plans embraced a permanent residence in the
community where we should determine to locate as renters,
and as the lease was to be for three years instead of one,
Mrs. Black had been the first to consent to a reduction to
seven dollars per acre: Charles' offer. She had even thrown
in a cypress brake of several thousand trees, with permission
to cut from it all the timber for our purposes we might wish,
including the manufacture of all kinds of lumber for the
market. This, to Charles, was one of the best features of his
bargain. For, as he declared, should the crop from any cause
fail, the profits from this branch of the business could be relied upon to save us from any very great losses. He would
" make one hand wash the other," whatever might come.
And a flush of honest pride came over his face, while he continued : " Besides, my dear boy, you know I neither chew,
smoke, drink, nor use profane language, and when they inquired whether you were the same sort of fellow, I was able
to say that I knew you pretty well, and the only bad habit
you had, to my knowledge, was smoking."

" Well," said I, for my curiosity was aroused to know what
sort of people they were, anyway, " What said they to that?"

" The mother said it was a pity, for she believed the tobacco
habit was a hurtful one. She knew it to be a filthy one.
Then one of the young ladies inquired whether it was a pipe
or cigar you smoked   On my telling them I never knew you
to smoke a pipe, she seemed pleased, for she said: ' Oh! well,
ma, that is not so bad, I am sure.' She pronounced ma, as if
it were spelled *maw ;* and sure, as if spelled *shooah.* Ha!
ha !"

" You know my only introduction was a letter from Mrs.
——, to whom we are strangers, who introduced me as one
whom she had known for only about a month. But when I
was ready to come away, one of Mrs. Black's guests placed

nearly a thousand dollars in cash in my hand to expend for
him in the purchase of supplies for his plantation. I tell
you, Albert, it does make a difference in our relations with
the world, what sort of people one is dealing with. I mean
as to personal habits. I am sure it has had great weight with
Mrs. Black. She is quite refined and cultivated, but a shrewd
business woman with it all. In fact she is the 'man of the
house ;' the old Colonel is somewhat dissipated. Why, she
as good as told me she would rather rent her place to gentlemen—you know they always say gentlemen—of correct habits
and high principles, at seven dollars per acre, than to others
at double the money. In fact she made many pleasant
speeches to me, and never once appeared to hesitate to accord
me perfect social intercourse in her family. She rather
encouraged me, I fancied, to pay some attention to the
eldest of her two daughters. To be sure, they were all rank,
fire-eating rebels, except, possibly, Mrs. Black; yet every
evening she managed to have one or more of her lady friends
to dinner or in the parlor, and allowed me to see that she
felt gratified by my presence in her house and my courteous
manner toward her friends."

My brother's pleasure at finding the women of Yazoo so
accomplished and agreeable was, I am sure, solely from the
human desire for agreeable social companionship, and his
representations in that particular helped to banish my doubts
as to the place he had selected for our new home. The next
day we separated, he to the North for supplies, and the evening following I took the "good steamer" Martin Walt for
Tokeba, via Yazoo City, where I was to remain at least over
the Sunday following.

I was then twenty-three. Charles was ten years older.
Neither of us had ever married. If I had ever thought
upon the subject, certainly it then was the one thought
farthest from my mind. Charles, I am certain, never once
thought of seeking a wife there. My faith in him was limit-
less. He was the successful boy of our family. He never

made mistakes. I cannot now recall any undertaking of his
life, up to that time, in which he had not succeeded according to his plans, and his confidence in the future of Yazoo
City amounted to enthusiasm. I had been but illy able to
disguise my own as he advanced from point to point in the
unfolding of his plans as to Tokeba, Yazoo, and the great
Delta.

Alas, my brother ! He has been dead now five years, and
these events occurred eighteen years ago. But the perfect
figure of this man of perfect health, perfect honor, and perfect faith in our enterprise and in mankind, as he appeared
to me on that last evening of our stay together in Vicksburg, is as fresh and as accurately imaged before me this
moment as then.

CHAPTER II.

FIRST LESSONS—COLONEL J. J. U. BLACK AS TEACHER.

TOKEBA* PLANTATION, in 1865, contained nine hundred acres "open" land, "more or less," for so it was described in the contract, which the lawyers of Mrs. Charlotte Black, wife of Colonel J. J. U. Black, wrote out, and which, having been signed by the Colonel as "agent in fact" for Mrs. Black, "of the first part," and by Charles, one of the "parties of the second part," lay in their hands awaiting my signature. In that instrument we promised to pay to Mrs. Black, for Tokeba, seven dollars per acre per annum for a term of three years, one-half of the annual rental to be paid in advance. It was upon the west bank of the Yazoo River, and lay in a compact body, bounded on the north by a bayou, from which it derived its name, and upon the south by the cypress brake. It was two and a half miles above Yazoo City, which nestled at the foot of the bluffs that crowded to the water's edge at that point, on the east bank of the river.

From my station on Peak Tenariffe, the very day of my arrival, I was able to see where the plantation lay from a small opening in the vast forest of gum and cypress that covered the alluvium, which stretched away toward the west, far beyond the Mississippi River, eighty miles distant, as the crow flies.

*An Indian word, though some said it was a corruption of "took a bar." It had once been famous ground for bear hunting.

I had been heartily welcomed by the Black family. They would not allow me to remain at the hotel, where I had taken lodgings upon leaving the Martin Walt that glorious Sabbath morning, but insisted I should make their home mine "for the present."

My first impression of them was favorable. The next morning, bright and early, the Colonel, mounted on a little, old gray horse, and myself, mounted on a smart, mouse-colored mule, were off for the plantation. Our route lay over the alluvion fringing the east bank of the river for many miles, along the point of land formed by a bend which the river makes for the accommodation of Tokeba.

That the bend is really for that purpose is clear, from the fact that after touching the northeast corner of the place in its westward course, at the mouth of the bayou, it proceeds to scallop its eastern end in such a manner as to make the family residence-site, midway its width, a point of view from which the sluggish stream may be followed with the eye, toward the northeast a considerable distance above the bayou's mouth, and toward the southeast quite to the town, through the densely overhanging trees.

At Yazoo City, after butting itself against the bluffs, the river takes off at a sharp angle toward the west, with greatly increased velocity, into the alluvion again, through which, resuming its sluggish flow, it ploughs its way without further interruption until, attracted by the hills, it touches them again at Liverpool.

As in the former case, at this point it resumes its westerly course, with velocity again quickened until it has left the bluff in the rear, and then, attaining its normal flow, it passes into the sombre, level plain. After passing Haines' Bluff, where Sherman and portions of his army once crossed, it glides gently, with an almost imperceptible movement of its turgid waters, over the grave of Fernando de Soto, for so the legend says, into the bosom of the great "Father of Waters."

We had gone scarcely a mile when the Colonel began to halloa: " Ho-ou-ou-ou-pee ! " long drawn out. It sounded in the cool, clear air through the forest, shrill and loud as a blast from a hunter's horn. Long practice had made him expert. His horse understood its meaning, pricked up his ears and struck into a smart canter. It was the Colonel's call to the ferryman on Tokeba, and was repeated every minute or two, so that when we reached the ferry-landing the "flat," guided and propelled by an old black man, touched our shore. The ferryman, bent in body and with legs all awry, promptly scrambled out and made the flat fast to a peg in the ground, pending which the following conversation took place:

" Good-morning, Bristol," said Colonel Black cheerily.

" Good-mornin', marstah," was the man's response

" This gentleman is Captain Morgan's brother, Bristol. We're going over to take a look at Tokeba this morning. How's aunt—"

But at this point he abruptly ceased speaking, and turning upon the freedman a most wrathful countenance, exclaimed :

" Hi, you black rascal ! Don't go putting on the airs of a gentleman about me. D'ye-y'hear ? Mind that !"

At the first word Bristol seized his long pole, scrambled on to the flat, upon which we had led our horses, and humbly ejaculating: " Ye-a-as, Mars Jeems," began pushing us out into the stream.

Meanwhile the Colonel continued: " These Yankees have come down, y'here, to make money, G—d d—n* you. D'you ever see a Yankee who didn't love money ? You'll have to quit yo' d—d free nigger notions around them, d'ye-y'hear? and me too, or by G—d I'll see ye all in hell befoah I'll give ye a recommend to them."

---

*It will be impossible for me to present to the reader a perfect likeness of Colonel Black. He was a slave-holder, a rebel, my host, my landlord, and my most implacable foe. He has been dead some years. I long ago foregave him. Under ordinary circumstances I would cover all his faults with that mantle of charity which belongs of right to ordinary mortals after death. But Colonel Black was so conspicuous a personage at a time when the foundations of a newer and better civilization were being laid there, that I should be false to essential truths were I, from feelings of delicacy, or of regard for sensitive readers, to fail to paint him in native colors.

What had the poor fellow done ? For the life of me, I
had not observed anything to criticise in his deportment.
When the Colonel made known to him who I was, he had
straightened himself up as well as his wabbling legs would
permit, taken his hat off, and gravely bowed to me, saying:
"Good-mornin', Massa Kunnel," with an attempt at dignity that made him appear ridiculous, to be sure; but what
of that ?

Colonel Black consumed the time of our trip over, in im
parting to me the information that he knew "the whole
damned nigro * tribe. Give them an inch and they'll take
an ell. They can be governed only by fear. You'll not be
able to do any thing with them unless you start right. They
are by nature a lazy, thieving, treacherous people. I wouldn't
trust one of them. This fellow, Bristol, is tainted, like all
the rest, with those damned notions about freedom, which
you damned Yankees "——

Here he checked himself, apologized, and resumed:

"It is true that Bristol did not run off with the rest to
the first Yankee soldiers that came along. The grand rascal
had good reasons for not doing so. He was my carpenter—
a sort of jack-of-all-trades, and has kept this ferry so long,
I reckon he preferred to remain on the place where he is sho'
of a living. But he is not a whit better than the rest."

Landing at the mouth of the bayou, we rode out to the
gin-house, only a few rods distant, thence over the spot he
said Charles had selected for a mill-site, thence to the
"quarter," two hundred yards further on, and from the quarter
thence to the knoll where stood the family residence, em-
bowered in China and magnolia trees. From here we rode
over the plantation, stretching back from the river fully two
miles, up and along the bayou, which bounded it on the
north; thence to the cypress brake on the south, whence,
tired and hungry, we returned by the route we came to town,
and a late dinner.

---

* Englishmen say "negro." Many Yankees and "poor white trash" have accustomed themselves to say "nigger" or "darkey." The real Southern lady or gentleman pronounces the word with a snap, denoting mastery, thus, "nigro."

The plantation was all Charles had claimed for it. Such trees as there were in the brake I had never seen before. Many of them were six to eight feet in diameter above the bulging roots, and ran up skyward straight as an arrow, eighty feet or more to the first limb. That which impressed me most, however, was the deserted "quarter." There were cabins of one and two rooms for a force of one hundred and twenty-five or more hands. Only two of them were now occupied. In one was an old man, no longer "serviceable," but who was taking care of and supporting his mother who, they said, was several years more than a century old. In the other were Sallie and her nursing babe. She was not more than thirty-two, and had lost a leg.

"The only able-bodied persons on the place were Anderson Henderson and his wife Judy, who occupied apartments at the great-house (the family residence)," the Colonel said, rather harshly.

During our ride Colonel Black endeavored to entertain me with incidents in the life of a slave-owner. These were illustrative of the "humanity" and "chivalry" of the master, and of the barbarity of the slave.

The story of the trip, however, the one of which he seemed to have stored the fondest recollections, was an account of his canvass before the war as the nominee of the "Old-line Whigs," for a seat in the State Senate.

It was made by him on horseback with two mules following behind, upon which he had packed "that gal, Sal, by G—d, sir," together with an ample supply of whisky and tobacco. That was before Sallie lost her leg, and when she was a "likely gal." Thus equipped he was able to offer to the suffragans of Yazoo weightier arguments than his opponent on the Democratic ticket, for he could bid them "choose to their taste" from the greater variety of the "creature comforts" which he "toted about" with him. "By G—d, sir,

that did the business for me, and I was the first Whig Senator ever sent to the legislature from this county."*

I remember but one other incident which in his estimate
equaled this one in occasion for merriment, or that furnished
me with so much food for thought. It was recalled to him
by the wrecks of several large steamboats lying in the river
as we rode past them.

"I stood right up there on my po'ch, by G—d, sir," said
he. "They had taken the alarm and left their landing below,
thinking to get out of reach of Ross' Cavalry by hiding up
y'here, where they thought themselves protected from any
large body of our troops by the low country. But a mere
handful of our fellows made a detour above, came down upon
them suddenly out of the thick timber yan, and caught the
rascals off their guard. Several of them were on the wheel
repairing it at the time. They were black Yankees, every one
of them, by G—d, sir, and looked for all the world like the
row of black birds, that they were. They were the first nigger troops sent into this section, and were putting the very
d—l into the heads of our nigros. There was no earthly
reason why Ross should not have captured them and hung
them all long before. But our people never thought well of
Ross, anyway. He did not amount to much, by G—d, sir—
except to steal stock and cotton. Well, as I was saying,
these black rascals were on the wheel— it was a stern-wheeler
—working away like a pacel of d—n lazy niggers lolling in
the sun, as they were; good for nothing as soldiers. Soldiers
h—l ! Well, by G—d, sir, they looked for all the world like
a string of black birds, ha ! ha ! ha ! Well, as I was saying,
five of them, by G—d, sir, ha ! ha ! ha !—d—n 'f I don't
forget whether 'twas five or six, but all the same, anyhow,
they were all nigros but one—tumbled over into the water
from the first volley and the balance surrendered, by G—d, sir.

---

* On the threshold of this narrative I beg the reader to remember that I have set out
to tell the whole truth about the state of society in Yazoo. At this late date therefore,
it is but right that the facts be stated in language so plain that the average American
woman, or man, may readily comprehend how I was impressed by personal contact with
the people of Yazoo.

It was one of the neatest captures I ever witnessed, or read about. It was a little tough on the poor, d—d Yankees, ha ! ha ! ha !—Yo're not a Yankee, yo're a Western man. It was not a regular force of our troops. . It was a po'tion of Captain Ramie's independent company."

These " stories " caused me to wonder greatly whether this man had exhibited the same side to my brother, that he was now without reserve uncovering to me. I could not bring myself to think he had. Of course, the last incident was of war, but he could have related it with less of the relish that a wolf is supposed to have for choice lamb, and as to the other—well, I will not characterize it.

Before we started that morning the Colonel invited me to his sideboard. On my refusal he declared "that a morning dram" was essential to health in that climate. On our return. in the evening he again invited me, insisting that an " evening dram," just before dinner, was absolutely requisite to " proper digestion" in that climate. He repeated his visits to the sideboard quite often during the evening until bed-time, when he implored me to drink with him, declaring that I would not be able to endure the climate without a " nightcap " to induce sound and healthful sleep.

I thought I saw that this habit was a sore affliction to Mrs. Black, and I know that his rudeness to me in inviting me so often to the sideboard, after being informed by my repeated refusals that I would not drink, greatly humiliated her. Indeed, she indignantly protested against it.

This habit of Colonel Black was not of recent origin, as he himself declared. It had grown up with him. He was an honest advocate of the regular use of whisky, " as a stimulant." I have said an honest advocate, for so he appeared to be, and his drams seemed to have no other effect on him than to inflate his ideas of his own importance, and to open his hand in a generous hospitality; the only offensive feature of which was his failure to comprehend how an old soldier could get on in this world without whisky. His only response to

my declaration that I had served all through the war, from
the first Bull Run to Appomattox, without having taken " so
much as one dram of any kind of liquor," was a long, dazed
stare.

The following morning I accompanied him to the office of
Mrs. Black's lawyers, where I examined the contract, found
my brother's well-known signature, and under it placed my
own.*

While I was engaged with the lawyers, the Colonel went
out upon the streets, and by the time our legal business was
concluded a number of his friends had dropped in. On all
sides there was apparently a desire to give me a hearty welcome to Yazoo, and I spent some time in pleasant conversation with them

The sideboard, however, in the shape of a huge demijohn, kept in the back room, formed as great an attraction to
Colonel Black's friends here as at his residence. Those who
called were cordially invited to " step into the back room "
by one or other of the attorneys, and the Colonel helped himself " right smart." In this respect the situation was somewhat embarrassing to me. I would not take anything, and
my repeated refusals became a subject for general remark.
All agreed that that fact alone would sufficiently distinguish
me from old residents of that section to gratify any desire
for notoriety that I might possess; and predicted that before
I had lived there six months I would have learned the folly of
my way, and would take my "social glass" like the rest of them.
Of course, all this was in a vein of pleasant badinage, and
merely illustrative of the " open-handed hospitality of Yazooans;" for so it seemed to be. I found both of Mrs. Black's
lawyers to be courteous and apparently skillful attorneys.
Their office was in a one-story structure, opening out on Main
Street. It was a sort of rendezvous for the " leading citizens " of the county, as well as of the town.

---

* It was Mrs. Black, and not the Colonel, we were dealing with, and I thought we
should be able to get on with her.

I also observed that the opinions of these lawyers upon almost all subjects in which planters and merchants were interested at that time, were received as law by those who sought them, and I could not fail to see that the legal profession, in which they were evidently the local autocrats, was highly esteemed in Yazoo. They did not seem to care to discuss the war. Others did, and as many as said anything upon the subject agreed that the "wah is over," the "nigros are free;" "we wor whipped!" "we don't want any mo' of it in ourn." The silence of these astute lawyers and an occasional shrug or wise look, struck me as indicating a mental reservation, at least, on their part, in their sort of involuntary acquiescence in the opinion prevailing on this point.

At dinner that day Mrs Black and her daughters, having learned of my ability to stand out against one of "the ways of the country," expressed their gratification in terms that could not be mistaken.

CHAPTER III.

A FIRST DAY WITH THE FREEDMEN OF YAZOO—WHAT WAS ACCOM-
PLISHED BY THE WAR.

IT had been arranged by Charles and myself before we
separated at Vicksburg, that during his absence I should
endeavor to gather together the labor required for Tokeba.
Should he be able to arrange for a saw-mill it was our purpose to bring trained men from the North to operate it.

The cotton harvest closes with the year. In the days of
slavery, therefore, the holiday season was undoubtedly the
best for such an undertaking, and 1 was advised by the Colonel and nearly all old residents with whom I counseled upon
the subject, that it would still be the best season for my
purposes. The war had completely overturned their labor
system, however, as all agreed. I argued that it had or would
overturn this custom also.*

There were daily many freedmen in town in search of
work. But Colonel Black assured me that these were mostly
restless, "no-account nigros," who were taking advantage
of their freedom to leave their masters, or were of those who
had "run off' with the Yankees," and were waiting for their
" forty acres of land and a mule."

I did not lack for advisers, and was struck with the unanimity of sentiment and opinion upon this subject. But the

---

* Of course I did not then realize how far-reaching in its consequences to the planting
and commercial interests of the cotton territory would be any change of this custom.

holidays were rapidly approaching, and as many Northerners were prospecting for favorable locations on the Yazoo River, I deemed it wise to set about my task without further delay.

In the crowd of freed people I had observed standing about the street corners, or in front of store-doors, there were few seeking homes for themselves alone. Most of them appeared well-behaved, orderly, able-bodied, and as though they had not long been idle. On closer inquiry I found that many of them had homes and had but recently quit work. In such cases the family remained with the old master, and their abandonment of him was wholly dependent upon the success of their representative in his efforts to find an employer for himself and them. In no case was he willing to hire himself for more than a brief period without his family. This feature of the situation struck me forcibly as worthy of more consideration than I had given to the general subject of labor. The few men and women without families that I could get to go for a term of three years, or even one year to the plantation, appeared to me dissipated and unreliable.

I had expected to be able to go into the labor market, and buy and pay for the labor required for Tokeba in the ordinary way—the one in which I had been reared. It had not occurred to either Charles or myself, while discussing the subject of labor for Tokeba, that, in order to secure a force of one hundred or so hands for the place, it would be necessary to make provision for food and clothes for any greater number than was actually required for its cultivation.

Both Colonel and Mrs. Black assured me that this had always been a chief obstacle to the profitable cultivation of cotton, except where their owners combined the business of breeding slaves with planting. This branch of the slave industry of the South had been less generally availed of by Mississippi planters than by their brethren in Virginia, for example. But the necessities of their labor system were gradually driving the planters of the cotton States into the practice. The supply from the grand old " mother of statesmen" was not equal to the growing demand. Besides, the laborers were made more contented thereby. Of course they "live together like the lower animals," Colonel Black would say, " and the desire to raise a family was purely a sensual one." It gratified the cupidity of the master in another way, also, for it often happened that there would be " a surplus that could be turned into money."

Now this phase of the question shocked me, and, strange to say, I realized for the first time the true inwardness of slavery; I say strange, because I had been born and bred a hater of slavery, and up to this moment had supposed that I knew what it was. Alas! I was only beginning to learn. Here, upon the very threshold, I was met with that problem which lay at the root of the American system of slavery, and was required to solve it or abandon all attempts to plant cotton. This was evident.

Neither Colonel Black nor his wife appeared to sympathize with me in the dilemma in which I found myself. The reason was, that they could not take in the same objects from the point of view that I did. Indeed, they could not put themselves in my place at all. It is all clear enough to me now. It puzzled me somewhat then. From my point of view their emancipation brought to the slaves liberty of choice, within only such proper restraints as were imposed upon all. I had never doubted that, left to himself, the slave would prefer that his wife should not work in the fields, but attend to her children and household affairs; that he would insist upon school facilities for his children, and would gladly do the toiling necessary to these ends. But here were rugged, brawny men, every one of whom insisted upon my employing their wives and children as field hands, as a condition of their consent to work for us; and here was our landlord and his good, Christian wife trying to aid me in the solution of this problem, by explaining certain features of one which we all agreed had already been solved by the war. Such was the only result of my first day among the freed people of Yazoo.

When next I went among them, to the first man who asked me also to employ his wife and children to work in the fields I put this question:

" Why will you freedmen all insist that your wives shall work in the field?" He seemed not to understand me, so I repeated it. The poor fellow looked about him as though to see whether we were likely to be overheard, and replied:

" Bees you a Yankee? I know you is, do, kase I dun seed it. Laws! Kunnel; I specs yo' is a Kunnel. We col'ud folks is too po'. Mars ain't dun tole us we is free yit, an' we got no money, an' no close, nur nuffin, 'cept'n what we eat and what we wahr. We dun heerd 'bout de Yankees comin' 'bout de Azoo, an' brerer Jon'than he 'lowd mount ez well come down y'hea and see fur ouah own self."

" Well," said I, " should you go with us we will pay you wages, you know, and that will enable you to support your wife."

" How much ye 'low ter pay me?" inquired the freed-man.

" Fifteen dollars per month."

" He! Dat's heep mo' money den I dun seed dis blessed yeah. But ye see, Kunnel, nun on us niggers got no lan', nur no mooles, nur nuffin, 'cep'n wot we eat an' wot we wahr, an' Uncle Jon'than, he 'low'd ef 'twar so dat de Yan-kee's comin' in y'hea, and we is all free, dat de o'omin folks an' all on um jes go 'way frum dah. He 'low'd, he did, dat we all better wuk, little an big, t'wel we got hole some ob dis y'hea lan' what we is a stan'in' on, and I 'low'd ter do jes dat er way fust, Kunnel. Ole Uncle Si, he 'low'd niggers nebber will own no lan'. Kase dey ain't nun fur um, an' de white folks won' nebber gi'e us nun daern, nur sell us nun nuther; kase dey 'feered de bottum rail mout come on de top. But de Yankee sojas wor dar lookin' arter 'fedrit cotting an' Gobment mooles, jes fo' de s'render, an' dey 'low'd dat we all mout own lan' jes 'e same ez de white folks, wen we dun buy it, an' pay fur it out'en ouah own money. But Uncle Si, he 'clar' dem Yankees no 'count no

way. Kase nun on 'um comed dar in de ole Homes
County,* whar we uns all wor wukin' fur ole Mars, jez 'e
same ez 'fo' de wah, any mo'. "

"You see, Mars Kunnel, niggers got no larnin', no how, an'
dem Homes County niggers dar whar we is, nebber heern de
wah wor ober t'wel young Mars Henry 'low'd he nebber g'wain
back ter Richmon' no mo', kase Mars Lee dun s'render.
Den we 'low'd dey wor whipped, an' nebber g'wain tell us niggers. But den, nigger got eyes, an' he y'eah mighty long dis-
tanze, too. So Uncle Jon'than he rund off de Satu'day
comin' an' peered like he nebber would come back no mo',
t'wel one night he jes' drapped down frum de hebbens like
he wor' a angel, an' dar comed 'long two Yankee sojas wid
da guns an' da pistils an' da shinin' buttons, an' 'low'd, ef
Mars lib any whar 'round dat er way? Ole Mars, he dun
y'eah de fuss an' de dogs a barkin', an' Jon'than's wife she
bust out a shoutin,' kase she duu yeah Jon'than a walkin'
'bout in de kitchin, an' she knowed his step fo' dat day.
Den de sojas dey holla 'bout de dog, an' swo' dey shoot um
ef dey doan call um off. Ole Mars done went out dar den,
mighty peert, an' call de dogs off, an' tie um up, an' spoke
to de sojas, an' wor mighty perlite, too, an' tole um, 'Gen-
'lemens, doan be afeerd, dey woan bite, cep'n yo' is niggers,
deez is nigger dogs, dey is;' an' den one de sojas he sot down
he musket on de groun', an' say, sais he, 'Ole man, yo'
got no fodder for dees y'here animools?' I tho't I'd di' a laffin',
or buss, kase Mars wor a preacher, he wor, an' he nebber
use de kuss wud hisself, an' dar dem sojas jez a cussin' an' a
dammin' de dogs an' ole Mars, an' a tellin' of um how dey 'low'd
dey g'wain help da self, an' broke de doah ef he wouldn' make
hase an' gie um de key. An' fo' God! dey tuck de key, an' dey
'low'd de fodder an' de co'n no 'count, an' poad out de
wheat ole Mars dun bin sabin' gin plantin' time fur ter sow,
an' jes turned de mooles looze on-ter it, jez ez do dar wor
nuffn' tu good fur dem ar Yankee mooles. Den dey ax ole
Mars fur dem fo' bale 'fedrit cotting he wor a hidin' dar, an' if

* This county adjoins Yazoo County on the northeast.

he got no Gobment mooles on de place, an' 'low'd dey had
orders fur ter sarch troo der premumses.   Den de wun whar
'peer'd ter be de boss, he 'low'd dey wor hongry, an' ole Mars
he d'clar de cook dun lef' um dat very minit—long wud Uncle Jon'than.   Den dey 'low'd dey doan' mine dat—dey help
da self.   Den de Missus she 'low'd ef dey jes wait dar a
minit, she make out ter git dem suffin' fur ter eat, an' ole
Mars he ax um in de parlor, an' done poke de fire, an' dar he
sot, honey, jes a talkin' an' a talkin' wid dose ar Yankees,
jez ez do he heep glad de wah been ober, and de niggers wor
free, an' when Missus done sot de table, an' make de kof-
fee, an' fry de baken, an' roaz sum taters, he gie a prar like
he praise de Lor' da God A'mighty fur sendin' ob de Yankees, an' de co'n an' de baken, an' relieben' ob um da 'sponsibil-
'ty on day souls ob all de niggers.   Den de sojas, when dey
done eat'n', au' kotch up da mooles, an' turn da wagon roun',
au' stop down de road apiece, brerer Jon'than an' Aunt Nancy
dey wor dar wid da traps, an' dey tuck um on day wagon an'
dey drove down ter Goodman by the railroad, whar de
Yankee reg'men' wor, an' brerer Jon'than he stop dar, an' I
comed y'hea, kase we 'low'd ter git wuk, an' den brerer Jon-
than sen' wud fur our feller servanz dar in de ole Homes
County; kase dey all foun' out dey is free now."

The foregoing was drawn out of Pomp by the questions I
from time to time put to him, until I had obtained the whole
story of his escape, and of that of his fellow-servants, from
that slavery which all agreed was annihilated at Appomattox.

Of course I had expected to find the freed people all poor
and many needy.   The little I had seen of them while serving in Virginia had prepared me for that.   But I had not
realized what the words poor, needy, meant.   The man before
me was not more than thirty-five.   He had a wife and five
children.

There he stood, a man full six feet tall, with brawny muscles and a frank, honest, open countenance.   His hat was a
mere remnant of one.   His coat, made of some sort of homespun cotton, had been patched with so many different colors

and kinds of cloth, it was difficult to make out the texture of
the original garment. His pants, of some sort of bagging
stuff, had received less care, for the original patches were
worn until they hung in strings, and his shoes, brogans, of
the color of raw hide, glazed with wear, made but a feeble
pretence at covering his feet.

This man, all his life, had been the slave of a minister of
the gospel of the Son of God, and had faithfully served him.
When the war came, his young master, Henry, this minister's
son, had enrolled himself in a regiment of infantry, and
served in the rebel army of northern Virginia to its close.
He had been twice severely wounded, and had been at home
on that account several weeks when Lee's army surrendered.
Nearly all the young white men in his county and many of the
old ones had rendered similar service. During their absence
this man before me had remained, faithfully serving his master, and the year before the surrender he and his wife and
his children—for they had all worked in the field who were
old enough to do so—had planted, cultivated, and harvested
a large crop, for which that minister had received the proceeds,
and up to the moment himself, Uncle Jonathan and Aunt
Nancy ran away, they had been similarly engaged. All he
had received for this service was his food and what I saw
upon his person. Yet this man looked forward to a future
which, to him, was full of promise; a future in which he saw
himself the possible owner of land, if only he could find
honest employment for himself, wife and children in the cotton and corn fields. Neither in his speech nor in his manner
was there any sign of bitterness toward his old master, nor
any desire to take by force any part of his past earnings,
nor wish to have any part of the land of another that he
could not pay for, nor any disposition to ask any lands or
mules or food from the Government, or from private citizens,
as a forfeit or a gift. This man might beg for work; he would
never beg for bread; neither would he steal it. He now
appears to me as I saw him then, a nobleman in the highest
sense of the word.

CHAPTER IV.

JEALOUS "JOHNNY REBS"—COL. J. J. U. BLACK IN A NEW ROLE.

I DID not mention the interview with my sable nobleman to Colonel Black or to the ladies, nor my reflections upon it either, while at dinner that day or ever afterward; from regard for their feelings—and—well, the war was over. I thought it a very serious matter, however, and it raised a flood of apprehension in my mind, the sequel to which may appear further on in this narrative. I had a sort of feeling that it was an exceptional case; I hoped it might prove so. This hope was strengthened by my subsequent experiences that day. For there were but very few in town who were not better clothed than the Holmes County "runaway." Whenever I asked the question, "why do you wish to leave your old master?" the response generally was a sullen, far away look, or simply:

"Ole marstah an' me doan 'gree no mo'."*

Occasionally one would reply in plain English: "I'm free now and I want to work for my own self."

As a rule this latter class were quite comfortably dressed, and bore the appearance of having had good treatment. They held up their heads and did not have that timid, shy look, which so many wore whose old homes were farther back toward the interior.

*I was not long in finding out the importance of the form in which I put my questions to the freed people, "Why do you wish to leave your old master?" was apprehended by them as implying that they were under some sort of obligation to that personage.

The true explanation of this did not occur to me for some time afterward. I am now certain that it was entirely due to the fact that they had seen, talked with, and probably spent some time in the employ of Yankee planters on the Mississippi, or had been with the Yankee soldiers. However, there were not very many of that class in Yazoo then.

Some of the ladies whom I met at the Colonel's, also his daughters, thought I ought not to be doing this work myself.

" It must be very disagreeable," said one.

" Don't you 'low to have an overseer ? " said another, " I reckon you'll have to have one."

On two occasions, while thus seeking labor for Tokeba, the Colonel accompanied me. I observed that whenever he addressed a freedman he would say : " Here, you, boy ! " or " Hi ! boy." Sometimes in his blandest manner he would salute one thus : " Well, Mr. Washington," or " Mr. Julius Augustus," or " Cæsar," as the case might be, " how do you do to-day ? How's your good lady ? "

This I accepted as a hint to me not to be nice in my manner of addresssing the freed people—that I should fall in with the ways of the country.* I do not recollect a single instance when this manner of Colonel Black's was resented by the freed people in any other way than by a sullen drooping of the eyes, accompanied by a grin of submission. The Colonel, however, soon became satisfied that I was either not an apt pupil, or that he was not very well fitted to be my instructor in such matters, and abandoned all further efforts in that direction, venting his spleen in an extra number of oaths. It speedily became known to the planters who came to town, as well as to the townspeople, that I was " the Yankee who had rented the Black plantation "—and that I was " Colonel Black's Yankee guest."

Now this latter fact was of the utmost importance: First, because the Black family, being of the bluest old South Carolina stock, were at the very top of the best society of Yazoo.

*The fact is, it was intended as a criticism upon my manner.

There were those who did not like the Colonel, but there was no doubt of his standing. The Stockdales were in trade —some of them—and, though a very distinguished family, this fact placed them on a round in the social ladder at least one below the Blacks. The sheriff, the judges and all in the trades or professions recognized this fact. The only rivals the Blacks had were the very great planters. Second, as Colonel Black's guest I was absolutely protected against insult, and could go where I pleased. These facts made me quite a conspicuous figure, and quite an important personage in the little town.

I had not been long engaged in the work of hiring the labor for Tokeba before it became evident to me that my manner toward freed people was being unfavorably commented upon by the "best citizens."*

Occasionally, some planter in town on similar business as my own, observing me in conversation with a group of freed people, would stop, and, after listening a short while, speak to some one he might know and ask who I was. Upon being informed he would mutter: "I thought so;" then walk on a few steps, halt, turn about, scowl gloomily upon us, and always turn finally to go away, with a nervous jerk of his head or shoulder, or some deprecatory wave of the hand.

I well recollect once when thus engaged, a man whom I shall call Wicks, because it as completely disguises his real name as any I can think of would. Ben Wicks, owner of several thousand of acres of cotton land, and formerly of a thousand or so of slaves, offensively and violently elbowed his way right in among a group with whom I was arranging for their hire, and exclaimed :

" What er you all doing y'here? You nigros better go back whar ye b'long, and quit running after these y'here d—n Yankees."

*The freed people at that time were just beginning to adopt surnames, and, out of regard to the custom of the country, I had purposely avoided addressing them by any other title than that given to them by their late owners, as Pomp, Tom, Dick, etc. It was not possible, however, for me to so soon acquire the style of address, and the manner of the Southron.

" Hi, yo black rascal !" he continued, in a still more veno-
mous tone, if possible, and addressing a freedman in the group
who had on a blue military cap and coat : " Yo'r kind'l be
d—n skase about y'here befo' a gret while." Then, without
having apparently looked at me, he walked angrily away.

I could then no more than conjecture what the cause was
of his indignation and disgust. It was evident that *he* did
not mean to be civil to me because I was Colonel Black's
guest.

But few of the residents of the town then carried weapons
exposed. Those who kept them on their persons wore them
concealed. But a great majority of the country white people
wore theirs strapped outside their pants, and many outside
their coats. They generally came to town on horseback, in
groups of from two or three to six or eight, sometimes even
a greater number, and dressed in old Confederate gray, or
what appeared to be homespun goods. A great part of them
carried saddle-bags, and frequently a demijohn.

Sometimes, as they rode out or passed by where I might be
standing, some one of them would shout out to another, some
epithet applied to Yankees, in a sufficiently loud tone for me
distinctly to hear. I always construed such demonstrations,
however, as due to a very " natural feeling " toward their
" conquerors," and in this category I classed every disagreeable incident of that character.

Another cause of ill-feeling toward me I discovered to be
in the fact that, whereas I was succeeding beyond my expectations in re-stocking Tokeba, many old planters, or their
overseers, were not having any success at all, and it was being acknowledged on all sides, what indeed had long been
feared by the native planters, that the freedmen preferred
to hire to the " new-comers," even at less wages than native
planters were offering. This fact was made a pretext for
unfriendly criticism of the means employed by the new-comers
to " entice the nigros from their masters," as it was called.

The fact is, I did not have to use persuasion at all. My

chief difficulty was to select from the great number willing to go with me the very best, and, unlike most of the natives, I inquired into the habits of the men and women who offered; whether they were given to drunkenness or other vicious practices, and it was whispered about that I had applied another test, to wit, whether they could read or write ! But this rumor, I was satisfied, was started by some wag for a jest.

All this information about my conduct reached me through Colonel and Mrs. Black, who appeared to watch over me with anxious solicitude. One morning at breakfast this solicitude manifested itself in open but friendly criticism.

The Colonel began by assuring me of his desire that I should endeavor to make myself popular with " our people." He had commended my brother and myself to his neighbors and friends, as worthy of full confidence and respect in every way ; and it was only because he could plainly see that I was unacquainted with the habits and customs of the people I had cast my lot with, that he ventured to speak. Then he told me that several of his acquaintances had spoken to him of the " unfavorable impression I had made by my treatment of the nigros on the street, and my manner of speech while among them." Some of these rumors were exceedingly disagreeble to himself. It was quite natural—he could understand—that my curiosity should tempt me " to listen to the tales of the nigros about their masters and mistresses," considering where I was raised, and that it was all new to me. But he regretted exceedingly to say that the nigros themselves were quoting me as their friend, as against their old masters, and if what some of them reported of my remarks to them was true, I was not only doing myself a great injury, but should be regarded by the community as willfully engaged in stirring up bad blood between the races. Mrs. Black declared she did not believe the stories afloat, and was heartily glad I was succeeding so admirably. The young ladies *could* not believe them. It was unbecoming in a gentleman, and they had steadily resented any reference to it by their associates.

I protested I had not thought of such a thing. I had come there to better my condition, and trusted I might be able to assist in helping to develop and improve the country, the impoverished and undeveloped condition of which had so often formed the theme of our table talks. It was impossible for me to disguise the fact, however, that I could see that the colored people liked me, and it would be quite natural for them to comment, and I had no doubt in an exaggerated way, upon my manner toward them. I had observed a disposition among them to appear more independent when talking with me than with Colonel Black, for example. But it would be out of place in me to rebuke them for expressing dissatisfaction with their old masters, who may have been cruel to them, as they themselves knew had often been the case. "But," I said, "I have not encouraged any of them to speak disrespectfully of any one, certainly not of ladies, nor would I ever be guilty of such an indiscretion, not to use a harsher term."

Mrs. Black promptly assured me that she knew I was misrepresented, and simply by way of offering corroborating testimony she declared, that only the day before Major Snodgrass had said in conversation with her upon the same point, that he had frequently observed me on the street and in conversation with the "nigros," and had never seen the slightest impropriety nor heard the least objectionable word from my lips. Quite the contrary. My "manner toward the nigros, my speech, and my bearing was always dignified and, though kindly, it was all the more commendable." He thought my course a wise one, if it was assumed, and if he could find another man just like me he would be only too glad to take him for a partner in his own plantation. He was satisfied he would then be able to command all the labor he could use with profit. Besides, while she believed the "nigros" would always remain as they were, the "natural servants of the whites," she agreed with the further opinion of Major Snodgrass, that they could "not too soon recognize as a *fact* the overthrow of slavery, which made it necessary that a *new* system of labor be established, and if the nigro was to be free to choose his own mistress or master, it would become necessary for their masters to treat them with some measure of kindness and respect. She was not sure but both would in the end be benefitted by the change."

The Colonel grew somewhat nervous under his wife's speech, and finally interrupted her to say that the Major's "doctrine was fallacious ; that if put into practice it would result in the ruin of the nigro, who could be governed only through fear, and that I should find that I was casting my pearls before swine, by G—d, who would take advantage of my kindness to eat or steal me out of house and home." He said he knew some of the "nigros" I had already sent out to the place, and they were " always a sassy, impudent, good-for-nothing set; grand rascals, sir; the last one of them, by G—d, sir."

Very soon after this conversation occurred, the Holmes County "runaway" reported himself, wife, and children, Uncle J mathan, his wife, their children, and two other grown persons and their several children. They had gone straight to Tokeba, and each family had already selected a cabin. But they had no furniture, and had for bedding and house-stuff only what they could "tote" away from the old place. Several of their number were nearly white, and fully three-fourths of the remainder were of mixed blood. Those of the lightest complexion were quite well dressed. So also were two or three of the blacks. But Uncle Jonathan and his son-in-law, Pomp, and their wives and children were wretchedly clad. They had "slipped off" in the night. This appeared to be the prudent course, because several young men in their neighborhood had organized a sort of patrol* for the purpose of preventing any " rising " that the blacks might contemplate, since the night that the two Yankee soldiers

---

* This was the beginning of that organization in Mississippi which afterward became known by the name of ku-klux-klan—click, cluck, clack, or the three sharp sounds caused by the cocking of a gun.

were out there; and had whipped one young man of the company in a most cruel manner, because he was "found away from home" without a pass, and were said to have threatened to kill Jonathan and Pomp, should they ever show themselves in those parts again.

It was out of the question for me to provide them with bedding at once. I had made no provision for such an emergency. All the other families had brought their beds with them, such as they were. But this was not a serious matter at all with these pioneers. They cut cane, gathered leaves from the woods and from other sources wholly unknown to me, and soon had beds, tables and stools. These, with two or three skillets the party brought with them, enabled them to get on after a fashion.

I was unable to make out from their account of it just what a "rising" meant. But I had not long to wait for an explanation.

CHAPTER V.

A "NIGRO" INSURRECTION AND A FOOL'S ERRAND.

THE next day but one following the arrival of Uncle Jonathan and his party, Colonel Black came in from down
town rather earlier than usual. He asked for "Mistress
Black," and being informed by Rose, the colored cook, that
"Missus in her room, Mars Jeems," he went directly to her.

There was an air of mysterious importance about him that
attracted my notice. His interview with Mrs. Black was protracted until the usual dinner hour had passed.

When at last all appeared, they were in such an atmosphere
of secrecy and mystery that I felt uncomfortable. Observing
this, I suppose, the Colonel seized an opportunity, afforded by
the absence from the dining-room of the colored servant, to
hint at the cause of it, which only served to increase my embarrassment.

In our table-talk previously there had been occasional
references to the danger of negro insurrections, "now that
the nigro is free"—a suggestion I had always combatted,
however. On this occasion the only topic of conversation
had reference solely to "servile insurrections" of ancient
times, and it was wonderful to see what a fund of information each member of this family, including Mr. ——, their
guest, possessed upon this subject.

The "Virginia slave insurrection" was brought forward,
and discussed in all its details; "servile insurrections among

the Romans" were recalled, and the Colonel brought to
light, with a manner which seemed to indicate an abnormal
appetite for blood-curdling historical incidents, an insurrec
tion that occurred in Tyre a thousand years before Christ,
when the king, the queen, the nobles and many thousands of
the slaveholding and non-slaveholding class were murdered,
only their wives and daughters being spared, to become the
wives and concubines of their former slaves.

By the time dinner was concluded, the ladies wore very
white faces indeed, and dread expectancy hung like a pall
over the whole household, excepting only the "nigro servants,"
who went about their work as usual.

Adjourning to the sitting-room the Colonel informed me,
after a somewhat lengthy prelude, that a plot had been discovered—"a deep, damnable conspiracy by the nigros, to
rise and kill all the white people from the cradle up."

The alarm among the ladies had now reached a pitch where
one of them, who was " not a Yankee," notwithstanding she
was " bred and bohn " one, and had been a governess in the
family before the war, but now was a sort of dependent, of
" uncertain age," would doubtless have gone into hysterics,
but for the courageous offer of one of her former charges to
stand by her to the last.

Up to this time I had remained steadfast in my skepticism.
But the earnest, sincere manner of the Colonel and of
Mrs. Black, coupled with the anxiety and the tears of the
young ladies, who hung together in a cluster, as if preparing
to meet their fate in each other's arms, lent to the spell wrought
by the recitals of horrors to which I had listened a new power
that overcame my judgment, and, forgetting my previous experiences, forgetting Pomp, Jonathan, Bristol, all, I passed
under this influence, and unhesitatingly volunteered to aid
in defending them against such a fate.

But I had no weapon. One was quickly provided, however, by one of the young ladies, and it was discovered that
there were in the house, besides, a pistol for each male mem-

ber of the family, a double-barrelled shotgun and a breech-loading rifle.

Taking " time by the forelock," the Colonel said, a number of " leading citizens," among them Mrs. Black's lawyers, had " called a public meeting for consultation, and to prepare to meet the emergency." " Fo'ewahned " was to be " foreahmed with all brave people," and he said he would be glad to have me accompany him to the place of meeting, where I should learn all the details of the conspiracy that had thus far been unearthed.

To this day, I am not able to say that the alarm manifested by every white member of the family at this time was feigned. It was all so natural, and their conversation relative to the cause of it seemed so sincere, it had all the effect upon me of a real danger.

I promptly accepted the Colonel's invitation, declaring that, in such an emergency, prevention was better than any cure that could be applied, and that the leaders, when discovered, ought to be tried and upon proof of guilt should be punished severely.

Arriving at the place we found the meeting already organized. There were about twenty-five, perhaps thirty, persons present, all white men, and residents of the town and the immediate vicinity. It had evidently been hastily assembled.

At the moment we entered the chairman, one of Mrs. Black's lawyers, was engaged in recalling incidents within the memory of his hearers, illustrative of " the blood-thirsty nature of the African, when once he had reached the point of daring to raise his hand against a white man," and he dwelt at some length on the " slave insurrection in Virginia," winding up with a vivid picture of the " horrors of Santo Domingo."

He was followed by Colonel Black, and he by another person, who spent some minutes in an effort to show that insurrections were common with " all servile peoples; " instanced the numerous "Roman slave insurrections, and one which occurred in Tyre, when the slaves rose and killed the king; the

queen, all the nobles, and many thousands of the master-class,
sparing their wives and daughters, whom they married. He
for one would not dare attempt to foretell the horrors
likely to result from an uprising of the nigros of the South."

At this point the meeting became greatly excited. But
one of those present, whose name I cannot now recall, asked
what proof there was that an uprising of any kind was contemplated by the blacks. Strange to say none had yet been
produced, and so far as I knew, no reference had yet been
made to the matter of proof by any of the speakers.

This struck me at the time as being a little queer. But
stranger still, not having been called for, I had myself
not thought of it. I, however, had observed the similarity
between Colonel Black's table-talk on insurrections and that
of the speakers, who all recalled the same historical incidents,
though somewhat unlike in details.

At this point the chairman called upon Mr. Gosling to
state to the meeting what he knew or had heard of the purposes of the blacks.

Mr. Gosling kept the ferry at the Yazoo City landing. He
was a little, old, " weazen-faced " man, with a squeaky voice,
of the class which before the war was not more than one if
any degree above the "poor white trash " of that section. I
recollect well the air of importance that he assumed on rising,
which, with his evident embarrassment, made him appear
quite ridiculous indeed. He could not sufficiently well keep
his thoughts in line for intelligent apprehension, when he
finally succeeded in uttering them, and would have failed
utterly, no doubt, had not Colonel Black and the other of
Mrs. Black's lawyers prompted him.

He was unable to give the names of the conspirators, or to
say when the rising would take place. But he had his sus-
picions, and they were grounded on the fact that the negroes were becoming very impudent indeed, not only
towards himself and members of his family; he had observed
their actions while crossing over on his ferry, and had heard

them "use thirtenin words." He had also frequently "saw them talkin' together in groups," and many more were now using the ferry at night than formerly.

When called on for the language he had heard them employ he confessed that it was always of a "dub'ous kind." He remembered that he frequently "heerd talkin'" between them, in which the Yankees up the river on the Payne plantations were contrasted with their old masters, greatly to the damage of the masters, and he had "heern um swar," and had "overheern um say kill with dark and thirtenin looks." To the inquiry as to whether he knew of the "nigros carrying ahms," he was able to speak with certainty. He declared, in substance that he had "heerd um say the niggers on the Payne pluntashons was ahmd with gov*ment* guns." He did not mean "Confedrit ahmy guns." And on several occasions he had "crossed niggers a totin' Springfiel', or Enfiel' rifles. Some had side ahms, an' woah Fed'ral unifohms." He had asked some of these, "Whar they b'longed, an' they done sassed him—told him 'twas none yo' bizness."

He had taken the trouble to find out, however, and they all lived "up thar with them ar' Yankees on the Payne pluntashons." He had not been particular to "demand" passes of those he had crossed in the day time, because in the unsettled condition of the country it was impossible that all should have them. But he had, on several occasions, demanded passes of those crossing at night, and some had told him that "passes done played out now."

When Mr. Gosling closed, the other and the elder of Mrs. Black's lawyers gravely arose, and, in a most dignified manner, expressed his regrets that some Federal officers had discharged their "nigro regiments in our midst" and allowed them to keep their weapons. The people of the South had "surrendered in good faith," and would "not violate their paroles," and while it was exceedingly annoying to have to "submit to such indignicies," which he could not but feel were imposed upon "our people" by the "malice of some inferior Federal officer," such acts should not be taken as indicating the policy of the "Government at Washington," and he hoped they would not be so construed. For one he cautioned the people to keep calm, and by all means not allow their "indignation at these outrages" to lead them into rash or inconsiderate action. He did not see what they could do but submit. But it was their "duty, as good citizens, to be at all times on guard," for "nigros were easily imposed upon," and one or two "evil-disposed persons in the community" could easily "excite them to acts of vengeance." Should the "outbreak begin," the punishment ought to be "swift and certain," in order to "teach them that they cannot hope to raise themselves above the white man and rule him."

At this point Colonel Black, who had left the room while Mr. Gosling was giving in his evidence, returned, bringing with him a "nigger," as he was called, though he was nearly white, and, I observed, a cripple. He needed no introduction. They all knew Dave Cottonridge. Colonel Black announced that Dave had important information to communicate, and he would like the chairman to allow him the privilege of giving it to the meeting in his own way.

Leaning upon his cane, Dave informed them that he had "done y'heard ole Aunt Maria" say that 'white folks better look shahp, heep mo' mischuff in the nigro * than white folks ever dreamed of; that the darkies up the river could read, some of them, and had been holdin' meet'ns and sayin' many hard things about their old masters." He also said, by way of a clincher, that old Uncle Sandy (this was Mr. Gosling's ferryman) had told him that old Aunt Suky had " 'lowd how Unkle Ike " (her husband) " had 'low'd that them nigros over the river mighty onsartin, and wouldn't be surprised to y'hear the cradles a groanin' by an' by."

During this recital the meeting became very much excited again, except that portion which appeared to be the leaders,

---

*Mr. Cottonridge, though once a slave, had served in the Confederate army, and pronounced negro like a "real gentleman."

and, as I afterward knew, the instigators of it. I saw nothing in the so-called evidence to justify the excitement, however, and may have, in some way, discovered the fact to Colonel Black. For he arose at this juncture and explained that the importance of the testimony before the meeting could be understood only by those who were " acquainted with the nigro character and with their mode of imparting to each other information relating to any common purpose among them."

He cited the " records of history relating to nigro insurrections, particularly the Virginia insurrection, from which it appeared that, for some time before it occurred, similar expressions had been employed by the nigros."

While he was thus talking I could see that he was being closely followed by the audience, and I observed signs of emphatic approval of what he said, as much as to say: " That's it exactly. We know what it all means; these dark looks; these meetings; these speeches, with a hidden meaning; he's good enough to do it, any way," and so forth. I did not take in the situation then; not all of it, nor any considerable portion of it. In fact, I have since often wondered what it was prevented me from seeing through it all. I have sometimes thought that I might have seen more clearly, even then, but for a certain feeling of gallantry all of us possess in a greater or less degree toward the opposite sex, and but for what followed.

Having said this much by way of dispelling any doubts I might have of the character of these proofs, Colonel Black announced to the audience that there was present, by his invitation, one who had been an officer in the Federal army; " my guest and a gentleman who has recently cast his lot with our people." He would like very much, and he had no doubt the meeting would be glad, to hear his views upon the situation.

The meeting voted unanimously that I be invited to speak, and to give them " the benefit of my advice." I was extremely

anxious to be thought well of by the people of Yazoo. I fully
intended to make my permanent home there. I was young,
ambitious for success, and, as I now well know, very green.

The situation, however, was extremely embarrassing. My
father had warned me, when I enlisted for three months, in
April, 1861, just after the firing on Fort Sumter, that the
war would not close until the slaves had all been freed, and
he dedicated me in a certain sense to that service, to fight for
the slave—" God's poor." I had *volunteered* to do this; I had
abandoned my preparations for college to do this; I had
believed in the " cause" of the negro, as against his " master,"
the white man. But I arose, and said to this meeting,
quite tamely I am now sure, that " I had been exceedingly
pained by this occurrence; that I had come to Yazoo for the
purpose of making my home, in what I considered one of the
richest districts in the world, in natural resources of soil,
climate, and so forth, and should be found with the foremost
in putting down the insurrection should one occur, and they
could command my services at any time, and in any way
deemed best to prevent such a calamity. I, however, could
not agree with those who had spoken upon the subject; I did
not believe that the people who had just been ' made free at
so great cost' would ' throw it all away by such an attempt.'"
I was certain it could never amount to anything more. I
was not at all convinced by the evidence before the meeting
that an insurrection was contemplated. " However," I said,
" I am inexperienced, and know nothing by contact with
them of the negro character; therefore, I should be advised
by those who at least ought to know."

There was some stamping of feet when I sat down, and the
chairman called on Colonel Black, whom he observed in an
attitude as of a wish to say something, who proceeded to
commend me for " the stand " I had taken. He felt certain
that those " who raised him " knew best what was " for the
good of the nigro," and best knew his character. He knew
that they were a " dark, ungrateful, treacherous people," and

being ignorant as well as degraded, it would be only natural
for the rascals to assume that their " freedom had made them
all white," and to insist upon " complete social equality."
As that could only result in the " degradation of the white
race to the level of their own, it became the duty of every
white man to meet them upon the very threshold of their
demands and let them know for good and all that though
God, for some reason known only to Himself, had permitted
their emancipation, He had, for some equally wise reason,
not changed the color of their skin, the kink in their wool,
or the length of their heels," and that " these differences "
would and " ought to perpetuate their subjection to the Caucasian."

In conclusion, he did not think there was " immediate
danger," and, as it was evident " from the temper of the
meeting that it was deemed unwise at that particular
juncture to resort to summary means of redress," as it
might be " misconstrued by the canting, hypocritical humanitarians of the North, who were just now all powerful in
affairs, owing to the unfortunate *manner* of Mr. Lincoln's
death." He would advise that the " military authorities be
first directly appealed to for such protection as the exi-
gencies of the occasion required, before they took matters into their own hands." He, therefore, moved that a
committee of three be appointed by the chair, " to proceed
to Vicksburg and lay all the facts before the commanding
general of the district, and beg him to send troops, in
charge of a discreet officer," to Yazoo at once, or to allow
them to " organize a home garrison or patrol " for the " protection of the lives of their wives and daughters."

The motion was adopted unanimously, and the chairman
appointed Colonel Black and two others. But, upon request
of the Colonel, I was substituted for one of these, with the
suggestion that I be the chairman. I begged to be excused.
But the Colonel and the chairman of the meeting insisted
that it would be but " natural for the commanding general to

heed what I might say, rather more than anything they could, as I was, in a sense, his comrade, and could not be suspected of any ulterior purpose or sinister design, and could speak from personal knowledge of the excited state of the public mind."

Thus persuaded, I consented. A committee were appointed to draft the petition, and, as time was precious, they were empowered to place that document, when prepared, in the hands of our committee, without waiting for a formal approval of it by the meeting. Then, after appointing a "night patrol" to act "in conjunction with the city marshal and police," the meeting broke up.

I found myself quite a hero by the time I reached the Colonel's home, where several ladies had gathered, and were discussing the situation. Observing their terror, I volunteered to remain on guard at the house that night as an additional protection to the ladies. But after bedewing me with their thanks, they refused me that privilege, on the ground that I needed rest preparatory to the journey on the morrow. And so, after an half hour more on "the horrors of Santo Domingo," I retired for the night with a loaded pistol under my pillow.

There was a boat at the landing early the following morning, and an attempt was made to charter it to convey the "distinguished committee" on their errand of love. But that fell through. The attempt, however, cost us a delay of quite two hours, so that it was ten o'clock before the Colonel and myself got off to make the trip by land. This, being a short cut, was only about sixty five miles. Seated in an old, rickety, army ambulance, behind two "poky" mules driven by a "po' white," we made, I am sure, quite an attractive if not a distinguished appearance. To cap the climax, just as we started it began to pour down rain, and in spite of our outside protectors we were very soon nicely soaked. This induced my companion to soak himself inwardly with a different kind of protector that he had not neglected to bring with him, and which lay curled up within a large black bottle, stowed away,

when not in use, in the saddle-bags along with other necessary
articles for the journey, which Aunt Rose had provided
That morning on our way down town we met several who
had been at the meeting the night before, and who, after the
usual salutations, went about their business. I had not failed
to remark the absence of all excitement in the town, and that
the people were engaged about as usual. Nor had the negroes
appeared to me any. more "mysterious" or "dark" looking
than before the meeting. Just before starting one of our committee discovered that he ought not to spare the time from
his business, and therefore had concluded that it was not necessary that he should go. The plan to charter the steamer
fell through for want of the sum for its use demanded
by the captain.* Just before darkness came on, having
made about forty miles, we put up at the house of a planter
by the way, who "hadn't y'hearn no talk 'mongst my niggers
'bout any risin'," though he "wouldn't be surprised to
y'hear most anything, now they is free," and who, after giving us a supper on hoe-cake, bacon, greens and coffee, and
after taking several "night-caps" with the Colonel, gave us a
room together for the night, in which there was only one bed.
Being young I could stand almost anything, though it
proved a hard night for the Colonel.

The following morning, after breakfasting on coffee, bacon
and hoe-cake, with the addition of a chicken, cooked with the
bacon, in lieu of the greens, we got off early for the remainder of our journey.

Arriving at Vicksburg, one of the first steps in the direction of the object of our mission was an invitation from the
Colonel to accompany him in an effort to find some old acquaintances. He met several of these on the main street.
In every instance his manner of introducing me, after the
usual formula, was about as follows :

"Well, by G—d, sir, he's a Yankee but a gentleman,
and my guest, by G—d, sir. Let's take something," or, "will

* There came a time when this plan of chartering a steamer whenever the negroes
were "about to rise" was more popular in Yazoo.

yo' join us," or, " we've but just arrived, after a long journey
overland in the rain, by G—d, sir, and I'm thirsty.   Won't
yo' join us ?"

As I always refused to "join" he found it necessary each
time to apologize for me, by saying: " Oh! he's all right.
He'll get out of that befoah he's been with me a six month.
He's a gentleman, by G—d, sir, and is going to become one
of us;" or, " he hasn't learned ouah ways yet.   He means no
offense by it;" and he always vouched for my "standing."

I thought I saw that these remarks of the Colonel were
each time in response to a questioning look of his acquaintance, which seemed to say: " Who have you here; a
Yank ? " and I became satisfied, afterward, that these explanations were also intended to put his acquaintances on
their guard while in my presence.

I observed, too, that they rarely went into a saloon, but to
a drug or other store, dry goods or grocery; always drank
whisky liberally, and never, or hardly ever, paid for it.   It was
a bore to me from the beginning, of course, and as the Colonel's acquaintances were legion, as soon as I could do so
without offense, I excused myself, leaving him to finish his
" rounds " alone.   Alone in my room it was not long before I
began to feel very mean indeed.

When Colonel Black returned he was just enough " loaded
up" to deprive him of a measure, at least, of his cunning, and
he allowed me to see that he suspected my loyalty to our expedition and became inquisitive.   Not wishing to court a
rupture, however, I did not allow him to see what was passing in my mind.

The next morning he notified me that as neither of us was
acquainted with the General, he had acted upon the advice of
some friends and taken the liberty of inviting the " distinguished divine," the Rev. Dr. Augustus Lobby, to introduce
us.   When this tail end to our committee of " distinguished citizens," as the morning papers called us, arrived,
we went to headquarters, for I was in for it, and obtained

an interview with the General. We found him in bad humor. He declared he had been doing scarcely anything for two weeks but receiving delegations from other parts of the State on similar business.* He would listen to what we had to say, but wished us to understand that his mind was already made up. He had no soldiers for "such purposes." He did not believe an insurrection was contemplated, and he should " protect the freed people to the utmost limit of his ability and authority."

The Rev. Dr., however, was equal to the emergency. In the style of an ancient Roman senator addressing his captors —barring that ancient's defiance—he proceeded to sketch a history of " servile insurrections in ancient and modern times." There had, as yet, it was true, been " no general massacre " of whites by the blacks on our soil, as there had been " in Santo Domingo." But the one which occurred in Virginia had " put the people on their guard," so that measures had been adopted, that had grown into "customs with our people," and which, by " always anticipating them," had " prevented a general rising of the nigros." Then he pressed upon the mind of the commanding general of the district "the greatly-exposed condition of the whites by reason of the abnormal state of affairs existing since the wah, and that in remote and unprotected country districts, brave men, delicate women, tender children and dependents, on their bended knees, were at this moment pleading with a merciful God, while their husbands, fathers, and brethren were interceding with *him* for the means of preventing so dreadful a catastrophe. In such an emergency property shriveled into nothingness. In his hands were the means of preventing the slaughter of the white race, and there should not be a moment's delay in applying them. He was glad to have the honah and the pleasuah of introducing to him the committee of distinguished gentlemen present. They represented

---

*It might be interesting to know just how far these representations respecting so-called contemplated risings by the freed people influenced Mr. Seward and others in Mr. Johnson's Cabinet during the winter of 1865.

all classes of the people, and would be able to lay before him
the facts upon which their apprehensions were grounded;
and he would crave the careful and unbiased attention of the
commanding general. He was glad to be able to add as
an evidence of the absence of all *sectional* feeling in this
movement, that one of the distinguished gentlemen, he was
informed, had commanded a regiment on the same side as
himself, in the late unhappy wah, and was, therefore, in a
sense, his comrade. Surely he would hear *him*. The other,
he had personally known for years as the head of a most
interesting family, a high-toned, upright, Christian gentleman, and a loyal, patriotic citizen."

In justice to the people of the South, I ought, perhaps, to
tarry here a moment in order to present a clearer cast of this
divine. For, in some respects, he was the typical divine of
the South. He well represented, possibly a minority—but
certainly an influential and distinguished one—of those who
occupied the pulpit previous to the war, and who did their
share in firing the Southern heart, and uttering prophecies
against the Union. He was a man of coarse, but commanding figure; bold and loud-mouthed speech, with periods long,
and rhetorically balanced, imperious and authoritative in
manner, as though accustomed figuratively, and on occasion
literally, to use the plantation lash; with rather an unusual
development of intellectual ability, though accompanied with
evidence of more or less subservience to the lower passions
of our human nature. Indeed, if it be not irreverent to say so,
a man, out of whose face and features libidinous, vindictive
and brutal passions seemed, at turn, to be looking. The
reader may judge of the power and influence of such a man
before the war and during all its varying vicissitudes, as he
stood a self-poised clerical leader to encourage the hearts of
the people.

Colonel Black followed. He laid great stress upon my
" knowledge of the situation, " the " terror of our people,"
their " helpless condition," etc. Then he began to sketch the
" history of servile insurrections," the " horrors of Santo

Domingo," and to describe and illustrate the "treacherous nature of the nigro." He would have, doubtless, resumed his sketch of historical servile insurrections but was interrupted by the General with the remark, that his "engagements" were of a "most pressing nature," and what more we had to say could be "put in writing." Then he abruptly dismissed us, greatly to the indignation of the Colonel and the chagrin of the Rev. Dr. Augustus Lobby, who declared that he had "small hope from the outset of making much impression upon *him*."

Leaving our petition with the Adjutant we withdrew, and soon the Colonel and I were on our way back to Yazoo.

But all the soul had gone out of him. He could hardly speak without an oath, and roundly berated the whole civilized world; declaring that we had "fallen upon desperate times."

But sandwiched as I had been between my reverend friend and my profane friend, the Colonel, the reader may readily imagine the relief I felt, and should have mercy. I was not the only one deceived that year by the same means. Indeed, I afterward learned that I had not only the Hon. Carl Schurz for company, I also had U. S. Grant. After making that discovery I felt better. But what was the object this people had in view in that "movement?"

I ought to add that our journey back was less rapid, and, when at last we drove over the base of Tenariffe and into town after midnight of the day following, the profoundest quiet prevailed there. There was not a soul astir, not even a policeman, and as to the "special patrol," the freedman at the stable where our conveyance was obtained, did not know there was one.

At the home of Colonel Black they were sleeping so soundly that it was with difficulty we could obtain entrance, and it was Aunt Rose who let us in. When at last I was snug in bed I thanked God that He had, thus early in my life in the "Sunny South," enabled me to look into the secret places of a "kind master's" and a "repentant rebel's" heart, and to know, for a certainty, that I had been on a fool's errand.

CHAPTER VI.

THE Colonel's trip had been too much for him. He was
not at breakfast the next morning. The remainder of
the family were, and as chirrupy and careless of danger as
ever I had known them. I did detect an aversion to any
discussion of the " insurrection," however, and it seemed to
me that they all looked a little "sheepish like" when I spoke
of it. Certain it is that they had only very mild thanks for
my devotion, and the topic of conversation that morning, as
indeed, during the greater part of the remainder of my stay
there, was chiefly of their progenitors, of whom they never
ceased to feel proud.

They came of an old South Carolina family, and were
able, though but faintly, to trace their lineage back to William the Conqueror on one side, and to an old Scotch laird
on the other. Still, as Americans, they had never considered
the fact worth mentioning until now, when the " leveling process, inaugurated by the radicals," was undermining and
destroying the "props that had heretofore sustained as chivalrous a people as had ever risen to bless the world in the tide
of time."

While passing the usual hour or so in the sitting-room with
the young ladies that evening, one of them, looking up from
her crocheting, or whatever it was, with a rather bewitching
smile playing around the corners of her mouth, and much

mischief peeping from out the rims of her large eyes over which long lashes hung like drapery, poutingly inquired:

" Colonel Mawgan, there weren't very many like you in the Yankee ahmy, was there ? "*

I am sure I may readily be excused from recording here what my answer was, and my reader be content with the following, from the same young Miss:

" Well, if he weren't a baboon why was he such a hairy man ? " This of " Abe Lincoln," and—

" What made him love the nigros so ? " and the expression of her face became a profound study.

Again—

" We all were so very happy, and ouah nigros so contented and happy, too! How could you all wish to steal them from us ? "

And—

" How could you all fight against we all for them ? I won't believe yo' did. Yo' don't look a bit like that. Paw says you all fought for the Union, not to take our slaves away from us. Yo'r not a Yankee, yo'r from the West, arn't ye?"

Then—

" But I can't understand it at all, anyway. I don't believe any of we all do. Paw was a Union man and talked strong against the wah, till he had to go with his State, and Judge Syam and paw and maw all 'low we could have kept our nigros only foah President Davis breaking up the Union."

And again—

" But what you all g'wain to do with them, now they are all free ? They can't take car' themselves, po' things ! We all will have to provide foa'h them just the same as befo' the wah."

Not getting very much comfort out of my responses she finally somewhat peevishly exclaimed :

" Well, they'll always be just what they are—*servants*, and I reckon it won't be a great while befo' we'll have them back on ouah hands again. Yo'll see ! "

* The war had interrupted the school training of others as well as myself.

Now I had seen enough of the world to know that "babes,"
oftener than their elders, speak out with fidelity not only
what is in their own minds, but also what is passing in the
minds of their parents, and notwithstanding just a hint of
diplomacy in the attitude and manner of my fair interlocutor,
I had an idea that Miss Sue had let out the true state of her
own, the judge's, and her parents' views on the " negro question," so I ventured to ask her :

" In that event, what will you all do with them, Miss Sue?"

Evidently she was not prepared to answer so far-reaching
an interrogatory, for she began to reply with some embarrassment :

" I—reckon—the—South can take car' of its own.   But
why should that concern you all ?   Paw says the Yankees
wor' always meddling in ouah affairs, after they sold their
nigros to we all.   He! ha! ha!"

Miss Sue evidently believed that she had utterly demol-
ished me, for, recovering her embarrassment as she proceeded,
she broke out in a triumphant laugh at the close.

" But, Miss Sue, you will not be able to sell your negroes
to any one, now that the whole world nearly has abolished
slavery."

" Sell them !"   " Why !"——

But I came to her relief.   " Perhaps you won't wish to
sell them when they shall have all fallen back on your hands
again !"

" Judge Syam says we may not be permitted to sell them
like we all could befo' the wah, 'count of some amendment
or other to the laws which you all g'wain to force on we all.
He 'lows he shall be just as well satisfied if you all only leave
us alone and let us manage them owah own way.   And paw
says you all boun' to pay we all foah our nigros anyway, because they wor our property, and you all knew when yo'
stole them from us that yo' had no right to do it.   You all
just wanted them for soldiers to fight we all with.   'Spect yo'
wor tired a-fighting we all anyway.   No one but Yankees
ever would have done such a mean thing."

Miss Sue's indignation, gathering heat from the furnace of my questions, was rapidly passing into anger, and her cooing, attractive manner had changed into one of repulsion to me. I preferred her other mood, and so began:

" Oh, well, Miss Sue, we have all suffered by the war. There have been many things said and done on our side as well as yours, that should never have been. For my own part I am glad the war is over. I believe these other questions will settle themselves, don't you ?"

Miss Sue brightened instantly. " Yes," said she, " and we'll settle them foah the good of our nigros as much as foah our own, too, foah we all *raised* them and know thar ways, and they are used to ouah'n."

Evidently Miss Sue *could* not apprehend my meaning. It was so with the entire Black family. It was so with their neighbors—white neighbors. Black, or colored people, were in no sense neighbors. They were *servants*. It was so all around.

With the former master class their former slaves were still " our nigros." And in the eyes of that class the freed people were identical in character and destiny with " our slaves."

The change which I had given to the direction of our conversation had a most charming effect upon all present. They had all joined in what was going on between Miss Sue and myself, and had chilled toward me in sympathy with her. And, now that I had hung out the white flag, they continued to follow her. So that we soon become quite agreeable to each other again, resolved to have peace at any cost. That is, I was so resolved. I couldn't afford strife, and could see no good likely to result from contending with them.

CHAPTER VII.

COLONEL BLACK'S LIBRARY—A NEW DEPARTURE—TOKEBA'S
JAIL—MORE DIPLOMACY—A SOUTHERNER'S INSTINCTS.

THE incidents reported in the three last chapters convinced
me that I had been the subject of conversation with the
people, white, light, and black, to a greater extent than any
one ignorant as I was of their ways could have foreseen, and
I feared it might lead to disagreeable consequences.

I could not like the Colonel, try ever so hard. I could
like the girls; they were so unlike the typical girl of the far
South my fancy had created. Though not strong charactered
like our real good Yankee girls, as I thought, they were
nice. I liked Mrs. Black, too, though I could see that she
was sorely tried by me.

The literature of the family library was quite ancient.
Dryden, Scott, Shakespeare, Pope, Swift, Byron, and Johnson were to be found there. Also Voltaire and Paine, Adams,
Madison and Jefferson were there; but Calhoun, Webster,
Clay, and Benton appeared to be the favorites. Besides several old volumes of the Congressional Globe and Agricultural
Reports, there were works on African slavery, in defense of
that institution, and on the origin and destiny of the dark
races. Of course, I looked in vain for a scrap from such advanced thinkers as Gerrit Smith, Garrison, Phillips, Sumner,
Lowell, or Whittier, or even Seward or Emerson.

The Colonel was a fatalist, and often quoted from Pope.
A familiar line was the following:

"All discord, harmony not understoood:
All partial evil, universal good; * * *
      * * * Whatever is, is right."

They never had family prayers, so far as I could discover; and, though Mrs. Black was inclined to "high church" in her religious views, she rarely attended any place of worship. The Colonel never.   Being a stranger, and everything there so different from what I had been accustomed to in civil life at the old home, I did not press upon them my wish to attend some place of worship.   I had been reared a Baptist, and might have preferred to worship there with that denomination, but the Blacks disliked the very name of Baptists.

I could get along with the family well enough.   The accommodations were excellent.   In the parlor their neighbors, male and female, were courteous enough, and socially very companionable indeed.   I would not "talk politics." The war was over with me, in deed and in truth.   I was there to make money, it is true, but the getting of money was not my only object.   In my view fully as much comfort, even pleasure, could be extracted from the getting of money as from the thing itself, and with much greater profit to the head and heart if pursued with a right motive.   But I thought I saw trouble ahead if I should persist in my quest for laborers upon the streets of Yazoo City.   Wishing to avoid that, I resolved to seek elsewhere for them.

While at Vicksburg, I had heard that large camps formerly occupied by Federal soldiers, were now full of freed people who were dependent for support upon government aid, and I resolved to try my luck in that quarter.

At one of those camps on the Mississippi River, just above Vicksburg, I found many of Colonel Black's former slaves. From their number I was quickly able to select all the labor we were likely to need.

The camp was on an island, where I was compelled to remain all night, and it was then and there, and from the lips of these "runaways," from Tokeba, that I first learned the truth about both the Colonel and Mrs. Black.

There was no hesitation on the part of the runaways, either in their recognition of me or their talk about the old home

place, for my dress, complexion and speech could not well be
disguised.   They took to me at once, and manifested their joy
at the prospect of going back to Tokeba to work for the
" Yankees," in various ways.   Indeed, they had already heard
" the wud put out " that " ole Mars Jeems h'd done gone
rent Tokeba to de Yankees."   But they could hardly believe
" de tale, kase why! Mars Jeems wor' so mighty down on de
Yankees, he done swor' of'n, dat no d—n Yank should eb'r
put dey feet ont'er Tokeba.   He'd shed de las' drap ob he
blocd fus', an' meet dem all in hell's fire an' b'imstun.   Fo'
God he said it! Kunnel, of'n an' of'n, b'efo Gen'l Herron
com'd dat ar' way.   Den we all l'f um, an' been long wid' de
Yankees dat day ter dis.   Did ye see dat are ole jail dar on
Tok'ba ?

"No." I had seen no *jail* on Tokeba.

"Well, den, it's dah all same, 'low he nebber tote it arway.
'Twas dar when we all le'f um, sartin.   Mars Jeems nebber
tole ye widout ye ax him, an' den he mout a tole ye hit wor
only a chick'n coop, 'cept'n' he know'd you mount a know'd
better'n dat.   Kase dat are ja'l look no mo' like a chick'n coop
an' it do like de ole Mars' own gret house, hit don't; an' it
look no mo' like Mars' house an' it do like Heb'n, I's spects.
Fur dar no wind'us in it, any whar, an' de sides all nuth'n
'cept'n squar, monstus logs so't de po'h nigger nebber see
whar ter broke fro'um.   Dars ole Brister!   Did yo' see Brister ?   Well, he good fur nuth'n cept'n choin' bout, kase his
legs, ye know.   Wall, Brister he mout' tole ye all bout'n
dat ar' jail, ef'n ye ax *him*."

This all sounded to me so like the stories I had read before the war, and to which I had sometimes listened from the
contrabands, who came into our camps while war was being
fought, that I became deeply interested, and nearly the whole
night was spent around a huge log-fire listening to the history of Tokeba from the lips of the slaves who had wrought
it out of the dense wilderness years before the war.

It is truly marvellous how their association with the Yankee soldiers had unlocked the lips of these poor, wretched people. They were in no special way unlike the thousands huddled together in the camps in and about Vicksburg and above and below that place, as I could see. Merely the fact that they were in the deserted camps of the Grand Army, beyond the presence of the master class, had lent to their bearing an erectness, their speech a directness and frankness that was in striking contrast with that of most of their fellows in Yazoo.

I had met at Yazoo City several of the old slaves of Colonel Black, and had already employed some of them, but from none had I heard any of these stories of cruel treatment by their old master and mistress.

What shocked me most, however, was the unanimous opinion of these people that Mrs. Black was more cruel and tyrannical than the Colonel, and their accounts of cruel floggings, brandings and starvings inflicted upon them by order of Mrs. Black were simply incredible. My estimate of that lady, based upon what I had seen in her own home, forbade belief in such stories, and I secretly attributed them to a habit of recounting their wrongs to Federal soldiers, until they had learned to exaggerate them in order to deepen a soldier's sympathy for themselves.

Of the numerous tales was one which painted the Colonel as having ordered several—I forget the number now—of his slaves to be locked up in the jail, supplied with cornmeal and water only, and then himself going on a trip to New Orleans, where he remained for several days with the key of the jail in his pocket. No one, not even the overseer, dared release them or give them food could it have been got to them, and so when the Colonel returned one or two had already died, some died soon after, and others were crippled for life. The cries and groans of the sufferers both night and day, were enough to make the whole place mad. But in such terror were they all of Colonel Black when angered, no one dared to interfere in behalf of the sufferers.

Returning to Yazoo, I at once informed Colonel Black of my success, and that I had brought back his old servants.

His face at once became a study worthy a master artist. However, his philosophical temperament triumphed over his wrath
and indignation before these found audible expression, and
I could judge of his feelings and of the thoughts passing in
his mind only by the lights and shadows as they alternated
in the general play of his features. Finally, he broke out in
a most comical laugh, and, with a round of ridiculous oaths,
declared that I had now "capped the climax," for of all the
" worthless, good-for-nothing, thieving gang," there was " not
one, by G—d, sir, from old Aggaby to that scape-grace boy
of Sal's, worth a tinker's baubee."

" Well! well!" said he, " I had heard they were in an old
military camp somewhere about Vicksburg, nearly starved to
death, and I had been expecting them to turn up befoah long
and beg me to take them back. But I never would have
done it, by G—d, sir. They all ran off in one night and took
away with them all they could tote with the first lot of d—n
Yankee —— of Federals that came to this place! Take
them back if you choose! But, d—n them, they should
have starved befo' I would have done it." And much more
he said in the same strain. Spoke of his great kindness to
them, and how ungratefully they had acknowledged it.

That night he was quite drunk before bedtime, and the
ladies, having been informed of what I had done, acted as
though they felt " hurt " about something. From that time
on, that was a dull house to me.*

In pursuit of further politic measures, I resolved to move
myself to Tokeba. By this means I could not be accused of
disrespect to my hostess, whatever might happen. As I now
recollect, it was not more than two or three days after this
that Mrs. Black invited me to dine with the family, adding,
that some " prominent gentlemen " would be present. They
were the former sheriff and a judge of one of the local
courts. The talk from the first was almost entirely of a polit-

---

* The truth is, Colonel Black was piqued because his old slaves preferred me over
himself. There had not been a time that he would not have most gladly welcomed
them all back to Tokeba. Without intending to do so, I had mortally wounded him
in his pride, and "wronged" his family.

cal nature, and after a somewhat bitter arraignment of Congress, and a general denunciation of the Freedman's Bureau
and the Civil Rights Bill, in which all, except myself, had
taken part, the ex-sheriff bluntly asked me for my views.

During my stay at Colonel Black's I had purposely avoided
taking any conspicuous part in the frequent discussions upon
the merits of public men or measures that occurred. I had
no taste for partisan politics. I had not been a student of
our national nor of their local affairs. The fact is, all my
studies in that direction had begun and had ended with
slavery. In that respect I had been a " one-idea man "—or
boy, for I was but eighteen when I enlisted. I had often
been tempted to resent the frequent allusions by the Colonel
and his family and their guests, male and female, to Lincoln,
as a " baboon;" Seward, " the traitor;" Butler, " the beast,
the wretch, the reviler of women;" Sumner, "the miscegenationist ;" Stanton, " the tyrant," the " bloody tyrant;"
Stevens, " the incendiary;" Ben Wade, " the hog," and so
on through the whole list of our heroes at that time. And I
had heard them one and all equally often extol Lee as
" general, statesman, patriot, and noble gentleman," compared with whom Grant was a "satyr;" and others of the rebel
leaders held up as " examples worthy of emulation for all
time."

As, however, such speeches, whether uttered by old or
young, male or female, were always accompanied with what
to me, at that time, was their antidote, viz: " but we were
overpowered," and " we have surrendered in good faith," up-
to this time, I had been able to keep down my feelings.
Day after day I had been in a way compelled to listen to
opinions, all to the effect that had it not been for fire-eaters
like Calhoun and Toombs on one side, and Thad. Stevens
and John Brown on the other; or, had these men all been
taken out and hanged, as only John Brown was, the war could
have been averted; that it was the " supeariah skill of Lee,"
and the " supeariah virtues of ouah soldiers," that had en-

abled the South to prolong the war against "Lincoln's hirelings," until, "fo'ced by numbers," and "overpowered," they
had "sahrendered" without being conquered; and, while
praising Grant for his "terms to Lee and ouah brave soldiers,"
they attributed his generosity to a "secret knowledge" that it
would "never do to drive such brave men to the wall" by
"sevearah terms," for they would have died to the last man
before they would have made a "humiliating sahrendah," or
in any way have compromised the "honah of the South;" and
I had held my peace, under the spell of the plea from press
and pulpit North, that it would take *time* to heal the "sore
places of the war;" and, after all, this was "but talk," often
without any foundation other than an "impulse of disappointment," or of "chagrin" at their defeat. It must be so,
I thought, for, as a rule, those who uttered such language in
my presence would apologize immediately after and beg me
to forget it.

Of one thing I was certain. They were "whipped." Nor was
there anywhere apparent any regret that the war had ended.
On the contrary, all were glad of it, and the great majority while
in my presence approved the overthrow of slavery. It had
been a source of no possible "advantage to the master," they
said, or to the country. On the contrary it had brought "only
woes."

The only anxiety apparent was for the "nigro." All agreed
that his destiny "must be left to the wisdom of their former
masters," who alone "understood the nigro character," and
were, therefore, "the only persons competent to make the
laws for his government." I had opinions on all these questions, more or less formed, only I had not expressed them.

My answer to this direct invitation to do so must have
satisfied them that I was not a politician in any sense of that
word. For as all appeared to expect an answer, I resolved
to speak pla'nly and loyally.

As to the Freedman's Bureau, I knew nothing whatever
of its workings; had never examined the law, and was not
competent to judge of the necessity of such a law as they had
described. If there was an agent of the Bureau in the State,

I had not met him. I, however, believed that the freedman
would eventually enjoy all the rights of citizenship. I had,
as they had already been informed, been a soldier, and of
the kind, who " ran at the first Bull Run," it was true, but was
nevertheless able to answer " here," when the Yankee roll
was called for the last time at Appomattox, by General Grant.
I had not been a " hireling " for thirteen dollars a month
during those years—though that was the pay I received in
the beginning of it. They had, I regretted to say, misconstrued my silence on former occasions. Grant, in my opinion, was an able general and a most merciful conqueror.
Butler was a patriot, and the right man in the right place.
The men who followed Grant were not hirelings; those who
followed Sherman were no more barbarians than he, and he
had given first lessons in merciful warfare. Lincoln was a
truly great man; Sumner, a scholar and statesman of spotless
purity of character; and all the rest deserved the thanks of
mankind.

I said much more and perhaps I put it just a little stronger
than I have here reported. I am sure, however, that my
manner was entirely respectful and temperate.

Mrs. Black at last came to my succor, declaring that she
had always more admired the abolitionists than those whom
we termed " dough-faces," for they were false to their " section," and having " betrayed " the South into the war, left
them to fight it out alone. Indeed, she wouldn't be at all
surprised to find that after all Mr. Sumner was a " real gentleman." She was especially bitter toward " that *tailor*, Andy
Johnson," who, as a " Southern man," should have remained
true to his " home and fireside." However, he would be found
to be " sound on the nigro question." Of this she had no
doubt, and to my astonishment the whole company were of
the same opinion. They felt sure that Mr. Johnson would
adhere to his " well-known " sentiments toward the " nigro,"
and should it ever come to " a wah of races," he would certainly be found on the side of the white man, wherever others
of his party might go.

CHAPTER VIII.

CHARLES' RETURN—REMINISCENCES—SMOKY TOKEBA—WHISKY
AS A MEDICINE.

THE incidents reported in the former chapter occurred only a few days prior to my brother's return. Of course, I told him of them and dwelt significantly upon the temper of the people. He had often allowed me to see that he had great faith in my ability to win friends. At school I had always been a match for the best of my fellows in a wrestle, "side holt," "square holt," or "rough and tumble." I had as often as any other carried off the prize in my class and in our debating and other societies. I had enlisted in the ranks in spite of the suggestion of my father and of influential friends that if I would wait for a later regiment I could go as a commissioned officer. And I had got my first promotion, from "high private" to sergeant, upon the request of my company, by a vote of fully four fifths of the privates, over all the corporals, of whom a majority voted for me for the vacancy. Therefore, he was somewhat surprised at what I told him, and I could plainly see also annoyed. In seeking for an explanation of it he "prodded" me with all manner of questions, putting much stress upon the way in which I had conducted the financial part of the business at my end of the line.

Had I gone in debt? Had I paid my way? Had I had any misunderstanding with any of them about any of the details of the contract? Had I signed that instrument? Of course, I had paid the rent, as promised?

I was able to give entirely satisfactory answers to all of these interrogatories, even to so exacting and rigid an examiner as my brother. And as to the last question, I reminded him that I had written, informing him of the fact, on the evening of the day I made the payment, three thousand one hundred and fifty dollars—being the first installment, as per contract, and on the day prescribed by its terms; also, that I had in my letter mentioned Mrs. Black's grateful acknowledgment of it to me, as I placed the money in her own hands ; how she almost broke down with joy, and declared that it was a perfect God-send to her, as she had hardly known for weeks where the next day's supply of food was coming from, and that the first use to which she would put a part of it would be the purchase of a barrel—a whole barrel—of flour and some necessary articles for her children, of all which they had been so long deprived. *

But we were in for it, and would make the best of it. Besides, whatever their feelings might be, they were only natural after all. If for no other reason, their poverty would, for a time at least, compel compliance with the new order of things. During this time, the tide of immigration which, Charles observed, was setting strongly southward, especially, the more thrifty and intelligent portion from the East, of itself would, in a very few years, work a complete change in the elements of society. Charles had no fear. There might be some annoyances, growing out of the natural feelings of the two races toward each other, under the circumstances. But even these would disappear with improved conditions; and my brother rallied me somewhat on my failure to get on with Southerners. As for himself, he had found them very agreeable people. He was certain they were equally well pleased with himself ; had already promised to time his projected trip to New Orleans to suit the convenience of Mrs. Black, who would visit that city the following week, for the pur-

* Having no apparent income or means of support, it had been a cause of some anxiety to me how they managed to live so well. Mrs. Black's confessions upon receipt of so much money, all in a lump, while making me feel that I had been a burden to them, were, nevertheless, quite a relief. Their pride had suggested to them the means for successfully hiding from me their actual condition, financially. As to those means, the reader may learn more further on.

pose of putting the young ladies under the training of an
accomplished instructor in the special studies desirable at their
age.   And so he did, and had a pleasant trip, too, he afterward informed me.   But though he was at the house several
times after this at dinner, I cannot now recall that I ever
received an invitation to go there.   I am quite sure I never
dined at the house after my experience with the ex-sheriff, as
I have related.

My brother's negotiations at the North succeeded beyond
his anticipations.   He arranged with an old lumberman to
come down at once and bring with him his saw-mill, fixtures
and entire force of skilled hands, and very soon things were
so lively on Tokeba that occupation banished not only the
apprehensions which my experience during his absence had
awakened, but all thought of " insurrections " or of the ladies
whom I had so gallantly defended for the moment; and we
were all kept as busy as our personal supervision of the work
going on at Tokeba made necessary.

As the business was wholly new to us and our employees
all strangers, it may be readily seen that we really had no
time for anything else.

In less than ninety days things were " just smoking " on
Tokeba, as Charles, in one of his happy veins, declared.
There stood the saw-mill, just where Charles had planned for
it, and it proved to be the very best kind of a site.   As there
had been no overflow to enable us to get the logs from our
brake, we had purchased them of "up river *swampers*," and there
they were, in " booms " or tied with ropes to trees by the river
bank, in " cribs," just as Charles painted it to me before our
parting at Vicksburg, and the old mill was just " singing
away lively."   It could be heard on a calm day at Yazoo
City, more than two miles away.   On the plantation our
hands were doing equally well, and the best of feeling
existed between the laborers and ourselves.   Although we
had been delayed by ice in the upper Mississippi in getting
down the mules purchased for the place, there they were now,
with plows behind them, and jolly, singing freedmen and

women—the women would work and liked to plow—behind
the plows, while " Mose " and " Cephas " and " little Maria "
and " Susan " " toted " water for the plow-people, and
" trash-cleaners " and burners in the van.

" Old Uncle Bristol " still kept the ferry and worked in the
carpenter shop, repairing plow-frames or making new ones,
while the kling-klang of the anvil at the blacksmith's shop
kept him to his task; for the work of the blacksmith was
crowding him.

Altogether it *was* " just smoking " on Tokeba. The mill
could not supply the local demand for lumber, which we
readily sold in town, delivered on the levee or to steamers
that took it from the mill for customers at way landings on
the Yazoo River, at prices ranging from thirty-five to eighty
dollars per thousand feet, according to kind and quality.
Neighbors from far and near passing Tokeba would rein in
their horses, halt, take a look at things, and ride on evidently in a brown study. Having no leisure for entertaining them, " nor anything good to drink," we seldom invited
them to alight*—we were busy.

Mr. Moss, our partner from Illinois, was so well satisfied
with the way things were going, that he returned home to
look after his business there, leaving his interests entirely in
our charge.

The merchants in Yazoo City, anxious for our custom, held
out such inducements as led us to make our purchases of
general supplies for the place and for our hands in that town,
instead of sending abroad for them, and their orders on us
for lumber for their other customers often exceeded our
weekly bills with them for supplies for Tokeba. Ours was
the only saw-mill in operation in that region, and for a time
proved a real blessing to Yazoo City and the country round
about. We were not asking credit ourselves, being able to
pay our way as we went, either with greenbacks, which
were quite popular in Yazoo at the time of which I write,
or with good cypress lumber, which was almost as popular as
greenbacks.

*This was a violation of one of the ways of the country, but it was business.

Considering their misfortunes in the war and the unsettled condition of the country, it was quite natural that many men of property should not at all times have the money by them with which to pay for the lumber they wished to order from us, and as we intended to make our home in Yazoo we never hesitated to give credit to such persons. Thus we were able to confer favors upon individuals, as well as many benefits upon the community, and things looked rosy-hued enough to enable me to still further magnify the many virtues of my brother; his far-seeing business sagacity, particularly his push and grit.

The general health of the place was good, but as our force was a large one, there were all the time some sick, so we fell into so much of the ways of the country as made it fashionable to have a regular salaried physician. This gentleman was of the old school, a most honorable man and skillful doctor, who resided at Yazoo City and made regularly stated visits to the place.

Neither Charles nor myself used liquor of any kind, and would not have it on the place except as a medicine and when prescribed by our plantation physician. The doctor often advised us in all candor not to fail to take a stiff dram whenever we got out about our business of a morning before the sun had time to dispel the dews and poisonous vapors from the river. But as that would have necessitated our regular use of whisky, since we were out with the sun *every* morning, we refused to act upon his advice in that particular. Charles often declared that we enjoyed much better health and greater freedom from chills and fevers, than any of those in our neighborhood who drank liquors. I am quite sure he did, and the fact was observed by others; even our physician sort of half way admitted that we were better off without " the stuff" than with it. But it was customary in that locality to prescribe it as a tonic for the prevention of malarial poisoning. On the same theory, I suppose, that they prescribed whisky for the bite of a rattlesnake.

CHAPTER IX.

BLUSHES—MORE OF THE WAYS OF THE COUNTRY—A DEEPER
DEEP THAN MORMONISM.

DURING the winter and spring of 1866 nothing occurred to mar the *entente cordiale* which circumstances, aided by our saw-mill, had established between " those Yankees on Tokeba " and " our people." *

We were too much absorbed in our business to heed or care for what was passing in the political or social world. As yet there had appeared no social hostility toward any of our firm, and we mingled with our neighbors and with the town people with no feeling on our part that we were in any way specially objectionable persons. Not many of our acquaintances came to Tokeba, however; a fact we supposed to be due to our lack of leisure for entertaining them.

But there were persons who visited the place very often. It was some time before we learned their true character or their object. They were females. In complexion they ranged from pure Caucasian, so far as I could see, to mulattoes or brownskins. They were always neatly and sometimes quite tastefully dressed. Ostensibly they came to see old acquaintances among the force, and generally made some excuse to come to the " great house;" to talk with the people in the yard, beg a shrub or flower, or to seek information of " the Captain " or of " the Colonel." They sometimes made

* From the day of my arrival in Yazoo to this date, summer of 1866, I had not heard the phrase " our people " used by the native whites in any other sense than one which embraced themselves alone. Neither freed people nor Yankees were meant to be included in it.

themselves quite conspicuous by passing the office as many as
two or three times of an evening, and in other ways.

Our office was Colonel Black's old "study," and stood by
itself in a clump of China trees, separated from the family
residence, but in the same yard. No matter which of us
happened to be in, these visitors were sure to stop and make
some inquiry about their "old feller-servants," or some
trifling matter. We always treated them kindly, sometimes
placed chairs for them, and interrogated them about their hopes
and prospects, now they were free.

One day when two of those women were sitting thus together, one of them boldly exclaimed :

"Colonel, it 'pears to me yo' are a long time taking a
hint ! "

Her speech was in every whit as good English as that of
the average white lady there, and her manners equally
refined and subdued. She was a very comely person, too. I
have often wondered why I was so dull of comprehension. I
had never suspected what their frequent visits meant. To me
they were all freed people. All poor, all needy—needing land,
money, clothes, bread, meat, no more than the dignity of self-
respect, which everywhere, in all times and with all peoples,
has been the chief want of slaves. But yesterday they were
all slaves, and I had not yet learned to discriminate, besides
I had no other idea than that these people would look to the
Yankees for light, as they had done for liberty, and while it
was neither my business nor my inclination at that time to
become their instructor, I could not so far humiliate and degrade myself as to fail of trying to be an example for them
in my private life and habits. Perhaps, too, my bringing up
had something to do with it. To be sure I had been through
the war and had seen much of "the world" for a young man.
The truth is, however, such a thing as was about to present
itself had never before entered my thoughts. Therefore, I
plainly asked her what she meant. She replied :

"Any one might know yo' are a Yankee."

Then the other :

"All de Yankees not dat 'er way." At which they both laughed. But this left me more in the dark than ever. Being disposed to pursue the inquiry, I said curiously:

"In what respect do Yankees differ so widely from Southerners?"

Then the "dark" one—

" Colonel, is yo' married?"

" No; and don't wish to be."

"Is de Captain, yo'r brother?"

" No."

" Is he youah own deah brother?"

" Yes."

" Doan yo' all fin' heap lonesome up y'here by yur own self?"

" Not at all lonesome—too busy."

" My! Yo' Yankees nebber will hab no fun, t'wel yo' own dis yar whole blessed worl'! Yo' alwus so mighty busy an' peart."

" I like to work," I rejoined.

" Wuck! he! he! laws! Yo' doan wuck, I knows, Look at his han's, Liz."

And Lizzie—for that was the fair one's name—

" And see his face! No mo' sunburnt than mine is, he! he! he! Ain't he han'some!"

This was too much. I was not accustomed to that kind of fire, and couldn't face it. So, turning to my desk with some embarrassment, I resumed my work.

"He! Laws! See um blush!" ejaculated the "dark" one through her merry laughter.

But Lizzie got up at once, blushing herself, hung her head and walked away. The "dark" one followed. *

A few days after this incident, while at the "quarter" with medicines for the sick, an elderly woman who did not work in the field, the wife of one of our best hands, as I passed by, was standing in her cabin door. She beckoned to me and asked me to please come in. Thinking some one of

* I afterward learned that Lizzie was the concubine of a white merchant in town, and the dark one of a neighboring planter.

the family had been taken ill, I approached her. She withdrew inside, hastily put things to rights, and in a somewhat flurried tone and manner hoped I would forgive her
if she was wrong; she meant only to make me happy.
Then she explained that she had been noticing the Captain and me ever since she "put foot on Tok'ba." She "had
'low'd to speak to me the very first chance." She was " mor'n
glad " Captain and I would have nothing to do with " doze ar
town gals, 'twan't necessary."

" Dar is jes ez good gals an' better tu, I 'spect, y'here on
de plantation, honey."

I was beginning to get my eyes open by this time, and
impatiently started to leave her.

She begged me to stop a minute, and went on to explain
that " I must not think myself too good for de colored gals;
'fo' God, the best gen'lemens in de Azoo County nebber think
deyselves too good ! An' dey ha' wives too. Mighty quar,
bein' yo' is sich a likely gen'leman—an' not one dem gals
cept'n' dey is in lub wid ye, too ; white no mor'n de black, I
tell ye ! I'z hearn um talk, an' I knows ! he ! 'Deed h'it war
a mighty pity ! 'Twouldn't make no differn' ef yo' iz got a
gal up to de norf whar yo' come frum, boun' ter hab one
y'here, too; yo' y'hea' me ? I knows that, honey." Then
she bluntly asked me how I liked her " gal " Rose ?

Now Rose was her daughter, was only fourteen, and,
though a pure African, was one of the most perfect natural
beauties I had ever seen. I had not then, nor have I since,
seen such exquisite arms and hands.

Now I understood perfectly why it was Rose had been
sent on so many errands to our rooms, by day and by night.
This revelation made me sick, and I hastily left the woman,
forgetting my errand to the quarter, and so was obliged immediately to retrace my steps. Having to pass the woman's
house again, I found her standing in the same place as before.
But this time I refused to respond to her beckoning call for
me. On my return she came out and met me in the way,
and, in a tone of entreaty, begged me to forgive her " ef I

hu't yo' feelin's, honey," and, by way of apology, said, she had never been with the Yankees before and "ha' not larnt yo' ways."

This woman's husband was a preacher, and he frequently gave his hearers lessons in practical morality, of which the following may be accepted as a fair specimen:

" Paul mount plant, Apolous wah-too (water); but de increaze come frum wha' ye do."

Although he was a " reformer " amongst his people, it was evident that he had neglected his own fireside, or did not understand the Scripture he often attempted to quote.

Thus I was every day learning; and every day brought fresh cares and increased anxiety. As time passed, I found myself asking myself :

" Well! what kind of a country is this, anyway ? "

My interest in their fate induced me to observe these poor people closely. There were not many like Rose's mother, I was glad to find, and so I learned to discriminate. Yet the level of morality was low indeed, and it was clear to me that new influences must be introduced among them ; new ideas, new aims, new purposes; and to that end the hopes aroused in their hearts by emancipation must be nourished.

" They must be taught to think," I said.

We had promised them a school, but had not been able to obtain a suitable person to teach it, and the subject had been deferred.

By reason of Charles' age and greater experience, his attention had been chiefly called to the lumber interests, and it had fallen to my lot to keep the books, see to the sick, issue the rations, and attend to such part of our business in the town as did not require the personal supervision of the senior member. For this reason Charles was not in town as often as I, nor so well known to the people of the country round. Besides, I outranked him in military title. Thus it came about that I was recognized by the people of Yazoo City and county as the representative of our firm, if not the head of it

CHAPTER X.

A DEEPER DEEP—THE WOLF SHOWS HIS TEETH.

WE were not getting on with Colonel Black quite as smoothly as we could have wished. The following will serve to illustrate some of the annoyances to which he subjected us:

It was not long after the incidents related in the foregoing chapter that, happening in town one day, on one of those numerous errands connected with the supplying of the place, Colonel Black met me, and calling me aside into a small court, where we were out of hearing of the passers-by on the street, but in plain view of a group of men lounging at a store front, with an air of deep mystery and importance, informed me that it was rumored in the town that one day while his guest I had told Mistress Black that a "nigro wench" was as "good as a white lady."

I had never said any such thing, but resolved to keep silent until I had learned more of his purpose on this occasion. Accordingly, after a brief pause, he reminded me of the pains Mrs. Black and himself had been to, in order that our introduction to Yazoo should lack nothing of the elements requisite to insure us a good start in our new home, and of the high regard in which we were held by his neighbors and friends, as evinced by their entrusting me with an important commission so soon after my arrival.* All this had been due

---

*This was none other than our Vicksburg fool's errand.

to us as "high-toned, honorable gentlemen," and was creditable
to themselves, for they all recognized the absolute necessity
of encouraging Northern men with brains and money to come
amongst them if they would ever hope to repair the "ravages
of the wah," and he was glad, indeed, to see that such influential Yankee journals as the New York *Tribune* were doing all
they could to aid the " stricken South " in that direction.

" But," he continued, "ouah people are very sensitive upon
one question, and cannot tolerate in ouah midst any division of
sentiment upon it, or opinion either, without tearing down
the only props remaining to ouah social fabric, by G—d, sir,
and consenting to the destruction of all present prospects for
any tol'able solution of the great labor question thrust upon
us by Lincoln's proclamation. The nigros are free, thank God,
and not yo' all Yankees, by G—d, sir!" And I thought I saw
a gleam of malice in his cold, grey eyes. " For even yo' must
admit that we could have kept ouah nigros had we not seceded,
and that we never would a done, by G—d, sir, had it not
been for a few d—d hot-heads, who were ambitious foah leadership." Now his face began to turn purple.

" I knew from the outset that secession was but a piece of
d—n foolishness, and meant emancipation, and I opposed it,
by G—d, sir. But now that he's free, we have nothing to
hope from any policy that does not leave the control of the
nigro to the wisdom of his fo'mer masters, by G—d, sir."
And a number of rapid thumps with his cane upon the ground
evinced his sincerity no less than his earnestness. " And we
are bound to look upon any man as a public enemy, by G—d,
sir, I care not who he is or whence he comes, who does nct
consent to this. Yo' have had no experience with the nigro,
and, by G—d, sir, yo' can't be expected to know the nature
of the beast."

Then resuming his assumed air of gentle dignity:

"In your treatment of him, therefore, yo' must allow me
to say yo' ought to govern yo'r conduct by the opinions and
wishes of we all who do know him. The nigro is an animal,

by G—d; and by G—d sir, he must be kept in his place; and who knows better how to manage a horse or a steer than one who is familiar with his raising ?   Allow me to make my meaning plain," said he; " only yesterday Aunt Sukie, whom I raised from a child, and who suckled my children—" at this point his hands began to tremble, and he sobbed audibly—" came down to visit her daughter Rose.*   Whatever it was passed between them the Good Master only knows, for this morning, by G—d, sir, when she brought me my toddy, she called me Colonel Black.   The hussy !   By G—d, sir, she did not repeat the insult."

And his eyes flashed his indignation.   " One of my neighbors has told me he has had the same experience with one of his gals, by G—d, sir; only she refused to call him ' master,' and has since run off.   By G—d, sir, this thing must stop, or we all will be ruined.   Only let the rascals know they can do these things, and it won't be long befo' they'll have their heels upon ouah necks, and be telling us what we shall and what we shan't do, by G—d, sir.   It will all end in asking us to marry them, and then, sir, by G—d, hell itself will be to pay, sir-r-r-r !"

It was evident that the Colonel was not only losing his self-control, but was getting very much tangled up in his ideas as well as utterances, else I did not catch his meaning.

During this harangue he had stopped several times as though to give me a chance to say something.   This time he halted somewhat longer than usual.   But though it was a great annoyance to me to have to listen to his tirade, I stubbornly refused to say one word in response.   He must have observed my restlessness, however, for when he resumed, it was in a greatly modified tone and manner, and the sardonical leer which blackened his face as he came to the close of the last sentence gave place to a supercilious grin.

" Why," said he, " my deah sir, I recognize the fact that ouah ways, at first blush, may appeah distasteful to yo' who

---

* It was well known in town that Rose was the Colonel's favorite concubine. But this I learned afterward.

wor raised on the high God-and-morality notions of Wendell
Phillips and Henry Ward Beecher, but, by G—d, sir, it will
be easier for yo' to adapt yo'r ways to ouahs than for we all to
change. You must be governed by the example of the apostle
of old and while in Rome do as Romans do, by G—d, sir-r-r.
Why, sir! must we surrender our cherished theories and
dearest interests to please a handful of Yankee immigrants,
by G—d, sir-r? By——I beg yo' pardon, sir, those who come
amongst us? No, sir-r-r, by G—d, sir-r-r-r."

Still no response.

Then despairingly he again resumed, but in a whining tone:

"We were prosperous and happy, and at peace with ouah
nigros and all the world, before a lot of d—d fanatics took it
into their heads—got an *idee*, by G—d, sir—that slavery was
wrong. Wrong hell! The nigros wor' never so well off in
Timbuctoo or any of the wilds of their native jungles as with
us, by G—d, sir-r-r-r. Wrong be d—d! And pretending to
have had an inspiration—inspiration hell! and that they wor'
commissioned by God A'mighty to destroy it, by G—d, sir—
that shows that they were fanatics—with a little handful of
our impracticables like Calhoun and Bob Toombs, of Gawga,
fell into a rage over the discussion of abstract questions, and
drew the whole country after them like so many sheep, by
G—d, sir-r-r. I knew it would end that way, and was in
favor of hanging the last one of 'em, by G—d, sir. And if
we'd a had a king instead of an old jackass in the President's
cha'r at Washington, we'd a done it too, by G—d, sir-r-r-r.
Wrong! why, by G—d, sir, the nigros wor' barbarians.
They knew nothing—could no more than chatter like so many
monkeys, by G—d, sir, and we were not only christianizing
them, we were educating them for the only thing they'll ever
be any account foh; servants, by G—d, sir-r-r. I tell yo' sir,
now as then, the prosperity of the country and the peace of
this Union depends on we all being left to manage ouah nigros
in ouah own way, by G—d, sir-r-r-r-r-r."

But as the Colonel was likely never to let go, and the situa-

tion was becoming too monotonous to be longer endured, I
gave way and exclaimed, rather impatiently I fear:

"Well, who has proposed to hinder you?"

This staggered him. But he quickly rallied, and a smile
lit up his sinister countenance as he sneeringly replied:

"Well, sir, by G—d, sir, yo' may not understand the effect
of youah own example. It was only a few days ago that I
saw you as I passed by Tokeba at work with some nigros
repairing a fence. And Mistress Black says that the other
day she drove on to Tokeba to see how things wor' going,
and, by G—d, sir, yo' brother was working at the mill with the
nigros, and came to speak to her in his shirt sleeves, by G—d,
sir. I learn that you all allow yo'r nigros to call you Colonel
Morgan. By G—d, sir, they shall call me Master ! Besides,
it's all over town that yo' have been heard to call youah
blacksmith's wife Mrs. Smith. Mrs. hell ! By G—d, sir, this
must be stopped or yo' all will be ruined." Now he was in
a passion again. When it had partly subsided he continued:
"Mistress Black and I have made every excuse for you all
that we could think off to allay the apprehensions of ouah people. If their fears are allowed to grow it may lead to disastrous consequences. You alone can correct this state of things.
For yo' and youah brother not only have the appearance and
manners of gentlemen, by G—d, sir, yo' have the standing also. It is that, by G—d, sir, that makes yo'r exam_
ple so pernicious. Yo' all are quoted everywhere as the
nigro's friend. Friend hell ! It will not be inconsistent,
yo'll allow me, with the dignity of a gentleman, nor with
even youah notions of things, to publish a ceahd * over youah
own name, denying yo' *meant* in what yo' said to Mistress
Black, that a nigro was as good as a white gentleman,† that
will set everything straight. For Mistress Black and I'll
take good car' to explain your treatment of yo'r nigros. It
is not to be expected that you all can get accustomed to ouah
ways all at once."

---

* Why publish a card? We may see farther on.
† He was getting mixed again.

At this point he ceased speaking, and it was again more than evident that he expected me to say something. But I had resolved not again to break silence, and he resumed savagely:

"As youah friend and well-wishah, by G—d, sir, I deem it absolutely necessary for yo' to publish some so't of denial of such d—d stories as are floating around, by G—d, if you expect to live among our people in peace, sir-r-r-r-r."

This sounded too much like a threat to admit of further seeming indifference on my part, so I said:

"Colonel Black, you say the negroes are free?"

"Yes, by G—d, sir," he exclaimed excitedly.

"Well, you'll grant that I am a free man, too, will you not?"

"Well, sir, by G—d, sir, what d'yo' mean, sir-r-r-r?"

But I kept cool, saying only:

"We hold the lease of Tokeba for three years from the legal owner on a contract to pay a certain annual rental. We have paid the rent according to contract, and we have a right to the management of that place. I grant to you and to all the right to control your own labor in your own way without interference from me. I claim for our firm only such privileges as we cheerfully accord to others. We believe that we can get more and better labor for the same money out of our hands by treating them as though they too had rights"—at this point the clouds began to deepen on his face—" than if we treated them as though they were brutes." And now he leaned with both hands upon his stick—a heavy hickory—in front of him, trembling with wrath. "We have meant no more by it than our similar treatment of white men would mean." Now he began to grin.

"We have not dreamed that it would be considered revolutionary, nor even thought of it in that light. But we may as well understand each other on this subject. I am sure that no member of our firm is sorry for what we have done in this regard. Recollect, it is our money, not yours, now running Tokeba. We recognize the obligation each individual member of society is under, so to conduct himself that he shall not jeopardize the good of others while pursuing his own ends. Therefore, we shall make no display of our views or example; at the same time we shall not hide our light under a bushel. We shall continue to treat our people as though they were worthy of their hire, so long as they shall continue so, in *our* opinion; and a *large share* of a laborer's hire is respectful consideration from his employer."

At this point the Colonel grunted out " bah !" but I continued:

" We shall never forget that Mrs. Smith is a member of our community, nor can I understand why we should be disturbed in our lawful and peaceful pursuits by reason thereof."

The Colonel was completely beside himself. While listening to me he had grown red and white by turns, and as I concluded, he leaned forward on his cane, while his hands trembled as with palsy in his effort to control himself. The muscles of his face relaxed until a fiend-like grin appeared. Then turning on his heel he left me, with the simple taunt:

" Well, by G—d, sir; as you make yo'r bed yo' must lie. I took yo' for a *gentleman;* yo' are only a *scalawag.*"

As I passed out up the street the group of men by the store uttered deep groans.

CHAPTER XI.

LAMBS—I'M A GENTLEMAN, BY G—D, SIR—A NEW FUNCTION FOR
NASBY.

WHILE relating the foregoing *confab* with Colonel Black
to Charles, I thought I detected a slight accent of disappointment in his tone and manner—perhaps it was petu-
lance. He had himself lost much of his trust in the sincerity
of their welcome to us. But he told me that he had called
on Mrs. Black only a day or two after her visit to the place
and apologized for his inability* at the time to extend to her
such courtesies as the occasion required. She had assured
him, however, that no apology was necessary, and in proof
of the sincerity of her approval of his close attention to business instead of leaving it to others, informed him that she
had resented a remark by one of her acquaintances, who,
when Mrs. Black related to her the incident, exclaimed—
" Working at the mill with his nigros !—came out to speak
to you in his shirt-sleeves!—how dare he! Why, I thought
he was a gentleman !!" and Mrs. Black declared to him she
had given her friend to understand that she admired " Captain Morgan all the more for this very independence," and,
she had suggested to that friend that Southern gentlemen
would do well to follow his example.

After some further discussion as to the significance of Colonel Black's harangue at me, he came to the conclusion that

---

* The log-carrier was off its track.

the " old fellow " must have been drinking more than usual, and it would not be worth our while to heed his " nonsense."

" But why should they groan after me, Charles ?"

" O, well! let's not talk about it," said he, " 'twon't amoun t to anything. You'll see."

At the outset everybody had said we should not be able to get on without an overseer. The overseer was an indispensable auxiliary to a plantation force, everybody said— except the freed people, whom we had neglected to consult. So we had employed one. But it was not more than a week or two, however, after the interview which I have related with Colonel Black that the overseer began to complain of Uncle David and his family—said they were " lazy, sassy, and good-for-nothing." And shortly after this Uncle David began to hint that—

" 'Peers like Mr. Small wuckin' the crap mighty quar," and—

" Low! Mr. Small nebber make a crap b'fo' dis y'ar. Can't fool me."

He would have spoken of it before, only he didn't know whether we would " 'low " him to. And, later on, the overseer—

" That 'ere d—d nigger Dave ought 'er have some old time dis'pline; heap mischuf in that nigger; I'd like ter gie' 'im 'bout fohty lashes on his bar' back, well laid on; 'twould do 'im good."

And shortly after this Uncle David :

" Mr. Small g'wain ter ruin de crap, kase he doan put de dut up fast nuff. On some whar' hit need mo' dut he done tro' it away, an' whar hit doan need de dut now, he jest pile it up an' smothrin' de cotting."*

With such perplexities, added to our ordinary trials, the time passed until the summer was gone, leaving us no time at all for anything else. In the fall the yellow fever and cholera broke out in New Orleans, spread rapidly to Vicksburg, and cases were reported in Yazoo City. During this

*We were never fully satisfied that David was wrong.

time we were in town but little, and there appeared to be a suspension of Colonel Black's hostile demonstrations toward us. The delay in getting our mules made us late with the planting. The year had not been a good one, either. From all these causes it was apparent the crops would be a failure, or nearly so.

Although Charles received no more invitations to dine with the Black family, he attended to the conduct of all matters of business with Colonel or Mrs. Black, so that ever after Colonel Black's unsuccessful attempt to make me publish a "ceahd," I seldom came in contact with any of them. Apparently, therefore, all social relations between the family and myself had been sundered.

But this was the least of my troubles. I felt no special sorrow on account of the gulf, or rather I should say, on account of the incidents which had discovered to me the gulf, existing between the Blacks and my brother and myself. Indeed *I* preferred that it should remain open. I felt sometimes more like placing a danger-signal to mark the fact rather than to make any effort to cover up, or even to bridge that gulf; for I felt certain there could be no peace between us and them without our unqualified surrender to their wishes and "ways." But there still remained a doubt in my mind whether the Black family truly represented the sentiments and convictions of the best citizens of the place. Charles was certain they did not, and was equally emphatic in the assertion of his opinion that Black was a "harmless, drunken old coot," whom no one would follow and no decent man could respect. There were the Stockdales, Major Snodgrass, Judge Isam, and others, all men of temperate habits, and good morals, substantial citizens. Surely such men would never follow the leadership of "old Black."

We had not intended to credit out much lumber, nor did we. But it was quite impossible to decline the orders of men who appeared to be large property-owners and of gilt-edged business reputation, high-toned, honorable gentlemen, and by fall we had out several bills of this character. In all such cases it had been our custom to ask payment whenever, from any cause, we were in need of money. We did not always succeed in getting it. Some of it remains unpaid to this day; but *that* is of no consequence *now*. Even then the fear that we might never be able to collect it was of less consequence than some other things which I will here endeavor to illustrate.

It was late in the fall, after quite a severe and prolonged " spell of the ague," and while I was barely able to ride on horseback. But Captain Telsub's bill was overdue. We needed cash; and so I called at that gentleman's drug store, and presented our bill to him. He had received the lumber and already put it to the uses for which he intended it. He was in his counting-room at the time, received me pleasantly, and, saying that they were short of funds just then, begged me to send or call again. I informed him that he need not " put himself out " to pay the bill at once, but to indicate when he would be prepared to meet it, and I would cheerfully oblige him.

I am sure there was nothing in my manner to betray any doubt of his intention to pay, for I had none; nor did his manner discover to me any resentment on his part. It was arranged that I might call or send for the money at any time after the Saturday following, and I bade him good-day.

Passing out upon the street, on my way to the post-office, I had not gone more than half the square, when I heard my name spoken, and some one walking quite rapidly behind me. I half turned, stopped, and, leaning on my sun-shade, which I was at the time using as a cane, waited until he came up; for I saw it was the Captain. Although he appeared a little " flustered," there was no show of violence in his manner But, as he came nearer, his face grew red, and he began:—

" What in the hell do you mean, you Yankee s—of a b—? By G—d, sir, I'll have you to bear in mind that I pay my debts; I'm a gentleman, by G—d, sir, and if you don't know it, I'll teach you how to conduct yourself toward one, d—n you."

Now, this sudden and unexpected assault quite upset me. I was a non-combatant; had been brought up by parents who believed in the law of love, and in the power of gentleness and truth to protect the innocent anywhere. I had never raised my hand against any human being.

But had it been otherwise, in my feeble state I could have been no match for the large, powerfully-built man who now confronted me with his great fists almost under my nose. Almost in mortal terror I replied in a half-dazed sort of way:

" Well, sir, a gentleman would hardly assault one in my condition in such a manner as this."

But before the sentence was uttered, he hit me such a blow under my ear that I fell to the pavement. Then he jumped upon me and continued his strokes upon my head and face, while the crowd of " gentlemen," whom I had observed in and about his store as I came out, gathered in a sort of a ring around us, shouting: " Fair play, here! Fair play! Kill the d—n Yankee! Kill him, d—n him."

But at this juncture the ring parted, scattered, and the postmaster, who had been a Federal officer, in company with two other Yankee ex-army officers, who were planting near our place, rushed in, picked me up, and carrying me to the post-office, washed the blood from my face, " poured oil upon my bruises," and, after doing all they could to comfort me, insisted that I must abandon my puritanical notions there, and never be seen in public without weapons of some sort; that *they* carried them, and they had taken pains to let the fact be known; that I would not have been attacked had it been known that I was armed, etc.

CHAPTER XII.

A COUNCIL OF LAMBS—THAT " NIGGER SCHOOL "—" OLD MOR-
GAN"—" POLECAT MORGAN."

THAT night, while we sat by the great fire-place in our sitting
room in the old " mansion " on Tokeba, overlooking the
turbid Yazoo, sullenly winding its way through the gloaming,
I gave Charles an account of this " affair " with Captain
Telsub. Many things had occurred of an unpleasant nature
during the few months that had passed since we began house-
keeping on Tokeba—Charles and I—which I had not cared
to mention, remembering his predilections.

But the situation, it appeared to me, was becoming critical,
and I could no longer hide my anxiety from him. I had
observed a change in his manner of late, however, as I thought;
an absence of that buoyancy of spirit which had character-
ized him at the outset, and this evening he seemed more
abstracted than usual. For some minutes he had been sitting
square in front of the fire-place, steadily looking into it, and
whistling some unknown air in a pitch that was barely audible.
I had been wondering what sort of " spell " it could be that
had overcome him, when one of our carpenters, a white man,
who had formed quite an extensive acquaintance among the
loungers in town, called, and being seated, Charles said to
him :

" Tom, I wish you would tell the Colonel what you have
told me."

"Well, Cap'n, there's no more to it than I've told ye already, unless it's my opinion you want."

"Well, let's have your opinion, then."

"I think they'll raid the place."

"Pshaw!" said Charles, "you don't believe that, do you? What has put that into their heads?"

"Well, Cap'n, they all treat me well enough—always have, 'cept'n when that bully tried to make me say that if you was bound to build that nigger school-house, I'd bolt and not strike a lick on it."

Thus I soon found out what the trouble was. Some days prior to this, Charles had told me of a contract he had made with a commissioner of the Freedman's Bureau to furnish the lumber for a school-building in town, for the freed people.

The situation was this: The freed people had long been anxious to have a church of their own, but did not feel able to pay the cost of such a one as they desired. This commissioner had seen and arranged with their leaders to contribute to the cost of one, if they would consent that it might also be used as a school-building.* In furtherance of this plan, Charles, after consulting with Mr. Moss, had subscribed liberally to the fund.

The building was to be an addition, merely, to the little old shanty previously occupied by them, and was not to cost above $1,200; a plain, board structure. The first raft of lumber for it had already been floated down the river to the Yazoo City levee, and piled upon the bank. It had been arranged that building operations should commence at once. But as the Bureau commissioner could get none of the mechanics in the place to do that part of the work "for love or money," Charles had contracted to have our carpenters do

---

* Sometime afterward I learned that a movement had been for some months under way among the freed people, looking to their separation from the "white folks'" churches, where their position had always been a servile one, and that the white folks had been making very strenuous exertions indeed to prevent such a result. They were not willing, of course, to receive their former slaves into full Christian fellowship, nor were they willing to tear down the railing in their places of worship which marked the arbitrary line that the master-class had drawn between white and black worshippers. They wished them all to continue, at least in their worship of God, the same as "in the good old days befo' the wah."

it, and Tom was bossing the job. In Tom's opinion, they were going to raid the plantation, hoping by that means to remove the cause of "this outrage," as they were pleased to term it.

They had at first threatened to "kill any d—d Yankee s— of a b——" who would "dare to strike a lick" on such a job. But there were six of our white mill hands, all told, who had been in the Federal army ; they were "heeled,"* too, and were not going to be "bluffed."

That very day they had laid the foundation and commenced to build. None of them had been harmed, however, and Tom's opinion as to the purpose of the "rebs," as he called them, to "raid Tokeba," was based on remarks he had heard made by a crowd of loungers who had hung about there the greater part of the day.

While this talk was going on between Charles, Tom and myself, Uncle Stephen called with a long story about what one of his "feller-servants of slave time" had overheard between his young masters, the substance of which was, that the Yankees must be all "driven out" or the country would be "ruined," and something about a plan to "raid the Morgans."†

Uncle Stephen's fellow-servant lived with his old master in Holmes County, twenty-five or more miles away.

While Stephen was making his "report," two of our Yankee neighbors dropped in and soon after another. One of them had been an officer of negro troops and afterwards of the Freedman's Bureau. The feeling against him had become so bitter that he did not often venture to town. He related to us instances of outrage upon himself, which, though not amounting to violence, satisfied him that his life was in peril. And from what he said, it appeared that upon one pretext or another, all the other Northern settlers in the neighborhood had been grossly insulted.

In reply to Charles' inquiry as to the probable cause of all

* Armed with pistols.
† The kuklux germ in that county had been developing.

this feeling, the ex-bureau officer declared it had all the time existed, and was open now only because of the fight between the President and the known leaders of his party; that the rebels felt sure of Johnson's secret, if not open encouragement, and believed they would have to hold out but a short while before he would be able, by a judicious use of his patronage, to control Congress when it should assemble. This Yankee neighbor had a correspondent in Washington who kept him posted in such matters.

Brother Charles and I had heard that there was a difference of some sort between the President and the national leaders of the Republican party, but had not followed it up, and knew nothing of its scope or probable effect. We had given no thought whatever to politics. We had neglected to subscribe for any of the Northern journals, or local papers for that matter. The fact is, we had given ourselves wholly to our business, and had no time for anything else.

All agreed that the assault upon me was likely to be repeated, and that other Northerners were in equal danger. It was also agreed that the crowd had scattered on the approach of the postmaster and friends solely because *he* was a Yankee *in office* and supposed to have influence. He had been appointed during the " era of good feeling," and because no one else having the requisite capacity for the office could be found who could take the required oath. They had no fear of the Northern settler *out of office.* He was not so likely to have " influence with the Johnson administration." The ex-bureau officer attributed his security thus far in part to the fact that the postmaster was his partner in planting.

When all were gone, I asked Charles what he thought of the situation ? After a long sigh, he told me he felt that it was becoming serious; that the " bureau man " had returned to Vicksburg for the purpose of having an agent stationed in our town at once, and, if necessary, troops, to prevent actual interference with the building of the school-house, which, he declared, was imminent. Then he told me that he

went down with the first load of lumber for the school-house
and that their arrival had been heralded through town, where
he found the feeling against him was so bitter he was hooted.
They had called out after him, as he passed up the main street,
"Old Morgan"—"Old Yankee Morgan !" "Hi!" and " Polecat Morgan ! "

Within a very few days after this event, a number of revolvers found their way to Tokeba, and, as the hands had
been given to understand that we had no objections to their
having weapons, Uncle Taylor brought out his old army rifle
and handled it with such dexterity and skill in the manual,
of arms, that he became quite a hero at Tokeba.

CHAPTER XIII.

TAFFY, WOMEN AND WINE *vs.* THE ARMY OF THE UNITED STATES
—THE STRAW THAT BROKE OUR CAMEL'S BACK—A STALWART
FRIEND.

NOT many·days after the incident which closes the foregoing chapter, a squad of Federal troops arrived at Yazoo
City. It was understood that they had been sent there by
direction of General O. O. Howard to prevent interference
with the erection of a school-house for the freed people.

The angry, snarling wolves all at once became lambs, in
manners and appearance, and the proud " American eagle "
ruffled his own feathers until they stood erect, in indignant
protestation against the " outrage " put upon " we all best
citizens " by the hostile presence "in ouah midst " of " ahmed
soldiery" in a time of "profound peace." The officer in command of the squad was something more than " a gentleman,
by G—d, sir," he was " discreet." From the moment they
"sot eyes onto him" and got a glimpse of his face Yazoo's "best
citizens," females and males, began to coddle him, and dined
and wined that "discreet Yankee ahmy officer," *ad nauseam*
for us, though as the sequel proved greatly to *his* delectation.
They were powerless to prevent their coming, now they
were there. Therefore it would be the part of wisdom
to make the visit of these " Yankee soldiers " as harmless as
under the circumstances would be possible. Secretly they

cursed General Howard and held him, not Mr. Johnson—it
was *Mr.* Johnson now—responsible for the " outrage." But
to this officer they spoke of General Howard as a most patriotic, gallant, and worthy gentleman, " no doubt." And
they insisted that he had been " misled " in the matter by
the representations of his agent, who, they declared had
" sneaked in and sneaked out " of the town after " mixing "
with the " nigros " and had not consulted the " best citizens "
about the school for " our nigros." They hotly and with
great indignation denied that they had attempted in any
way to interfere with " the people," who were at work on the
school-house—they had never thought of such a thing ! On
the contrary they had long seen the " *necessity* for just such
a building," and had striven to induce " our nigros " to save
their money and build one. But " the nigro," as " everybody"
knew, was an " improvident creature at best," and besides,
lacked the " capacity to plan " such an enterprise or to carry
it out after it had been planned " for him."

" No such reports," they said, " would ever got out about
Yazoo County" had it not been for a " pa'cel" of Yankee
" adventurers " who were " scheming " to gain the confidence of " our nigros" only " to fleece them."

" The wah is over, and we all have surrendered in good
faith," said they further, " and the presence of these soldiers
is a reflection upon ouah honah, by G—d, sir," and—

" We all are too po' to take upon ouah own selves " the
cost of educating them.

" All our nigros free now, as we all are," and it was but
natural that they should be " only too happy " to have the
aid of the " General Government" in the schooling of " our
nigros."

I have no doubt these arguments would have taken effect
upon this officer without the aid of wine. As it was the
wine or the women—or perhaps it was his inherent " cussedness"—kept him aloof from the freed people, and from " them
Yankee adventurers up the river." In fact he failed to call

upon any of the Northern settlers in the region, and his time was so taken up by the best citizens that he had none to spare the " adventurers."

Then, too, Colonel Black and his friends managed the whole thing so adroitly there was perfect peace in Yazoo; there were no longer anywhere apparent any signs of ill-feeling towards the negroes; no groups of angry, threatening whites at the landing when a raft of lumber arrived for the " nigger school;" nor about " the people " who were at work on the school-house that was to be, and Charles declared that he could walk all the way from the levee to the post-office and not hear his name called nor yet a polecat's. So, without consulting with us, or with the ex-bureau agent, or with any of " we all Yankees," so far as I was able to learn, this very " discreet " officer of the United States army reported to his superior that there was no need for him or his soldiers there, and he and they were soon afterward recalled. But our point had been gained. The building had been completed and a teacher, furnished by the Bureau, duly installed before the officer could " tear himself away " from such " hospitable, high-toned " people as welcomed *him*—and was he not a Yankee ?—to Yazoo City.

Thus the plans of Tom's " rebs," instead of being executed on Tokeba, or on the " nigger school," had been " toted " out on the shoulders of " high-toned, chivalrous, honorable, Southern gentlemen," and in the laps of fair women, and buried; yes, buried; for those troops were regulars.

I felt that I was rapidly finding out more of the ways of Colonel Black and his friends, than it was well for my peace of mind to know. But there was one feature of their recent exploits, when taken in connection with the object of my " fool's errand," that puzzled me above any other in the course of my experience there up to that time. In the former instance they had acted as though extremely desirous of having Federal troops sent to Yazoo. *Now*, they were extremely anxious that they should be kept away, and appeared to feel themselves wronged by their presence. In the former instance they had harnessed me into their traces in a laborious effort to obtain them. Now, they held me in a measure responsible for what they termed the " outrage " inflicted upon the " best citizens " of the county by their presence in it.

What could it mean?

Less than one year before these same best citizens—and they were so held—were pleading with the commanding general of the district for these very troops, and for just another such officer to be sent there for the purpose of protecting the " white " women from enforced marriage with "nigros," and the "men, women, and children, from the cradle up," against a " deep, dark, damnable plot," on the part of " our nigros," to " rise " and kill them all.

Then they had been able to make a "tool," if not a fool of me, and had enticed me into the fire after their scorched chestnuts. They had found me out now, and, if "we *all* Yankees" had not yet learned their ways thoroughly enough to enable us to detect their point of departure from ours, I had, the ex-bureau agent had, some others had also, and Charles was in a fair way of doing so. Therefore, they had no use for the troops now. Their presence was a " menace." But was it because they had found us out, and we had learned too much of their ways to be further deceived?

Although at that time I was only a beginner in the study of the customs and laws of Yazoo, I was fully aware of the fact that it had always been unlawful to teach a negro to read and write. That was an historical fact. If not still unlawful, the fact was due to the power of the United States. I had abundant evidence of the respect the best citizens of Yazoo had for that power, when made manifest to them in the person of armed soldiers. But for that same power in the person of a freedman, they appeared to have naught but contempt. Indeed, they resented any such manifestation of it as an outrage; and the existence of it in the persons of " we all Yankees " had, apparently, served only to light our steps into a trap which any day might be sprung upon ou bare feet. At all events, it was clear to me that their respect for that "discreet Yankee ahmy" lieutenant was born of fear and not of love, or even of regard for his person, or for the government he represented; therefore they had resorted to cajolery and hypocrisy to deceive and mislead him.

But my difficulty remained. For in the few months intervening between my "fool's errand" and now, "we all Yankees" had undergone no change as I could see, and, to all appearances, the freed-people were just the same, or nearly so, as then, and so far as I could learn the only " rising " now threatened by the " blacks " was a longing aspiration afte r knowledge.

Had I appeared in the Yazoo City *Banner* with a "ceahd " charging that the only "rising " the best people of Yazoo County had any interest in, or could be induced to tolerate, would be one in which the negroes should be held and treated as felons, murderers, treacherous, blood-thirsty wretches, because it would afford the high-toned gentlemen of the county a pretext for a " vindication " of the superiority of the Caucasian race over the negroes, it would have been a true statement of the case at that time, in my opinion. But it could not have cleared away my difficulty:

" Why were the best citizens of Yazoo County now bitterly hostile to the presence of Yankee soldiers, in charge o a discreet officer, when less than a year before they had with such a semblance of zeal petitioned to have them sent there?"

There was nothing in Yazoo County to afford me any light whatever upon the subject, and it was some time afterward that I found the true key to the mystery.

Our crop that year was a failure. The proceeds barely paid for gathering and working it. The saw-mill, however, had been doing a good business right along, and in this crisis proved to be our stalwart friend. It lifted us over the rocks upon which several Northern planters foundered, and in spite of the overflow that deluged the Yazoo bottoms that winter.

In June following, we had as fine a " stand" of cotton on six hundred acres of Tokeba, as had ever been seen on the plantation. At least so Colonel Black's former slaves declared. In one respect the overflow had proved a blessing to us, for it enabled us to " float" a large number of as fine cypress trees as were ever brought out of the " brakes " in that region, and the mill was just " coining money " for us.

All this demonstrated the wisdom of Charles' plan of making " one hand wash the other," and I had greater faith than ever in his business sagacity. Our experiences in another direction, however, had increased his confidence in what he was pleased to call my " political acumen." But that was because I had, during the first year, better opportunities than he for learning the " ways of the country."

Our partner, Mr. Moss, was just beginning to realize the truth. He was absent North a great part of the time, and during his visits to us the native whites took particular pains, whenever he met them, on the river packets, or in town, to treat him with consideration. Therefore, he had been slow to comprehend some features of the situation.

In compliance with our promise to have a school on the place, the old quarter jail had been torn down and the same logs used in the building of a house for that purpose. Colonel Black's old slaves recognized and greatly enjoyed the "poetic justice " in this use of that jail.

We had not been able to procure a teacher in Yazoo, and the school had been delayed until our sister Mollie, who had just graduated, and was soon to be married, should visit us. Now, she was coming, and wrote that she expected that an old friend would accompany her, in the hope of improving her health by the travel and a winter in the " Sunny South."

We knew the young lady and her family well, and it was arranged that she should undertake, with Mollie's help, to teach the school; just to have something to do.

This was the " straw that broke the camel's back—" " a white lady teaching a nigger school ! ! ! "

They were both ostracized from the first. But one " white Southern lady" called during their sojourn with us, and rumor said she was " engaged to a Yank."

It was " monstrous ! " It was " incendiarism ! " It would put the " very devil " in the heads of " our nigros," said the best citizens. And whenever they happened to see this " nigger school marm," they would say:

" It's an outrage to subject the young lady to the consequences of such a calling," and they savagely denounced us as responsible for the " crime " against her " sex and her race."

She was a real good Yankee girl; a sweet-faced, sweet-tempered, lovely, Christian woman. At her home, Lura Starke was admired and loved by all. She possessed, among other virtues, the courage of true womanhood; or, rather I should say, the virtues she inherited had blossomed under the care of loving, worthy parents, into the true womanly graces. Therefore, she did not heed these reproaches, and made no protest against being called a " nigger school marm."

Sister Mollie and she went over to town one Sunday to church. They never ventured again. Mollie declared that during prayer she heard some ladies whispering to each other, that she was a polecat.

From this time on it was simply an accident if one of us returned from an errand in town without having been grossly insulted. On meeting us white women would gather their skirts about them and turn away. White men often huddled in groups at the post-office to obstruct our way to or from the window, where we got our mail, or stretched themselves across the sidewalk to prevent our passing up or down, and frequently commanded whichever one of us it happened to be, to " walk in the street with the niggers."*

*" Good nigros" still walked in the middle of the street with " other cattle," as was the practice in slave times.

CHAPTER XIV.

YAZOO JUSTICE IN 1867—TEN DOLLARS AND A "LICK" FOR A
YEAR'S HARD WORK—WAS IT IN SELF-DEFENSE?—QUESTIONS
REMAINING UNSETTLED TO THIS DAY—O'OOPHIE—POLECAT.

WE had occasion to send one of our teams to an adjoining
county after the "plunder," as the "household goods"
and "gods" of the freed people were called, of some people
who had come to us for the New Year. There had been some
mule-stealing in that neighborhood; and more because Pomp,
the driver, would be safer with than without one, we allowed
him to take a Colt's revolver with him. He started off with
it fastened in a belt under his coat. The following morning
Pomp returned with the goods all right, but minus the
weapon, and plus a very woe-begone countenance, indeed.*
After hearing his story I mounted, and, taking him with me,
readily discovered the "robbers," who were attending to
their business in the town, just like other honest men. They
did not deny that they had taken the pistol. On the contrary
they informed me that if I wished to recover it I had better
see a magistrate.

To a magistrate I went, stated the case and demanded
their arrest. The justice promptly complied. But before
the warrants, charging them with an "assault" on Pomp,
and "highway robbery" against the "peace and dignity of
the State of Mississippi," could be served upon them, the

* They were planters in the neighborhood whom Pomp well knew, and had got up to
ride with him and thus taken him unawares.

robbers appeared in court with counsel, and blandly " 'low'd" they had only performed their "duty as good citizens," when they " seized " the weapon.

Upon the hearing Pomp was allowed to " state "—the court would decide afterward whether he was a competent witness—that I had given him the weapon, and being called upon I was allowed to "testify" that I had; that it was the private property of my brother, and that Pomp had been allowed to carry it with him for use in case he should need it to defend himself or the team against mule thieves.

The defendants plead the " statute " in such cases, and were promptly discharged. Whereupon Pomp was arrested, charged with carrying a " deadly weapon " against the "peace and dignity " of the State, found guilty, and fined " ten dollars, or thirty days in jail."

Then I was arrested, charged with having given him the weapon, " against the peace and dignity of the State of Mississippi," was found guilty, and fined "fifty dollars, or thirty days in jail ;" being the lowest penalty the justice said he was allowed by the statute to impose.

During the proceedings, I had demanded to be shown the statute under which they were justified, and had been gratified. There it was, plain as day, within the lids of the "Acts of the Legislature " of the State, published by authority.*

Pomp could not read, yet he did not appear so greatly puzzled as I who could. Looking about the court-room and observing that not only the court himself, but also the "robbers" and a large part of the spectators, carried weapons, I called his honor's attention to the fact, and reminded him that although *Pomp* was a " freedman, free negro or mulatto," he was our teamster, our servant, and we had merely given him the weapon to be used in case of need in protecting our property, and it was not charged that *I* was not a "white man."

The court, however, informed me that in that case I should have sent a white man; that the statute had been

* The reader will learn more of this and other Yazoo laws as we proceed.

wisely framed for the protection of the community against
most disastrous consequences to society, certain to follow any
violation whatever of the principles which the statute recognized as essential to the welfare of both races, viz: their
complete separation, and the subjection of the inferior to
the superior. He, however, would instruct the officer to
allow us a reasonable time in which to pay the fine. He did
not wish to degrade me by a "commitment," as the statute
was "purely corrective."

I at once sought out the ex-bureau agent, who informed
me that the statute under which I had been fined, with other
similar acts of the legislature of the State, had been declared "null and void " by the Federal authorities, because
they were in conflict with the Civil Rights Act of Congress,* and all I need do would be to write to the commanding general and state the facts to him. This I did, and, in
a few days, received an official letter from headquarters,
inclosing a formal document signed by His Excellency Benjamin G. Humphreys, Governor of the State of Mississippi,
in which the commanding general was informed in effect that
His Excellency had previously advised all executive and
judicial officers of the State not to attempt to enforce the statutes complained of, pending the operation of the Federal
statutes, with which they were in conflict.

I presented this document to the magistrate, and claimed
exemption from payment of the fines imposed upon Pomp
and myself. He did not appear to have any desire to read it.
Nor was he in the least disconcerted by it. On the contrary,
he acted as though he knew it all the while, and, as though
my employment of the Federal power to defeat the will of
my neighbors and fellow-citizens had deepened the contempt
he had previously felt for me. However, from this on, we
preferred " Federal " to "local " government at Tokeba, and
Charles and I both determined to know more " law " in the
future, whatever the consequences might be to our business.

* This was the Civil Rights Act of 1866.

This resolution was quickened, no doubt, by outrages upon the freedmen, or upon Northern settlers themselves, which were reported to us or of which we were witnesses.

As to those inflicted upon the freedmen, the following may be taken as a fair sample :

The first is a "settlement" between a planter and one of his freedmen. It took place at the store of Mr. Fountain Barksdale, with whom we were having large dealings, and while I was making some purchases there.

The planter had just sold and received from Mr. Barksdale the money for several bales of cotton, which had been hauled to town upon a wagon at that moment standing at the store front. With the money in his hands the planter called to the driver of the wagon—

"Hi! yo', boy! Come y'here!"

The freedman, with his long ox whip in one hand and hat in the other, walked promptly into the store, where the planter handed him a ten-dollar bill. He had evidently expected more money, for the smile which had lighted up his face gave way to one of disappointment, and, in an attitude of abject humility, he inquired—

"Am dis all, marsa ?" The only reply was a ringing blow with the planter's hand upon his upturned face, followed by an order to—

"Go home, boy."

Without the least apparent resentment the man gathered himself up, walked back to the wagon, and started the team homeward.

Of the several white persons present, there was not one who appeared to have any sympathy for the freedman, nor any who appeared to question the perfect propriety of the planter's conduct.

On my way home from town one day I saw in the road coming toward me an old freedman, leading by the hand a little girl. The moment he saw me he "shied" off the highway into the bushes like a frightened steer.

I called after him—

"What's the matter, Uncle?" It must have been something in the tone of my voice or form of my speech, for he stopped, hesitated, and after a brief pause as though in doubt as to something, he replied:

"Nuth'n', marsa." Then I—

"Don't be afraid; what's the matter? why do you leave the road?"

He advanced toward me hesitatingly, leading the girl. Then I told him my name and where I lived.

His face brightened at once, and he came up until he stood by my horse's head, the girl still holding on to him, and he said:

"Beez yo' de Yankee Kunnel whar live on Marsa Black's plantation?"

"Yes."

"Beez yo' de gemen de white folks war a talkin' right smart about?"

"Yes, I guess so."

"Well, den, I reckon yo' is. Bless de Lord!"

By this I could half imagine the trouble, for I had observed that the girl's frock was stained and stiff with blood that had flowed from deep gashes upon her head, neck, and shoulders, and I said to him:

"Tell me all about it, Uncle." In response to this invitation, the man approached until he stood at the side of my horse, where, with his hand at times resting on the stirrup of the saddle, and at other times engaged in wiping the tears from his eyes, he told me his story in a tone of voice that equally with his manner, indicated his perfect trust in me.

Briefly told, this negro's master, "Mars Si," he called him, only the night before had beaten the little girl at his side, his daughter, nearly to "def's do," and, while his son, Andrew, the following morning, was "a stan'in' thar in he own doah, doin' nuffin' 'cepn' watchin' Mars Si, fur ter keep um off'n' de gal, Mars Si done shot de boy t'wel he wor dead."

They had run away from the plantation, the old man and
his daughter, and traveled on foot through the swamps on
their way to town in search " ob 'jest." Uncle Isam, that was
his name, was on a quest for justice. He had " done heerd
dar wor a booro in de Azoo City," and hoped to find what
he wanted there.

General Bell, formerly of the Mississippi River Marine
Brigade, was " trying " to plant on a place near Tokeba. I
should pass his residence on my way home. There was no
longer a bureau in town for the freed people. I so informed
Isam and requested him to accompany me to the General's
home, where we would all talk the matter over, and advise
him what to do.

I knew there was little to hope from the law officers at
Yazoo City, and did not know but Isam would do better to
abandon his quest altogether. But after General Bell had
heard the story, he accompanied Isam to town, resolved to
ascertain for a certainty whether or not any notice would be
taken of the matter. A warrant was sworn out by Isam,
charging his employer with murder, and placed in the hands
of the sheriff for execution.

Three days afterward, being in town, I met this sheriff,
who informed me that he had " business on the creek"—that
was " Mars Si's home"—which would necessitate a journey
there, and on his return he would bring Captain Cambee—
that was Mars Si—in with him. But the case was neglected
until Mars Si came in voluntarily and gave himself up.

On the hearing before the same justice who had fined
Pomp and me, it was proved by six witnesses " for the State"
that on the night before the killing, Mars Si arrived home
" nigh on to midnight;" that the girl who had been set to
watch for his coming, while her mistress slept, had fallen
asleep herself and was not prompt to admit him; that on
being admitted he flew at the girl with his stick and beat her
until her screams, heard at the quarter, a hundred or more
yards distant, brought her father, who took her in his arms and

carried her to his home; that the following morning Mars Si,
accompanied by one of his neighbors, and both armed with
guns, was advancing on Isam's house to force the girl to return home with him; seeing which, Isam's son, who stood
in the door on the watch, turned as if to re-enter " an' shet
de do';" that as the son began this movement, Mars Si
raised his gun and shot him dead.

For the defense, it was shown on the testimony of Mars Si
himself and his neighbor, that " as Mars Si approached to
recover the gal, the son turned like he wor g'wan to take
down his gun "—a squirrel gun which was hanging on the
wall inside the house—and Mars Si thereupon fired " in self-
defense." All agreed that the fatal wound was in the front
and side. Mars Si admitted the " chastisement " of the evening before; that the father had taken the girl away; that she
was but thirteen years of age ; that he was advancing on the
house to recover her, accompanied by his neighbor ; that
both were armed with double-barrelled shotguns, and that it
was Cambee's shot which killed the boy. Mars Si's lawyer, an
old one, testified that he had known Captain Cambee for many
years before the war; that he was an old citizen of the county,
highly connected and greatly respected ; that he had been
known as a kind master, and was " a high-toned, honorable
gentleman," and then announced that the defense rested their
cause.

The attorney for the prosecution, retained by Isam after
great difficulty, began his speech by offering as an apology
for appearing for Isam, the fact that "there are strangers in
our midst, and my refusal to appear for this nigro might be
misconstrued to the injury of our people." But, he had
" never appeared in a cause so repugnant to all his finer
feelings," and so forth.

The attorney for the defense appreciated the situation, and
the feelings of the opposing counsel. Here was "a high-toned,
honorable gentleman in jeopardy of his life on the testimony of nigros. They would not deny the killing. They

justified it. But they had fallen upon strange times. The most that could be made of the charge was manslaughter. They would plead guilty to that. It was within the knowledge of the court that by the laws of the commonwealth, the only testimony offered by the State was inadmissible. However, they were for the present under the rule of a military despotism. He appreciated the delicate duty imposed upon his honor; he was under duress, and they would consent to bail."

So Mars Si, having given Mr. Stockdale and another well-known and leading citizen as surety for appearance when wanted, was released and that was the end of it.

"Never indicted?"

"No."

"Nothing further ever done about it?"

"No."

General Bell and I were present at this hearing. The court-room was packed with whites, and as we left the hall and passed down the stairway the spectators groaned aloud. Some shouted, "O'oophe!" "O'oophe!" "polecat!" "polecat!"

Had it not been for the remnant of fear remaining that a way might be found for their punishment, in such a case, we should doubtless have been hanged.

These and similar events, occurring in the winter of 1866-'67 and spring of 1867, took effect upon our partner, Mr. Moss, and, by June following, of the nineteen ex-Federal officers and soldiers in that county, engaged, some in planting, some in merchandising, and some in manufacturing, there was not one who had not been the victim of such outrages, or a witness of them. So, that as a class we were a unit in opinion and feeling as to the purposes of the late rebels respecting their former slaves.

CHAPTER XV.

ARMY WORMS AND OTHER WORMS—OUR STALWART FRIEND LAS
SOED—ANOTHER KIND OF FOOL'S ERRAND—HOW TO GET " RID
A THE D——N YANKEES "—HURRAH FOR COL. J. J. U. BLACK—
WAS COLONEL BLACK " AGENT IN FACT "?

DURING the first days of September, Uncle David thought he saw signs of the army worm in his "crap." David was planting "on shares" that year.

In less than ten days, nearly all of the six hundred acres looked as though they had been swept by fire; all the green leaves and shoots had been eaten off, and the crop was ruined. Only our "stalwart friend" remained steadfast.

We had already shipped several cargoes of lumber to Vicksburg, one to New Orleans, and were getting ready another one for that market. I have not the exact figures, but there must have been at least half a million feet of lumber piled in our yard at the mill, nearly a million of shingles, and in logs in the river ready for the mill there were fully a million more feet of lumber.

None of this property, not even the saw-mill, was in any way liable under the terms of our contract with Mrs. Black for any part of the rent-money for Tokeba.

Although the crop was a failure, in all probability there would be enough corn and cotton made to pay the rent. Besides, there were upon the plantation, belonging to our firm, several head of work cattle, twenty-nine head of horses and mules, and wagons and plows, harness, etc., etc. The only lien of any kind against this property was that of the landlord for his rent.

Notwithstanding these evidences of our ability to pay the rent when it should become due, one day, shortly after the army worm disappeared, Colonel Finley, the sheriff, came to Tokeba and informed my brother that Colonel Black, as agent in fact of his wife, had been before a magistrate and made oath that he had reason to suspect and did verily believe we were about to remove our property beyond the jurisdiction of Yazoo County, " for the purpose of defrauding" him of his rent. Whereupon an attachment writ had been issued, commanding the sheriff to seize the *saw-mill and fixtures,* logs, lumber, shingles, etc., and hold them, subject to the further orders of that magistrate's court. He had called for the purpose of executing the writ.

The purpose of this proceeding was evident. When Colonel Black made that oath, he knew that if we had desired to do so, it would have been impossible for us to remove the property levied on into the adjoining county—the nearest being more than twenty miles distant—in less time than one week. When the magistrate issued the writ, and when the sheriff executed it, that fact was as evident to them as to Colonel Black or to ourselves. Yet they had done these things. Their only motive was our destruction. It was plain there existed no other; for if Colonel Black sought this remedy in good faith and for the sole purpose of securing the rent-money for Mrs. Black, why had he left the only property upon the place, which we could have run off in a night, viz: the horses, mules and other cattle, and levied upon our " stalwart friend"? Had his only object been to collect the rent, by allowing us to keep the mill running, we readily could have paid it out of the orders for lumber already on hand and from the proceeds of the cargo we were about to send to New Orleans. But this he would not permit, and the sheriff not only forbade us to operate the mill; he also put a guard over it to make sure that we did not.   It was evident that Colonel Black, the magistrate, and the sheriff had conspired together to destroy us.*

But we had made some few friends during our brief residence in the county, and, notwithstanding the ugly front of the enemy, we resolved to contest with the conspirators their *power* to destroy us, as well as their right to this writ for money not yet due.   But at the moment when we thought we were about to defeat them by replevin, the sheriff made another visit to Tokeba, and shortly afterward another, until the writs covered all our property, even including the growing and ungathered crops, and amounted to the whole of the rental for the coming year 1868, in addition to the last installment of the rental for 1867, which itself was not yet due·

The end of it all was that the enemy triumphed, the sheriff sold our property, and the rent remained unpaid still.

" Unpaid ? "

" Yes, unpaid."

" Why ? "

" Because, after the sheriff got his fees, there was not money enough left from the proceeds of the sale to pay it. Then, too, the property did not sell very well.   For example, a wagon which cost one hundred and twenty-five dollars sold for twenty-eight dollars; mules that cost us one hundred and thirty dollars per head only the year before in St. Louis were knocked off, some of them to Black, at twenty-five to fifty-five dollars per head, and the mill, with fixtures, which had cost us, as it stood when attached, nearly eleven thousand dollars, was sold to Colonel Black for *one hundred dollars.* The logs had been allowed to break loose from their cribs and float away.   The lumber and shingles went for a mere song— I forget the amount—while much of the crop was allowed to go to waste."

* Two years later the records of the bankrupt court showed that at the time they became sureties on the bond which Colonel Black had to make in order to obtain his writs of attachment every one of his bondsmen was insolvent.

" Why did we permit all this ? "

" We did not; we tried hard to prevent it."

" How was it done !"

" According to law;" and the law of Yazoo on the subject was similar to that of many States of the Union, North as well as South. The difficulty was not in the law, but in the character of our neighbors. We had never pretended to very great skill in matters of law, but we had good counsel—a native lawyer—and we were acting according to his instructions when we sought for a remedy by replevin. To enable us to obtain a hearing in a superior court this was the first and an essential step. But before we could take that step it was necessary that we should give a bond in double the amount attached for. Therefore having procured our bondsmen for double the amount sued for under the first levy, to prevent us replevying the mill and resuming work with it, Colonel Black got out the additional writs for the next year's rental, which ran up the amount of the bond to a point which of itself was calculated to frighten off any who might be disposed to befriend us. Besides, the sheriff required of our sureties an oath that they were severally worth the amount for which they were to sign in *real estate*, over and above all their just debts and all liabilities.

On attempting to give this bond we found that the contest had extended beyond the limits of a judicial proceeding. It was no longer between Colonel Black and our firm, but between " we all Southerners " and "them d—d Yankees up the river." Even the parties by whose aid we were to have made the first bond, shrank away, excusing themselves by saying that to be publicly known as our friends would ruin their own business. Every Northern planter was either in the same dilemma as ourselves or had already gone down, and had left the country, or was about to do so.

We could not find a real estate owner in the county who would befriend us. There were some who would gladly have done so, but they durst not.

At last, and when the limit of time allowed under the law by the magistrate, in which to give bond and replevy, was about to expire, by the advice of our attorney I armed myself with letters from several of the wealthiest and most worthy citizens of the town and neighborhood, and went to see the commanding general.* After stating the facts to him I laid before that gentleman the letters of our Northern neighbors, alleging that we were being persecuted because we were "Northern men, and loyal." I also placed before him the letters of Mr. Fountain Barksdale, Mr. Hiram Harrison, and Messrs. Kellogg & Co., three of the largest commission merchants and dealers in Yazoo City, setting forth that our business with each of them had amounted to several thousand dollars; that we had met all of our obligations promptly, and that we were respectable, reliable, and honorable business men; also, that the proceedings against us were oppressive and uncalled for.

Upon this showing General Ord granted an order for a stay of ten days, that he might investigate the matter. This gave us a breathing spell; time for renewed efforts; and upon the advice of our counsel I set out to see the judge of our Circuit Court, then in an adjoining county, while Charles posted off to raise money.

When I had placed before the judge all the facts that I had laid before General Ord he promptly set the cause for a special hearing before himself, whenever we should enter into bond equal to the amount of rent that would be due at the close of the year 1867, but when I got back to Yazoo City I found that Colonel Black and his friends had seized upon what they styled an "outrageous interference with the civil authorities by a military despot in a time of profound peace," as affording them all a pretext for still further inflaming themselves and their "anti-Yankee" allies against us. They were ready to make it "a personal matter, by G—d, sir," with any one who might appear to sympathize with us

*E. O. C. Ord.

in any way, so that it became impossible to make even the small amount of bond now required to enable us to get a hearing in court.

Upon report of an officer sent by himself to Yazoo, to investigate our case, General Ord granted an extension of his former order for ten days. Meanwhile, having succeeded in raising a sum of money equal to the amount on the bond, Charles took it to the sheriff and offered it to him in lieu of securities. But after consulting with Mrs. Black's lawyers, he flatly refused to accept the money. Then Charles went with the money first to one and then another of the merchants who had given us the letters referred to, and with each of whom, save one,* their own books showed a balance in our favor in the transactions of more than a year, and said to them : " Take this money, put it in your safe and lock it up, or, if you please, use it as your own, and make this bond for us."

All refused. Not because they had changed their minds as to the merits of the case, but, as each declared, to do so would ruin their own business.

We were now at the end of our pursuit of a legal remedy. It seemed that the feeling against us increased in just proportion to the zeal and skill with which we pursued after our rights, and so it did. Our partner gave out in the race first, I next. Charles was last to give up.

Finding that we could not prevent the sale, Charles proposed to be present and buy in the property, or at least make it sell for what it was worth. But a new obstacle confronted us, none of our friends North would risk any more money in Mississippi.

Charles had obtained the money for the bond on a promise to secure it on the property when it should be released. But the situation was now changed—at least more clearly apparent. If by its aid, the aid of the circuit judge of our district, and that of the commanding general, we were not able to

---

* In this case we owed $100—not yet due.

obtain our "day in court," what right had we to suppose
that there would be any protection for the property, after
Colonel Black and the sheriff should lose their interest in
preserving it?

We were forced to admit that there was but one answer to
the question, and that it would be as impossible for us to secure
the conviction of the man who might fire our mill, lumber
and cotton, turn our logs loose in the night, steal our mules,
kill either or all of us, as it had been to replevin the property
in the first instance. And, as the "anti-Yankee" element
had shown itself not only willing, but able to carry out their
plans in that case, would they not be able to do so in the other?

There was but one answer to that question either. Therefore our friend thought he would keep his money. Thus it
came about that, when the mill was sold, Colonel Black was
the only bidder, which demonstrated to Mr. Moss, Charles and
myself, the futility of laws that are against "the will of the
people," and that in Yazoo County the "anti-Yankee" element constituted the people.* For as the sheriff triumphantly conducted our animals over Mr. Gosling's ferry, and up
through town to the stable where they were to be sold, men,
women and children shouted as they passed by, " Hurrah!
Hurrah! for Colonel Black!" and they said to each other,
while they shook hands over it, " we'll get rid a the d—d
Yankees now."

---

*During this struggle, Mrs. Charlotte Black gave no sign that she disapproved of the
conduct of her agent in fact. While some of those with whom we had been on friendly
terms ventured to say *to us* that they disapproved, there was not one who said so
openly, and whenever we met them they passed by with a sort of sneak-thief expression of face and of manner. All seemed to say, " You should do as *we* Romans do."

CHAPTER XVI.

REFLECTIONS—AN APPOMATTOX " STRAW "—CHARLES' " NEW
IDEA "—SHALL WE SURRENDER, RUN AWAY, OR FIGHT IT OUT
ON THAT LINE—WEIGHTY REASONS WHY THE BATTLE SHOULD
CONTINUE.

WHILE Colonel Black and his allies were engaged in root-
ing out so many of the Northern settlers in Yazoo as they
could get under by hook or by crook, the reconstruction acts
of Congress were being put into effect in Mississippi. Registrars had been appointed for Yazoo County. A general registration of all persons entitled under those acts to vote had
been concluded, and proclamation had been made of an election to be held for the selection of delegates to a convention
to frame a constitution, etc. At this forthcoming election
colored men—black, light and white—were to be allowed to
vote along with their former masters.

Had I been called upon two years before to decide for myself whether the freed people ought to be allowed to vote, I
presume I should have replied : " Yes, why not ? " and
doubtless should have dismissed the subject with that. Had
I been, at the same time, called upon to answer the question for the country, I presume I should have replied:
" Really, I have not considered the question fully; " for such
is the conservatism of responsibility. If pressed I doubtless
should have said : " The freedmen are human beings like the

rest of us; I shall claim no rights for myself that I am not perfectly willing to accord to all others." If pressed further it is quite likely I should have added: "Yes, all who are qualified." But had the alternative been presented to me, and I required to decide the question for the whole country—"the ballot for the negro or not"—I am quite certain I should have demanded some qualification.

Up to this time, 1867, I had voted but once in my life, and that was while lying in the trenches before Petersburg; a vote that was counted in Wisconsin.

The issue then was: "Shall we surrender to the rebels, or continue the fight until they surrender to us ? "

On one side was George B. McClellan, a discarded Union general; on the other, Abraham Lincoln. I voted to continue the fight.

I was able to recollect that in 1860 the issue was " for " extension or " against " extension of slavery, and that I had carried a torchlight alongside of those who opposed the extension of that " sum of all villainies." Though not old enough to vote, I could " help to swell the ranks," they said. At the age of eighteen I was in the ranks, with a musket on my shoulder, on my way to Bull Run, where I might at least " stop a bullet " toward putting down the " slave-holders' rebellion," they said. At twenty-two I had witnessed the surrender at Appomattox, and, with " my regiment," had been assigned the distinction of escort for the captured headquarters' train of General Lee, who, with his staff, as paroled prisoners of war, preceded us on our return march.

True, I was able to recall that, while on this march a paroled Confederate brigadier became so offended with me that he would not continue under my " protection " any longer, because I had said I believed the freed slaves would become good citizens, in reply to his request for my views on what should be the future status of " ouah nigros." His flashing eyes and "shinin'" buttons had made a deeper impression upon my mind, however, than the taunt he threw back at me as he rode on : " Young man, I am older than you are. Remember what I say. The South will regain by superiah strategy and statesmanship what it has lost by appealing to ahms."

" Superior statesmanship ! " I only laughed quietly, and allowed it to pass without a word, for he had the appearance of only a dress parade brigadier. To be sure I had recently been feeling the effects of this " superiah " strategy ; but, having come into a limited knowledge of the nature of the contest going on between " Andy " Johnson on one side and the statesmen of the nation on the other, I had learned that these statesmen had been able to " sit down " on Johnson as effectually as Grant and our army had on the honest, manly rebels at Petersburg and Appomattox. Therefore, notwithstanding our rough experiences, my faith in the present *power* of the North was equalled only by the knowledge of it, which I had gained at Appomattox but little more than two years before.

There, where that power had been so signally demonstrated,* we had taken a " bond of fate " for the fulfillment of their promise to behave themselves, and allowed the rebels, as we said, " to go back home, brethren, and go to work for a living," as we Yanks had always done and expected always to continue to do.

My faith in the fidelity of the North to its high purposes, and in the *promises* of the nation to the emancipated slaves, was not a whit less than was my faith in its power. By actual contact with them, I had come into a more perfect knowledge of the true character of " conquered " rebels— especially of slave-holding rebels. And in the same manner I had come to form a juster estimate of the character and capacity of the African in America.

After only two years' contact with him I was able to answer the question—" the ballot for the negro, or not for him"—not only for myself, but also for the country; for, I said, any means

---

* Our children will more justly appreciate the magnitude of the task, accomplished when Lee surrendered.

that will enable us to live here in peace, and enjoy the fruits
of our toil, can but be helpful and good for the whole country.
Therefore, with the call for this election, there came to Charles
and myself a hope of succor through the power of the ballot,
backed as it was by the power of the nation. We began
to canvass the situation as to the prospect of an application
of the means afforded by the "reconstruction plan" for a
restoration to ourselves, and to secure to the freed people the
right to life, liberty and the pursuit of happiness.

In proof of the capacity of the negro to enjoy these privileges we had only to look to Tokeba; for during the two
years we had been together as "masters and servants," as
a whole, our hands had demonstrated their possession of the
very best qualities of natural manhood and womanhood.
Lewd, "bad" women came no more, or at rare intervals, to
Tokeba. During those two years, of the plantation force of
more than one hundred and twenty-five only one had been
drunk; only one had been caught stealing—that was Aggaby
—and concubinage had been utterly routed; "Voudoo"
had disappeared; Uncle Stephen had been taught a new text;
Rose, still a "pure" girl, was able to read and write, and her
mother had determined to make a true "woman" rather than
a "lady" of her; Uncle Bristol, Uncle Jonathan, and Pomp
wore new clothes and held their heads up, though Bristol
could not yet straighten out his legs;* Uncle David had
become his own overseer, and Uncle Anderson Henderson,
during the whole period, had been Charles' most trusted and
faithful mill-hand, while his Judy was universally respected
at the quarter and by ourselves as a model wife.

During this time we had kept out of debt, except to friends
and relatives residing in the North, of whom we had received
pecuniary aid, and excepting the wages due to our hands.
Our friends in the North could not "understand things" at
all, and the sudden winding up of our business—especially the
manner of it—was incomprehensible to them. Had we
"no *courts* in Mississippi?" some inquired.

*This affliction was said to be a legacy from that old quarter jail.

" What had we done to bring down upon our business the wrath of the entire community ?" some said ; others: " No business to have gone down there among those rebels;" while there were those who intimated that " the boys" after all, " had done badly," " no use denying it ;" " if there wern't a screw loose somewhere they would have had *some* friends; needn't talk to me." It would be impossible to bring a whole community against faithful, industrious, and honorable " business men, with the backing we had at the start, unless there was," they said. We could reply to these questionings and insinuations only by silence. We had " failed," that was certain. We could feel it in our bones.

CHAPTER XVII.

CHARLES' TWENTY MILLIONS GONE GLIMMERING—SWEET CONSOLA-
TION—FAME, AND HOW TO WIN IT IN YAZOO—TRUE FRIENDS.

THE fulfillment of my brother's prophecy seemed to me a
long way off ; for by the close of 1867 the " tide of immigration " had ceased to flow southward. Indeed, it was
flowing away from Yazoo. But there was one consolation—
yes, a real consolation—left to us ; for when at last we gave
up the struggle with Colonel Black, " agent in fact " for Mrs.
Charlotte Black, and that lady's lawyers, we discovered that
the negroes on the plantation were all loyal to us. Uncle
David, Uncle Anderson, Uncle Stephen, Uncle Aggaby, Uncle
Bristol, Mr. Smith and *Mrs*. Smith, and all the other uncles
and aunts, voluntarily came forward, each and every one, and
forgave us what we owed them ! Some with oaths, some sob-
bing and others crying, begged us to not go back " to the
North "—they had learned to pronounce the North correctly
—and leave them there alone.

During the two years we had been on Tokeba the fame of
our acts had spread far, carried partly on the tongues of
" ole marsa," who ceased in his cursing of the " free nigros,"
or " that d—d radical Congress," or " that d—d free nigro
bureau," only to curse " them d—d nigger-loving, radical
Yankee incendiaries " on Tokeba, and partly in the hearts
and prayers of such as Jonathan, Pomp, Isam, Mrs. Smith
and others. And now, when the new voters began to look

about for candidates to make the new constitution, delegations of them from far and near came and urged us to be their "leaders." Even " yan in de ole Holmes County" sent a delegation.

Our firm had sunk on Tokeba nearly fifty thousand dollars. Mr. Moss, our Illinois partner, thoroughly disgusted, returned North at once. Charles was on the point of doing so, and I think would have left Yazoo and all his bright visions to Colonel Black and his allies at that time, but for the noble conduct of our hands, which had altered the nature of our obligation to them.

My brother had changed very much, and I could see was growing older, but there was all the physical vigor of the two years before. His strictly temperate habits and careful dieting had brought him safely through acclimation, with scarcely more than an occasional chill. So one day, after the first shock of Black's treatment had passed, he said to me :

" Albert, it is evident that Congress is having a pretty hard fight with Andy and these rebels "—he called them rebels now—" and should the plan of reconstruction they have adopted fail to carry the South, there is no telling what the consequences may be to the nation. I am too old "—he was thirty-four—" and too set in my ways ever to hope to succeed in politics, but you are young and have a long future before you. Suppose you go to the convention; help to give us a free constitution—you can copy after Massachusetts or Ohio—start a loyal government, and I will remain here and see what I can do toward getting a new start. There are greater natural advantages here, from a business point of view, than anywhere else in the world. All we need is to let these rebels see that their slaves are free in fact, and that they were really whipped. Then things will settle down again to the ways of peace, and this country will prosper."

I had not thought of such a thing as he suggested. I was not old enough; had no knowledge of public men or affairs other than military. Besides, the fight was going to be a long

and bitter one.   It would require the ablest and best men to
be found.   The adoption of a new constitution and the setting
up of a new government under it would, in my opinion, be
but the beginning of the conflict, which would continue
until the negroes were in a position, by reason of their property,
education, and experiences, to protect themselves.   I did
not look for immigration again to set southward for many
years.

"It is to be a life-work, my brother," I said; and I felt
certain he was better fitted for it than I.   But he would not
listen to my suggestion that he become a candidate himself,
and reiterating his often-repeated apothegm : "The place to
look for a thing is that where it was lost," strongly urged me
to go to the convention.   He preferred a private life.

While we were debating this question, three Northerners,
all ex-Federal officers, announced themselves as candidates on
a ticket they called " the Republican ticket."   In discussing
the question with the Northerners, we had discovered quite a
division of opinion among them as to the policy to be pursued in the creation of the new government.   Some declared
that there were none of the native whites who could be trusted
to aid in doing the work, not one; and the freedmen were
too ignorant and inexperienced.   There were others who believed that it would be organizing for certain defeat, and that
it would not be correct in principle to ignore the native population altogether.

When asked to name some Southerner who could be relied
on I suggested Major Snodgrass.   The ex-bureau agent suggested another.   But strong objections were urged to both
these men.   Then I suggested that if not one native white
man could be found, a negro ought to be put upon the ticket.
At first this suggestion was laughed at.   This aroused me to
defend my idea, and I said:

"Why, gentlemen, the freed people are about the only
true friends we have here; remove them out of the country
and you will have removed the necessity for a convention.

How absurd, then, to laugh at my suggestion !   And if it be true that Major Snodgrass cannot be trusted, it is plainly our duty to convince the people most concerned at the very out-set, that we may be beyond question.   Therefore, allow them to select one of their number to go to the convention, just to look on, if for nothing else."   There were no freedmen present, and not one of our number was able to say whether there were any who desired to have one of their number on the ticket.

" Besides," as was declared, " we don't want either rebels or negroes in that convention."   An opportunity is offered us Northern men to take control of the State and run it " loyal end foremost."   There was enough talent in the State at large, they said, to do it; and the loyal people of the nation would stand by them, as they believed, to the end.

"But," said I, " suppose after you shall have set up a 'loyal' State government, the rebs should conclude that they pre-ferred their former slaves, whom they know well, rather than Yankees, for their rulers, and should nominate and with the aid of the freed people, elect them to fill the offices.   Then after you shall have left the State, as likely you will gladly do, in such a case, what if these same rebels should turn right around and put out the freedmen with officers elected from among themselves, how far will you have got in establishing a new order of things down here?"

Now I had had no experience whatever in political affairs, but these objections to their plan suggested themselves to me at once.

They replied that no such contingency could arise, for having once got control, a way would be found to keep it. Besides, as they argued, the freed people would remain loyal to them, because they were indebted to them for their free-dom, and the rebels would die before they could be brought to vote for the negroes.   The ex-bureau agent and one other agreed with me.

When I related these interviews to Charles he became

more urgent than ever in his wishes that I should go to the convention, and I began to feel that it might be my duty to do so.

The ex-bureau agent and myself held several consultations together upon the subject, and he agreed to see Major Snodgrass and the gentleman he had himself mentioned, and endeavor to induce one of them to come out on a ticket with us for the convention. One of them at first thought well of the idea, but after several days' delay he concluded that he would have to "sacrifice" too much in doing so to justify the step. During this delay a delegation of freedmen from Yazoo City came to me and asked me to consent to be a candidate on a ticket with one of their number. This I promised to do if they could induce some one of the native whites to take the other place. They replied that they had visited me at the suggestion of certain poor white men, who did not dare to be known as moving in the matter themselves, but would come out openly as soon as the ice had been broken by the new government.

Major Snodgrass was a wealthy planter and would, I believed, be a fair representative of the native "property" class, and a faithful one too. I believe those freedmen made an honest effort to induce the Major to allow them to put his name on their ticket. But he refused, and after some time spent in a fruitless search for a native white man willing to accept the place, I consented to stand on a ticket with a freedman, a blacksmith named William Leonard, and Charles W. Clark, an ex-Union officer, who had been "trying" to plant in that neighborhood. The opposing ticket had been in the field two or three weeks, and the candidates had done some canvassing in the country districts as well as in Yazoo City.

It was on the last day before the election that our ticket was launched, so there would be no time for speech-making or other "campaign work."

But that was a "mighty" interesting campaign for all that, and some of the fruits of it remain to this day. That

Yazoo graveyard cannot hide them all. They still live and thrive, and, whether in the midst of timid children huddled together in a "nigger school," or among that band of jolly revellers surrounding that Yazoo jail last Christmas eve, with tongues lolling, and hands red with the blood of those young men whom that election inspired with courage to hope for kinship with freemen, the fruits of that day's work will stand forever, to mock, when their fear cometh upon them, the "high-toned, honorable gentlemen, by G—d, sir," of the "banner county of Mississippi," who that day passed by on the other side and scoffed at the poor, blind Samson depositing his first ballot in a box that was held out to him upon the point of a bayonet.

CHAPTER XVIII.

A SECOND DAY AMONG THE FREED PEOPLE IN YAZOO—WHEN, WHERE, HOW AND WHY I BECAME A "DICTATOR."—AN ELEC-TION IN YAZOO WHEN "ONLY NIGGERS" VOTE.

IT is an historical fact, well known, of course, that the recon-struction acts of Congress were passed to "laws of the United States" over the spiteful vetoes of that "tailor, Andy" Johnson. It was not then, however, nor is it yet, so gener-ally well known as it should be, that those acts were also passed in spite of all the patronage of the President's great office, and that the agents appointed to execute them were more or less in sympathy with the fierce opposition to them which in the South existed among the former slave-holding class, with rare exceptions, and in the North assuredly extended beyond the ranks of the Democratic party, so called.

In Yazoo, among "we all adventurers," it was enough to know that those acts had become laws. As for myself, I knew as little as one well could, and know anything of the fierce stress through which they had passed. That they voiced the mind and the heart of the nation upon the questions they were intended and confidently (?) expected to solve,* I had no doubt. Therefore I was not bothered with any such ques-tions as :

---

*The country has yet to learn that those much-maligned acts have succeeded in accom-plishing God's purposes toward the negro far beyond the expectations of their framers.

" How will your action in consenting to be a candidate upon a ticket with a ' nigger ' affect your standing with respectable people ? "

Indeed, the only question that had given me any trouble was of an entirely different sort. It would have been stated thus: " Should you run away from this fight, and disaster befall the national cause, what will your old comrades in arms, and all the loyal people of the country say, who are acquainted with the true state of things here and with your known feelings and principles ?"

Physically I had all my life been a coward. I presume this resulted from my training; for when a lad at school my father had warned me that he meant to punish me severely whenever it should come to his knowledge that I had been " fighting" with my school fellows—a " barbarous practice," he said; and I well recollect that on one occasion I had seized a big Irish boy, who had been teasing my younger brother, and thrown him to the ground, where I held him firmly until he not only begged for mercy, but over and over promised not to do so any more. And I had justified myself to my father by presenting the proof that I had not *struck* the boy. Although the matter cost father much anxious thought and was a subject of prayer for several days, he finally reached the conclusion that, in that case, I had but executed the will of the Lord; leaving the question as to whether I had done it in a proper manner for further consideration.

During all my experience in the army I was never once able to get myself in range of the enemy's guns, except by the sheer force of my will over my physical members, which were always stricken as with palsy " just before the battle," however firm they might become when once the " ball '' had opened. Therefore, though I had a faint conception of the *character* of the enemy, massed behind the opposition to " nigro voting," no sooner had my resolution to become a " nigger candidate " been announced, than I at once felt all the physical symptoms premonitory of the "imminent deadly breach" between myself and "all the world"—in Yazoo.

Under and by virtue of the authority vested in him by the *laws of the United States*, the commanding general had appointed three registrars for Yazoo County, whose duty it was, by those same laws, to make a list of the persons residing in that county, who, under the law, were entitled to vote, and for several weeks prior to the conclusion I had reached as to my duty in the premises, these registrars had been preparing such a list. It had been completed, and the commanding general had issued his proclamation, according to law, setting the time when the election would be holden and prescribing the manner of conducting it.

Under that proclamation the election would be held by those registrars, assisted by a corps of judges and clerks chosen from among the citizens of the county. According to the law it was requisite that one of those registrars should be present at each polling place one whole day, and, as there were fifteen polling-places it followed of necessity that the election for the entire county would require five days, and it had been so arranged.

For some time before it was to commence, printed posters had been distributed throughout the county and put up at all the cross-roads and polling-places, in addition to the usual notice in the local newspapers.

As our decision was not arrived at until the day before the election was to commence, and we could do nothing without tickets, it was apparent that an election was likely to be held in three precincts of the county before we could get "before the people." Besides, on examining our exchequer, we found there was not enough cash on hand with which to pay for printing the tickets. At one of the newspaper offices they flatly refused to print them for us without the cash in advance. But we succeeded at last, by promising " not to tell," in getting a rather poverty-stricken " devil " to guarantee to have " a part " of the five thousand we wished "struck off" ready "'gin night come on," to start with, and arrangements were soon made for forwarding the balance as our necessities might require.

Captain Clark got possession of a small lot and entered on his part of the work of the campaign, during the first day of the election. But it was night before I got my supply, and was started off on horseback to travel twenty-seven miles to the place where the election for the following day, on my part of the line, was to be held.

One of a "delegation" of freedmen who had attended the meeting the night before accompanied me. He was employed on the plantation of Captain Bullfinch, a strong Union man during the war, and now a secret friend of our cause, whose residence was in the "hill country," about mid-way our journey. It was late at night when we arrived at the plantation. Here my guide insisted that I should stop for the night and go on to the polling-place the following day. He knew his "old marsa's" feelings toward the Yankees. No sooner had we reined in our horses, than the guide ran to the great house and aroused the Captain, who appeared in person, at the front door, and welcomed me heartily. Then the guide left us at once, as I supposed, to put up our horses. I was mistaken, however, for in less than fifteen minutes, several of the better class of the Captain's force were gathered about the porch to see and shake hands with their "great friend." The Captain enjoyed it as much as I, and appeared to encourage them in what they did. Indeed, his wife and another lady of his household, having been "warned" came down, and joined in the welcome.

The fact is, my guide had "sont" word by a fellow-servant that I would accompany him.

They had all remained up until after ten o'clock expecting me, and had retired only when they had given up my coming that night. When I remarked that the guide had neglected to inform me that I was "expected," the Captain's wife replied that he had been instructed to ; it had better "not be known."

After an elegant breakfast, and I was about to ride on, both the Captain and his wife begged me to make their house a "refuge" for myself and friends whenever I might wish, and to command their services at any time, when to oblige me in any way would not require too great a "sacrifice"[*] on their part.

This man owned nearly six thousand acres of land in the county; worked on his different plantations more than a hundred and fifty people, was a good, kind, patriotic citizen, and yet did not dare let it be published abroad that he had entertained "a Yankee" at his house, though the "rebels" had "surrendered" two years and more before.

It had been "sun up" an hour before I got off. The ride was about fourteen miles. But I was at the polling-place before the voters began to arrive. Inquiring of the officers of election the supposed cause of their tardiness, I found that none could account for it. There had been only about one-fourth, or possibly one-third, of the registered voters of the precinct at the polling-place the day before who had voted, they said, and what struck me as more unaccountable still, was their assurance that "none of the whites were voting." Several of Captain Bullfinch's people had accompanied me, and after reflecting a few moments, I asked them for their opinion of the cause.

"Dey is afeer'd, Kunnel, de colud people is, an' da doan know yo' is y'here with dem. 'Sides, de white folks don' 'low'd dar aint g'wain ter be no 'lection, no how."

"Ah! ha! that's it, eh!"

"Yes, sah, Mars Kunnel, dat's jes de way h'it ar', kase I done heerd um say down ter Benton, ter Mars Leedam's sto' how dey g'wain fur ter keep all day niggars frum votin' on da own 'count, kase dey wouldn't vote no how. 'Twan't no 'lection, dey 'low'd."

"Well," said I, calling him by name, "you go one way to some of your old fellow-servants;" and then to another one,

*Too great a sacrifice of reputation and possibly of property.

"you go another, and tell them all to come here, I wish to see them."*

In a moment they were off, on a fast trot, and I started out myself, following a blind path to see what I might be able to do in the way of helping to find the "lost" suffragans of Yazoo. I had proceeded about a mile, when, looking across a large open field, I saw what appeared to be a freedman, standing on the brow of a little hill "Now," I said to myself, "I'll call this man, and see if I can't enlist him in the search." Waving my hat toward him, in token of my wish to have him come to me, he started as if to do so, but in a very halting manner.   Then I alighted, hitched my horse and advanced to meet him.   As we approached, I could see that he was in great fear about something, and I spoke up in a kindly voice:

"Uncle, why are you not at the election?"

The change in his manner reminded me of Uncle Isam, as he replied :

"Doan know, marsa."

"Have you registered?"

"Yes, marsa; done got my paper."

"Where is it?"

"Low'd——Beez yo' de gen'leman whar gi'e it to me?"

"No, my name is Morgan."

At this, the change in his manner still further reminded me of Uncle Isam, especially as he came close up.

"Beez yo' de Colonel Morgan, whar lib yan in de 'Azoo City ? "

"Yes."

"Wull, I d'clar'! Dey done 'low'd yo' is dead wid de col'ra. Bress de Good Marsta, do, yo' ain't. 'Low'd yo' might be de Kunnel when I done seed ye a coming yan, kase we done heerd frum one ouah feller-servants yo' cloze by Benton. Mighty likely yo' mount a come dis y'here way."

But there were other surprises in store for me; for, see-

* Now the "ball" had opened.

ing his free and changed manner, several freedmen, who had remained hidden just over the hill from whence he had come, and entirely out of view until now, showed themselves. First, only their heads, as though peering at us, and now their bodies, standing. We walked up to them, when I found quite a large number, still lying upon the ground beyond the hill in a clump of trees.

These "outposts," becoming satisfied that I was, in fact, the person they had all heard so much about, but "nebber seed t'wel yit," shouted to those over the hill to come and join us, which they very promptly did. From their number I chose out several, whom I sent off after more, and the rest of us started for the polling-place. One of the number had a gun, a bird gun, which I requested him to take back home, assuring him that the Government at Washington was holding this election. At all events, there would be no need of such weapons at the polls, and he most cheerfully complied.

While on my way back to the polling-place, these poor people could not do enough for me, it seemed. They un-hitched my horse, held my stirrup, and waited on me with as much deference, respect, and devotion, as if in their souls they felt that I was their deliverer.

I also gathered from them, as we walked along to the poll-ing-place, among other things, that they had been told by their masters that there would be no election, and as if to prove the truth of this assertion, their masters had them-selves remained at home. Some of these freedmen said they had heard threats made to the effect that if they went to the polling-places they would be killed. But, without previous concert, they had started to go, and falling in with each other on their several ways, they had become quite a numerous company by the time they reached the field where I found them. Here they had halted to talk the subject over, and had resolved to send one of their number on to the polling-place to " sarch for de troof." This was the man whom I first spied. Among their number was a preacher, who had

recently attended conference, where he had been told of the
proposed election, and how it would be conducted.

Arriving at the place of voting we found several freedmen
there who had been "warned" by the two whom I had sent out
and quite a goodly number besides.   My opponent had captured
some of these, however, and secured their votes for himself.
On my arrival there in the morning, he appeared as much
at a loss to understand why the people generally had not turned
out to vote as any one else.   Nor had he made any effort to
find out—at least none such as I was making—and when
the crowd which came with me arrived, of course he set out
to capture them from me.

Mounting a wagon standing near the cross-roads grocery,
he began his efforts in that direction by a speech, which he
opened thus :

"Fellow-citizens and my colored friends."   Then addressing himself altogether to the freedmen he informed *them*
that he had no quarrel with " the white gentlemen present ;"
that he had been in the Federal army and was a Yankee the
same as his opponent ; that his opponent was a gentleman
and all that, but he was a very young man, and without
experience in public affairs, while, as they could all see, *he*
was a man well advanced in years.   He also informed them
that he had outranked me in the army, and that he was the
regular "Republican candidate ;" his ticket was the only
Republican ticket in the field.   Then he reminded them that
Mr. Lincoln, whose proclamation had made them all free,
was a Republican ; also of their duty to stand by the party
that made them free, and then announced the platform on
which the Republican—the " great Republican party "—stood,
upon which he should stand " until death."   It favored free
speech, free men, free schools; it favored the right of the
colored men to vote, the opening of the courts to them, and
that they should receive fair wages ; that whipping, brand-
ing and hunting them with hounds, and all that sort of thing
should stop ; that colored people should be allowed to own

land and their wives and daughters like other people, or
words to that effect. He concluded his remarks by informing the " colored friends " that the colored man on our ticket
was a blacksmith, without property or education—could
scarcely read or write, if he could do either at all, and that
he could not be of any service in the convention more than
to vote.

During the delivery of this speech there had been but slight
manifestations of approval or sympathy from the freed
people. They had remained almost as impassive as clay.
When he ceased I got up on the wagon and replied briefly,
in substance as follows :

" Fellow citizens : My platform is much the same as General Greenleaf's. I have never voted any other than the
Republican ticket, and am a Republican." Then I explained
that I could not see any difference in the tickets in point of
" regularity," as we had all nominated ourselves, so to speak;
that the difference between the General and myself was very
great, yet very simple. I wished to see *all* men have and enjoy
the *right* to vote, to hold office, be equals in the eye of the law.
I wished to see free schools for all, courts and highways for
all, fair wages for all, and lands for all who would work and
earn them.   " I wish to see you *all*, you, your wives and your
daughters, living so above just reproach and so protected by the
laws that no white, black, or other kind of man or woman
either will dare to interfere with your enjoyment of each
other's company." And, as to the colored man on our ticket,
I explained that we had striven very hard to induce a native
white man to stand, but had not succeeded in finding any
who would ; that we had done the next best thing we could
think of, and put a freedman in the place. We would have
been glad to have had but one " Yankee " on the ticket.
Could we have got a native to stand then we would have had
a ticket made up from all classes, and could have gone
forward like a band of brethren in the work of reconstructing
the State. I declared that I did not seek the office for myself,

but for a principle; one which they might not all readily comprehend at first, but I hoped and believed they would eventually do so.

There could not have been more than a half dozen white men present, but I had addressed my remarks to them as much as to the colored people.

From the moment I began the interest of the freed people in my speech was apparent to all, and that interest continued to increase until they voiced their approval somewhat as follows :

" Dat's de talk, gen'lemens; yo' 'heah me. Dar! I tole ye hit wor' de Kunnel from de fust. Can't fool me.* Now yo's a tellin' de troof," etc.

Seeing my success, my opponent undertook to entice them to his support by offering to treat. But he signally failed in that also. The few white men present looked on with the supremest indifference, if not contempt.

At the polling-place the next day there were a great many whites and two or three hundred freedmen. Having heard of the failure of their plan to "fool the darkies," they were now bent on coaxing, buying, or intimidating them at the polls, and the " pulling and hauling " process began early in the day. Failing to coax or to buy them from voting, later in the day they began to threaten the freedmen.

The lists of names of all who had registered were in the hands of the judges, who caused the name of each one to be checked off at the moment of casting the ballot, so that it was impossible to prevent their old masters from knowing the fact that such a one had voted. Therefore, all who would vote subjected themselves to such vengeance as their old masters might choose to inflict.

During the day there was some speech-making by the late rebels, by my opponent, and by myself. The crowd was listening to me, when an old white man, who had elbowed his way until he was close up in front, inquired :

* Some one Had told him I was not Colonel Morgan, of Yazoo City, but another of the same name, who had come from Jackson.

" What yo' all g'wain ter do with our niggers, now you all done stole um f'om we all ? "

" Make men of them," I replied.

" Men, hell ! "

" Yes, men; we're not in favor of opposing any honest effort in that direction, at all events."

" Well, how ye g'wain ter make men outen of um ?"

" Build school-houses and educate them."

" Edecate niggers ! Yo' mount ez well try ter larn a mool ter read an' write, ez ter try ter larn a nigger."

" Well, we propose to make the trial."

" Yo' all 'low ye can larn a nigger ter read an' write ?"

" Yes."

" Yo' lie ! d—n yo' ! "

CHAPTER XIX.

THE FOLLY OF WISDOM—COURAGE OF MY NEW FRIENDS—A TRI-
UMPHANT " VINDICATION "—AN " HONEST " DIFFERENCE OF
OPINION—UNHEEDED WARNINGS.

THE poor ignorant fellow who closed the last chapter was
merely a tool for a crowd of " genteel " white planters,
hanging upon the outskirts of the audience and making fun
of us while cheering him on.

Meanwhile the freedmen had warmed up, and as many as
had sticks in their hands crowded close around me as though
they would make a wall of their bodies for my protection.

When the intruder gave the lie, several of the older and
calmer freedmen about me exclaimed:

" Doan pay no 'tention to 'im, Kunnel. He no 'count, no
way. Jes' stan' yo' groun' an' we'll die by ye."

As that was the prevailing custom, the freedmen evidently
feared I should resent the speech of my interlocutor. But I
had no such idea, and kept right on with my talk. Finding
they could not draw me into a personal quarrel, the " genteel " planters gave up the day, and all rode off, halloaing
and cursing " that d—d radical Congress," the " Yankees,"
the " ungrateful nigros," and almost everything else.

After the polls closed, and I was riding toward the polling-place of the next day, it being not yet dark, a shot, fired
from near the roadside, passed whizzing by, so close to my

head that I distinctly felt the force of the bullet. But it
was not billeted with my name. It was long after dark when
I reached Benton, but there were as many as three hundred
freedmen awaiting my arrival just beyond the town, alongside the public highway. They had sent a " runner " to meet
me, and to ask me to make them a speech. They said they
had been unable to obtain any other place of meeting.

After talking a few moments to them, I rode out to the
home of Captain Bullfinch, where I was hospitably received
and entertained. It was the first time since I had left him,
nearly two days before, that I had been thus received by a
white man. The following day, the incidents at Benton were
quite similar to those of the day preceding. Our trials were not
less on the next day, nor on the day following at Yazoo City,
where this election was brought to a close. When the ballots
were all counted it was found that the question, "Convention
or no convention," was decided in the affirmative, by a vote
of more than eighteen hundred "for," to only three "against."
The three votes "against" convention had probably been cast
in obedience to a feature of the " plan " of the " anti-Yankee "
element, which may appear further on in this narrative. It
was also found that the " Morgan ticket" was elected by a
vote of quite fifteen hundred, to less than four hundred for
the " Yankee's ticket," as my opponents ticket came to be
called. The result staggered the natives.

They had hoped to succeed in their plan of deceiving the
negroes as to the importance of their votes upon that question
by staying away from the polls themselves. When they discovered that they had failed, they deluded themselves into
the belief that they could, by making fair promises to " our
nigros," persuade them to have faith in their sincerity. And
they showed their utter ignorance of the character of the *free*
negro, by trying to bribe him not to vote, when the other
two means had failed ; and they added to their duplicity,
treachery and ignorance, still another quality, viz., brutality,
when at last they resorted to intimidation to accomplish their

purpose. This election demonstrated their possession of still another trait, viz., bossism.

I knew that there were more than two hundred white men in that county who had sympathized with the Union cause during the war, and whose best judgment approved the Congressional plan of reconstruction, and they would have voted "for" convention could they have done so without the danger of incurring the same hostility that had been visited upon us.

"Were they moral cowards ?"

"No."

The most prominent of their number had been hung to a tree until he promised to pull down from his house-top the American flag which he had unfurled there during the canvass for the "secession convention," in 1860. And there had never been atonement made, nor any redress offered. He could not vote at this election a *secret* ballot, because those same men who had "grapevined" him in 1860, stood by to warn him that "nobody but niggers" were voting at this election. "Take care, remember 1860."

The anti-reconstructionists preferred that the negroes should vote the "Yankee ticket," if they voted any, and throughout the county so advised them. Their reason for this was that should it be elected they might be able to say that a "foreign" government had been set over them, through which pretense they could more certainly hold their own ranks together. But in almost every instance such advice operated to secure more votes for the "Morgan ticket," and when the election was over the chairman of the "white man's" committee assured me that he had discovered his "mistake" too late. I might, however, be certain that should I ever again offer myself as a candidate for office in the county, he would not repeat it. This man further assured me that he was "amazed" at the intelligence exhibited by the negroes; confessed himself "mistaken" in his estimate of their character; confessed that he and his friends had "intended" to deceive them,

believing it to be for the best good of all to do so ; confessed
that I had conducted my campaign "with perfect fairness,"
that he would have done just as I did had he been in my
place, barring my refusal to fight; that had he been a "nigro"
he would have done precisely as the negroes had, and voted
for me; and that the white people could justify themselves in
their course, only upon the ground : First, that they had had
no voice in framing the laws under which the "so-called election " had been held ; secondly, that they had purchased and
"owned the nigro or raised him," and could not be expected
to consent to his sudden elevation to the rank of equal citizenship with themselves upon the request of strangers; and third,
the Southern people do not believe that the North is sincere
in the effort put forth to " force nigro equality " on the South,
and do believe that it is altogether prompted by a fear among
the radical leaders that the Emancipation Proclamation is null
and void ; that the war on the part of the North upon the
South was an unconstitutional war ; that they, the radicals,
will lose their power in a few years, unless they can make up
for defections, which are certain in the North as soon as the
war feeling dies down a little, by additions from the South,
and as the defection of " Andy " Johnson has shown that they
cannot hope to gain that from the whites of the South they
mean to lasso the whites with the negro vote and keep them
in subjection until they shall have fully accomplished their
purposes.

And then this Yazoo white statesman, laughingly continued: " And as for you, and all like you, who join your faith
to these radicals and to the nigro, they will have no more
use for you then than they now have for the paper in their
waste baskets.   Then it will be our turn, and woe be to you."

I thanked this man for his advice, and for the very sincere
manner he had manifested, but assured him that I would
abide the consequences, and in such an event, would never
come to him, nor to any who believed with him for succor
nor for sympathy.

" It's an honest difference of opinion," I said, " and you

must allow me to hope, that while this is going on, we shall have large and voluntary accessions from your side to ours, right here, in Yazoo, and shall then be able to take care of ourselves."

Then he—

"Don't you fool yourself, young man. *We don't intend to allow you to gain any from our side that we can't get back when we all shall need them.*"

CHAPTER XX.

DELIVERER AND DICTATOR—COUNTING THE COST—LES MISERA-
BLES—STRAW FOR BRICKS.

IT was through the trials and by such means as I have
herein faithfully recounted that I became known to the
whites of Mississippi as a " dictator," and among the blacks as
a " saviour." The convention was carried in the State and
the delegates would assemble January 7th following, 1868, at
Jackson, the capital.

During this campaign I did not expend so much as one cent
for " treats," or for any purpose calculated to induce any one
to vote our ticket. The total expenses of the campaign
amounted to fifty-five dollars for tickets, and six dollars for
horse hire. Of this amount twenty dollars thirty-three and
one-third cents was my share.

Recovering from the first shock of their defeat, the native
whites resolved upon a new course. For a time it had
seemed that they were divided in their plans ; for one party
said : " Now let's wait and see what the convention does
before we decide on our policy." The other said : " D—n
the convention. Let's drive it from the State."

The former volunteered their advice to me, as to the course
I should pursue to win the support of a " respectable following." The other endeavored by flattery and by proffers of
a mock sympathy for the defeated candidates upon the " Yankee ticket," to win them to open hostility to the Yankees

upon the "Morgan ticket," and to the whole body of the freed people. This disguste l those very worthy but short-sighted men more than their defeat had done, and so two of the three left the county, protesting that it was "beyond hope of re-demption."

Meanwhile, reduced in circumstances as I was, I suc-ceeded, by the sale of a quantity of refuse lumber that had been overlooked by Colonel Black, in raising money enough to purchase a suit of clothes to wear to the convention, and to pay my expenses in going there and for a week or so after my arrival at the capital.

On the morning of my departure I waited at the post-office in the company of the postmaster and other friends, black and white—negroes and Yankees all—until the stage drove up. When it came, I took my seat along with other passengers, male and female, some of whom were natives and some drummers for Northern mercantile houses. The white women appeared not to know me. The native white men did, and to my cheerful salutation, "Good-morning, all —room for me?" they scowled and barely nodded. But the drummers returned my salutation cheerily and one of them "hitched along," making room for me to sit down. But I was not to be allowed to go in peace; for, espying me as I got up into the stage, a handful of white urchins began halloa-ing, "O'oophie!" "O'oophie!" "polecat!" The drummers seemed not to know what this meant nor to whom, if to any one, it was directed; and one of them inquired of me about it.

But at that moment there appeared a dozen or more loungers near the corner, some of them full-grown men, others half-grown, who approached the stage door, and, making horrid grimaces, ejaculated: "Halloa, polecat!"* "Whar ye goin', polecat! g'wain ter de nigger convention?" "Ha ! ha! ha! He! he! he!" "Well, good-bye, Morgan. Take

*The epithet, "carpet-bagger," had not yet been invented, or, if coined, had not yet reached the Yazoo channels of trade in such things. The "honor" of its invention is claimed for Virginia by some, and for Horace Greeley by others. However that may be, the epithet represents not so much a mollified state of feeling on the part of the "enemy," as a change in their diplomatic methods, adopted for effect upon the "jury" at the North, then and ever since, in a measure, sitting at their (the enemy's) trial.

good car' yo'self. Haw! haw! haw?" Then the driver hav_
ing got his mail on board, cracked his whip, and away we
sped on our journey of twenty-six miles to the railway station. But from the moment the boys began to shout,
"O'oophie," the " white ladies" showed signs of uneasiness.
One of them coughed, while the white native " gentlemen "
fiercely scowled. When the loungers appeared at the stage-
door, and joined in the outcry, these native " gentlemen "
smiled approvingly upon them. By the time we were off,
above the crack of the driver's whip and the rumbling of
the stage, arose the shouts of this rabble, " O'oophie !" " polecat!" " Morgan!" " O'oophie!" until we were out of hearing
of them. Of course I was relieved of the necessity of an-
swering the drummer's inquiry. He had already joined the
rabble, and during our ride together, which was as far as the
next station, Benton, where he left us for the purpose of introducing his firm to the merchants of that " berg," as he informed us, he was the most offensive in his speech and man -
ner of the whole company. All the drummers " cut " me at
once, and my ride was anything but a pleasant one.

At Benton there were similar cries after me as at Yazoo
City, when we started ; also at Deasonville, the next station, and at the railway depot. On entering the car my
identity was made known to other delegates on board, who
were *en route* from counties in the northern part of the State
by these very cries; for nearly all of them had passed through
a similar experience. In fact none of us were spared now
that we were on board of the train, but were marked for all
manner of jest, scorn, or violent abuse, according to the temper and gifts of our fellow-passengers, some of whom were
en route to the capital to " see the fun." Very naturally
these " outcasts " came together and formed a group by ourselves ; for, all the world over, " misery loves company."

The scope of this narrative will not admit of any reference to my experiences during this period outside the limits
of Yazoo County, nor during my term of four years in the
State Senate afterward.

Somehow, my experiences as a planter, with the courts, and with the Yazoo County bar had given me an uncontrollable desire for the study of the law, with a view to adopting it as a profession, and I applied myself assiduously to that end. I lacked the collegiate training which would have enabled me to grasp more readily the intricacies of the profession, but I had already had that experience with men and their affairs which I believed would, in a large measure, make up for this defect.

Then, too, behind this ambition was a consciousness that I had failed to obtain this higher training, not from lack of thirst for knowledge, but from a still nobler inheritance, which I venture to call a spirit of youthful patriotism and a willingness to sacrifice self in the service of others. I felt sure that this consciousness would enable me to batter down such obstacles as I could not overleap while pursuing the goal of my ambition.

" Where there's a will there's always a way " I said; and so it came about, that within a period of eighteen months from the date of my election to the convention, I was admitted to practise law in the courts of Mississippi; a result achieved after an examination by a committee of three of the oldest members of the Yazoo bar, and upon their recommendation. It was cause for no little self-gratulation that one of this committee was the surviving member of the firm who were Mrs. Black's lawyers.

During this time Charles and I passed through the most trying period of our experience in Yazoo. It was a season of trial, however, which bore more heavily upon him than me, and called out all the virtues of his grand character.

After my departure for the convention, he succeeded in obtaining board in the home of a resident of the town—a widow lady of rare good breeding, benevolence and courage. Her husband had been a planter of considerable means. The loss of their slave property and other misfortunes had stripped them of the bulk of their worldly possessions, however, and at his death she found herself in such straitened circumstances that she felt justified in opening her house " even to Yankees." She was a Christian lady, devoted to her church duties and the care of her family, consisting of two girls and two boys, and her great ambition was to educate a son for the medical profession. No lady in the county was more highly thought of than she. But in an hour, as it were, this noble woman, battling for her children and her daily bread, was made an outcast. It came about in this way:

The postmaster, who was a Yankee, and the other Northern men had previously been received by her as boarders. But within sixty days from the admission to her house of General Greenleaf and Charles, the feeling in Yazoo had increased until it became such a reign of terror that even General Alvin C. Gillem, President Johnson's personal friend and trusted commanding general of the department, was induced to send a squad of troops there for the protection of the freedmen and loyalists. But the officer in command of these soldiers, upon his arrival, was seized by Colonel Black and his friends, " anti-Yankees," and welcomed at their houses, dined, wined, and petted by both sexes, until he became the drunken tool that he was for the furtherance of their purposes.

When they had thus wrought upon him, there was sent to that Southern widow lady the following note of warning:

" Mrs. ———, you are keeping a den of infamy, which will be burnt down if you don't purge it out. An outraged Southern community won't stand it long. Beware ! ! K. K. K."

This lady became hotly indignant at the outrage, and for a brief space resented it.

Of her nine regular and transient Yankee boarders but two used any kind of intoxicating liquors, and only three used tobacco. Three were college graduates; one had commanded a brigade; two had been colonels of regiment; two had been captains of companies. One of these captains had been a quartermaster on the staff of General Thomas. Those men had brought into and invested in the county sums of money aggregating not less than one hundred thousand dollars; probably it was more than two hundred thousand.

Upon receipt of the kuklux warning, their landlady openly declared that she had never welcomed to her house more perfect gentlemen. The authors of that "warning" message knew that, and it was that fact which prompted and, in Yazoo, justified their action; for it was these very qualities that made them powerful in resources for resisting the purposes of the old slave-holders, and made their example "dangerous to the institutions of the South." Therefore, the best "old time" citizens of Yazoo rudely brushed this brave lady to one side and opened hostilities in earnest.

By way of illustrating the greater effectiveness of their resources, they "allowed" the officer in command of the troops to get drunk off their liquors and then to be seen "drunk upon the streets." *

Thus shorn of their strength the soldiers were wrought upon with ease; made drunk like their officer—but in the low groceries, instead of the elegant homes of Colonel Black and his friends—and then cunningly guided to the so-called "den of infamy," where, after a scene of debauch in front of the house, they were "permitted" to fire off their pistols with just sufficient accuracy of aim to miss my brother, who opened the door at that moment, and perforate the doorfacing of the front entrance-way. Then these United States soldiers were skillfully "withdrawn" to their quarters, and shortly afterward from the county, on the ground that their commander had reported no cause of their presence there for the protection of the freedmen, or any one else.

Prompted by a desire to defend their landlady, Charles and General Greenleaf sought for quarters elsewhere in the town. But now a new difficulty presented itself. There were more

---

* Having accomplished this much, they could enforce *complaisance*; for should he rebel against their wishes or *humors* Colonel Black and his friends would only have to "make complaint to the headquarters" and prove that he had been seen drunk upon the public streets of the town, to have secured his withdrawal from there, and, doubtless, a public exposure of his "weakness."

than fifty widow ladies in the town, who were dependent upon their own exertions for a livelihood. Some kept boarders, some rented rooms, while others served at sewing, or such other employment as they could obtain for themselves and their children. Of their number there was not one who did not need, and under any other circumstances would not gladly have received these gentlemen as boarders or roomers. But now there was not one who durst do so. There were numerous houses, offices, or rooms for rent in the town. Yet it was not until after considerable manœuvring that these gentlemen were able to procure a lodging place. This was a suite of rooms near a livery stable, over the office of a lawyer, who plumed himself somewhat on his ancestry. They were obtained only through the intercession of a third party, a man who, at the time, was an officer of the United States. For the protection of the owner of those rooms, it had been allowed to "leak out" that they had been obtained by indirect means.*

Now that a lodging place had been secured, still another difficulty presented itself, viz : how to obtain food and service. None of the hotels, restaurants, boarding-houses or private-houses, owned or controlled by the whites, would oblige them.

It began to look as though they would be starved into a "surrender." It had been understood that if Mrs. —— would dismiss Charles and the General from her house she might keep the others.† She had protested earnestly against the demand, but Charles and the General believed they could not, in justice to her, allow the lady to continue the contest. Having surrendered this outpost, the anti-reconstructionists supposed that persistence in their policy of ostracism and in-

---

* There was still remaining in Yazoo so much respect for a Federal officer, as to make it tolerably safe for one having the requisite courage to do so, to take upon himself the odium such a responsibility entailed, should it become necessary. At all events this officer could at that time better bear such a burden than the Unionist, from whom the rooms were rented.

† Having abandoned all open, active interference in the political affairs of the county, those Northern men were no longer special objects of attack from the anti-reconstructionists. Of course, the person of the postmaster, being a Yankee *in* office, and that a Federal office, was sacred.

timidation would necessarily compel their full surrender or
their retreat from the county. But they were again to be
foiled ; this time by the freed people. No sooner had they
learned of this fresh outrage upon their friends, than a negro
woman came forward and volunteered not only to provide the
food, but also to cook and serve it for them *at actual cost.*

To their warning of the probable consequences to herself
of such service to them, this woman replied :

" Captain, I'z cooked fur my ole marstah all my days, an'
he nebber gin me so much as a new dress when I quit um.
Kase I wor free now. Sence dat I'z been cookin' fur de white
genelmens an' a furnishin' of um thar food, an' I 'low I can
do jez 'e same fur yo' all. Kase I'm ole now, got no mo'n a
few yar ter stay y'here on dis si' de dark riber ob death, no
how; an' my son, yo' all knows *him*, he sais, sais he, ' Mammy,
nary schools in dis y'here Azoo County 'fo' de Morgans
come'd ter dis yar Azoo City, an' sho's yo' boh'n ef dey
goze frum y'here, dat day de schools go wid um,' an' so dey
would. I noes um. Kan't fool me, 'f I iz a nigger an' ain't
got no larnin'. Jeems ha' got some, thank de blessed God
A'mighty and yo' all Yankees. Doan yo' min' me, honey, jez
yo' say yo'l nebber be too proud ter eat arter ole Aunt Sarah,
an' I'l take car' on yo' all, honey, bless ye."

This grand old woman, the General told me afterward, spoke,
looked, and acted "just as though she were asking a favor"
of these outcasts ; and they granted it. But she had continued at this service not more than a few days, when, having
to carry the food some distance, the enemy began first to coax,
then to try to bribe, then to threaten, and all these failing,
they actually intercepted her upon the street and spilled her
dishes.

Certain freedmen, however, having foreseen such a result,
one of them, a shoemaker, and a sort of pet with the whites,
had been able to secure a room upon the ground floor of the
same building in which the outcasts lodged, and had moved
himself, family, and shop into it, so that when Aunt Sarah

could no longer perform the service, this shoemaker's wife
volunteered to supply her place. This was upon his own
motion, and for that reason was the more appreciated by the
outcasts. By reason of the close proximity of this shoemaker's shop, and of a stairway which led from it to the
back gallery of the rooms of the Yankee outcasts, the food
could be got to them without danger of being intercepted by
"the enemy." But that enemy's resources were equal to this
emergency, for those "anti-Yankees" not only withdrew their
custom from this "nigger cobbler"—for such he had now
become—their merchants refused to sell him food supplies
for his "Yankee boarders."

And now there was a new, and, to these outcasts, a wholly
unforeseen way opened for their succor.

In spite of the edict of the merchants the supplies were
not cut off. It was some time before Charles and the General were afforded any explanation of the mystery. When at
last it came, it proved a source of great comfort to them, for
it demonstrated the significance of their example no less than
the absolute necessity for it, if free institutions were ever to
take the place of the slaveocratic dynasty that the war had
disarmed ; for those provisions had been furnished secretly,
some by the freed people, delivered through their wash-woman,
who succeeded in running them through the blockade by hiding them under the clothes in her basket; some by a certain
merchant in the town, while the rest had found their way
at night to the hands of the shoemaker from boisterous, bull-
dozing "anti-Yankees," who, in their hearts, still retained
their old love for the Union cause.

About this time I visited them. Their quarters had been
transformed into an arsenal. There were two breech-loading
Spencer rifles, a double-barrelled shot-gun and two revolvers,
near by the head of the bed in which they slept. Their windows were barred with iron, and the only door of their apartments was doubly bolted with a huge brace for additional
support. It was during this visit that I learned the facts

above narrated, and the additional fact that they were hourly expecting a violent attack from the enemy, who, foiled in their effort to *starve* them out, were now planning to *drive* them out or *kill* them. The latter alternative it seemed had not been fully determined upon, and I was on the eve of learning why for myself.

The incidents of my trip all the way from the capital to Yazoo City, were but a repetition of those on the occasion of my trip from Yazoo City to the capital, " only a little more so," as the driver of the stage put it to the postmaster afterward. It was a little more so ; for this time I was refused meals at all the eating places but one, and a drummer for a New York firm wanted " to whip the scalawag," and announced to our fellow-passengers that " such proceedings as I witnessed in that radical black-and-tan convention, gentlemen, wouldn't be tolerated over night in our State." He obtained liberal orders for his house at all the towns on the road and at Yazoo City, and announced to his customers at the latter place, that he was glad he would be able to say to the people of the North when he returned, that the published accounts of " outrages in the South upon Northern gentlemen are d—d lies."

At Deasonville I should doubtless have been mobbed but for the alacrity of the driver, an old Unionist and a secret friend, who gathered the reins and rapidly drove on, when he saw the signs of it in the threatening actions of the white loungers there, one of whom having struck at me, was " reaching for his hip pocket." Having remained in my seat he did not dare to shoot after the stage had started, for fear of hitting other passengers. My arrival at Yazoo City created a sensation. As the stage came rattling over the plank-road and down the bluffs into the town below, some white loungers on the corner identified me from the other passengers in the stage, one of whom shouted back in response to their inquiry: " Is that Morgan ?" " Yes, here he is, we've got him—the young one." This arrested the

attention of others, and soon the cry, " O'oophie !" " O'oophie!"
" polecat !" " scalawag !" was sounded along the length of the
street, rallying the white boys from their marbles or other
play, and causing a crowd to assemble.

But the driver had the foresight to stop me at the corner
near the little " Yankee stronghold;" for such had the quarters occupied by General Greenleaf and Charles really become—and thus enabled me to elude the mob.

CHAPTER XX

THE TRUE VALUE OF FRIENDSHIP—NONE BUT BLACK AMERICANS.
ON GUARD TO-NIGHT—AN UNCOVERED SECRET—"SNAKES"
AND THEIR USES.

IN those days it was deemed the safer policy by all Republican members of that State convention, to travel incognito and give no notice of their intentions. On this occasion I had arranged with my colleague to ask leave for me to go after I should have started, and as I left by the half-past two A. M. train, I was able to make the stage line by daylight, thus preventing telegraphic discovery of my whereabouts to the enemy at Yazoo City, or at points on the way. So they had not expected me at Yazoo on that day. I had not been a half hour within the stronghold, wher it was besieged by a small army of *friends*, all colored mer but one; for now even Northerners found it more to their *interest* not to recognize the outcasts socially, by calling upon them at their stronghold. But the welcome of such as came was worth some sacrifice; for it at least was genuine; besides, it required some courage to boldly visit us in that place with any other than hostile intentions. To be sure, these were negroes. They were nevertheless brave and sincere friends.

They had heard of my "fight" in the convention, they said; had heard how the Democrats had defied the president of that body, the sergeant-at-arms, and even "Stanton's hirelings." How they had drawn pistols, and failed to shoot me only because I was "a coward" and would not "draw and defend myself." And they had heard how a negro, Charles Caldwell, with a little handful of his friends, armed only with pistols, had rallied to my side and made them scamper.

"That's right, Kunnel, stan' yo'r groun'; but doan shoot; doan preten' like yo' iz a g'waiu ter shoot, kase dat jes what dey'l git ye 'f ye does. Dey done said it. I hearn um talk, yan in Barksdale's sto' an' Dave Woolridge's saloon. Dey is boun' ter git yo', jes giv' um de leas' bit 'f a chance. Min' dat; and if'n yo' is killed, den whar will we all be ? Yo' jes take car' yo' own se'f, Kunnel; yo' y'hea' me ? I done said it, kase I noes; jes' yo' keep still and stan' up like yo' iz a stan'in' an' we'll take care ob yo' brother an' de gen'l if we die fuss."

Such expressions as these came from all sides.

That night I made a discovery. Just outside the sleeping-room, on the porch, which was closed in on three sides and facing the only narrow stairway from the street to the porch, fully a dozen men, negroes, stood guard all night. There were but two pistols among them—old ones at that. They were armed with stout hickory clubs. That night I made another discovery. It was after ten o'clock, and when the last of our brave friends had quietly gone away. A wonderful solemnity rested over the stronghold, unbroken, save by an occasional " shuffling " of the men " on' guard," and a noise which sounded like the low ebb and flow of a rather animated conversation going on beyond brick walls. I asked Charles what that muffled sound was.

" Shall we uncover our secret to the radical delegate to the black-and-tan convention from the 'Azoo ? " was his response, directed to the General.

" Certainly. Why not ? I guess we can trust him with our lives, our fortune, and our sacred honahs, by G—d, sir," was that outcast's reply, delivered with great mock solemnity of manner.

B y this time my curiosity was up.

" Shan't we administer the iron-clad oath first ?" said my brother, in great seriousness.

Then the General—

" Well, you know him better than I."

" Yes, he's my brother, that's a fact; but this is a solemn and weighty proceeding, and, you know, the only ' Americans on guard to-night' are negroes, and I am not brother to the negro—though if this siege continues much longer I shall wish I were. Throughout the civilized world espionage of the enemy is considered proper, nay, the *right* of either party upon the other. In a case like this, where the disparity in numbers is so great as exists between this little garrison and the besieging party, the General and myself have thought we might be justified in obtaining information of the enemy by any means in our power—even to peeping through a key-hole, when by so doing we could overlook a council of grand, Cyclops, and, by placing our ears near enough, overhear their discussions."

At this moment certain proceedings instituted by Charles took place near the centre of the room, enabling us to hear from below, such words as " Morgan" —— " Stanton," —— " d—n fool," " d—n coward," and similar expressions, but we could not connect them, and I was wrought up to a high pitch of excitement by this surprise, and my curiosity to know the end of it. It was plain, too, that both Charles and the General were expecting to obtain " valuable information to-night," and Charles remarked on the change in the tones that came from the office below :

" Something has happened to throw a damper over their prospects," he said; " their speech is not so boisterous as heretofore, and lacks confidence."

" Well, Mr. Master of-Ceremonies, ' lets at 'em,' as Sheridan said at Five Forks, the moment all was ready." This from me to Charles; for I was getting out of patience.

But my brother was a natural-born tease, and seemed bent

on illustrating the fact then and there, for he continued:
" Be aisy, me b'y, an' wa-it 'til I finish. Di ye moin thim
lethers I'v been a wroitin' 'til the pilot; av coorse yi duz, an'
the spalpanes a callin' uf me a loier, an' a demandin' av the
noimes of me infoirmint ur me infoirmints, an' a thirtnin
moi with a lahyer if I refoost."

But by this time, certain other mysterious proceedings, instituted by him as this bit of play was going on, culminated,
and lifting quite out of its place one of the planks in the floor
of the room, exposing a bunch of cotton, Charles whispered—
" Well, feth, an' I'll shoah 'im 'til ye in a minit jus'. Be
aisy now. Di ye say 'im ?—the spalpanes !"

And suiting the action to the word he raised the cotton
from its place long enough to enable me to see into the room
below.

At the moment the cotton was withdrawn there had been
a lull in the conversation of the "gentlemen" in that room, one
of whom I now saw sat in a plain chair, tipped against the
wall, in such a manner as to bring us face to face, and I involuntarily sprang back, fearing he might see me.

" O, he's too drunk to see anybody now," whispered the
General, and on looking again I concluded he might be, for
both arms hung loosely at his side, and his pipe was ready to
drop from his mouth.

" That's his position every night," said Charles.

It was the lawyer with " an ancestry."

On looking from the other side the aperture, I saw four
men seated round a plain board table. One of them was Judge
Isam, another Captain Telsub, another Aurelius Bings, Esq.,
and the other was Major Sweet. An empty black bottle
lay on one end of the table, while another nearly empty,
stood upon the other end, and several half-smoked cigars and
pipes were strewn upon its surface, and on the floor near by.
They were all so near drunk that their speech was maudlin
and aimless.

One, while I was looking, raised his head from the table

where it had rested a moment, and faintly gave utterance to the following: " D—n—hic—Stanton."

One younger and less drunken, replied: " D—n Andy Johnson, by G—d ! If he wan't such a coward he'd 'rested the d—n tyrant and put 'im in irons. Then all hell couldn't a' stopped him ! "

" Well," piped the third, " how'd yo' go about—hic—a restin' a scalawag—hic— with that G—d d—n rump a Congress—a-hic-a-hic—a hind 'im, and the d—n—hic-hic—d—n bull—hic—bull-bull-dog—hic-hic-hic—Grant—the s— of a b— on top of him—hic. Lets-take-a-drink. By G—d—hic. Here's ter Grant ! May the—hic—coons—hic-hic—eat 'im. The s— of a b—! Hurrah for—hic-hic—hell ! By G—d ! "

This speech closed in so loud a tone that it roused him of the ancestry, and he eased his chair to the floor, got up, started toward the table—I presume to take a drink—and fell sprawling upon the floor. This created quite a rumpus, and the scene, as a whole, became so ridiculous that it was with difficulty I could restrain myself from laughing.

There they were, Yazoo's best citizens, the leaders of the ku-klux-klan of that county, the night after receiving the news of Stanton's victory over Johnson, all upon the floor drunk; stumbling, pulling and hauling one another in their efforts to help their fallen comrade to regain his feet, while their cursing and hurrahing added bedlam to this scene of " hell upon earth."

The lights had been turned low in our room by General Greenleaf before he came and joined us at the "key-hole," which fact had reduced to minimum the risks of our being seen had they been sober. Now that they were so drunken, we felt perfect safety from detection, and so watched their performance until we were tired of it.

There was no use to go to bed, for court the god of sleep with whatever charm we might, he could not have been won against such odds, and so we were forced to pass the greater part of the night in the presence of this " torment," without any means of redress whatever.

Shortly after midnight a light-complexioned freed-woman entered without knocking, and, gathering up one of these "chivalrous Southern gentlemen, by G—d, sir," led him off home. A half hour or so later a freedman came and led away another. Still later, two others go off, "arm in arm," and in each instance they had departed cursing Stanton, the "scalawag;" or Johnson, the "coward;" or Grant, the "butcher."

When all had gone, a slender, fair colored girl entered, put the room to rights, spread the bed, pulled off the boots of her "lord and master"—him of "an ancestry"—helped that "gentleman" to bed, and—then made herself perfectly at home. But at this point, Charles quietly replaced the cotton, readjusted the floor planks, the General turned up the lampwick, and we all looked each other in the face.

Observing my astonishment, the General remarked : "Why, young man, that's nothing when you get used to it. Just you wait until two or three of them happen to arrive at the same time, or when instead of sending a 'trusty old family servant,' the 'missus' happens to come herself."

"Den yo'l see de fur fly," exclaimed Charles! It was he who had discovered this means of "espionage upon the enemy," and he seemed to fairly gloat over the fact.

"And you have had no scruples ?" But the General, divining my thought, interrupted me.

"Scruples be"—— he was about to say d—d, but caught himself and proceeded : "We made that discovery while in pursuit of the highest aspiration of the human soul, to wit? a desire to save life."

"How's that ?" I asked. "I prefer Charles should have the honor of the discovery. It belongs to him, and he can tell you all about it better than I."

"It was the night following the day that Captain Telsub struck the General," began Charles, now in real seriousness, "and we both barely escaped with our lives, as I wrote The Pilot. Hearing groans and cries, and a hoarse voice as of some one pleading for dear life in the room below, and believing that the savages had captured one of our crew, and were about to offer him in sacrifice to appease the wrath of their gods, we, the General and I, decided on making a hole through the floor here,"—and he indicated a point near the corner of the room—" but Uncle Peter, who was present at the time, was opposed to that place, and insisted upon this one for the opening.   You doubtless observed that by putting the face close down between the joist quite over the opening in the under ceiling, you had a perfect view of the entire room, and that as the table about which they sat was in the centre of the room, you were immediately over the heads of those surrounding it.   Furthermore, that as Peter put it, ' Marsa ku-klux nebber 'low ter look fur coon y'here.' "

" But after you had made your port-hole, how about the *prisoner?* " I said, when Charles stopped, as though he had finished his story.

" O, certainly; I forgot him.   It was only the Captain— him of 'an ancestry'—the ' snakes' had him."

But now I was in a deeper mystery than ever.   The General cleared it all away, however, as he added, after leaving Charles to enjoy the pleasure of my anxiety and suspense a brief moment:

"Snakes in his boots, Colonel!   Don't you see? "

Then Charles—

" And that poor girl, Rarety, * was doing her level best to comfort him.   Finally, she went for a doctor, and, after he came, Judge Isam dropped in, and together they succeeded, about one o'clock in the morning, in getting opium enough, or whatever it was, down him to induce sleep."

" 'Twan't opium, Captain," interrupted the General, " it was whisky.   You see the poor fellow was anxious to keep sober long enough to have a hand in the hanging of them d—n Yankees, and that brought on the attack.   He wan't used to it."

* This was the name of the one I had seen enter last.

"Then you didn't have to shoot?"

"No; oh, no. You ought to have seen Peter, though! He knew from the first, but didn't want to give ' de white gen-'lmens away *dat er* way.' So he had helped us to see for ourselves."

"Do you really believe they would have hung you?" I asked.

"Yes, sir, I do."

"How could they dare to do such a thing?"

"Well, *we* wouldn't believe them at first," said Charles, breaking in upon the General. "But for several days before we had been receiving warnings through our colored friends that the enemy were getting ready to do so. One of these warnings came from this very girl, Rarety; another came from a waiter in Dave Woolridge's saloon; another from Barksdale's residence, through one of the maids. All these informants agreed that we would not be harmed in our bodies unless we drew our weapons. But, if we drew our weapons, we were to be arrested, locked up in jail, and then taken out at night and hung by the K. K. K.'s. Well, these warnings became so frequent and repeated, from the same sources, just before the day on which the event was to occur, that we agreed to take whatever might come, and make no resistance, unless it should be at the last moment. Accordingly on that day, after a gang of them had pursued us all the way from our stronghold to the post-office, and from the post-office back again, insulting us every step of the way, and forcing us to walk in the middle of the street, where we belonged they said, Captain Telsub struck the General square in the face. For a moment I thought he would forget; but he did not, and we got inside our refuge in safety. Then they followed up our steps, banged against the door, threw stones at our windows, and raised the devil generally. Their leader warned them that they must break no doors or windows, however, and they shortly withdrew."

"No wonder the Captain had snakes in his boots," I said, when Charles ceased. "I should think they might nestle and grow in the boots of all of them."

"That's half what's the matter with them all now," said the General. "It's so long since they've been allowed to whip a darkey here in town, in the good, old-fashioned way, that they have all gone stark mad."

CHAPTER XXII.

WHEAT AMONG TARES—A HUMAN HORNET—A "NEW-COMER"
OF THE RIGHT SORT FOR YAZOO—HOW "OUR FRIENDS UP
NORTH" FURNISHED POWDER FOR "WE ALL" DOWN SOUTH
TO BURN UNDER THE NOSES OF BRAVE EX-UNION SOLDIERS—
A "NEST OF VIPERS."

THE following day was Sunday. There was still another
surprise in store for me.

Charles had written to me about his Sabbath-school, but I
was wholly unprepared for what I was to witness.

About the hour for the school to assemble full a dozen stalwart freedmen, all armed with stout hickory, or other hard-
wood sticks, appeared upon the sidewalk, in front of the
"Yankee stronghold." This was the signal of departure for
the church, the little church which we had helped to build,
and Charles and General Greenleaf* buckled their weapons
about them and joined the group.

Being the most "distinguished" and *important* personage,
on account of my official station, I was assigned the "post
of honor," which was none other than the centre of the
group—for better protection, they said—and, flanked by two
freedmen, who went on ahead as advance guard, Charles
and the General, side by side, led the procession, which followed in military order. Thus escorted, we reached the
church in safety and walked upon the sidewalk, too.

---

* I had not yet been able to get my own consent to carry such a weapon.

Inside the church was a motley gathering indeed. There must have been fully two hundred children who were under sixteen years of age; from pure white, with blue eyes and flaxen hair, to coal-black boys and girls. There they were, poorly clad, but with clean bodies—Charles taught that cleanliness was next to godliness, and they had taken the lesson from his lips as coming directly from their Father in heaven. There were not teachers enough. One a "Southern Unionist," Charles, the General, and the wife of the Freedman's Bureau agent, were the only "white teachers." There were but few of the colored adults at that time with sufficient learning to act as teachers even in such a school. But such as there were, were utilized to the best advantage.

One feature of this school attracted my attention. The pastor, a very light colored man, who had been a slave until freedom came for all, and all the officers of the church, were present either as scholars or teachers. The exercises were simple. A song was sung, followed with prayer by my brother. Then another song, followed by the lessons for the day, after which there was more singing, and then the General made a brief talk,* and when he closed he informed the school that I would talk to them if they would like to hear me.

Then the pastor gravely rose, and, with tears filling his eyes, briefly informed the school of some things that he had heard of me during my absence at Jackson, and said he believed the Lord had raised up " Captain Morgan, Gen'ral Greenleaf, and de Kunnel like he raised up Moses 'mong de childun of Israel," though not of them, to lead them. Then, raising his eyes towards heaven, he uttered the most affecting prayer I ever listened to. There were few *words*, but they came straight from a *good* heart.

From the moment we entered the church, the crowd of white boys that had followed us all the way from the stronghold, hung about the building, some pushing against the doors, held fast by doorkeepers on the inside, some lifting

*I was deeply grateful for the change that his experience had wrought in this former opponent of mine. He could now talk to the freed people without any halting in his speech or manner.

themselves up by the window-sills until they could see in, when they would utter "cat-calls" and make grimaces, while some threw stones upon the roof. They had heard the announcement that I was to talk to the school, and at once began to fill the windows. When the pastor began his prayer they groaned. Then this " nigro preacher " prayed for them, their parents; that Yazoo City might be made a God-fearing town; and he threw so much pathos and entreaty into his words, the boys themselves became silent.

But the moment I began to talk they made such a din that I could not be heard. I ceased speaking, and, turning to Charles. suggested they be invited inside, and that enough of the school vacate their seats to make room. I thought I would like to talk to those boys too.

But the pastor promptly replied that they had tried tha course at the start, and the only result was to increase the disturbance.

Then I suggested that the police be called.

The General said he had tried several times to get police attendance, and failed.

" What shall be done, then ? " I asked.

" *It is simply a question of endurance,*" said my brother. " Let us suspend a few moments, and they'll get tired and get down from the windows."

Throughout the exercises the audience had kept perfectly quiet, and there was no excitement whatever. I remarked this to Charles.

" Oh, they're used to it," said he. " It's this way every Sabbath, only worse. One day they forced open the door and came in, and we had to adjourn for the day."

" Where do you suppose Dixon* and his gang are to-day ? " inquired the General of Charles.

" They've doubtless heard of Stanton's victory, and are waiting for orders," replied this chief of the outcasts.

" *Guess that's it,*" responded the other, with much feeling.

* He was a " new-comer," but from Virginia, and had but just come into the county.

In a few moments the boys had all disappeared from the windows, and were howling and "cat-calling" in the streets. Then I finished my talk, the school was dismissed, and we returned in the manner we came.

As we neared the stronghold a young, girlish-faced man with thin lips, light hair, and no larger than most boys at fourteen — "a human hornet" was Charles' description — "bolted" straight from the opposite side of the street, pushed himself rapidly through the ranks of the "guard," jostling me nearly to the gutter, and then walked away as rapidly as he had come. This was Henry Dixon, and this was a new feature of his policy ; for both the General and Charles declared to me that he usually had a "gang" of young men with him, the young Stockdales, Blacks and Isams.

The next day when I took stage for the railroad to return to Jackson, the white boys were out as usual. This time they had a new epithet for me. It was "carpet-bagger." *

But the men failed to put in an appearance. Indeed, my entire trip was quite free from serious annoyance from adults.†

The only drummer on board was a representative of a Memphis house. It was not necessary that he should abuse me in order to show where *his* sympathies were. He was well known in Yazoo.

The change in the conduct of the membership of the ku-klux-klan organization was so great that the Northerners who during the reign of terror had held themselves aloof from that " Den of Yankee vipers," as the K. K. K.'s termed the quarters where my brother and General Greenleaf had their " office," dining-room, and lodgings, once more returned to *counsel* and *advise* the gallant garrison. Even certain of the anti-reconstructionists condescended to " speak " to the General and to Charles when they happened to meet them on the street.

* In Yazoo, the fact that the mint in which that epithet was coined, was located in the North, ay, in the heart of the North, or what was thought there in Yazoo to be the same thing, viz : the Tribune office or sanctum in New York City, justified these best boys of the best citizens of that town, in giving to that word a pronunciation smacking of triumphant jollity, thus—key-ah pit-ba-ah-ger-r-r !

† The kuklux were awaiting orders.

The " Unionist" over the way removed the lock from his cistern, and the stronghold by the exercise of proper discretion could be provisioned in the daytime.

The main body of the whites, however, continued to frown fiercely upon the outcasts, and the female portion to lift their skirts and cross over to the other side of the street, whenever they saw Charles or the General approaching. By way of emphasizing their contempt for these "carpet-baggers," they, the white females, made it a point to exhibit, on every such occasion, especial courtesy and politeness of demeanor toward all other Northerners. This was intended to *shame* the garrison into a surrender. Indeed, this change was so great that since the night when the grand Cyclops celebrated in such a dolorous manner the triumph of Stanton over Johnson, it had not been necessary to maintain a guard over the stronghold while the garrison slept.

CHAPTER XXIII.

CHARLES HAS A NEW EXPERIENCE—·A SLIGHT INDISCRETION
AND A TRIAL—COURAGEOUS GENERAL GREENLEAF, AND TRUE
FRIENDS—MORE STRAW FOR BRICKS.

AS the work of the convention at Jackson progressed, and
the time approached when that body should adjourn and
the result of its labors be submitted to the people* for their
rejection or approval, Charles and General Greenleaf commenced organizing Loyal League Clubs and also the Republican party throughout the county.

The Loyal League Clubs established by them were organized in conformity to the constitution and by-laws of the
National League in every particular. Their meetings were
secret, and the outcasts were surprised by the number of
applicants for membership from the old Unionist element in
the county.

About this time *The Clarion*, a newspaper published at
the State capital, and edited by Ethel Barksdale, who, with
Hons. W. P. Harris, A. G. Brown and a majority of the
leading minds of the anti-reconstruction element of the State,
had banded together in what they themselves styled the Central " Democratic Association," of the State of Mississippi,
published the following :

* The convention which passed the ordinance of secession in Mississippi, refused to
submit its work to the people for approval. The Johnson reconstruction convention of 1865, also refused to submit its work to the people. Had the convention which
framed the first Free State Constitution for the State, followed the examples thus set
them, there would have been no necessity for this work. But thus has it ever been.
The men who frame *free* constitutions have nothing to conceal, and have never yet
been afraid to allow the people to know what they have done, how they have done it,
and why.

" THE LOYAL LEAGUE CONSPIRACY *

"The following resolutions speak for themselves. They were offered
by Hon. W. P. Harris in the Democratic Association in this city on
Saturday evening last, and unanimously adopted. We advise similar
action by the Conservatives throughout the State :

"RESOLUTIONS.

" Whereas a secret, oath-bound organization, in violation of the laws
of the State,† exists in this city, known as the Loyal League, which
we believe to be not only mischievous, but well calculated to disturb
the peace and good order of society; now, therefore, be it—

"*Resolved*, Without intending in any manner to interfere with the
political rights of citizens of any class or parties in the exercise of the
elective franchise, that we will not hereafter employ, countenance, or
support in any manner any man, white or black, who is known to
belong to the Loyal League, and who determines to continue a member thereof.

"*Resolved*, That we, the Southern people do hereby pledge ourselves
to protect those freedmen who have the boldness and good sense to
avow themselves the friends of law and order, and that we will, by
all means, peaceably if we may, forcibly if we must, protect, defend,
and support them in preference to those who have arrayed themselves
against the laws of the State and their true friends.

"*Resolved*, That our respect for a colored man is far above that which
we entertain for any Northern man or renegade Southern man, who
avows doctrines favorable to,or in encouragement of,the Loyal League,
which society we know to be in direct violation of the laws of the
State, and that we will not countenance any white man, from whatever latitude he may come, or dignifiy him with our recognition who
affiliates with this organization.

" *Resolved*, That we are a law-abiding people, and that we will do
nothing in violation of law or good morals, and will use our utmost
endeavors to protect and defend the same, and earnestly appeal to the
whole community to join us in the maintenance of the rights we avow.

" *Resolved*, That all towns. villages, or communities in the State of
Mississippi, where Loyal Leagues exist, are earnestly requested to
adopt similar resolutions.''

* The reader should remember that many of the best men of the nation were members of this league.

† The only " law of the State " which the League violated was that one defining and
punishing unlawful a-semblies of negroes. See Revised Code, Mississippi Slave Code,
of 1857, page 247, which reads as follows :
" ARTICLE 51. All meetings or assemblies of slaves, or free negroes or mulattoes mixing and associating with such slaves, above the number of five, including such free
negroes and mulattoes, at any place of public resort, or at any meeting-house or houses,
in the night, or at any school for teaching them reading or writing, either in the day
time or night, under whatsoever pretext, shall be deemed an unlawful assembly.''
* * *
The punishment for the violation of this law, by this same article, was "not more
than thirty-nine lashes on the bare back."
But as to these laws see hereinafter.

The revival of the reign of terror in Yazoo was one of the first fruits of those resolutions. The change was so sudden that the garrison was surprised.* The first sign of the approaching storm was observed by Charles one morning when he entered the post-office for his mail. It came from a group of well-known boys and young men lounging about that corner, who revived their old cries of " O'oophie !" "polecat !" " old Morgan !" etc., etc., and as he came out and passed down the street they followed him.

Some of them had pistols, and one, just as they passed by some " ladies " standing in the front of a door on Main street tried to trip my brother and throw him down, to the great delight of these fair ones. He must cross the bayou just above "Mr. Goosie's ferry," and, this crowd of howling, teasing, cursing, " cat-calling " white youth pursued him into the ferry-boat, a long flat boat. Up to this time Charles had controlled himself perfectly. He had his revolver buckled to his person outside, and not concealed. They had several times called out to him, " Why don't you stan' yo' groun' an' fight like a gentleman ?" and had repeatedly called upon him to defend himself. Merchants standing in their store-fronts, and their clerks had hallooed this cry after him; but he had kept cool, and gone quietly on his course.

As the ferryman was shoving the flat from the bank one of these white boys—son of one of the " leading citizens "—seized the ferryman's pole, and, raising it, made a " rush " for Charles, followed by the whole crowd, as though they meant to drive him from the further end of the flat into the rapidly running stream, where, without help, he would have been in great danger of drowning. Divining their purpose, Charles drew his weapon, and ordered them to "halt! come nearer and I'll fire !" He had not even then lost any part of perfect self-control, and stood as calm and self-possessed as if talking to the Sabbath-school. But alas! he had drawn a " deadly weapon "—had " exhibited it in a threatening

*During the brief era of good feeling Yazoo had become so quiet that the outcasts abandoned their habit of going together whenever they went out.

manner." The " boys " at once ceased their pursuit, retired
to their end of the flat, and Charles went on his way.

Whenever in this country that time shall come that the
declarations of one or more of those who fought to destroy
the Union, or for *slavery*, or who sat in the council chamber
of treason, or of rebellion even, against our flag, shall be
taken by the people of the whole country, or of one-half of
it, as worthy of credit above the statements on honor of
one who served in the army of the Union from the beginning until the close of the late glorious war, receiving honorable wounds and merited promotion, and against whose
fame no stain has rested, then the people of this country will
deserve to have a king set over them, and God in wrath shall
give them one.

The following is from the Yazoo *Banner* of May, 1868.
I beg my readers to remember that I do not bring it forward
here to corroborate my account of this event in my brother's
life, nor shall I employ any similar papers for such a purpose
nor in proof of any statement I may make. I use this one
because in itself it presents pictures of life in Yazoo that I
can neither hope to excel nor imitate :

SONG.

AIR—*If you belong to Gideon's Band.*

Old Morgan came to the Southern land,
Old Morgan came to the Southern land,
Old Morgan came to the Southern land,
With a little carpet-bag in his hand.

CHORUS.

If you belong to the Ku Klux Klan,
Here's my heart and here's my hand,
If you belong to the Ku Klux Klan,
We are marching for a home.

Old Morgan thought he would get bigger,
Old Morgan thought he would get bigger,
Old Morgan thought he would get bigger,
By running a saw-mill with a nigger.
If you belong to the Ku Klux Klan, &c.

The crop it failed and the saw-mill busted,
The crop it failed and the saw-mill busted,
The crop it failed and the saw-mill busted,
And the nigger got very badly wusted.
      If you belong to the Ku Klux Klan, &c.

And Morgan is a gay old rat,
And Morgan is a gay old rat,
And Morgan is a gay old rat,
And the boys they called him a " polecat."
      If you belong to the Ku Klux Klan, &c.

But some close at his heels would tag,
But some close at his heels would tag,
But some close at his heels would tag,
And call this hero " scalawag."
      If you belong to the Ku Klux Klan, &c.

Old Morgan went to the bayou bridge,
Old Morgan went to the bayou bridge,
Old Morgan went to the bayou bridge,
And with some little Ku Kluxes had a scrimmidge.
      If you belong to the Ku Klux Klan, &c.

Old Morgan stepped into the flat,
Old Morgan stepped into the flat,
Old Morgan stepped into the flat,
And knocked a little Ku Klux into a cocked-hat, and the
    little Ku Klux didn't like that so very well, and another
    little Ku Klux picked up a spike pole to hit old Morgan zip,
    and Old Morgan drew a horse pistol out of his pantaloons,
    and cocked it on the little coons, and the little Ku Klux that
    had picked up the spike pole dropped it very soon, and old
    Morgan turned and run out of the flat, and the little Ku
    Kluxes hollered " run, polecat."
      If you belong to the Ku Klux Klan, &c.

Returning the next day to town, my brother was met by
an officer who had a writ of some sort for his " apprehension."
Charles asked to be informed of the nature of the charge
upon which he was to be arrested. This the officer at first
declined to grant. But he shortly yielded, and announced
that the order for his arrest was based upon the affidavit of
———, a son of one of the most prominent physicians of the
county, which affidavit charged my brother with " carrying
a concealed deadly weapon," " exhibiting a deadly weapon,"

"violating city ordinance," "disturbing the peace, and
assault."

Charles recognized the man as "a proper officer to make an
arrest," and while denying the charges, he declared himself
a law-abiding citizen, submitted to the demand of this officer
without a murmur, was taken before the mayor, tried, and
on the testimony of the "prosecuting witness," together with
several of the youths who were engaged with him, Mr.
Goosie and his ferryman (the only persons who were present), was found guilty, fined on each count, and charged
"with all costs," the whole amounting to more than sixty
dollars.*

Pending that *trial*, General Greenleaf, the postmaster, and
the freed people, together with some Northerners, who
contributed secretly, "took up a collection," and thus raised
the whole amount of the fine and costs, and paid the same
promptly. They supposed that would be the end of that
proceeding. To assist in raising the money a few of the
principal ones had held a consultation, which was attended
by some Northerners, whose blood had been roused by
the outrages upon the chief of the outcasts, and by some few
Unionists, as well as negroes. General Greenleaf had the
hardihood to remind those present that the practice of carrying weapons was universal among the whites, as all could
see, and he also declared that the aggressors, as every one
in the town well knew, were the prosecutors themselves.

---

*From the Yazoo *Banner* of May, 1868:—" The trial consumed two days, and was protracted late into Saturday night. The examination took great latitude, Morgan being
allowed to show the state of public feeling against him, that he was a persecuted man ;
that his life was threatened, and that he was justified in carrying concealed weapons in
self-defense. The Very Rev. Tolbert Gibbs was a prominent witness for the defense,
and revealed many very strange and wonderful things he had heard about plots that
were laid, "inductions dangerous," to kill him and his friend Morgan, of which
scarcely a word was believed by any one who heard him.

    *   *   *   *   *   *   *   *   *

"The prosecution, represented by Judge Hudson, pressed him at every point with
efficient ability and vigor, and although for two days he bore the ordeal with consum-
mate coolness and audacity, towards the close of the trial he seemed to have become
cowed, and cringed like a poor cur. It was difficult to repress a feeling of sympathy for
the depraved creature, as he realized that all his arts and devices had failed, and felt
the iron grasp of justice tightening upon him.

"He was found guilty of every charge, and fined as follows : For the assault and bat-
tery, $10 ; for carrying concealed weapons, $20 ; for unlawful exhibition of a deadly
weapon, $5, with costs, amounting to $26. We submit, with all due respect, that the
punishment in our opinion is by no means commensurate with the offense, and besides,
the mayor had no right to punish for the unlawful exhibition of a deadly weapon,
which is an indictable offense, of which the circuit court has jurisdiction. When the
grand jury meets Morgan will learn that there is some little law yet left in Mississippi."

The only conclusion to be reached from the proceeding, therefore, was, that the prosecution, as well as the persecution which preceded it, had been designed by the enemies of reconstruction, and of the United States, to injure the leader of the Republicans, and, if possible, to destroy him.

In this the General but expressed the sentiments and opinions of the meeting, as was clearly shown from the speeches of others who took part. But all carefully avoided any reflection upon the court. In fact, all agreed that the mayor had but performed his duty under the laws. Nevertheless, they also agreed that those same laws, in justice, should be enforced upon all alike. Otherwise, there could possibly be no protection for the loyalists. Efforts had been frequently made to obtain protection from the police against such mobs as had pursued my brother that morning, without avail, and the General declared that my brother and himself had adopted the practice of carrying weapons as a last resort, and only in self-defence. The demonstrations about the building in which the meeting was being held became so violent during these proceedings, that when at last the sum required had been raised, and the meeting adjourned, nearly all present gathered in a body around the General, against whom the wrath of the enemy, nearly all of whom were armed with pistols or knives, and some with both, was now chiefly directed.

The sequel showed that they meant to " get him too," by the same means as had been employed to entrap my brother. Only, those who now pursued the General were the kuklux fathers of the young kukluxes who had pursued Charles.

So determined were they to aggravate him to make some sort of defence that they actually spat upon him, threw stones at him, and, finally, getting close enough for the purpose, they struck him several times, and once squarely in the face.*

* From the Yazoo *Banner* of May, 1868 :—" The words were scarcely cold when, as he was escorted down the street by some dozen of his admiring audience, a gentleman insulted him once and again, and the hound dared not resent it. He sneaked along to another part of the town where another gentleman insulted him, and he dared not resent it. Perhaps he has learned from this, that if Southern gentlemen do not usually treat such incendiaries with all the contempt and insult which their baseness so well merits, it is because they are restrained by self respect. And perhaps the colored audience, who heard the foul and false aspersions cast on our people, and then saw their calumniator twice display his own pitiful cowardice, will learn from this how much reliance is to be placed on these apostles of incendiarism."

CHAPTER XXIV.

AT LAST !—A MURDERER'S CELL !—THAT YAZOO JAIL IN 1868—
WHAT MR. BARKSDALE DID—THE GOOD SAMARITAN—UNCLE
JONATHAN SEES THE KUKLUX—THE WICKED FLEE WHEN NONE
PURSUE.

THE threat of the *Banner* proved but the expression of
the will of the kuklux. For not long after *that* trial
of my brother, another writ was issued, and he was taken
again into custody on the very same charge upon which he
had been tried by the mayor and fined, as I have shown.
Bail was offered, but at that moment the same counsel who
had prosecuted in the former case came forward and demanded that no person should be received as surety except
such as could swear that they were worth the " amount of
the bond in *real estate*, over and above their just debts and *all
liabilities whatsoever*."

When General Greenleaf came into the county, in 1865,
it was said he paid twenty thousand dollars in gold for his
interest in the plantation he then purchased in company with
another Yankee.

There were at the moment three other Yankees in the
town who had invested similar amounts, yet, altogether, they
could not now make that bond : only three hundred dollars.
They volunteered to make up the amount in money, and
deposit it for security for my brother's appearance at court,

but this was refused. Then the officer took Charles to jail. It had become the "common jail" now, and stress was placed upon the word common by the enemy, who shook hands with each other, and fairly gloated over their "victory." It was afternoon, and the march to the jail was amid the jeers, curses, and hurrahs of the anti-reconstructionists. Everybody said that although a little pale, he showed no signs of fear, and walked by the side of the officer through the mob of howling "best citizens" and "poor white trash" as calmly as if he were going on some ordinary business-errand, in ordinary times. Some freedmen afterward told me they saw a smile on his face as he passed through the gate into the jail-building, and that he spoke in a cheerful tone.

But his friends were not idle. The freedmen, under the leadership of the pastor of the little church we helped to build, with several of its officers and others, caused word to be sent to their friends in the country round to come to town forthwith, and in a short while the guard of the stronghold, with augmented numbers, was on duty within easy reach of the jail, armed with their hard-wood sticks.

The General and the other Northerners were no less active, for they had information direct from Dave Woolridge's saloon and from other sources, that the Captain would be taken out and hanged during that night ; and, from some words they had heard, and certain actions of Captain Telsub, Judge Isam and Colonel Black, they were satisfied it was not to be done by the ku-klux-klan of Yazoo.

From the moment this information reached the General, he began to work on the agent of the Freedman's Bureau—one had recently been sent there—a very worthy officer but an extremely timid man, to convince him that it was his duty to interfere to save Charles. He protested he would gladly do so, but there was no law for it under the instructions of the new commanding-general of the department, and he would be recalled and perhaps dismissed if he exceeded his instructions even in this emergency. Besides he did not

believe the rebels intended to do more than frighten Charles
and compel him to forego his efforts to organize the party.
That much had indeed been hinted to him—the agent. For
his part he saw no use in it, anyway.

"It is perfect folly for you gentlemen to continue your
struggle here, with the President and the commanding-general
against you. I'd abandon it altogether if I were in your
places, and then we'll have peace here at all events," said he.
But the General was not dismayed. He got other Northerners to go and see the agent, and, learning of the General's
efforts in that direction, the freedmen began to go to him.

While the town-officer was taking my brother to jail, it was
discovered that neither the sheriff, Colonel Finley, nor any
of his deputies were in town, and some said they had not
been at their office since the evening before.

During the afternoon the General learned that certain " old,
and trusty faithful family servants " had seen certain signs,
and heard certain words, that prepared them for the news of
Charles' second arrest. Also, that they had " done sont "
word to certain of their friends, who had been out " warning."

This fact put a still more serious aspect upon the situation;
for if what he had heard as coming from certain "family
servants " was true, the sheriff and his deputies had purposely absented themselves. But there was a surprise in
store for them all. The General had not thought of sending to
the country for the freed people *to come to town*, and to me,
and to all others ever afterward protested that he had no
more knowledge of their coming than " the man in the
moon," nor had he done anything to prompt such a step. But
shortly after the discovery of the sheriff's absence, the number of anxious freedmen in town suddenly increased, and
before dark had become a crowd. They were very orderly;
no great excitement was apparent, but they were very determined, and " stan' yo' groun' General, stan' yo' groun,' we'll
die by ye," was heard by the General from all sides whenever
he appeared upon the streets.

At last it was said the "niggers" were moving on the jail with the determination to take my brother out—rescue him —and soon a shout was heard "Take 'im out!" "Take Captain Morgan out that ar jail!'" These shouts reached the ears of Mr. Fountain Barksdale. Now Mr. Barksdale was at the topmost round of the Yazoo business world. He knew all about the cause of these shouts. He knew that my brother was an honorable man, a law-abiding citizen, and innocent of any fault in this matter. So Mr. Barksdale began to think. He took off his spectacles and wiped them. At that moment one of his numerous clerks rushed in with the news that the "niggers" were going to burn the town unless Captain Mogan should be at once released. Mr. Barksdale was a nervous man. He did not wait to hear more, nor for his hat, but rushed almost frantically out upon the street and in the direction of the jail, shouting in his well-known thin, tenor voice, "Turn him out! Turn Captain Morgan out a there! Where's the sheriff? Where's the sheriff? Where's the mayor? Turn him out! He's no business there! Turn him out, I say!" He had gone nearly the length of Main street in that manner, appealing to nearly every "leading citizen" whom he met on the way, and often to the negroes themselves, crying out all the time : "Take him out! He's no business there! Take him out!" He had forgotten his spectacles, and carried them in his hand. He was also bareheaded. He appeared to have forgotten everything but "Captain Morgan," and "Take him out" and "fire the town." Fair women threw their arms about him ejaculating : "Oh, Mr. Barksdale, save us! Save us!" "Our nigros!" "Our nigros!" "Burn the city." "Burn the city!" "Our nigros!"

With the appearance of such an ally as Mr. Barksdale, the freedmen became almost wild with joy, and fell in by his side or behind him, and joined in the shout, "Take 'im out a there!"

But there was no officer to be found. It was getting late,

and the General and other Northerners had gone to make a
final appeal to the bureau agent. This time with effect; for
that officer himself began to see that it was indeed a serious
matter. He at once sought out Colonel Black and Judge
Isam, and said to them :

"I give you notice that if Captain Morgan is harmed to-
night, in anyway, by anybody, I will make a written report
to General Grant, through General Howard, and shall hold
you two gentlemen responsible for whatever may happen."

Then Colonel Black :

"What authority, by G—d, sir, have you for interfering
in this matter? He is there by the decree of the courts of
the land; by G—d, sir! He's a low-down, contemptible
meddler, sir, consorting with our nigros, and inciting them
to insurrection, by G—d, sir; and, by G—d sir, an outraged
Southern community won't stand it any longer, sir, by G—d
sir! He's no nigro."

But the General and other friends were close by, and, for
once, the agent stood up "like a man."

"Well, put your order in writing," said the Judge.

"I make no *order* in the premises; I merely inform you of
what I will do in case Captain Morgan is harmed in anyway."

"But your superior officer is General Gillem; by G—d,
sir," shouted Colonel Black.

"I know that, gentlemen; but Captain Morgan is an old
Union soldier, a gentleman above reproach from you, or any
like you, and is not a low-down fellow, nor an inciter of insurrections, and I shall take good care that what I may have to
say in this case shall not be pigeon-holed on the way to
Washington."

"By G—d, sir, d—n you." This was Colonel Black talking now, and he had lost his head. "We'll have you dismissed, by G—d, sir. We'll have you dismissed."

"Dismiss and be d—d," replied the agent. "I now believe
you do intend violence on Captain Morgan. Mark you, I'll

be there, and you'll have at least two to hang," and the agent
returned to his office.*

Within an half hour or so afterward Charles, accompanied
by the General and the " guard" of the "stronghold," walked
into the agent's office to thank him for his services.

" No officer with you ? "

" No."

"Have you made the bond ? "

" No."

" IIow came you here, then ? "

" Walked."

Charles was in one of his teasing moods now, and it was
the agent's turn to feel surprised.

" Well, how did you get out? "

" They opened the door, said they had no further use for
me there, so I walked out," responded the outcast.

" Well, I declare ! " exclaimed the agent. " What d—n
fools they are, to be sure."

When he had reached this point in his account of this event
to me afterward Charles ceased for a moment. The General
who was present, asked :

" Why not finish the story, and tell the Colonel what
Uncle Jonathan saw that night ? "

" I'm going to. I think it may be well to caution him that
Jonathan's story is discredited by Colonel Black and the
sheriff, and, as they are high-toned, honorable gentlemen, by
G—d, sir, it were better not to repeat it."

" Well, what did Jonathan see ? " I asked.

" The kuklux."

" You'll recollect, Albert," he continued, " that when we
all left Tokeba, Uncle Jonathan got a little patch over near
the mouth of the bayou that comes down from the piny road.
Well, the day after my confinement in the *common* jail,

* At the time the agent had not been made aware of what Mr. Barksdale was doing,
therefore, his conduct was rather heroic, for Colonel Black and his allies at Jackson,
within that "Central Democratic Association," were more powerful with General
Gillem in such matters than any one else outside of Washington.

Uncle Jonathan came into our stronghold, looking as if half
scared to death. He had seen the kuklux. He knew it
must be them. There were many men, "a long string," on
horseback. They had ridden far and rapidly, for their horses
were foaming. Some carried guns. They came to the foot
of the bluffs, where they met a man coming from town, with
whom they conversed for some minutes, and then, with ranks
somewhat demoralized, they turned about and rode away.*
But I was no longer *in* the common jail of Yazoo, under
a *charge* of assault with intent to kill; therefore they could
do nothing, that they could justify through the Associated
Press dispatches, and the headquarters of the commandant
of this district, and thus my life was spared."

*That same day we heard similar accounts from two other sources.

Carolyn Highgate Morgan, circa 1870. From the Angela Morgan Papers, Bentley Historical Collection, University of Michigan.

Carolyn Highgate Morgan, circa 1900. From the Angela Morgan Papers, Bentley Historical Collection, University of Michigan.

Captain Albert Talmon Morgan, 1865. From the Angela
Morgan Papers, Bentley Historical Collection, University of
Michigan.

Albert Talmon Morgan in Mississippi, circa 1870. From the Angela Morgan Papers, Bentley Historical Collection, University of Michigan.

Albert Talmon Morgan, circa 1896. From the Angela Morgan Papers, Bentley Historical Museum, University of Michigan.

CHAPTER XXV.

BOYS, WHY DON'T YOU GET AWAY FROM THERE ?—LETTERS FROM
THE OLD HOME—CHARLES' FEVER—NEVER SAY DIE!

I DON'T think I ever before saw Charles in quite so savage a mood as he was at the close of his account of that "trial," and the subsequent proceedings. He paced up and down the floor of the stronghold for two mortal hours, during which he delivered himself of the most bitter invective against our Government that I ever listened to, or ever read; and what surprised me most was the perfect sympathy existing between him and the General

Yet nearly a week had passed since the occasion of it transpired. It seemed that the more we discussed it the more savage they became, and I feared they might never cool off.

During the so-called trial the General telegraphed the fact to me and asked for pecuniary aid; as much as $300. I at once wired our sister Helen and a brother the facts of the case and thus obtained the money.* But the mails brought her letter, one from another sister, a brother, and one from father and mother. "Why do you boys remain there?" was the burden of each. "Our mother is nearly distracted," Helen wrote; and father reminded us of some wholesome advice he had volunteered at the outset of our journey

* There being no money in the State treasury and the Governor having refused to recognize the legality of the convention, no warrants were permitted to be drawn in favor of any member or officer of that body. The collection of a tax levied by the convention had been enjoined by the Central Democratic Association, and, therefore, I had as yet drawn no money from the State for my services.

Southward, and ventured to repeat a part of it. " Why don't you leave that God-forsaken country ! "

There was one other. It's author couldn't " understand it at all." I had already told Charles of these letters, and he had received one from Helen—and a brave good woman she was—our " best sister." But she had written: " *Charles, why don't you come home?* "

So, now, when his fever of wrath was at its height, I again called his attention to these letters, and handed him mother's.

The superscription was in the strong, ancient, well-known characters of our father, and the fact did not escape Charles' eye. His hand trembled for a moment as he crumpled the envelope, and then, quite petulantly, opened and began to read.

The first part was mother's. She began, almost at the beginning, to remind us how much she had suffered while her three "soldier boys" were at the front, Charles, William, and myself; of our long service; of her joy at our return, scarred, but whole in limb; how she had hoped to pass her last days in peace, with her children around her, and all that. But peace had not come to her, and she thought she had suffered enough and that we had done our share. She had not long to live, anyway. We could do no good for ourselves nor any one else where we were. Therefore, why not come home ?

Then father. I believe he was one of the truest men that ever lived. His neighbors used to call him " honest George Morgan." His father and our mother's father fought in the Revolution. They had willingly given three of their sons to the war for the preservation of the liberties their fathers had won from the British. I had no recollection of having seen tears in Charles' eyes but twice before. This was the third time. As he proceeded with mother's letter, they stood trembling upon his eye-lids, but only for a brief space; then they flowed like great drops of grateful rain, and thus his fever passed away. But, when he came to that " other " letter I thought I saw symptoms of its return; for he rose from the bed, upon which he had thrown himself—our only bed—and again paced the floor.

" Don't understand it all! No; they don't any of them understand. They couldn't understand dear old 'Pap' Thomas, nor Grant, nor Sherman; they couldn't understand Stanton nor Lincoln; they can't understand us! During the war they were so wrapped up in big prices for their wheat and in buying and selling, they couldn't find time to keep up with current history. Now they are so tamed by their fears that these poor, half-starved, half-naked, unarmed negroes *may* rise and slaughter their old masters and mistresses for what they have done to them in the past, and so full of tenderness and pity for whisky-guzzling, tobacco-smoking, swine-eating, scrofulous, lecherous, cowardly rebels, that they have forgotten our wounds; forgotten our generosity to these same rebels when our bayonets were at their throats, and to-day, if one of us should be shot down like a dog, or hung to a lamp-post, so that it were done in the *common* jail, or while under some foul charge, these same kind people would never be able to understand it, and would go down to their graves feeling that, somehow, we were in the wrong. I tell you, Albert, we must fight this thing out, if it takes our lives. The country don't understand it at all, and they won't understand it until we have furnished them proof upon proof, and they have come to see with their own eyes that the last state of the sick man of the South is worse than the first. Think of it! the negroes' only refuge is the Bureau, and you know how feeble, uncertain and treacherous are the means of protection that affords them. But here we are, without even so much as that—unless by a subterfuge, when the agent happens to be a man with some little of the milk of human kindness in his breast, and enough sand in his gizzard to support his backbone in a game of bluff. These same poor, despised negroes, after all, are our only protection, and they have proved their courage and fidelity to my entire satisfaction.

I thought this was a good place for me to put in a word, so I said:

" Then you won't desert them and go home ? "

" Desert them ? " cried he. " From this time forth every black man in Yazoo is my brother, and every black woman, not excepting poor Rarety, is my sister. God bless them! I would have as soon deserted Thomas at Nashville as desert them now."

" And I Meade at Gettysburg ! " I involuntarily exclaimed. My brother's eloquence had made forget his " fever."

" And I Grant on the Chickahominy, by G—d ! " shouted the General, whose oath came out so round and full that it seemed to fit the place.*

Then we sang the "Star Spangled Banner," "John Brown's Body," and other patriotic airs, until Charles' " fever " had passed quite off again, and the shoemaker's wife came up to warn us that we were disturbing the man with " an ancestry " in the office below. He was recovering from a fresh attack of *mania-a-portu,* and our songs had very much the same effect on him that water has on a mad dog. So the council " broke up " of its own accord.

Pending the canvass of that year, the following from the Vicksburg *Times,* of June, 1868, is a specimen of the spirit which was commonly manifested by the whole Democratic press and leaders throughout the State. This spirit, very often accompanied by *violence,* was everywhere present:

" Others may do as they please, but if men will protect and shelter vipers, they must take the consequences. We shall prepare and publish a list of merchants who keep negro radicals as porters and laborers, and advise our people to avoid all such shops. Hotels who employ negro waiters and porters who belong to Loyal Leagues, will also be published, and the public warned against them. Draymen, hackmen, barbers, and all other negro laborers who belong to the Loyal League, shall in like manner be published. * * * The Southern Democrat who feeds a radical, white or black, is false to his race,

* The General's spiritual as well as his mental vision had been sharpened.

false to his country, false to God and false to himself.   He who supports them in any shape is a COWARD who disgraces the name of man."

Also the following, which was only a specimen instance of the intolerance and proscription of many of our leading business men.   It is from the New Orleans *Times,* a paper which applauded the stand taken by Captain Leathers, at that time of the steamboat Quitman, and backs him up by the following resolve of a Democratic club at Pointe Coupee:

"POINTE COUPEE, *August* 22, 1868.

" *To Capt. T. P. Leathers, of the Steamer General Quitman :*

"SIR: At a meeting of the Seymour and Blair Democratic Club of the Sixth Ward of the Parish of Pointe Coupee, held last evening, at the club rooms, at Red Store Landing, on motion of Mr. J. J. Plantivignes, and seconded by A. Provesty, Esq., the following resolution was unanimously adopted, viz:

"Whereas, it has become the settled policy of the Democracy of this State not to give employment or support of any kind to members of the radical party; and whereas, it is announced by the New Orleans press that Capt. T. P. Leathers, of the Vicksburg packet General Quitman, has discharged from employment on his steamer all persons not members of the Democratic party; therefore, be it

" *Resolved,* That the thanks of this club are due and are hereby returned to Captain T. P. Leathers, of the steamer General Quitman, for being the first among steamboatmen to take this important step, which is calculated to contribute largely to the success of the Democratic party in this State."

"And by virtue of a resolution to that effect, we are instructed to send you this copy of said resolution of thanks.

" By order of:

"JULES LA BAUT, *Pres't.*

" Very respectfully, yours,   " L. B. CLAIBORNE, *Secr'y.*

Commenting on this the Vicksburg *Times* added :

" The above example of Captain Leathers should be followed by every steamboat that comes to port, as it is the only security they have for frustrating the designs of unprincipled carpet-baggers, who are constantly prowling about among the colored race, in order to lead them astray.   However, Pointe Coupee is not the only parish that will vomit forth its voice of thunder in praise of the above resolution.   But we may hear from numerous others in parts of the State that the radicals little dream of."

CHAPTER XXVI.

DURING Charles' "fever" of the evening before no thought
of teasing him had once obtruded itself upon the sanctity
of his wrath; for we were all so wrapped within the presence
of outraged justice that, to me, the little room of the stronghold in which we were seemed a temple of the living God,
scintillant with His anger or radiant with His love, according
to the changes in my brother's eyes, which sometimes blazed
with indignation, and at others danced in the hot tears of a
sympathetic pity for the more deeply wronged colored people.
The place was holy ground ! Sanctified ! Not by the prat-
tle of tender, loving children, nor by the touch of holy,
gracious woman, blessed as these are and restful, but by God's
benediction resting on it. So, when the first rays of the
morning sun had lighted the sides of Peak Tenariffe not
more than half way to its base, the merry morning calls of
these two outcasts fell upon my drowsy ears, to prepare me
for the entrance of the shoemaker's wife, the advance courier
of breakfast.

A night of perfect rest had changed everything. The
sanctity of the stronghold had disappeared along with the
solemnity that had filled it the evening before; along also
with my dreams of home. Yes, home. For, although I had

tried very hard to, I had not yet been able to feel quite at home in Yazoo.

Observing my languor, Charles commenced rallying me about my habits; declared that my "elevation"* had, after all, had the same effect upon me as upon "ordinary mortals," and I—was "putting on airs."

Now, that was too good an opportunity for me to let pass, considering the circumstances, and so I fired back at him thus: "H-hem! Pretty good that for a jail-bird."

This proved an unfortunate remark for me, as well as for the General; for Charles at once drew himself within his "shell," and do what we might, we could not restore him to cheerfulness. That was indeed a sore subject to my brother. I do not recall any subsequent reference to it by either the General or myself during the remainder of his life in Yazoo. The kuklux seemed to appreciate the fact no less than we did, for neither the old ones nor the young ones ever mentioned the matter; certainly never in his presence.

By the time the new constitution was ready for submission to the "qualified registered voters of the State" for ratification or rejection, Charles, the General and a handful of Unionists, who, after Stanton's victory over Johnson, openly espoused the cause of reconstruction, had succeeded in organizing a Loyal League or a Republican club in nearly every centre of population in the county.

Thus, for the first time, there was a Republican party in Yazoo. The reader knows through what trial and by what sacrifice. Charles was its recognized head; its soul. The General, by common consent, was its chief counsellor, while the postmaster and other Northerners, together with the Unionists and the pastor of the little "nigro church" with its official membership, constituted the organizing force. The delegates to the convention were its representatives. Nine hundred and ninety-nine of every one thousand of its membership had never yet voted the Republican ticket.

*Meaning my election to that "black-and-tan convention."

Either they had been enjoined from doing so as in 1856 and 1860, by the " grape vine " process—which had been the case with the Unionists—or, they had been Democratic, Whig, or Free-Soil voters in States where men had liberty of choice in such matters, as was the case with many of the Northerners; or, as in the case of the freed people, the constitution, laws and customs of the State in which they existed, expressly withheld from them the right to do so on account of their race. Yet this party thus organized and so constituted was destined to give to the world an example in self-government toward which the future Republic will turn with grateful heart.

Let the incredulous reader withhold his smile or scorn until, in the course of this history, we shall have dug down to Elisha's bones. Then, if he be a lover of his country, of justice and of liberty, let him accompany the spirit of the immortal Lincoln from the dedication ceremonies at Gettysburg to that Yazoo grave-yard, and there again resolve, " that the government of the people, by the people and for the people shall not perish from the earth."

The following from the Vicksburg *Daily Times*, then one of the most prominent Democratic organs, is a fair sample of the newspaper editorials published in the State from the date of the passage of the reconstruction laws up to the assembling of our Constitutional Convention in January, 1868, and afterward.

" A GOOD RESOLUTION.

"The Democratic Club of Marion, Alabama, recently adopted unanimously the following resolution:

" *Resolved*, That the members of this club, in their social intercourse, will not recognize any man as a gentleman, or a friend to his country, who may accept any appointment to office under the reconstruction acts of the Congress of the United States.''

" This resolution is good, but does not go far enough. If our people will refuse to speak to, or hold any kind of intercourse with such scoundrels as Eggleston, Barry, McKee, Railsback, *et id omne genus*, much of their harm is gone forever. Would any sensible man exchange any kind of courtesies with the villains who burn his house or murder his family? We fancy not. And yet the despicable wretches who seek to place us under the domination of ignorant negroes—to force them upon us as our political. and social equals—affect to be terribly shocked that the Southern people should look upon them with scorn and abhorrence. This is the only true policy. Between the white men of the South and the advocates of negro suffrage, there should be a deep ditch and a high wall, and these obstacles should be as fixed as fate, and as impassable as the gulf which separated Dives from Lazarus, when the former was in hell, suffering all its torments, and the latter was experiencing the beatitude of Heaven. They should be made to feel that they are despised outcasts, cut off from all human fellowship and sympathy, and no companionship save that of the ignorant and besotted negroes they are seeking to use for their own base and selfish purposes. If the white men of the South will but adopt this policy—if they will neither speak to, or be spoken to by them, the negroes even will soon despise and scorn them as much as we do. Let this be done—let McKee, Speed, Barry, & Co., feel that the brand is upon them, that white and black alike avoid and loathe them—and our word for it the country will soon be rid of their presence. For ourselves personally, no man who favors negro suffrage and domination can be permitted to speak to us, to touch our hand, or receive in any manner the most ordinary courtesy or civility from us. Between them and us there can be nothing but hostility, eternal and undying, and there is not a murderer or thief in the world for whom we have not more respect than we have for the vagabonds who are seeking to impose negro rule upon the people of the South.

" The most abandoned criminal, the most cowardly murderer, the most despicable highwayman, that ever expiated their crimes on the gallows, in the State prison, or the galleys, are honorable and princely gentlemen compared to such wretched sneaks as Eggleston, Barry, McKee, Railsback, Speed, and the whole kennel of carpet-bag adventurers now lording it in Mississippi.''

General Eggleston was at this time president of the convention. He was a brother or cousin of the gentleman of that name who was some years in Congress from Ohio. He had emigrated to Mississippi in 1865, and invested largely in real estate. Barry, McKee, and Railsback were members of the convention, and Speed was a relative of the late Attorney-General Speed. He was then engaged in the practice of the law at Vicksburg.

CHAPTER XXVII.

A GENERAL ELECTION IN YAZOO—W. H. FOOTE VS. THE "HUMAN
HORNET"—NO LIVES LOST.

THAT general election in Mississippi, when all the people participated for the first time, will long be remembered in Yazoo.

The Governor and all State and county officers, with rare
exceptions, were opposed to any "reconstruction" of the
State, and zealous supporters of their own "plan," which
was founded upon the idea that, as the State had failed, by
rebellion, to take itself out of the Union, the only act necessary to entitle the people to share in the government of the
whole country, was the surrender of their arms.

True, this people had sent men to a representative body
so called, which upon the demand of Andrew Johnson, in
order to "disarm the adversary," as that President put it,
had resolved that, "The institution of slavery *having been**
destroyed in the State of Mississippi * * neither slavery,"
&c., "shall hereafter *exist.*"

By whom was that institution destroyed! By the "sovereign State?" No, never. By the "sovereign people" of
the State? No, never. What did they mean by such an
ordinance?

They did *not* mean to surrender by their own act their
legal claim to be reimbursed from the national treasury to the

* Italics by the author.

full extent of the market value of the slaves emancipate the will of the nation ; they did not mean to estop their successors from resolving that, after all, slavery *had not* been destroyed. They did mean to dodge the question, and they did it. They justified their tergiversation on the ground of " present duress." Thus they thought, felt and acted *then*.

This new constitution dodged nothing. Under its provisions the negro was a man, and all men were to be equal in their right to life, liberty and the pursuit of happiness. Recognizing the institution of concubinage prevailing in the State as more demoralizing to the family and more destructive of manhood and womanhood than even that slavery which had been ' "destroyed," this new constitution declared that:

" All persons who have not been married, but who are now living together, cohabiting as man and wife, shall be taken and held for all purposes in law as married, and their children, whether born before or after the ratification of this constitution, shall be legitimate, and the legislature may by law punish adultery and concubinage." (Sec. 22, Art. 12.)

Recognizing in the diverse elements composing the body politic, and the illiteracy and low civilization of the community, those dangerous germs that without restraint might, in a night, under favorable conditions, overspread the State with bankruptcy and ruin, this constitution declared further that :

"The credit of the State shall not be pledged or loaned in aid of any person, association or corporation; nor shall the State hereafter become a stockholder in any corporation or association." (Sec. 5, Art.12)

And

" The legislature shall not authorize any county, city or town to become a stockholder in or to loan its credit to any company, association or corporation, unless two-thirds of the qualified voters of such county, city or town at a special election, or regular election to be held therein, shall assent thereto." (Sec. 14, Art. 12.)

And

"The legislature shall never authorize any lottery, nor shall the sale of lottery tickets be allowed, nor shall any lottery heretofore authorized, be permitted to be drawn or tickets therein to be sold."

Excepting these provisions, and the spirit of the Thirteenth and Fourteenth Amendments to the National Constitution, relating to slavery and the qualifications of a voter which entered into its fibre, this new constitution would have been accepted without a dissenting voice by the people of California, Iowa, Wisconsin, Ohio, Pennsylvania, Massachusetts, or Maine, as the equal of their own in the propriety and wisdom of its provisions. Yet, the people of Yazoo divided upon it so bitterly that one portion of the whites became savages in their efforts to defeat it, while another lent themselves to all manner of devices, by cajolery, by bribery, and by intimidation, to the same purpose.

Opposed to them were Charles, the General, five other Northerners, a handful of Unionists, the freed people—the Republican party of Yazoo.

As the laws forbade freed people to own or acquire lands, there was but one plantation in the "hill portion" of the county where the Republican party could hold meetings, and there were but two in the "swamp portion." All other places of meeting were upon the broad highway, in the little negro church we helped to build, the Yankee stronghold, secretly in the cabins of the freed people, upon forbidden premises, or by secret meetings upon premises, the consent to occupy which had been secretly given.

Of the Democrats, one party rode through the county as K. K. K.'s, threatening and endeavoring to *scare* the freed people from their right to vote. They did not dare to kill, because of the sterling qualities of the Freedman's Bureau agent.* But freedmen were whipped and "bundled" out of their houses without warning and driven upon the highway.

On election day the "chairman" of the Democratic party and his numerous coadjutors fastened themselves upon Charles and the General, and assumed to be their "protectors" and "defenders" against calumny or personal violence, thinking by this means to arouse a suspicion in the minds of

---

* There was but one Republican hung during that campaign.

the freed people that, at the last moment, they had been either converted, bribed, or driven to join the side of "the people." And such reports were circulated far and near.

Merchants deliberately rolled out of their warehouses barrels of flour, huge sides of bacon, or pork, or tossed out pairs of shoes, boots, pants, coats, hats, dresses, nay, money, which was freely and openly tendered to the freed people, in consideration of their consent to be led to the polls by one of their former masters and there voted for what *they called* "the people's ticket." Lawyers, doctors, ministers, planters turned out personally and worked throughout the election as though they were working for life or for liberty.

Nay, more, fair women, old, and those of tender years, turnd out and cooked food, went upon the street, and personally solicited by coaxing and by coddling black and white negroes, votes for this "people's ticket."

"The human hornet" was omnipresent, irresistible, irrepressible. Now on horseback, hunting for voters coming from the country, now running towards Charles or the General, as though he would ride them down to give "the chairman" or some one of his aids an opportunity to interfere for their protection, Henry Dixon was a host in himself.

So persistent were "the chairman" and his aids in their attentions to Charles and the General, so often did they have to "interfere" to "protect" them, so completely were they hemmed in and deprived of the power of locomotion by the crowd pressing about them, the day must have been lost but for the sagacity, courage, and fidelity of the freedmen themselves.

One of these, W. H. Foote, was as active, zealous, and effective for the Republicans as Dixon was for the Democrats. He went everywhere—into the most violent and blood-thirsty crowds of whites—with head erect, brave words of cheer for friends, and only defiance for enemies. He was a "newcomer," and little known.*

* He was a native of Vicksburg.

His audacity shocked the " whites " as the sudden appearance of some unexpected and invincible force upon the battle-
field will shock a grand army about to clutch a great victory.
Planters, merchants, doctors, lawyers, all who did not know
him, said:

" Why ! look at that nigro; who is he ?   He has the audacity of a white man !   Where is he from ?"

Before they had time to rally, Foote would have accomplished his business—retaken some hapless freedman captured by the Democrats, inspired him to fidelity just as he
was ready to surrender, and would be gone to some other
quarter of the town on similar duty.

Hearing that a large body—about four hundred voters—
on their way in to vote, had been halted by Dixon and others
of his party, just over the brow of Peak Tenariffe, he procured a horse, rode out to the place, and, when met by Dixon
with a threat that if he interfered they would shoot him, he
replied: "Shoot and be d—d!" Then, turning to the
freedmen, he cried out, " Men, this is our day. The new
constitution is for our freedom as well as that of our former
masters. If ye reject it, ye reject liberty. Follow me!" They
all obeyed.

Dixon and his party had told these freedmen that Captain
Morgan, the General and all the other Yankees "done
sold out and left the country" that very morning, and,
if they went to town there would be bloodshed, because the
white people never would submit to be governed by their
slaves. Surprised and overwhelmed by the audacity of
Foote, nearly the whole party had deposited their ballots
before "the enemy" could recover. Then there would have
been bloodshed but for the cool head and brave heart of
Charles.

Learning of what had been done, the party that had held
him prisoner for above three hours broke, and joining their
comrades from other points were about to break the "line,"
as the long file of Republican voters which Foote had res-

cued, was called. Being released, and divining the cause, Charles pursued them, and arrived upon the ground just in time to place himself between the angry and now half-crazed whites and Foote and a handful of freedmen, who, armed mostly with sticks, were "stanin' thar groun'," and " talkin' back " to the whites in a manner most exasperating— to them. Seeing Charles' movement, several of the " guard " who had done but little else during the election but to keep near him and the General, and certain other very solid freed-men, gathered close in around him, literally making a shield for him of their bodies.

But his cool, calm, unimpassioned words—he had pur-posely left his pistol at home that day—stilled the storm after a brief spell. The whites put up their pistols. Foote and one or two of his party put up theirs. The sticks went back into service as canes, and, so, through similar trials, hair-breadth escapes, and exhibitions of sagacity, fidelity, and courage, the election passed and the day, in Yazoo, was won for the Republicans, without the loss of life.

CHAPTER XXVIII.

DO SOUTHERNERS HAVE PREJUDICE AGAINST COLOR—TWO MORE

BRICKS—AN APOLOGY.

AT that first *general* election in Yazoo I was not present, and the facts here given relative to it are faithfully set down as they were detailed to me subsequently over and over again by both the General and Charles, scores of the freedmen, and others, Republicans and Democrats.

There were several counties in the State without active capable Republican leadership.

Yazoo had more than her share, so I had been detailed for service in the State-at-lage. There is one county in the north of Mississippi where at the time of which I write the blacks outnumbered the whites two to one, and where there was a strong "Union element" before the war. In the course of my canvass it was announced that Judge Loring and myself would visit the county-seat of that county on a certain date "for the purpose of addressing the people upon the issues of the day"—our new constitution.

Arriving there on the day appointed we were surprised to find that, although public announcement of the meeting had been duly made, there was no one present nor any sign of preparation for the speaking.

After supper, guided by a genial host, we were seated on the ample gallery surrounding the low story-and-a-half hotel on three sides, enjoying our cigars just as the moon lifting herself above the grove of China trees which surrounded the court-house, deepened by contrast the mystic shadows that hung like a pall over the dense forest of cypress and gum which covered the lowlands between us and the Mississippi River. The notes of the mocking-bird reached our ears from the valley below. The soft and gentle air was odorous with the fragrance of sweet flowers. Our journey with horses had been long, our supper excellent and our cigars were luxurious. One after another the neighbors and townspeople dropped in —for the Yankees had come—took seats upon the porch, its long steps, in chairs upon the ground in front, upon benches scattered about, or, lay down upon the warm earth; all chatting about their goods, their crops, their horses, their neighbors, or politics. Nearly all were smoking like ourselves. There was no drunkenness nor any liquor drinking. Below us lay their homes and firesides.

They had heard there was to be a speaking there that day. "Oh! yes; but it was their busy season and they had not 'low'd to go nohow." "Why were none of the colored people out ? " the judge inquired of the principal lawyer of the place.

" Well, our people didn't think it was best."

In the course of a discussion between one of the physicians of the place, a person of undoubted skill and much learning in his profession, I drew out the acknowledgment that, after all, it was not so much the " disfranchising clauses " of the new constitution that " our people " objected to as another clause, viz: Section 22, of Article XII, relating to concubinage; for, while hotly replying to some criticisms 1 had advanced upon the nature of the canvass inaugurated by the leaders of the party opposed to the ratification of the new constitution, that popular physician exclaimed:

" Why, sir, that so-called constitution elevates every nigro wench in this State to the equality of ouah own daughters. The monstrous thing ! Look at it faw a moment ! Ever since Washington's time—and he understood it—the world wide fame of the fair ladies of the South faw beauty, faw refinement, and faw chastity has been ouah proudest boast. This vile thing you call a constitution robs us of that too."

" My good sir, how do you make that out ? "

" Possibly you all are ignorant of the effects of the work you've been doing down there at Jackson. But that only illustrates another objection ou' people have to anything you all may do.   Such work ought never to be entrusted to strangers, faw the very good and sufficient reason that they can't be expected to know the peculiarities of the people to be affected by it. Everybody who has resided in the South long enough to get acquainted with ou' people and thar ways must know that the nigro women have always stood between ouah daughters and the superabundant sexual energy of ouah hot-blooded youth.   And, by G—d, sir, youah so-called constitution tears down the restrictions that the fo'sight of ouah statesmen faw mo' than a century has placed upon the nigro race in ouah country.   And, if you all ratify it and it is fo'ced on the people of the State, all the d—n nigro wenches in the country will believe they're just as good as the finest lady in the land; and they'll think themselves too good faw thar place, and ouah young men'll be driven back upon the white ladies, and we'll have prostitution like you all have it in the North, and as it is known in other countries.   I tell you, sir, it'll raise h—l generally 'twixt ouah young men, and the nigros, too.   The end of it all will sho'ly be the degradation of ouah own ladies to the level of ouah wenches—the brutes ! "

During this speech neither the speaker nor any of his auditors appeared to be in jest.   On the contrary they were all in sober earnest, and while it was being delivered that *philosopher* was the center of interest.   Full twenty of his neighbors and fellow-townsmen heard this argument thus presented, and not a voice was raised in disapproval, or to modify in the slightest degree the force of the only inference to be drawn from it in its bearing upon the character of the women of the State, no less than the men.

Hardly were we comfortably in bed when we heard a knocking at the door, so faint at first that we did not know what it was. The Judge sprang out and opened it while I stood ready for defence. A young freedman crept in, trembling so from fear we could ill make out anything he said. At last, by putting this and that together, we learned that the freed people who had heard of the meeting would have atended only the "white geutlemens" sent word that there would be "a fight" in town that day.

There had never been a Republican meeting in the county, nor yet a school for colored children, and we afterward learned that fully half of the colored population did not know they were free.

I ought to add here, in justice to the women of the South and to myself no less, that I could not then have been brought to utter in support of any cause such reasoning as that physician advanced against our new constitution. Even now when the cause of truth, seeking to promote human liberty and happiness by meeting out simple justice to the negroes of the South, imperiously demands that I shall sacrifice my own pride, my own feelings and my own "interests" upon its holy altar, I have brought the incident forward and given it a place here only because it illustrates better than any other I might give, the utter absence of *prejudice against color* on the part of the *native* whites of Mississippi.

The reader will therefore pardon this digression from the general course of my narrative. I promised to confine it to Yazoo. I have ventured beyond that county in this instance only because the time, place and circumstances surrounding all the parties to the incident seem, to me, to make it fit in more snugly than any other I might mention, with the bricks that form the base of the completed structure.

CHAPTER XXIX.

"HOW ARE YEW, MORGIN? "—DEFEATED BUT NOT CAST DOWN—
TIMELY SUCCOR—" GRAND OLD FLAG."—IT IS OVER - -A SEARCH-
ING OF HEARTS.

ALTHOUGH Yazoo and a number of other counties were
carried for the constitution in the State, it failed of
ratification. And as soon as the struggle was over, I found
the " little garrison of the Yankee stronghold " in mourn-
ing. But the town was in holiday attire, and in place
of angry words, threatening gesture, fierce looks, and oppro-
brious epithets, I was greeted all the way there and upon
my arrival with only laughter and ridicule, accompanied
with requests intended to be sarcastic.

" How are *yew*, Morgin ?"

" Say, got any money left over from yo'r last investment?"

" What are convention warrants goin' at now ?"

" G'wain back on to Tokeba ?"

" How's the saw-mill business ?"

" Say ! the General's done gone dead."

" Got yo' carpet-bag packed ?"

" When ye g'wain to start ?"

" Have you found out what O'oophie means yet ?"

"Good-bye—ta, ta !"

The only response made by the little garrison was as complete a surprise to " the enemy " as any the anti-reconstructionists had yet suffered.

When they came down town next morning the first thing which attracted their notice was "the old flag," flying from a window of the stronghold.

There was no mistaking it. There it moved in all its original glory. "Not a stripe erased, nor star obscured." And from its folds rang out, in tones so loud and clear that none mistook their meaning, "The little garrison of the Yankee stronghold in Yazoo may die—it will never surrender."

This was the first "Yankee flag" that the air had been permitted to kiss in Yazoo since the "Yankee soldiers" of General Sherman withdrew from that region. The only one planted in the faces of Yazoo rebels by a private citizen since that one which the Unionist had hauled down in 1860, in obedience to the "will of the people" of Yazoo, enforced with a "grape vine."

The audacity of the little garrison proved not only their fidelity; it was also their shield.

Taken "all aback" by it the rebels lost their cunning. The white boys threw stones at the flag, white male rebels scoffed at it, white female rebels abandoned that street as if infected with small-pox; or if, as was sometimes the case, they were compelled by some emergency to pass that way, on approaching it they would lift their skirts, cross over to the other side of the street, turn up their noses, turn away their faces, and, it was said by themselves, hold their breath until they had passed through the region of atmosphere infected by it.

Grand old flag! for so it seemed to us then. Its silken folds and gay colors diverted from our heads the bolts which "the enemy" had forged, out of their malice and greed, with which to further afflict the garrison should it still refuse to surrender, and all unconsciously emptied them out again upon the heads of its traducers.

Grand old flag! for so it seemed to the freed people. Men, women and children who beheld it with upturned faces, moistened eyes and grateful hearts, while they gathered from its ringing tones the courage to hope or, as they often did, to stop in the street, lift from their heads the ragged covering they called a hat, and give three cheers for the "Flag of Freedom."

Grand old flag! for so the Unionists said when, as some did after a detour which took them through the livery stable, and up into the stronghold by the backway, they came to crave leave to kiss it.

" Grand old flag! "

Here is an editorial from the Meridian *Mercury*, of July 7th, 1868 :

"IT IS OVER.

" With a sigh of relief, thank God, we can announce that it is over; the election, the most disgusting, disgraceful, and degrading thing ever devised by the malice of man. Thank God, it is over ! and pray His Holy name to remove the sin-created and sin-creating thing, *negro suffrage*, the most abominable of all abominations; the ' sum of all villainies,' to which the sin of slavery is as snowy white to coal black; to remove it from the land, and sink the hell-deserving authors of it to everlasting perdition ! Confound them; blast them with His righteous anger, and sink them to the lowest depths—deeper down than the sympathy of the infernal spirits that inhabit the blazing regions of hell can ever reach—aye, down to the bottom of the ' bottomless pit,' were a righteous prayer of every good, God-fearing man and woman, and should ascend fervently to heaven, welling up from the depths of humbled but trusting hearts.

'' To say that the Great Ruler will not listen to the prayer, if we pray fervently and walk uprightly, and keep ourselves unspotted and free from all contamination with the accursed thing, and hate carpet-baggers and scalawagers, and proudly scorn to debase ourselves, as they do, to say that He will not listen to such a prayer, is to impugn God's justice. Let us all pray to God and keep our consciences clean, remembering that God permits them who will to defile themselves.

"And when we pray fervently and trustingly to God for help, let us not forget that He helps them that help themselves. If we expect heaven's [aid, we need not lie supinely and wait for it ; it will never come. God loves positive men, earnest men, working men ; and as fathers bestow the largest patrimony upon their sons who are working and thrifty, and cut off the worthless with a penny, so God's help comes to those who work in His cause.

" The first preparation for the great work before us is to shape and temper our firm resolves until they be hard as adamant and as true as steel. Then with the skull-and-cross-bones of the " Lost Cause " before us, we will swear that ' This is a white man's government;

and, trusting in our firm purpose, our good right arms and the God of Right, we will maintain it so!'

" If we falter now, we shall be damned ; and let us see to it, that he be damned who does falter. Out upon a recreant white man who turns his back upon his race to marshal and direct negroes who are howling like savages at the ballot-box in the work of degradation ! Condemn him ! Spit upon him !

"Now that it is over, let there be a searching of hearts. It can scarcely be possible that those who have participated in the late struggle have been contaminated with negro suffrage, or can look upon it with the least degree of allowance. Those even who have been most active and successful in the canvass with the negroes, and who in their enthusiasm may have been led to invoke God's blessing on the 'glorious colored Democracy,' should have the sternest face set against the abomination of negro suffrage. They have seen the monster, seen it good, and should have learned to hate it with intensity. But, let there be an inward searching of hearts, and if there be any weakness, any faltering in the cause of white supremacy, a manly struggle will overcome it.

"Could Salmon P. Chase have been in Meridian during the three days of our election, and seen what was to be seen, in his heart he must have been cured of his abominable notions of universal suffrage. Look back at the things we have passed through and be a white man.

" In whatever we do to maintain supremacy of race, remember it will and should recoil upon us, and defeat our ends and aims, if we forget to be forbearing with the negro, and just and honorable in all our dealings with him ; and yet, while we are all this, we must make him understand that we are the men we were when we held him in abject bondage, and make him feel that when forbearance ceases to be a virtue, he has aroused a power that will control him or destroy him.

" Thank God the election is over ! And now let us dismiss it from our minds as the paramount thought, resume our usual avocations, and strive again to make a living, and enough over to pay the taxes the negroes and their allies are pressing out of us by force of the arms of the Federal Government, as best we can, until the white men can assert their rights, and suppress the robbery.''

The editorial comments of at least one of the two Yazoo papers were equally felicitous. I had preserved them, but they have been lost or mislaid in the long years which have intervened.

CHAPTER XXX.

A " DEMOCRATIC SCHOOL " AND WHAT CAME OF IT—SLIGHT DIFFERENCES OF OPINION.

DURING that campaign, just before the day of the election, the anti-reconstructionists hit upon a new plan for capturing the votes of " our nigros." It was quite novel, as the following from the Yazoo *Banner* will show :

"DEMOCRATIC SCHOOL.

"YAZOO CITY, *June* 26, 1868.

"We the undersigned citizens of Yazoo City, promise to pay monthly the sums opposite our names for a school for the express purpose of educating the children of the members of the Colored Conservative Club of Yazoo City, provided the sum of fifty dollars is subscribed. The school to be controlled by a board of trustees selected by the club, and to continue for a session of five months :

Wm. Byrns...	$1 00 per month.	
J. L. Covert...	2 00 "	"
Charles C. Dyer..	1 00 "	"
M. Dusseldorf...........	1 00 "	"
M. B. Kellogg...........	1 00 "	"
M. Gusdofer...	1 00 "	".
Stern & Lurch........................	1 00 "	"
John Link..	1 00 "	"
John Kent...	1 00 "	"
Dr. H. B. Kidd.........................	1 00 "	"
Rosenthal & Deles..	2 00 "	"
Charles W. Boyd..	1 00 "	"
H. Halder & Bro...	1 00 "	"
James Cotter........................	1 00 "	".
G. W. Brantley..	1 00 "	"
W. H. Mangum......	1 00 "	"

H. C. Tyler	1 00	per month.
Joseph Schmitt	1 00	" "
N. G. Nye	1 00	" "
Ed. Drenning	1 00	" "
John T. Heth	1 00	" "
M. W. Smith	1 00	" "
W. S. Epperson	1 00	" "
S. J. Pepper	1 00	" "
W. H. Patterson	0 25	" "
S. Patterson	0 25	" "
W. Z. McCracken	1 00	" "
P. M. Doherty	1 00	" "
R. E. Craig	1 00	" "
F. Barksdale	1 00	" "
H. Harrison	1 00	" "
R. Power	1 00	" "
J. O. Hunter	1 00	" "
Peter Lander	1 00	" "
Stout & Patterson	1 00	" "
Alex. Smith	0 50	" "
J. N. Ratcliff	0 50	" "
M. Berry	1 00	" "
G. A. Gibbs	1 00	" "
G. Andrews	1 00	" "
Samuel W. Jones	1 00	" "
John Henley	1 00	" "
J. C. Prewett	1 00	" "
P. F. McGinly	1 00	" "
B. S. Hudson	1 00	" "
James Ellis	0 50	" "
W. Y. Gadberry	1 00	" "
E. B. Rundle	0 50	" "
P. Dever	0 50	" "
Thomas Ellis	1 00	" "
F. W. Battail	0 50	" "
Robert Bowman	1 00	" "
Cash	1 00	" "
H. S. Wilson	1 00	" "

It was the *Banner* of July 3, 1868. I am able to recognize in the list of names signed to that pledge some who after-ward became personal friends, some who became Republicans, and some most worthy men. But certainly one of the number was a "Grand Cyclops" of the kukluxes, and was present on that memorable occasion when news was received of Stanton's victory over Johnson.

I am sure that all who still survive—for some are dead—will pardon me for making use of their names, with which to adorn my narrative.

But there was to be no peace for that school. The bant-

ling came into existence in the midst of such a fire of wrath
against the Yankee stronghold of Yazoo, and all who affiliated
with its garrison, North or South, in any way, that it endured
but a sickly existence; there could not have been more than
a half dozen or so pupils at the start, and it never numbered
more than twenty. At the same time the school in the little
church we helped to build was overflowing.

The kind-hearted, sympathetic editor of the Ohio *Progress*
little dreamed, when he wrote, to what uses his warm lines
were to be put. But here they are, though my reader will
have to wade through the *Banner's* comments, before coming
to them.

From the Yazoo *Banner* of October 18, 1868 :

" OUR DEMOCRATIC COLORED SCHOOL—WHAT AN OHIO RADICAL
THINKS OF IT.

'· The school established by our citizens last summer for the benefit
of colored children generally, but more especially for the children of
colored Democrats, is, we are glad know, in a most flourishing condition. There are now about twenty pupils, all of whom, we are
informed by Mr. Richards, the teacher, are making fair progress in
their studies, and give most satisfactory evidence of substantial
improvement. The little darkies are delighted, their parents are
gratified at the interest thus displayed in behalf of their children by
their white friends, and in every way the institution may be declared
a decided success.

" But to show our people how their efforts to improve the colored
people and how their benevolence is appreciated by an Ohio radical,
we reproduce an article on the subject of our colored school from a
radical paper called the *Aid to Progress* which is published in the town
of Wilmington, Ohio. The editor of this paper, we believe, was
formerly a carpet-bagger, and was operating in Mississippi on the
ignorance and credulity of the negroes but a few months ago as a
means of earning a livelihood. But strange and unaccountable as it
may seem, he became weary of enduring the scorn and contumely of
respectable people and rummaging about negro quarters at night, and
accordingly returned to Ohio, where he became the editor of a mean,
dirty little radical newspaper.

" Noticing an article in the Vicksburg *Times*, in which it was stated
that a competent Democratic teacher was wanted to take charge of
the colored school in this place, and being accustomed, like every
other radical, to systematically maligning the Southern people and

tracing every act of theirs to an unworthy or dishonorable motive, he makes the following comments on the aforesaid notice:

" 'Let whoever reads the above remember that hundreds of men and women have been foully used, many of them murdered by those rebels, because they undertook after the surrender of the rebel armies to teach the ignorant negro. Thinking that they will be able to prevent them from acting with the party which gave them their freedom, these base wretches are now pretending to want them taught. Is there anything too criminal for modern Democracy to engage in? The negroes should of course be taught; but what is the motive by which this call for "a competent Democratic teacher" is prompted? The most damning that ever moved the heart of man. It is to use the vote and action of a human being as a means by which to enslave him. The treachery and villainy of those rebels stands without a parallel in the history of man. And yet there are honest men here in the North simple enough to believe that they can be trusted with the government of these States.' "

I have no doubt that everything *Aid to Progress* said upon this subject was equally as patriotic and sensible as the foregoing. But the *Banner* would not allow its readers to have any more of it, for on November 13, 1868, that paper closed the discussion thus:

" The Ohio radical editor, whose article on our colored school we copied and commented on some time ago, replies to us at some length, but as he says nothing worth noticing, we will let the ex-carpet bagger have the last word ; so, good-bye, scalawag ! "

My reader will not fail to note, however, that the writer in the *Banner* has dropped the word " Democratic," and now calls it a "colored school." But then, that was after the two elections which were to be held during the " five months," for which a school was pledged by all of the above signers, viz : our election in Mississippi, and the Presidential election had passed, and when Grant had become the choice of the nation for President. It is evident, however, that his respect for a " carpet-bagger " or a " scalawag " had not materially increased. I ought to add that the " Democratic school " thus established, did not long survive the election of 1868.

CHAPTER XXXI.

SOME OTHER THINGS ABOUT THE FLAG OF THE U. S. IN 1868, IN
YAZOO, MISSISSIPPI—STARING AT VACANCY—A DISCOVERY THAT
WAS NOT PATENTED—HOW, WHY AND WHEN "THE SOUTH
SOLIDFIED."

THE flag of the United States in 1868 brought to the little
garrison hemmed within that Yazoo stronghold a season of peace. For a little while, the lock which during the
campaign for the ratification of the constitution had been
restored by the Unionist over the way to its place on the
cistern was again removed, and the colored children could
gather together in the Sabbath-school that Charles and General Greenleaf had organized in the little church on the hill,
that we had helped to build, without serious consequences to
any one. Charles, the General or myself, could go to the
post-office for our mail all alone without peril of life or limb;
the shoemaker's wife could buy provisions *in the market,* and
the "guard" resume their usual occupation.

But the captain in the office below, with "an ancestry,"
was in a very bad way. He had been an opium-eater for
several years. The habit had grown upon him of late, until
it supplanted desire for strong drink and for tobacco; though
Rarety still cared for him and ministered to his comfort
variously. Shortly after the flag was flung to the breezes in

Yazoo, from our stronghold window, he was "observed to be worse." The lower edge of the bunting reached down so near his doorway, that he had to walk directly under its folds on passing out or into his lair. Its shadows flecked his door-sill, and at times darkened his window. It was more than he could stand. The deep sighs and low groanings as of a soul in purgatory, which for months had ascended through the ceiling and into the rooms above, where the Yankee outcasts slept, grew more frequent and pathetic as the agonizing fever for more of the subtle drug wrought out its spell upon the wretched sufferer.

Since that day when all three of us—Charles, the General and myself—had solemnly accepted kinship with the negroes, on thoughts of abandoning them and returning North had been allowed expression within the sacred precints of the stronghold, if indeed one ever existed. But the hours hung heavily upon our hands, and the already lengthened visage of my brother grew longer, and its expression more stern and sad. His seasons of abstraction, when he would sit staring at vacancy with an air of listless unconcern, the antithesis of his former self, grew more frequent, and lengthened from moments into hours. Rousing him from these spells I would challenge him for a walk. Our course always terminated upon the summit of one of the bluffs overlooking the lowlands.

In spite of the disasters which had befallen our plans, a few moments here would bring back to his cheek the old glow, into his mind the old vigor, and into his heart all the strength of our old hopes. It was during such times that we formed new plans. Our experience in the swamps had taught us that nature had wrought a system of drainage and of levees that no hand of man or brain could excel.

The entire Delta of the Mississippi is honeycombed with rivers and bayous, which constitute at all seasons of the year a natural outlet for any surplus water that can come through the channels above, augmented as they often are, by heavy falls of rain below them. And whether the tide flow in or out, these lateral ditches, so to speak, have and perform the same function; in the one case guiding the water pressed back by the down flowing torrents from above, out of the central channel and into the lagoons, brakes and lakes, which throughout the region are as numerous as the central channels or lateral ditches. In the centuries that have passed all these natural courses have become more or less clogged from natural causes, such as from accumulated vegetable growth, stumps of trees, logs, and from crumbled earth, etc., and therefore cannot act uninterruptedly. So it has come about that the pent up waters have swollen above the banks of these natural courses, and found a vent out upon the arable lands, destroying in their relentless, tireless encroachment many millions of hard-earned wealth, and even the necessities of life, in a single year, as often has been the case, since slavery found and occupied the inexhaustible soil of this wonderful country.

These overflows carry out of the channels and deposit upon their margins, on every occasion, the debris and the soils which they have dragged down from the mountains and the intervening plains, thus creating by the course of nature a system of levees, compared with which all the efforts of man must dwarf into littleness. I don't recollect, if I ever knew, which of us—Charles or I—made the discovery; I think it was simultaneous.

But certain it is, that he made the mathematical calculations which resulted in a demonstration to us that further leveeing was but a waste of effort, that the remedy lay in aiding the channels by straightening them, thereby increasing the velocity of the flow of the water in some instances; by narrowing or confining them, thereby forcing the current to deepen its own channel in some; by dredging in some; by removing the "obstruction" in all; and by a system of reservoirs upon the main channels above, as the Missouri and Ohio, from which the flow could be regulated in such a manner as to maintain for navigation an uniform depth of water in the current of the main channel the whole year round. By such means there would be constituted such artificial aids to the natural flow of the waters, the volume of which is each year increased as the great Basin is opened up for agricultural uses, as would forever remove all danger of overflow of the lowlands.

Then Charles would say, pointing to the vast region below: "Yonder lies an empire surpassing India, surpassing the Nile; unequaled."

And we would descend to the stronghold with a relish for dinner, however humble and scanty, as it often was.

Then neither of us had read Ellet's report of his survey of the Ohio River, nor Humphrey and Abbott's report of their survey of the Mississippi Nor had Captain Eads discovered to the country his scheme for removing the bar at the mouth of the last-named river.

The vote of Mississippi would not be counted at the ensuing election for President—thanks to the kuklux and anti-reconstructionists, who by fraud, violence and murder, had defeated our new constitution—unless, as many in Yazoo insisted ought to be done, the "sovereign white" people went forward and held the election in their own way, as in times before the war, and trusted to a Democratic President and Congress, which they affected to believe would be triumphantly elected by the North, to recognize its validity.

There was good reason for their faith in such a result; for of the numerous drummers for Northern mercantile houses whom I met in the State, I do not recollect but one who did not loudly proclaim his own faith in it.

To be sure, there were many who were not sincere in such professions. One of these candidly acknowledged to me that he believed Grant would be chosen. "But," said he, "when one is in Rome, he must do as the Romans do, especially if he has goods to sell."

Occasionally visitors from the North came to Yazoo, travellers, prospectors, and such as had relatives among the "old

citizens." These never came near us, and always appeared
to seek out for counsel, or for information relative to the
country, the very same "high-toned, honorable gentlemen,"
who had most heartily welcomed us in 1865, and they were
always taken in charge by them, just as we had been. We
often saw them thus together, walking the streets or riding
out to take a look at the country.

Whenever we met such parties, as was sometimes the case,
the strangers were almost certain to be informed that we
were " no-account fellows, who had come down there from
God only knew where, and by ' consorting' with nigros
' from choice,' had brought upon ourselves the scorn and contempt of all the ' best citizens.' " The only other thing we
had succeeded in, was our effort to " stir up strife between the
races." This we had accomplished so far as to entirely destroy the affection " our nigros" had always felt for their masters.

The logical effect of all that was to array against us the
feelings of all " new-comers" and visitors, and the open contempt which that class of persons were sure to manifest
toward the outcasts, was always "happily" utilized by the
anti-reconstructionists in still further solidifying the masses
of the whites against us, our example and our opinions, and
per consequence, against the Congressional plan of reconstruction; for, as those people had already had ample proof of
the estimation in which we were held by " discreet Federal
army officers " and soldiers, and by the " Northern mercantile classes," represented by their agents, and by the " commanding general," and by " the President," now that we
were despised and contemned by all travellers, visitors and
new-comers, why should not the Unionist of 1860 and the
masses of the poor whites conclude that we were indeed " no-
account fellows," and finally come to believe what had been
told them over and over again by the entire Southern press
and by *all* the white leaders, that the Congressional plan had
been engineered through Congress, and was being sustained

by only a handful of fanatics like Sumner and Stevens, together with the "licentious" and "free love" elements of the country, represented by such women as Harriet Beecher Stowe, and such men as Henry Ward Beecher. Besides these weighty influences, there were others equally worthy of consideration and equally if not more potential with the great mass of the white people.

It had not anywhere been denied that the South fought for independence as a means of better securing their "slave property," or that the North fought for the preservation of the Union, the emancipation of slaves having followed as one of the most unavoidable incidents of the struggle. And up to this time the Southern press had been largely taken up with quotations from the press of the North confirmatory of that view of the cause for the war, and of the chief result of it.

Every utterance by a Northern Republican of note, or by a Northern Republican journal, that was, in fact, hostile to emancipation or to negro suffrage, or that could be made to so appear, was quoted throughout the press of the South, and commented on with direct application to the local leaders in the reconstruction movement. Every Northern newspaper account of violence at the North upon negroes, or of hostility to them was copied by the Southern newspapers and turned upon the reconstructionists. Every account of a defalcation or of official misconduct by a Republican at the North; in fact, everything happening at the North which was likely to aid them in bringing the Republican party, or any of its members, into disrepute, whether of an official or private nature, of a political or social character, was copied from the Northern newspapers into the columns of the Southern journals, and always accompanied with suitable editorial comment, calculated to show by contrast the higher morality and superior virtues of the people of the South. More than this, old Unionists were coddled, and the fact was pointed out to them that, notwithstanding their "well-known fondness for the Yankees," they were no better off than "we all seces

sionists," nor "half as much thought of." Had they ever
been reimbursed for their losses? Had they been shown any
greater consideration than even the "chief of we all, ouah
President Davis?" And the Unionists were compelled to
admit that they had not been. They did not stop there. They
tried to coddle the negro; pointed out to him the fact that
he had as yet never received anything but promises from
the Yankees; read to them the "news from the North,"
showing how some hapless negro had been hung for marrying a white woman; how, perhaps, it was Fred. Douglass had
been refused a ride in the white folks' car, or a seat at the
white folks' table, " thar whar yo' god Mogin come frum;"
how some great Republican leader had spoken against
"nigros votin'," and never failed to conclude the interview
by asking the poor freedmen, homeless, landless, almost
naked, as so many of them were, "Whar yo' fohty acres o'
land and a mool, de Yankees done gi'e to you all ?"

Alas! the slave's dream of freedom had disappeared along
with that "sour apple tree" upon which "we all Yankees"
had so often hung "Jeff Davis," dropping only "apples of
Sodom" upon the bare head of the mystified freedman.
He could not answer his old master's criticisms of the Yankees.
He did not even try, but he never failed to resent, in some
manner, if in no other than a sullen silence, any criticism
upon General Greenleaf, Captain Morgan, or " de Kunnel."
He knew he had never been promised land nor mules by the
Yankees, certainly not by the General, my brother nor by
myself. He had never expected to acquire land in that way.
And that freedman knew, as " we all Yankees " well knew,
that his master's reference to it was but a bitter sarcasm.
That master knew that that freedman was entitled to something for his long years of unrequited toil, and his taunt was
nothing but the irony of the cruel wrongs the centuries had
inflicted upon the black man through the divine right of the
white man's power. All these facts, when taken together,
made it clear to the Unionists, with rare exceptions, that the

thing we sought for there in Yazoo, after the defeat of our new constitutiou, had little support anywhere, North as well as South, except among the negroes and a "baker's dozen" of fanatical leaders in Congress, whose strength with the Northern people would be found to lay with that dim and uncertain margin which existed between downright lunatics and shrewd far-seeing, self-seeking, money-making Yankees. Therefore the white race in Yazoo solidified.

To be sure there were then, as there are now, at least two parties among the whites. One believed that slavery was unconstitutionally destroyed, and that therefore the North would have to pay for the slaves—if only the South could hold out just a little longer. The other party was composed of those who had no faith in the sincerity of Northern professions of regard or sympathy for Unionists or negroes, and meant to "lookout for number one."

We believed, indeed felt certain, that we knew to the contrary. We believed, almost knew, that Grant would be elected. It was thus reduced to a question of endurance.

The last dollar that I had been able to raise by the sale of my warrants, received for per diem while a member of the constitutional convention, I had spent in defraying my expenses in the State canvass.

Charles had staked everything on Tokeba and in the sawmill, and we were both too proud to ask our friends for any more help.

The General had sent his wife and children to a place of refuge, and, although he had lost everything that he had invested there, he had received a small sum from some quarter, which he generously put into "the pot," thus keeping that prime essential "a boiling."

My "convention suit," however, was getting threadbare, and Charles sorely needed a new hat and a new pair of pants.

CHAPTER XXXII.

THE WAR OF THE BADGES—HEROIC COLORED WOMEN—HOW MIS-
SISSIPPIANS VOTED AS THEY FOUGHT IN 1868— MORE BRICKS.

IN spite of our poverty we kept the flag flying from the
window of the stronghold.

The freed people had observed that the Democrats were
wearing Seymour and Blair badges, and heroically started
a fund for the purchase of some Grant and Colfax badges.
The little garrison were able to contribute a few "last dimes"
for such a purpose, and with the aid of a handful of Northerners, poor as ourselves, and a few Unionists, a sufficient
amount was finally gotten together to pay for several hundred. They were at first entrusted to only the more courageous of the freedmen, but their number increased so rapidly
that very soon every Loyal League and every club possessed
as many as one or two, and at least one person on many of
of the plantations had one.

"Jes' to let um know we doan' 'low' ter s'render," as
Uncle Peter put it, these badges were to be worn squarely
upon the left breast, and as nearly over the heart as convenient. By changing about every patriotic freedman and
Unionist in the county would be able to wear one of the
badges at least one whole day before the election.

Now, the Democrats, old and young, male and female, had
worn their badges without any regard whatever for our feelings.

It has not been my purpose to fortify any statements I may make with "documentary evidence." However desirable such evidence may be deemed by some at this stage of our narrative, by the time the reader has followed me to the end, he will consent to waive his own desire for it. Nor do I now intend, by bringing forward the following, to violate this rule, but rather to supply the basic element of the narrative with an acid it may otherwise be found to want. It appeared in the local columns of *The Banner* in its very first issue after the arrival of " our badges," dated October, 1868, and runs as follows :

" A large number of Grant and Colfax badges have been distributed among the colored population of Yazoo City during the last week by the carpet-bag agents of radicalism. The freedmen are profusely decorated with "counterfeit presentiments " of the radical candidates for President and Vice-President, no doubt praising the liberality of their radical friends in presenting them with these little ornaments free of charge. They don't know that *we all* have to pay for them in the grinding exactions their party inflicts upon us."

There it is, *verbatim et literatim,* just as it stands to this day in the original now on file in my "scrap-book." Its full value will be better appreciated by the reader when the fact is made known that the only " exactions " *our party* had yet " inflicted upon we all " was in the nature of a tax levied by the convention to defray the expenses of per diem of its members—there being no money in the State treasury—and for stationery for its use, etc., the collection of which had been enjoined, and which the anti-reconstructionists had refused to pay.

These badges so excited the ire of " the enemy" that several of our brave friends got themselves into serious trouble on account of them. Woe to the hapless freedman caught wearing one beyond the shadow of the flag flaunting from the Yankee stronghold ! If upon the highway he was sometimes seized by the very first " repentant " rebel who met him and whipped or, at the least, robbed of the priceless treasure.

Some not only talked back, they also struck back, and the Bureau agent had a number of cases before him growing out of such conflicts.

Grave, dignified, " high-toned, honorable gentlemen " debated seriously whether those wearing them ought not to be arrested under the act of their legislature of 1865-'66 prescribing a fine or imprisonment or both in the discretion of the court for " insulting gestures largely, or acts" of " freedmen, free negroes, or mulattoes" against a white man, woman, or child, and many denounced the " practice " as "incendiary," and liable to incite a " wah of races."

" Mr." Foote, as he was called by the freedmen, " Foote," as he was termed by the whites, for his defiance of them, had wrung from even the Democrats so much concession to his dignity, bravely, almost defiantly, wore one, sometimes two, pinned to the lapel of his coat and insisted upon walking upon the pavement while doing so, in utter disregard of Dixon's oft-repeated commands to " walk in the middle of the street, where other niggers go."

These badges were the cause of domestic troubles almost without number; for if a freedman, having obtained one, lacked the courage to wear it at home on the plantation in the presence of "ole marsa and missus" or of " the overseer," his wife would often take it from him and bravely wear it upon her own breast. If in such cases the husband refused to surrender it, as was sometimes the case, and hid it from her or locked it up, she would walk all the way to town, as many as twenty or thirty miles sometimes, and buy, beg, or borrow one, and thus equipped return and wear it openly, in defiance of husband, master, mistress, or overseer.

It was " General Grant's picture ! " How perfectly they could always speak those words and these other, " Abraham Lincoln," even in those earlier days of freedom, and to refuse, neglect, or lack the courage to wear that badge in the clear, far-seeing thought of those poor, "rising" freedmen and women, amounted almost to a voluntary return to slavery. Those badges were also the cause of endless trouble in the families of the anti-reconstructionists ; for the white man's concubine, the mistress' maid, and their cook, were liable to appear in the family circle any day with "Grant's picture" upon their breasts. Their children, mingling and uniting together like any other "happy family," divided into hostile factions, and their quarrels and wranglings often led to bloodshed— from the nose of some over-sensitive white boy of the "recognized" side of the family, or from the backs or legs of some too presumptuous "brat" or "pickaninney" of the "unrecognized" side of the family.

Altogether we concluded that the investment had proved a paying one; for aside from the value of the badge as an auxiliary to "party discipline," it had effect similar to the old flag in diverting from the little Yankee garrison the thoughts of the enemy. But the day of our deliverance was at hand.

CHAPTER XXXIII.

REASONS FOR THEIR FAITH—CERTAIN CITIZENS OBJECT TO THE
RACKET OF THE K. K. K.'S AND AFTERWARD APOLOGIZE—DE-
LIVERANCE—HURRAH FOR GRANT! HURRAH FOR H—L!—" BOT-
TOM RAIL ON TOP"—UNCLE PETER'S WISDOM—MAGNANIMITY OF
FREEDMEN—A REMINISCENCE,

THE operations of the ku-klux-klan, as well as its organization up to this time, had been secretly carried on.

But now, so strong was their faith that the "Democratic
white man's national ticket" would be elected,* this organization began a series of public demonstrations—just before the
day of election—by way of preparation for future service,
as we feared.

* The Jackson *Clarion*, the official organ of the Mississippi Democracy of that date,
in its issue of May —, 1868, contained the following :

THE POLICY AND PROSPECTS OF THE NATIONAL DEMOCRACY.

"The intentions of the national Democracy, in the event of their triumph in the Presidential election, are thus foreshadowed by Colonel Forsyth, of the Mobile *Register*, in a
letter to his paper from Washington City. Our people will see how deep an interest
they have in the success of this grand old party of the Constitution in that election :

"I have taken a good deal of pains to learn what are the sentiments of leading Democrats as to the action of the party, should it win the administration in the November
contest, in reference to Federal policy toward the South. It was a question of the
largest practical interest, whether, should the Democracy come into power, it would
leave the whites of the South to struggle as best they could out of the mire of radical
reconstruction, or whether it would not at once lift them out by the strong hand of
Federal power. I get but one answer to the inquiry, and that is, that the Democracy
will be swift to sweep from the statute books the whole system of military and African
reconstruction as utterly null and void and of no effect, and at once to recognize the
existing white constitutions of the Southern States, and readmit the latter into their
full equality into the Union. I must confess that I did not personally need such assur-

Even at that early day, when gratitude for the negroes' services in the war was still a living thing, and when the hope that "They would probably help, in some trying time to come, to keep the jewel of liberty in the family of freedom,"* had neither been extinguished under the pressure of "great business and commercial interests," nor satisfied by the fulfillment of the prophecy, the "bloody shirt," known by another name then, had been made to do good service in the North. Therefore, the night riders of Yazoo had postponed the execution of their "decrees" against the little garrison of the Yazoo stronghold, fearing its effect upon the "God-and-morality party," and now confined their visits to the unprotected cabins of the freed people, some of whom they dragged from their beds, whipped, forced to surrender their badges, or to take an oath never again to meet with the Loyal Leagues, Republican clubs, or try to vote.

By that means, and by parading the streets until after midnight, blowing tin horns and beating tin pans, they expected to create such a terror in the minds of the freed people as would deter them from coming to the succor of the garrison in the Yankee stronghold, when the final assault should be made upon it.

But their "racket" had an opposite effect. It did not drive the freed people from the town nor prevent them visiting the stronghold in large numbers the two days preceding the election, and on that day, armed with their hard wood sticks. It did, however, disturb the "solid men" of the town in their slumbers, and the *Banner* warned them that they were misdirecting their efforts. That so incensed the "Grand Cy-

ances, for when policy and good faith both point to one course, the result is seldom doubtful. But some Southern friends did deem them necessary. I think that before Congress adjourns the Democrats in that body will make a further declaration and pledge to this effect. * * * * * * * *
"In uttering the results of my own belief, I am able to speak cheering words to our poeple of the future. I have not a doubt of the verity of a deep and widespread popular reaction against radicalism, and, if nothing untoward happens to check its progress, I am prepared to witness a revolution of the masses next November, the like of which has not been known in the annals of American politics. The white stomach is sick unto nausea of the party deification of the negro. It revolts at sharing the powers of Government with him.

* A. Lincoln to Gov. Hahn, March 13, 1864.

clops" that in its next issue that paper apologized as follows, to wit:

" THE KUKLUXES.

" In our local last week regarding the demonstration of the ku-kluxes, or whatever else they were, we meant no disrespect to the organization or its members. We highly approve of the principles and objects of the ku-klux-klan (if we rightly understand them) and all kindred organizations, and our animadversion was intended simply to apply to the unnecessary noise that accompanied the last turnout. We are still of the opinion that no earthly good can be accomplished by blowing tin horns and yelling through town at the dead hour of night."

But now our deliverance had come.

The first glimmer of light from the sun of the advancing new era which we beheld cast such a shadow over the faces of the Democrats that, employing a different figure from that of our " distinguished divine " (himself the " rising " com-mittee of which I was the " distinguished" chairman*) to illustrate the color of a " Yankee's heart," its reflection lighted up the faces of the freed people, old and young, not excepting even Dave Woolridge and Mr. Goosie's ferryman. There was no occult mystery in that fact nor evidence of any re-markable power of divination on the part of the freed people. The laws, customs, and practices of the country had for a century taught the negro to recognize in every white male a master, in every white female a mistress.

Long practice had made them expert in reading the faces of the white people, and their judgment upon the meaning of the various shadings in color, as they came and went, was unerring. The " Chairman of the County Democratic Com-mittee " and the " Grand Cyclops " were the first to receive the news and at once went off and got drunk. The Stock-dales and other "solid men " of the town sought for comfort

---

*During the sitting of the constitutional convention at Jackson, winter '67-8, I was informed by "native-born white ladies " residing in that city that some months after the war this divine preached a sermon there, in the course of which he described the heart of the Yankee as so black "charcoal would make a white mark upon it."

in the bosoms of their families, "recognized and unrecognized."

The white youths appeared on the street with their hands farther down in their pockets if possible than ever. The planters from the country got drunk before starting homeward, and yelled from the backs of their horses as they rode away, reeling to and fro in their saddles, "Hurrah for Grant!" "Hurrah, for hell!" "O'oophie!" "Polecat!" "Carpet-bagger!" and, if perchance they met a group of freedmen, they would stop—as some did—and, as gravely as. their maudlin tongues would permit, inform them:

"Bottom rail on top now, sho 'nuff."

Or perhaps inquire of them:

"What you all g'wain to do now with yo' god, Mawgin— make him Gov'nur?"

If the response was "Yes," as it often was, the rejoinder, as often as not, would be:

"That's right, stan' by yo' friends. Hurrah for Mawgin! Hurrah for hell! Ya-er-hah'r'r! O'oophie! Polecat!"

And ride on.

Its effect upon the freed people surprised every one, even the Yankee garrison, great as its faith was in the intentions, purposes, and manhood of the freed people. Neither the General, Charles, nor myself was prepared for so perfect a vindication of that trust as followed.

Instead of boisterous or even appropriate manifestations of joy at the election of General Grant, the only sign of their delight was manifested in their faces. There was hardly a suggestion from them of a jubilee gathering in honor of the event.

Instead of resenting the commands of Dixon and a few others to walk in the middle of the street, they would always promptly yield the sidewalk to them. Instead of refusing to "uncover and stand with your hat in hand while talking with a white gentleman," they would, as a rule, politely lift

off their hats on such occasions and, if the person were a
"white" lady, remain with the head uncovered until she
should move on. Instead of addressing the whites by their
proper or surnames they continued voluntarily the old practice.

Some of the whites affected to see in this the subtle mock-
ery of disguised insolence. Others insisted that it was due
to their inability to comprehend the great boon of freedom,
and still others that it portended the existence of some deep
laid plot to "rise" and "kill all the whites from the cradle
up."

To us the freedmen explained that it was a "great triber-
lation on ole massa and missus ter be 'bleeged ter give we
po' niggers all on us up. Kase dey done got oost t'wour
bein' deirn fur so long dat 'peers like 'twe'l broke da' hearts.
So nigger 'low he 'jes go long widouten hu'tin' da' feelin's,"
as Uncle Peter said.

"My color got no lan' yit, an' skasely no larnin', an' heap
better ha' de good will nor de bad will ole mars fur a spell
yit," Uncle David said.

"The colored people fear the Lord," said the pastor of the
little church on the hill that we helped to build, "and desire
to show their manners to everybody. 'Sides, my people
alwus did like the white people."

"It'll be a long time before the race'll get shut of all feeling
of dependence upon the white race. Great many of this
present generation never will. Besides as for me, though I
consider myself just as good as any white man that ever
lived, I was raised with the Southern people, and I don't expect them to grow out of their ways much faster than the
nigros do out of theirn," Mr. Foote explained.

On the day when Lee surrendered to Grant at Appomattox
I lay with many thousand Union veterans in a large open
field, just over the brow of the ridge, upon the opposite side
of which was now the famous "apple tree." When news
of the fact passed along the lines a solemn hush fell upon
the weary host. I felt no desire to cheer, I am sure, nor did

I witness any boisterous demonstrations on the part of our boys during the whole day. I fancied that I saw in this conduct of the colored people at Yazoo, some resemblance to that of our grand army at Appomattox, particularly in the absence of all evidence of the existence of a revengeful feeling. As for the garrison, the extra bolts and braces for doors, extra bars for the windows, and the guard of stalwart freedmen gradually disappeared, got lost, melted away, and nothing remained of its former " brazen character " but " the grand old flag," which still flaunted the breezes of Yazoo.

" Delicate white ladies " now walked timidly under its laughing folds. The white boys no longer threw stones at it, and we could leave it out flying all night with no fear of loss or injury to it.

CHAPTER XXXIV

CHARLES' NEW LEASE OF LIFE—UNCLE DAVID'S CRAP—IT MIGHT
HAVE BEEN—FEATURES OF THE CHANGE, WITH THE EXCEP-
TIONS TO THE RULE—A WAR REMINISCENCE—A SURPRISE.

CHARLES appeared to enjoy the change more than any
one else. He no longer had seasons when he seemed to
look only at vacancy. On the contrary, he had an object in
view which claimed his attention without variation, and
when Congress met he accompanied other members of a committee to Washington for the purpose of presenting the
" Mississippi case " to that body.

The General began to calculate the expense of getting his
family to town and setting up his rooftree there with only less
anxiety than he counted the days when the family would be
expected. He appeared to take rather more pains with his
toilet than formerly, and his hollow eyes and pinched cheeks
rapidly gave way to a more wholesome expression of countenance.

As for our faithful hands, who had sustained us no less
gallantly in our political struggle than formerly they had
done in our struggles on Tokeba, some had been able to eke
out a scanty living at odd jobs; some had hired themselves
under contracts made before the Bureau agent to native
planters in the neighborhood, or had succeeded in obtaining
small patches of land to work on their own account. Of this
last number, Uncle David was the most successful.

After leaving Tokeba—winter 1867-'8—he succeeded, through the protection of the Bureau agent, in renting fifteen acres of land, adjoining Mr. Gosling's, for which he paid, in advance, all the money he had or could beg or borrow, viz.: thirty-seven dollars and fifty cents. He had neither horse, mule, ox, cow, sheep, goat, nor pig; neither wagon, plow, ax, shovel, spade, rake, nor hoe; nothing but the new clothes he had purchased while on Tokeba, bed, chairs, and skillets, and the food which he shot in the woods, caught from the river, or " exchanged work " for. Yet, with the aid of his wife, Aunt Betty, and one daughter, this *black* secured as net proceeds of the year's work—

2,000 pounds cotton, at 2s. per pound, current rates then	$480
100 bushels corn, at $1 per bushel..	100
70 bushels of potatoes, at $1 per bushel.................................	70
Vegetables...	40
Fodder..	25
Total..	$715

David was sixty-eight years of age, Betty sixty, and the daughter sixteen.

As for the Northerners, of those who remained through the siege, one returned North, one opened a store in town, and one, who had "surrendered " early in the struggle, in company with some " ex-Confederates," went to Louisville and Cincinnati, where they gathered up a large number of ring-boned, spavined and otherwise crippled and broken-down horses, "fed them up " for a brief spell, and then brought them to Yazoo, " to sell to the darkies."

The year's crop of cotton exceeded any that had been grown in the bottoms for seven years. It was an extraordinary yield, and Charles and I could not help feeling that but for our fidelity to truth and the right in opening a school for the children of our hands, and in other matters, we would have shared in the wealth it brought; for the term for which we leased Tokeba ended with the year 1868.

But the election of Grant, even though he would not take

his office until March following, secured to the freed people, who had made ninety-nine out of every hundred pounds of it, a fair proportion of their share, except in some few instances where their employers or landlords still pleaded "the statute," which denied to a "freedman, free negro or mulatto" access to the courts, and enforced their view with the shot-gun or, as in many cases, ran the crop off to New Orleans, sold it, pocketed the money, and then told the laborers to "git up and git."

As for Colonel Black, having failed to secure the requisite labor to work Tokeba himself, he had lost a year's rent and one good year's crop, and walked the streets leaning upon his cane, with all the evil spirit subdued, and silent, except when whisky "spirits" had possession of him.

As for Mrs. Black, she mourned in sackcloth and ashes the "degeneracy of the times" and her "hard fate."

As for her daughters, one of them succeeded in marrying a Pennsylvania "Yankee," who had readily adapted himself to the "ways of the country," and who forthwith undertook to "run Tokeba."

As for the "Grand Cyclops," two continued in their practice of the law "in all the courts of Mississippi," and all of them agreed to "wait and see what would turn up next."

As for the "chairman of the Yazoo County Democratic Committee," he returned to his usual occupation, taking along with him the "human hornet," whom he carried under his arm.

As for the "radical delegates to the black-and-tan convention from Yazoo," Captain Clark accompanied Charles to Washington, the blacksmith rented a small building in Yazoo City, and with the remnant of his convention warrants opened a shop on his own account. And as for me—

On that first day of the battle of Gettysburg, after fighting from early morning to near nightfall, I received a wound which stretched me out upon a cot in a little room in Baltimore, so that for months I could not sit up nor turn over. When at last, the kind, skillful surgeon gave me leave to do so, and I was placed in a chair by an open window, from which I could see the hurrying throngs of men, women and children, the railway train arriving from a distance, the hills and forests beyond, a glorious November sunset, and heard the nurse say I would be allowed to " go home soon," I forgave the rebel who shot me, forgot the sores upon my back, everything in the thrill of the moment, and cried; so now, in this moment of restfulness and joy, I forgave " the chairman of the Yazoo County Democratic Committee," the Barksdales, Harrisons, and Kelloggs, their poor return for our firm's liberal patronage during our struggle with Colonel Black and his aiders and abettors; Dave Woolridge, who, through the " friendship of the whites," had added a hotel to his saloon, and now allowed me to know that I could have my meals at his house; even the captain with " an ancestry," though his nocturnal combats with bats, owls, lizards, and snakes, now became seriously frequent and annoying; and " the enemy," male and female, whom I had met in " better times," and under " more favorable auspices," who now began by ones and by twos to " see " me gradually as we passed upon the street, and I returned their salutations, however faint as at first they were, cordially. " The war is over," I said, " let us have peace."

I forgot Tokeba, the " black-and-tan convention," the kuklux, the blows, curses, epithets; the jibes, jeers, and the scorn; all, except the " human hornet," Ben Wicks, the planter of "many thousand acres and many hundred slaves" formerly; Major Bob Sweet, the bull-dozer; Harry Baltimore, the irreconcilable ; Joe Telsub, the K. K. K. commander ; Colonel Black, and a few others, who would neither allow me to forgive nor forget, but kept up to the end a spiteful and revengeful warfare.

I believe in my soul that their course was altogether prompted by my inability to forget our friends and the " Old Flag," which still flaunted from that window of my quarters —" stronghold " no longer.

The change in the character of our quarters—from a "stronghold" to "apartments"—which took place on the departure of my brother for Washington, came near costing the remnant of the little garrison their lives. This was the winter of 1868–'9. It occurred about midnight. The General and I had been more than usually absorbed in our legal studies, and had not yet retired. The first note of warning was a shuffling of feet upon the pavement below—the same where our "guard" to the Sabbath-school used to form—and a low, suppressed tone of command: "Halt," "right dress," "front," "order arms," "parade rest." While these commands were being hurriedly given, we sprang to the window, peeped out through the shutters, and saw not less than thirty, perhaps forty, men, all disguised in black hoods and gowns, so that they could not have been identified by a passer-by, and armed with guns and pistols, and what appeared to be wooden guns—such as are used in drill practice.

Although since the announcement of Grant's election our former precautions had been abandoned, we still kept our Spencers and revolvers within easy reach from the bed. Seizing these and hastily placing an additional prop against the door, we stood ready, "cocked and primed" for an attack almost by the time the klan were at a "parade rest." Their only way of approach to our rooms was up the narrow flight of steps between the adjoining building and that in which we were, immediately in front of them, or by going around through the yard of the livery stable and up a narrow, rickety stairway at the rear, which led from the ground to our back gallery. In either case they would have to cross the back gallery a few steps before reaching the door.

There was no stalwart "guard" there now. The occupant of the office below had vacated it or had been silenced. No sound came from that quarter and we waited in breathless suspense for the first warning of approach up the stairway. After waiting a moment and hearing none, and, fearing their purpose might be to fire the building, the General crossed

over to the front window to see what the kukluxes were
doing. He at once made a sign for me to come to him, which
I did. On looking out I saw one whom I took to be Captain
Telsub, of the "Cyclops," at the head of the file, in close, whispered conversation with several of the "line" who had
gathered about him. They appeared to be divided in opinion
about something ; for, as the Captain, who was apparently
in command, gesticulated in an animated manner with head
or hand toward the entrance of the stairway, as if he would
go up himself if others would follow, some of those about
him would point with equal emphasis toward the window,
through the cracks and holes in the plain board shutters of
which we were peering down upon them. It was some time
before we could make out what was meant by their pointing
toward the window. We felt certain they could not see us.
We could occasionally hear above the whispered voices a
muttering among the masks still in line, and several times
heard distinctly the words " by G—d," " d—n it," " h—l,"
" Spencers," " one," " two," " three," " half a dozen of um,"
&c. Finally, several of those in the "line" turned as though
they would go away, and the commander yielded, gave the
command " attention," " shoulder arms," " right face," and
then, uttering, altogether, a loud, deep groan, followed by
curses, they marched away silently as they came.

They had scarcely passed out of sight when we heard a
gentle tap at our door. Surprised by this, we did not answer
it directly. Then came another, accompanied with a low
tone, " Me, let me in."

It was the shoemaker. The kukluxes had disturbed
him, and he had arisen and peeped out, then seized his pistol
and listened, while his wife slipped out the back way—to
give the alarm to the " guard."

While thus listening, the shoemaker had been able to
satisfy himself that it was the rays of light coming through
our shutters, which had warned the band that we were not
asleep, and that fact had deterred them from their purpose.

Shortly afterward there were at least a dozen of our stalwart
friends on the back gallery, and in our rooms, the greater
part of whom remained all night. This was the last appearance of "the enemy" in disguise.

When next he rode on his raids, he needed no disguise
and marched in solid column, "nine hundred strong," armed
with Winchester rifles, needle guns, double-barrelled shot-guns,
and with ropes over the pummels of their saddles, and pistols
and knives in their belts.

CHAPTER XXXV.

SEQUELÆ—RENEWAL OF AN OLD ACQUAINTANCE—GET OUT A HERE—SCRAPS FROM HISTORY—REVELATIONS.

BUT I was yet to experience the sequel to that last visit of the kuklux. The General was out of town on some errand, and the only person present was Captain Bishop, a Northerner, who, seeing the way we were "just coining money" with our mill on Tokeba, in the year 1867, had brought down a portable steam saw-mill, and set it to buzzing in the brake adjoining ours. He, too, had passed through such a series of trials as had nearly bankrupted him, and, as others had sometimes done, had " come over" to lie on our bed, seek consolation from us, and minister to our craving for fellowship and intelligent sympathy.

He had fallen asleep, when there came a rather sharp knocking at the door. On opening it, I was startled by the presence there, on our rear gallery, of several of the irreconcilables, headed by Dave Woolridge and the " ex-sheriff "— he of my last dinner at the Blacks in the winter of '65-'66. In a bold, brusque manner those two leaders entered our room, the ex-sheriff slightly behind the "nigro." Whereupon the following dialogue took place between us:

" Colonel Mawgin, you've been slandering the white people of this Azoo County long enough, and I'm y'here to ask you to take it back, and by—"

Then the ex-sheriff—

"And ou' people—"

At that instant the manner of my callers had become so threatening that it amounted to a violent assault, especially when, half advancing, Dave made a movement as though to draw the long sword from his heavy cane* while he stood as if about to spring upon me; the ex-sheriff keeping well up with him, while those upon the gallery huddled at the door-way.

Taking in the situation at a glance, and without waiting for the ex-sheriff to finish his sentence, I sprang through the narrow doorway to the adjoining room—the sleeping apart-ment of the outcasts—seized a loaded navy revolver, and yelling to the sleeping Captain : "Come on, Bishop !" lev-elled it cocked at the ex-sheriff and shouted : "Get out of here ! "

Meanwhile, the Captain, who had been somewhat dis-turbed by their entrance, though still but half awake, stood at my back with a Spencer, and they "got." We followed only to meet our old stalwart "guard" hurrying through the rear yard and up the back steps as the last one of the kukluxes hustled down the narrow passageway on to the street in front.

Some explanation of the two last assaults upon our quarters may be desirable. We were still "consorting" with negros "from choice." The "desperate" element among the anti-reconstructionists—none of them having ever been regularly enrolled and in active service for the Confederate cause dur-ing the war—were still on a hunt for a "last ditch" in which to spill the "last drop" of their chivalric blood, "by G—d, sah." They were of the class who "lost all but honah, by G—d, sah, by the wah ! " and having "surrendered in good faith," were now as mad as March hares, because, by the election of that "butcher, Grant," payment for "that gal, Sal, by G—d, sir-r-r," had been relegated to some future new era,

---

* He usually carried about with him a heavy sword cane.

undefined and undefinable even in the horoscope of Yazooans, and where the chances of a verdict in their favor were "mo' than likely to be mighty onsartin," should that era ever dawn.

Their emissaries were in Washington, New York and all the great political and commercial centers, wringing their hands and shedding tears, figuratively, at the "probability" that the "barbarous nigros, inflamed by a desire for revenge," in the election of Grant, would find an "opportunity," and possibly, too, a "cover" for a "rising," when they would "kill all the white men, women and children, from the cradle up," and "marry their daughters." This "all-but-honah" crowd were constantly receiving "assurances" from their emissaries, that, after all, Grant's election did not mean that the "nigros" would be allowed to do any such thing; that Republicans, no less than Democrats, had "no more love for the nigger," when it came to that, than the "chivalrous Southron," nor half so much; and, at the "first signal of distress from the South," the Yankees would be found to respond as promptly to their "cry for help," as in former times they had responded to their demand to help "catch a runaway." Therefore, "the first outbreak against the peace and quiet of society, that assumed the form of insurrection, would signalize the destruction of the negro's cherished hopes, and the ruin of the race"—or his return to the subjection of the white man, which was all the same; therefore, they would give Grant "a fair trial."

As this may readily be taken as merely my opinion and not a statement of fact, I have thought I ought not to venture it here. But there are at hand so many reasons for it, and such an array of documentary and other evidence going to prove its correctness, I have thought that by bringing forward authenticated records in connection with it, the reader might come to see, that, after all it is not my opinion, but rather a perfectly logical deduction from the attendant facts and circumstances, in which case I should ask to be relieved from a possible charge of presumption.

" EXECUTIVE DEPARTMENT,
" JACKSON, MISS., *December* 9, 1867.

" Whereas, communications have been received at this office from gentlemen of high official and social position in different portions of the State, expressing serious apprehensions that combinations and conspiracies are being formed among the blacks to seize the lands and establish farms, expecting and hoping that Congress will arrange a plan of division and distribution, but unless this is done by January next they will proceed to help themselves, and are determined to go to war and are confident that they will be victors in any conflict with the whites, and furnish names of persons and places; and

"Whereas, similar communications have been received at headquarters Fourth Military District, and referred to me for my action, and the co-operation of the civil authorities of the State with the United States military in suppressing violence and maintaining order and peace;

" Now, therefore, I, Benjamin G. Humphreys, Governor of Mississippi, do issue this, my proclamation, admonishing the black race, that if any such hopes or expectations are entertained you have been grossly deceived, and if any such combinations or conspiracies have been formed to carry into effect such purposes by lawless violence, I now warn you that you cannot succeed.

" What is not known of your plans and conspiracies will be discovered and anticipated, and the first outbreak against the quiet and peace of society that assumes the form of insurrection will signalize the destruction of your cherished hopes and the ruin of your race."

When the convention met in the following January, I asked for the appointment of a committee to inquire into the grounds of the Governor's apprehensions. Having had some experience in " nigro risings " I preferred not to serve upon the committee, and was excused. After several weeks of persistent effort to get at the true state of the case, that committee submitted the following report :

[EXTRACT.]

" That they have taken every means in their power to inform themselves upon the subject they have been called upon to investigate. They have made diligent inquiry of different delegates in this convention coming from all parts of the State, and at no place within the limits of this State, before, at the time, or since the issuing of said proclamation, were there any indications of insubordination, riot, insurrection, or outbreak of any description whatever among that class of citizens referred to in said proclamation, but on the contrary a peaceable and orderly disposition worthy of the highest admiration has marked their conduct under the most trying circumstances, even where cruel wrongs have been wickedly inflicted upon them. They have also made inquiry of many citizens of the State not connected with the convention, touching the charges above referred to and everywhere they find the colored man true and loyal to the country.

"In conclusion your committee would beg leave to state that the alleged causes for issuing said proclamation were so utterly without foundation that they are at a loss to find any reasonable excuse for so doing, and that the fears and 'serious apprehensions that combinations and conspiracies are being formed among the blacks to seize the lands and establish farms' had their origin in the brains of evil-disposed 'gentlemen of high official and social positions' in different portions of the State, and nowhere else."

With their report the committee submitted the following official correspondence. The first extract is from the response of Governor Humphrey's to an inquiry of the committee:

"I presume you do not expect me to admit that the convention now in session in this city by virtue of the military bills passed by Congress, has any constitutional right to require me to account to it for my administration of the civil government of the State of Mississippi. I, however, acknowledge the constitutional right of all or any portion of the citizens of the State, in a peaceable manner, to assemble together for their common good and apply to those vested with the powers of government for redress of grievances, or other proper purposes, by petition, address, or remonstrance, and the correlative duty of all civil officers to furnish them all the information in their possession that pertains to their welfare and happiness, when respectfully requested so to do. I have no secrets I desire to withhold from any class of our people, white or black. My proclamation of the 9th of December, 1867, was issued at the urgent request of General Ord, Commander of the Fourth Military District, and all the information I have on the subject you desire to investigate was received from and through him; except a few letters received from prominent citizens, which I referred to him as soon as received, and which, I presume, are now in his possession. For obvious reasons, then, I must refer the committee to him, and if in his judgment a revelation of the sources of information will not be an act of bad faith to the informers, white and black, and prejudicial to the public service, and he will authorize a publication of all communications, public and private, I will cheerfully comply with his instructions on that subject.

"Very respectfully,

"BENJAMIN G. HUMPHREYS,
"*Governor of Mississippi.*

"To A. ALDERSON, *Chairman of Committee.*"

The following letters explain themselves :

"HOLLY SPRINGS, MISS., *February* 14, 1868.
" *To* A. ALDERSON, *Chairman of Committee, Misisssippi Constituticnal Convention.*

"SIR : I am in receipt of a letter from Gen. A. C. Gillem's headquarters, transmitting one from you, asking all the information I possess touching the facts that occasioned the issuing of that proclamation (referring to a recent proclamation of the Governor of Mississippi upon the subject of illegal combinatious, etc.) as far as consistent with my obligations to those from whom the communications were received. As I have turned over with the command of the Fourth Military District all the communications referred to, not even retaining copies, 1 have no means of furnishing you with the desired information.

"I am, sir, respectfully, your obedient servant,
"E. O. C. ORD,
"*Br. and Brv't Maj. Gen.*"

" HEADQUARTERS FOURTH MILITARY DISTRICT,
" MISSISSIPPI AND ARKANSAS,
" VICKSBURG, MISS., *March* 17, 1868.
"*Hon.* A. ALDERSON, *Chairman of Committee, Constitutional Convention for the State of Mississippi.*

"SIR : I am directed by the General commanding to acknowledge the receipt of your communication of the twenty-fourth ultimo, asking to be furnished with any information in his possession upon which the proclamation of His Excellency the Governor, referred to by you, was based, and in reply thereto, to inform you that the General commanding upon due consideration of the character of the reports made to his predecessor, General Ord, upon which the action was taken, finding that they partake of a confidential nature ; also, with the regard to the considerable evils and little good that would seem to result from their publication, he decides that it would be incompatible with his duty to comply with your request.

"At the same time the General commanding desires to inform you that he never shared in the belief that insurrection was meditated by any class of the inhabitants of this State.

"I am, sir, very respectfully, your obedient servant,
"JOHN TYLER,
"1st Lt., 43d Inf., Brv't Maj., U. S. A., A. A. A. G.*"

Now this was the same General Ord who had befriended our firm against Colonel Black and his allies. He was known during the reconstruction period as a faithful department commander. His sympathies have always been believed

I have understood, to be favorable to the Congressional plan of reconstruction. Yet, it would seem from the correspondence here quoted that he had either been deceived into entertaining a fear that the freedmen were, in fact, "about to rise," or had been tricked into a position where he was made to appear to have such fears. The evidence must have been very strong indeed to have aroused any such fears in the mind of General Ord, but at that time it was not at all difficult to obtain any amount of "proof" that the freed people were about to "rise," etc., and, as General Ord was comparatively a "new-comer," at least, had been but a very short while in command of that district, it is not improbable, in my views, that he was "taken in" in the same manner as more illustrious commanders before him had been. But now Grant was soon to "take his seat," as our friends termed the assumption of the robes of office, and "the enemy" wished to give him a "fair trial."

To this end, as the negro would not "rise" on his own motion, they would assume that he was about to do so, hang or shoot his "white-skinned leaders," and then when the poor, faithful, outraged colored people should come flocking to town to see what was the matter, or to "stand" by us if they died for it, those chivalrous Southrons could furnish the world with ample proof of the absolute correctness of their assumption, that the negro was indeed "about to rise," by raising the cry that they were coming in to burn the town, and then opening fire upon them, killing a half-dozen or more of them, and driving the remainder to the woods, where hunger would soon force them to return to their *masters*.

Should the Federal power afterward fail to interfere—the State authorities were pledged in advance not to—both they and the freed people would be satisfied with their "trial" of Grant, and the master class would rally to his standard, as formerly they had done to "Andy" Johnson's. And, as after *his* "trials," Johnson came to be known in the South as *Mr.* Johnson, instead of "that tailor Andy Johnson," it is cer-

tain, Grant, in the case I have supposed, would have come to
be known as "illustrious" President, rather than "that
butcher" Grant.

They would also by the same "trial" satisfy the freed people "that the United States military authorities of this district are not in sympathy with any emissaries, white or
black," that urge you to wear Grant and Colfax badges in
the face of Seymour and Blair badges worn by the kukluxes.

Their plan failed only because Captain Telsub could not
induce his cowardly followers to attack our quarters *while we
were awake.*

In the latter case the day following its occurrence the
ex-sheriff sent me word that I had mistaken the purpose of
his visit, and he wished to call and explain. I replied that I
would receive him should he come alone. He came trembling, as men with guilty consciences always do when they
meet the man they have deeply wronged, and fear his vengeance. I offered him a chair and begged him not to
"mention the matter." But he insisted upon explaining that
"white citizens have been hearing rumors for some days past
that you all had a large quantity of arms stored up there under
the nigro church, and we were appointed a committee to call
upon you for an explanation of the matter. Knowing that
you were a gentleman, as I certainly did, I told my neighbors when they came to talk to me about it that if they were
there you had nothing to do with it, for I always believed
you and the Captain meant well, and never did take sides
with Colonel Black in his persecutions of you all, and I told
my son ——."

But this was getting off the subject, and I brought him back
thus—

"You had heard the arms were stored under the little
church on the hill which we ——" But here he stopped me
and resumed his "apology."

But it was too tedious, and I bluntly asked him—.

" Why didn't you go and look under the church yourselves?
This is not a church."

" Well, I suggested to them we ought to see you first, and
have you exonerate yourself from the charge."

" Charge! What had you heard that I had to do with
it?"

" Oh, well, you know, Colonel, we all look upon you and
your brother as the leaders of the nigros, and"——

" Ah! I see, Mr. Fisher; let me tell you something. You
all never take a step in politics, since the war at least, but
you make a blunder* to start with. Let's you and me go
together, now, to the little church on the hill which we helped
to "——

" Oh, never mind; never mind that. I hope you don't
think that I believe the tale. It was my desire to serve you,
and clear your name before our people of the foul "——

" Come on, now, with me, Mr. Fisher, right now, and exonerate me afterward before your "——

He did not wait for me to finish my sentence, but at once
took his hat and abruptly left.

Now the truth is, this man was one of the " leading citizens," " best citizens " of Yazoo; member of the church
and " devoted Christian," as I understood at the time. He
came with his gang of desperadoes, shoving the negro in
advance, in order that my " taking off" by assassination in
broad day might be publicly explained as the act of " old and
faithful family servants," who, by striking at " the inciters of
it," had " vindicated" their masters from the "slanders"†
referred to by Dave, and, at the same time, had thwarted the
plans of the negroes to kill all the whites and "seize " lands,
marry their daughters, &c.

They had seized upon the moment when they knew the
General to be absent, and doubtless had not observed the
entrance of Captain Bishop; or was it to enable them to learn
the strength of the stronghold in weapons of defense ?

* I ought to have said fraud.

† The "slanders" were no doubt certain statements which Charles had been making
in Washington.

As in other similar instances, the " guard " got their warning from a waiter in Dave's saloon, and had, as they had so often done before, " rushed to the rescue."

I believed then, and have since been assured, by the indirect allusions of Dave's widow, and of those who were their confidants at the time, to these times, that Dave Woolridge himself knew who kept us posted and knowingly shielded the informer. Those of that kuklux band who still survive, should any there be, will doubt this statement. They had perfect confidence in Dave's loyalty to their cause. I do not *know* that he was not loyal. I believe he was all the while a good, though secret, friend to the little Yankee garrison.

In the case of another, who shall be nameless now, in whom they apparently had as perfect trust as in Mr. Woolridge, I do know; for his visit to the stronghold on a certain very dark night gave me the proof of his loyalty to our cause.

Then such persons did not dare to let their " own color " know even their thoughts, fearing accidental or involuntary exposure.

CHAPTER XXXVI.

ALL DOUBLED UP—CLEARING DITCHES—WAITING A VERDICT—A
SATRAP'S KNIFE—MAKING HAY—CHARLES GETS A PLUMB—A
PATRIOTIC FOOL.

BUT the incidents adverted to in the two last chapters,
while certifying to the desperation and the cunning, also
demonstrates the cowardice of the "last ditchers," who, forgetting their oft-repeated pledge to die in it, cleared that historical gully at one bound in their flight for the woods, upon
the inauguration of President Grant, one of the first acts of
whose administration was the appointment of Adelbert Ames,*
who had been on duty in the State for some time, to succeed
Alvin C. Gillem, Johnson's confidant, in the command of
the district.

This appointment was received by the kukluxes very
much as they had received the news of Grant's election, only
"it doubled them all up." The only sign anywhere visible
of resistance to his authority, was made by the governor,
Benjamin G. Humphreys, and he resisted only to the point
of drawing out a "show of force" in the form of two United
States soldiers, with fixed bayonets, who, one morning, showed
themselves at the capital, under command of one of the
"military satrap's† underlings." Then he graciously "surren-

---

* A lieutenant-colonel in the regular service, who had been, I believe, a major-gene-
ral of volunteers.
† General Ames at once made himself known to the K. K. K.'s as a satrap.

dered 'to overpowering force,' gave up the keys and muniments
of office, and retired to his plantation and the bosom of his
family—'recognized' and 'unrecognized,' where he remained
' under the shadow of a military despotism,' calmly biding
the time when ' disenthralled,' 'redeemed,' Mississippi should
be able to ' reassert herself,' and, pointing to the fact that ' our
people ' had never ' voluntarily ' surrendered those ' constitutional rights reserved by the States,' had never ' voluntarily '
emancipated ' our nigros,' had never ' voluntarily abdicated '
those offices to which the ' sovereign white ' people of the
State had elevated them, declare, that the former ' having
been' destroyed by the Yankees, and the latter having been
accomplished ' by force,' the entire proceeding lacked the
vitalizing power of constitutionality, and was, therefore, 'null
and void,' and of ' no effect.' "

Being so, and there being no grant of power in the Federal
Constitution " to coerce a State," what shall hinder a restoration of the old order of things—for the protection of the
lands and the " lives of the white men, women and children,
from the cradle up ?"

All the kukluxes of Yazoo at once imitated the example of their chief—the "human hornet" and three others alone
excepted—and peace reigned throughout the borders of Yazoo.

The remnant of the little garrison now abandoned their
old quarters. The General and his family began housekeep-
ing, and I, by express invitation of Mrs. Blank, took board
at the house of the lady whose home but little more than a
year before had been converted into a " den of infamy " by
the presence of my brother and the General.

General Ames' knife cut deep, but the hand at the helm
in Washington was as steady as Ames' surgery was courageous and skilful.

Charles and Captain Clark were still at the national capital. The new military commander who had heard of the
little " Yankee garrison of Yazoo," tendered to me the office
of sheriff and tax collector of the county.*

* Under the constitution and laws then in force the sheriff was ex-officio tax collector
of his county.

This I declined, somewhat to his surprise, and when a reason was asked, I said : "I shall prefer to be in the legislature, if I am to be in office, under the new regime."

"The sheriff's office in Yazoo County, I am told, is worth in fees and commissions six to ten thousand per year—is it not so ?"

"I believe it is."

"Your compensation as a member of the legislature is likely not to exceed a thousand per year."

"True," I replied. "But I do not wish office for the money there may be in it. Until the government to be set up in the stead of the old one shall be established, I shall prefer to be in the legislature, where I think I may be able to do more good.

From that moment this "satrap" became my steadfast friend. He asked me to suggest a name for the place, and also names for all the other offices to be filled in Yazoo County. I then suggested the name of F. P. Hillyard for sheriff.

"Who is he ? " said this commanding general.

"An old Unionist, and one who, though not very staunch, has nevertheless been friendly to our 'little garrison.' "

"Was he a slaveholder ?"

"Yes."

"Can you rely upon his loyalty to yourself and to our cause?"

"Yes, I think I can."

"Will not your brother wish to have it?"

"No, I think not. The rebels are very much more bitter toward him than me. Besides, he wishes to resume business, and I am sure neither of us will care to make it a family affair. Should I be nominated for the legislature he would prefer to have no office."

"I think you're making a mistake, but if you request it I'll appoint Mr. Hillyard."

I subsequently asked for it, and he was appointed.

General F. E. Franklin was appointed probate judge of the county, a Unionist was appointed to the office of chancery clerk, only second in fees to the sheriff's office, and when they had all been filled, the Unionists—all natives or ex-slave-holders—held all the " offices of profit" in the county.

Then the Northerners said—

"Morgan, you're a fool! " and " the enemy " said—" fool!" and the "chairman of the County Democratic Committee," said—" fool ! "

I borrowed money enough to see me through, until after the forthcoming election, and began the cultivation of my new field.

At this point, the general commanding asked me to tender to Charles, on his behalf, the office of sheriff and tax-collector for Washington County. That suited me, and I at once telegraphed my brother the fact, advising him to accept it.

He accepted.

Then I said, surely we may now have lasting peace in Yazoo, and I began to dig deeper in my new field.

CHAPTER XXXVII.

THE OLD STUBBLE-GROUND OF SLAVERY—A LEAF FROM HISTORY—
"OUT DAMNED SPOT."

THIS, my new field of labor, was now, 1869, the *old* stub-ble-ground of slavery. For four years Andrew Johnson had been chief husbandman. His co-laborers in Mississippi were the "high-toned, honorable gentlemen" of the "Central Democratic Association" of the State at large, and their sub-alterns of the ku-klux-klan, among whom, in Yazoo, were Colonel Black, Judge Isam, Ben Wicks, Major Sweet, Harry Baltimore, Captain Telsub, the human hornet, Mr. Gosling, Sheriff Finley, ex-Sheriff Fisher, Uncle Ike, and Dave Wool-ridge. His "organs" were such newspapers as the *Clarion*, Mr. Barksdale's paper; the Vicksburg *Times*, the *Mercury*, and our *Banner*. His chief civil executive officer in the State was Governor Humphreys. His political policy found expres-sion in his letter to the first reconstruction Governor of the State, wherein he favored the "extension " of the suffrage, in order to " disarm the adversary," and it was amply illus-trated in the numerous "nigro insurrections " that followed, the cunning and "statesmanship " of " we all," as displayed in their ability to appropriate the military power of the United States for the suppression of "risings " which were "about " to occur, and in the resources of " our people," as shown by the facilities which they enjoyed for compelling the freed

people to "rise" whenever occasion required additional ex-
pedients for convincing the Cabinet of *their* President, the
"jury" at the North, or for getting "rid of them d—n Yankee vipers" hemmed up in that Yazoo stronghold.

Up to this point in my narrative, my patient reader has
followed me in a summary of individual experiences with our
fellow-citizens in Yazoo. Here, upon the threshold of our
new era, I shall ask them to follow me with equal patience
through a summary of what the General and I, in our pursuit
of a better knowledge of law, found upon the official records
and between the lids of the statute books of Mississippi. It
will embrace the thing which the conspiracy above described
was, by the capture of Johnson, organized to protect, defend
and perpetuate. I promise to be brief.

I shall begin with the tax law, passed in 1865-'6.

One of the provisions of that law allowed the land owner
to assess himself—fix the taxable valuation of his lands for himself.* Another fixed the *rate* of tax upon lands at *one-tenth*
of one per cent. for "*State* purposes," while the rate upon all
personal property was fixed at *one-quarter* of one per cent.;
and power was given to the county to fix the rate for "county
purposes" upon the State levy as a basis, and not otherwise.

Another provision laid so great a tax upon all "privileges"
that all freedmen were practically excluded from the trades
and professions.

Still another provided for a tax on each poll, and gave to
county and municipal governments power to increase it
practically without limit.

These provisions resulted in such inequalities as the following—

All blacksmiths, bakers, butchers, brickmakers, carriage-
makers, carpenters, dealers in timber, lumber, or shingles,
printers, gunsmiths, saw-mills, shoemakers, tailors, tanners,
watchmakers, painters, milliners, &c., were required to pay
twenty-five cents on every hundred dollars' worth—not of

*Of course this was in obedience to the well-known assumption of chivalry, exclu-
sively enjoyed by Southrons.

capital invested in business, but of the *gross amount* of their *earnings*, and that not upon an estimate made by themselves, but, in the words of the law, " upon *their gross receipts*."

* " The county of Warren, including the city of Vicksburg, is the wealthiest community in the State ; and we have taken some pains to examine the tax-rolls of Warren County and to ascertain the practical workings of the barbarous system here. The following are the cases of the three largest landholders in the county:

Colonel Benson Blake and wife's total taxes on 8,506 acres of the best cotton land in the State, including a magnificent residence and the finest improvements in the county, all told is only $99 78

Colonel Joseph E. Davis' total taxes on 3,793 acres of bottom land, fronting on the Mississippi River, including the Hurricane Plantation, which he lately sold for $50,000, all told... 141 14

Heirs of General John A. Quitman, 6,810 acres of same sort of land, handsomely improved, including a plantation which was rented for $30,000 per annum the same year it was assessed—total taxes, all told.. 188 64

Here we have 19,109 acres of the most valuable cotton lands in the world, including plantations the most highly improved of any in the South, with palatial residences and steam gins, worth at the very small average price of $20 per acre, $382,180, paying a total tax of only $439.56

Mr. Charles Peine, on his livery stable, pays........................ ....$671 03
Messrs. Gray & Birchett, on their apothecary shop, pay.......... 502 85
Messrs. Herrick & Dirr, on their photograph gallery, pay........ 200 00
Mr. B. Stricker, the butcher, pays...................... .... 224 95
Mr. Fred Lloyd, another butcher, pays.. 243 70
Messrs. Kleinman & Beck, bricklayers, on their own work pay. 87 76
Mr. Gerard Bedenhard on his soda fountain, pays................ .... 115 88
Mr. Phillip Gilbert, shoemaker, pays.. 75 28
Mr. W. P. Crecy, on a salary of $1,200 per annum, clerk in Hardaways, with *no* property, pays.. 33 00
Mr. Vetch, a barber, and no property but his soap, shears, and razors, pays.. 107 63
Pompey Higgins, a colored drayman, on his dray and two mules, pays.. 33 82
And last though not least, the daily and weekly *Herald*, on their receipts, pay... 185 20

* The items here stated are taken *verbatim* from the political manual published in 1869 by Hon. J. S. Morris, of Mississippi, who was subsequently Attorney General of the State. They were, as I now recollect, first published in the Vicksburg *Republican*. And both the *Republican* and the manual were freely employed during the canvass of that year by Republican speakers throughout the State. I have never heard the correctness of the statements questioned. They are absolutely correct, and can be easily verified by any one who may doubt the fact.

Daily and weekly *Times*...................... .... 164 80

While the weekly *Republican* (having no daily as yet) denounces
    the robbery under a tax last year of...................................... 103 00

Our tax at the same rate for this year, owing to increase of
    business, would be not less than............................ 200 00

These "irregularities" were equally great and equally
oppressive of the poor in Yazoo County, and generally in the
State, as in Warren, as I myself discovered by a personal in-
spection of the records and by personal experience.

But the greatest hardship was from the poll tax. In many
instances in Yazoo City and County, freedmen, after working hard in the cotton field, or in the shop, the entire year
without other pay than food and clothes, except an occasional
mite for spending money, were arrested, "tried" and condemned for a failure to pay five dollars, sometimes ten dollars, upon their poll, and put at work in the chain gang, or
sold, to satisfy the amount! Thus much upon the subject of
taxation under the Johnson conspiracy.

We also discovered that that conspiracy had enacted a code
of *laws,* under and by virtue of which the freed people were
denied the right to reside in an incorporated town without
permission from the town authorities, to do "irregular or
job work" without a license, to testify in court against a
white man, to sit on grand or petit juries, to hold office, to
vote, to bear arms, to own or acquire land, or to lease land
or houses.

That code further provided that freed people might be
whipped by the court, or by the "master," "mistress," employer, or overseer.

Thus it will be seen that *by law* colored people were denied
the right to rise, were by law *kept in their places,* were *by
law* made subject to the property class, all of whom were
white. Having done that why not go just a little further?
So they went further, and in that same *law* expressly provided that "freedmen, free negroes, and mulattoes" might
be put up on the auction block and sold—

For non-payment of taxes;

For " running away; "

For failing to have an employer or regular employment on or before the second Monday of January;

For insulting " an employer," " master, " mistress," " overseer," or any of their children;

For " costs; "

For " damages; "

For " insulting gestures largely or acts."

They could be sold *for " committing any misdemeanor, the punishment of which is not specifically provided by law."*

Such is the language of the statute.

Nor yet is that all; they were forbidden to inter-*marry* with any white person. If they did it was a " felony," and punishable by " confinement in the penitentiary for life."

They were forbidden to assemble together in any number greater than five, "at any place of public resort, or at any meeting-house or houses in the night, or at any school for teaching them reading and writing, either in the daytime or night."* The punishment for a violation of this provision was " thirty-nine lashes on the bare back."

This code applied to white men in the following particulars only: If a white man *married* a negro or mulatto woman, he was liable to the same penalty as a freedman was for marrying a white woman.

If a white person was found " unlawfully assembling," or " usually associating" with a freedman on terms of " equality;"

* I have heard it denied that this was any part of those laws. But it was. The following is a true copy :
" ARTICLE 51. All meetings or assemblies of slaves, or free negroes or mulattoes mixing and associating with such slaves, above the number of five, including such free negroes and mulattoes, at any place of public resort, or at any meeting-house or houses, in the night, or at any school for teaching them reading or writing, either in the day time or night, under whatsoever pretext, shall be deemed an unlawful assembly, and any justice of the peace of the county or mayor or chief magistrate of any incorporated town wherein such asssemblage shall be held, either from his own knowledge or on the information of others, may issue his warrant to the proper officer to enter the house where such unlawful assemblage or meeting may be for the purpose of apprehending the offenders, dispersing the assemblage, and all slaves offending shall be tried in the manner hereinafter provided for the trial of slaves, and on conviction shall be punished by not more than thirty-nine lashes on the bare back.
" Provided, that nothing herein contained shall be construed to prevent any master or employer of slave from giving them permission in writing to go any place whatever for the purpose of religious worship, provided such worship be conducted by a regularly ordained or licensed white minister, or attended by two discreet and respectable white persons appointed for that purpose by some regular church or religious society."
Revised Code of 1857, page 247.

or "selling" or "lending," or "giving" him food, shelter or raiment, "when escaping from his master or mistress, or employer;" or for attempting to entice or persuade such a one to leave his or her master or mistress, or employer, he was liable to a fine and imprisonment.

If he was found "attempting to persuade or entice such a one to leave his or her master or mistress, or employer, *to go outside of the State,*" the fine and imprisonment was much greater.

In regulating the manner of making contracts with laborers, that code provided for their execution before any two respectable and disinterested *white* witnesses. There was but very little time allowed the laborer for recreation, or for looking after a new home and employer; for during the period from Christmas day to the second Monday of January, his employer would call in a couple of his neighbors to witness the new contracts, and all who refused to consent to the terms of such a contract as the *employer himself* wrote out, were threatened with arrest. If they still held out, and failed to find an employer (of course this was likely to be in a community where the white planters had a common interest), when the second Monday of January arrived, they were turned over to the neighborhood magistrate, fined, and as nine times out of ten they were unable to pay the fine, they were put up and sold. If unluckily the victim had money enough to pay the fine, he was none the less a "vagrant," immediately afterward, and would be again arrested, tried, found guilty and again fined. Of course by that time he had learned the "law," and either consented to the contract or allowed himself to be sold.

And then this conspiracy by that "tailor Andy" Johnson's legislature, declared :

"SEC. 4. *Be it further enacted,* That all the penal and criminal laws now in force in this State, defining offenses and prescribing the mode of punishment for crimes and misdemeanors committed by slaves, free negroes or mulattoes be, and the same are hereby, re-enacted, and declared to be in full force and effect against freedmen, free negroes and mulattoes, except so far as the mode and manner of trial and punishment have been changed or altered by law.

' SEC. 5. *Be it further enacted*, That if any freedman, free negro or mulatto, convicted of any of the misdemeanors provided against in this act, shall fail or refuse for the space of five days after conviction to pay the fine and costs imposed, such persons shall be hired out by the sheriff or other officers at public outcry, to any white person who will pay said fine and all costs, and take such convict for the shortest time.

"SEC. 6. *Be it further enacted*, That this act shall be in force and take effect from and after its passage.

" Approved, November 29, 1865."

[Pamphlet Acts of 1865, page 165.]

Under this law, men might not only be whipped by their employers, they also might be branded.

" You don't mean to say that under that code the laborer had no remedy at all ?"

" I do."

" Well, there was his old remedy left him, at all events; he could run away."

" Yes, that's a fact, and it was indeed an old remedy. But the free State of Canada was a long way off, and Fred. Douglass was still looked upon at the North as a person not fit to sit at table with white folks, to sleep in the same hotel, or to ride in the white folks' car, with some few exceptions. At all events, in Yazoo in 1865, 1866 and 1867, and up to the election of Grant, very few freedmen availed themselves of that remedy."

" Then they deserved just the treatment they got."

" Perhaps that is true, but let's see."

In his inaugural address, October 16, 1865, Governor Humphreys, said :

" The planter cannot venture upon the cultivation of the great staple, unless the laborer is compelled to comply with his contract,* remaining and performing his proper amount of labor, day after day, and week after week, through the whole year; and if he attempts to escape, he should be returned to his employer and forced to work, until the time for which he has contracted has expired."

*Made before *white* witnesses, as I have heretofore described.

Throughout that inaugural there was not one word upon the subject of compensation for all this *forced labor*.

That inaugural was subsequently put into effect in the shape of a *law* passed by these conspirators, which reads as follows:

" SEC. 1. *Be it enacted by the Legislature of the State of Mississippi,* That all runaways or those who *misspend what they earn* shall be deemed and considered *vagrants* under the provisions of this act, and on conviction thereof shall be ' fined not exceeding one hundred dollars, with all accruing costs, and be imprisoned, at the discretion of the court, not exceeding ten days.' "

This did not apply to whites.

" But these laws were not constitutional, nor in any sense valid."

That may be true, and Congress so declared in effect when it passed the Civil Rights bill of April, 1866, that law for which it was arraigned as a "partisan, usurping" body at the North, and as an " unconstitutional" or "rump" Congress at the South.

But neither Governor Humphreys nor any of his coadjutors in Mississippi were willing to concede that those laws were unconstitutional. They were, at least, perfectly willing that the question be left to the courts of Yazoo and of Mississippi, for in his special message to the legislature of that State of October, 1866, that Governor said:

" The civil rights bill passed by Congress* at its recent session conflicts directly with many of our State laws, * * * and has been a fruitful source of disturbance. Immediately after your adjournment in December, 1865,† I appointed * * * commissioners to visit Washington, lay these laws before the President, and request him to indicate which of them the military authorities would be allowed to nullify. The President gave full assurances that none of them should be nullified except by the civil courts of the land."

Therefore, in order to make sure that no freedman, woman, or child should " escape," that conspiracy passed a *law* making it the *duty* of " every civil officer " to arrest and " *carry back to his legal employers* " every escaping freedman, woman,

---

* Over Johnson's veto. remember.
† This was the date of my Vicksburg fool's errand.

or child, and offered a reward to "every person" who should do so in "the sum of five dollars and ten cents per mile from the place of arrest to the place of delivery."

In this manner that conspiracy at once nullified that Civil Rights bill of Congress, and set up their own *civil rights laws in its stead* *

Following is the full text of the Civil Rights bill of Congress, which was such a fruitful source of disturbance in Mississippi:

" An Act to protect all persons in the United States in their civil rights, and furnish the means of their vindication.

" *Be it enacted, etc.*, That all persons born in the United States, and not subject to any foreign power, including Indians not taxed, are hereby declared to be citizens of the United States ; and such citizens of every race and color, without regard to any previous condition of slavery or involuntary servitude, except as a punishment for crime, whereof the party shall have been duly convicted, shall have the same right in every State and Territory in the United States to make and enforce contracts ; to sue, be parties, and give evidence ; to inherit, purchase, lease, sell, hold and convey real and personal property ; and to full and equal benefit of all laws and proceedings for the security of person and property, as is enjoyed by white citizens, and shall be subject to like punishment, pains and penalties, and to none other, any law, statute, ordinance, regulation, or custom to the contrary notwithstanding.

" Sec. 2. That any person, who, under color of any law, statute, ordinance, regulation or custom, shall subject, or cause to be subjected, any inhabitant of any State or Territory to the deprivation of any right secured or protected by this act, or to different punishment, pains, or penalties, on account of such person having at any time been held in a condition of slavery or involuntary servitude, except as a punishment for crime, whereof the party shall have been duly convicted, or by reason of his color or race, than is prescribed for the punishment of white persons, shall be deemed guilty of a misdemeanor, and on conviction shall be punished by fine not exceeding one hundred dollars, or imprisonment not exceeding one year, or both in the discretion of the court."

The truth is, this conspiracy under the guise of conferring civil rights upon the freed people, involved them in a more terrible servitude than that which "all agreed" had "been

* For these laws, see Pamphlet Acts of the Legislature of Mississippi, 1865-'6 and '7, and the R. C. of 1857.

destroyed" by the war; for it exalted the white man above the position of owner, by taking away the responsibilities of ownership. It took from the freed slave all the hopes which had come into his heart by Mr. Lincoln's proclamation, and left him to feed upon the live coals of his old master's quickened lust and greed.

The only barrier to the strict enforcement of these provisions was the Freedman's Bureau, which during the greater part of the period from 1865 to 1869, in Mississippi, was presided over by a military commander whose sympathies were known to be with the conspirators. Thus it came about that their enforcement was intercepted only in localities where the subaltern in the Bureau had greater influence at headquarters in Washington than his superior, or clandestinely performed his duty when the dictates of a humanity common throughout the *civilized* world, wrung from him a spasm of manly interference, or when General Grant or Gen. O. O. Howard, or heroic Mr. Stanton ventured to brave the wrath of the conspirators and of the whole Democratic party of the nation, together with a large class of misguided Republicans who styled themselves "liberals," or as in most cases, "reformers."

In the county of Yazoo, under these provisions, men and women were cheated, swindled, robbed, whipped, hunted with blood-hounds, shot, killed; nay, more, men were robbed of their wives, their children, their sweethearts; fathers, brothers, sons, saw their mothers, wives, sisters, seduced, betrayed, raped, and, if Yazoo *law* afforded them any promise or hope of redress, Yazoo *practice* gave them no remedy whatever. The naked truth is, that the Congress of the United States took from that she-bear her cubs, and Andrew Johnson threw our lambs into the den.

CHAPTER XXXVIII.

A BRIEF SUMMARY—ANTICIPATIONS.

SUCH, then, was this old stubble-ground of slavery, grown rank in the cottonwood* planted by Andrew Johnson, while under the spell of that conspiracy.

I bear upon the little finger of my left hand a scar received in my first effort to whet a scythe. I had often seen one of the mowers cut a very pretty figure upon concluding his efforts to whet his scythe. At that instant when the last few rapid strokes of the stone at the point of the blade indicate that the left hand, which has patiently followed it all the way from the shank, may be released, he would seize the blade at the very tip by the same fingers which had steadied it upon its snath, standing upright, and by a dexterous twirl, cause the implement to describe a complete circle and come down flat upon its side to the ground with a ringing sound.

I admired this feat, and had watched the performer until I believed I had learned the "trick" of it, and so ventured to test my skill. But the rebellious point caught hold of the outside of my little finger and shaved off the skin nearly its entire length.

"I hope you'll learn from this lesson," said my father, "that scythes were not made for playthings."

* In the cotton region neglected fields are liable to grow up in cottonwood. When the growth is rank it is often more difficult to clear the field of it than at the first clearing, because of the numerous roots which run near the surface and project innumerable "knees" upward and out upon the ground.

I had learned to plow before I was fourteen, and well re‑
membered that it was a rule with father to plow deep in old
ground. I had learned to sell calico, weigh sugar, buy wheat,
settle cash, and keep accounts before I was sixteen, and never
knew father to sell a yard of anything, knowingly, that would
not " wash " for goods that would; sand the sugar, or weigh
the wheat in a hopper that had a false bottom, or upon scales
with false weights; make false entries in cash-book, or defraud
or oppress a debtor.

Although my father was a just and a good man, and my
mother the most patient, affectionate and devoted woman that
ever was, I had my faults, and knew them. I was not then,
nor do I pretend to be perfect now. But of one thing I felt
sure: what of ambition, lust, selfishness, or other evil I brought
home from the war with me, after more than four years at
the front, during the four subsequent years had all been
burned out of me in the crucible of fire in which I had been
tried.

The Sabbath-school on the hill, in the little church we
helped to build, was to me a sanctuary, our Yankee strong‑
hold, one of God's fortresses, and this new field a holy of
holies in God's temple upon earth, into which I dared not
venture with any other than robes of truth and righteousness.

If I had gone to the war to suppress an unholy and wicked
rebellion, and to free a portion of God's children from un‑
natural bonds, riveted by ungodly men, believing that the
service was God's service, so now I felt myself to be God's
servant in the work of clearing this old stubble-ground of
slavery. As such, I felt bound by every obligation of duty,
to stand erect in the face of error, to deliver my blows with
intent to kill, and leave the result to God.

Across the very threshold of this field lay the following
fundamental axiom of " the enemy," to wit:

" Experience has demonstrated that the white races are
the superior, the colored the inferior; " and also its corollary
in their system of political ethics, viz: " Therefore it is God's
will that the colored continue in subjection to the white races."

I had felt the full force of the effect of the enemy's attempt to re-establish in Yazoo and in the State the policy which was the logical outcome of that barbarous assumption. The consequences to me had been all the more disastrous because of Charles' assumption at the beginning ot our life in the South, that the rebels had been conquered at the moment they were disarmed; whereas the fact was, as they all, from "babes" to Colonel Black, persisted in maintaining, at all times and under all circumstances, that they had only been overpowered.

My experience had taught me, and theirs had convinced the General, Charles and Mr. Moss, and all the other Northerners in Yazoo, not excepting the one who had surrendered,* that Colonel Black and his allies were at all times able to demonstrate their right to voice the sentiments and the purposes of " we all " Southerners. At the same time, the physical endurance, industry, loyalty and trustful appreciation of our hands; the political foresight of the mass of the freed people of the county, as exhibited in their desire to have a native white man on their ticket, especially in discriminating against the purely "Yankee ticket;" the courage and devotion of the "guard" of the stronghold; the frenzy for knowledge of the great mass, and the fidelity and patriotism of all during those four years, had convinced me that the freed people of the county were the superiors of their former masters in physical strength, in manly courage, in political sagacity, and in love of country, and not inferior in any of the elements of good citizenship—general intelligence alone excepted. Therefore, applying my experience as a test, I was able to know that the conspiracy which had dominated Yazoo up to that moment, was for evil, and only evil; and that, as the conspirators embraced the intelligent class, it followed that the only way of reaching the citadel of the enemy's power lay through the intellects of the conspirators. Their policy relative to labor had proceeded upon the

* This man informed me months before his surrender was finally accepted by the enemy, that he had fought on that line as long as he could afford to; the "reserves were too far in the rear."

hypothesis that the most profitable laborer was the human machine, and they had rigidly excluded from them all knowledge except the merely mechanical art requisite to wield a hoe, or an ax, hold a plow or drive it, scrape cotton and pick it, wash potatoes and boil them, cut a steak and fry it, make a bed and—lie in it, or under it, according to the whim, caprice or desire of the owner of the bed and machine; with whom to see and at the same time not to see was enjoined as a duty; to perform, male and female, without the responsibilities attaching to a participant in the intrigues of which the machine was a prime factor, the menial services of social assassins and scavengers. The multiform complex-ities of a government whose corner-stone was such a policy, required for their elucidation " men learned above their fellows " in all the arts that policy engendered, and the maintenance of that policy required for these " learned men," a following apt in scenting, prompt in obeying and brutal in executing all the requirements of the chief conspirators, according *to their spirit.*

Of the total white population of the State in 1860, fifty-seven per cent. could neither read nor write, and thirty per cent. of this illiterate class were of that following. The sleuth-hounds of slavery, when that " divine institution" was " destroyed," they became carrion crows and fattened on its carcass. Having been without the means to purchase a slave, now that the slaves had become freedmen who could neither own nor lease lands, by taking advantage of their lighter complexions and of the " lien laws"* framed by their leaders, they could hypothecate the crops they *intended* to plant for the supplies requisite to feed and clothe the labor required to make the crop, *hire* freedmen and *compel* them to do the work required from January to Christmas, during the hours from dawn of day to darkness of night, of the entire period, refuse to pay or divide, and then walk over to the auction block and buy them in for another year as " runaways."

* Those laws enabled the planter to give a lien on the crops he expected to raise.

It was thus the enemy became united in a common interest, common purpose, and a common destiny, and, having become adepts at disguise and cowards at heart, they became kukluxes standing guard over their sacred mysteries. Had the kuklux possessed less intelligence they could have ranked as barbarians. Being the intelligent class they were savages.

How to reach their intellects and convince them that intelligent laborers were more profitable in the long run than ignorant ones became the question. Once convinced of this the doors of their citadel of power would fly open. The sword which hung over every approach to it could neither be scaled nor flanked. Political enginery would exhaust itself in efforts to that end.

Christianity scorned any other weapon of attack than the sword of truth, and commanded its soldiery to *strike home through shield and buckler to the bone and to the marrow in the bone.* Such a soldiery needed no mask—would be skillfu would be courageous, and the victory would perch upon the banners of those having the better-tempered blades.

Thus it came about that ours was the victory. And when at the close of the struggle we halted to take breath, looking about upon the field of battle, nothing remained of " the enemy's " defences but a foul stench.

CHAPTER XXXIX.

ABOUT GRANT'S " FAIR TRIAL "—ALSO OF CERTAIN EFFORTS TO
CAPTURE THE "ILLUSTRIOUS" SOLDIER BY INVADING HIS FAMILY
—A CHAPTER OF MISSISSIPPI STATE POLITICS—MR. BARKSDALE
BECOMES A " NATIONAL REPUBLICAN "—HOW IT ALL ENDED.

IN blank ignorance of the proceedings attending the forma-
tion of that conspiracy, and of its purposes, Charles and
I had attended to our business on Tokeba and the maturing
of our plans for the future development of the foundation of
that empire which was to be wrought out of the great deltas
of that marvellous valley—one which by the grace of God
shall yet be.

When at last we were wrecked and beaten upon by every
tempest from this seething political sea, thoughtful, patriotic
reader, is it to be wondered at that we seized upon the reconstruction measures of Congress as offering a safe harbor for
refuge ? that we put in there ? that we sought out the North
Star ? that we trusted to its calm, steady rays, as the sea-
tossed mariner does to the faithful indices of the magnet ?
and that, gathering together such parts of the common wreck
as could be found there upon that old stubble-ground, we
bound them together in one, and shoulder to shoulder with
the brave and true of our heroic crew, withstood the tide and
the tempest ?

It mattered nothing to us whether they were negro or mulatto, Northern or Southern, Irishman, Dutchman, Jew, rebel, white, yellow, or red. Were they loyal now? Were they true? Could they weep over the crimes against their colored fellow-citizens committed in the name of liberty, by this mottled tyrant and hybrid of slavery—that Mississippi conspiracy—as bitter tears as over the spectacle of " a white lady cooking her own bread ? "

Indeed and in truth this was a new field of labor. But there was a significance attached to the election of Grant to the Presidency which to us went further and meant much more than his personal triumph. It caused us to believe that the heart of the nation was in sympathy with the garrison of that Yazoo stronghold.

With me the " ball " had opened. I had passed the premonitory symptoms of the " imminent deadly breach." For months I had worn the scoffs, the curses, and the blows of the enemy as if they formed a crown, and now this crown had blossomed into a laurel wreath. This gave me not only faith in the future of Yazoo, it also gave me strength of purpose, of head, and of body, too.

So long as the anti-reconstructionists had openly and from policy no less than conviction, opposed the purpose of the nation toward their late slaves ; so long as the conspirators opposed all those principles which plainly had come to the top during the war, and by fidelity to which alone we had been able to win the victory over the cohorts of slavery, I had felt it to be my duty to treat the " disarmed " rebels as unworthy to lead in the work of laying the foundations of a free government in that State. Therefore as a member of the committee on " franchise," in our " black-and-tan convention," I had favored a clause relating to the qualifications of voters and for holding office, which would exclude from the enjoyment of those privileges until the inhibition should be removed by Congress, and that removal should be concurred in by our State legislature, all those persons so excluded in the amendments to the national Constitution.

That class had been thus disfranchised by Congress because of their treason and rebellion against the Union in the interest of slavery.

The motive which actuated " we all of that black-and-tan convention " had a juster foundation still. It was grounded in our knowledge, obtained by sore trial and heroic sacrifice, that nine of every ten of that class were still determined to win by their " superior sagacity and statesmanship" in the field of politics, what they had failed to accomplish upon the field of battle. We knew what we were doing. We were upon the ground. We were patriots, and not O'oophies, nor yet scalawags, nor even polecats. The consequences of our acts must fall upon our own heads. We could have purchased smiles, praise, even rich rewards in the shape of gifts from the enemy, had we been so craven as to be willing to treat with them. Not being so, we bared our heads to the pitiless storm. Some died under the terrors of it, others were shot, others hung, and at least one was burned. But now Grant was President. The knowledge of that fact literally suppressed the enemy. At the same time, it filled the blood of every loyalist in Mississippi with iron. Each and every one, no matter how weak and halting he had previously been, now became a reigning king, while the enemy groveled in the very dust. But yesterday they were defiant rebels. To-day they were repentant sinners, supplicating for mercy.

The men who had garrisoned that Yazoo stronghold were not tyrants. They bore the enemy no malice. For one, so strong was my faith in the power of the nation to work out its will in the South, I felt warranted in taking my stand upon the side of mercy. I have never regretted the fact that I did, for it was also the side of good State policy. The disfranchised class were so few in number that there would never be danger of their outvoting us. By leaving them to *pose* before their following as martyrs to a sacred cause they could work more trouble for us, now that the Government was certain to be given into our hands, than if relieved of that interesting character, they could possibly do by mere force of their numbers or of their virtues. So I became an enthusiastic advocate of "universal amnesty."

True it is, that the surrender of the enemy had been accompanied by many growls and vicious kicks, such as their efforts upon our stronghold before Grant had taken his seat and while Charles was in Washington. But this was while they still had Grant on "trial," and while they still hoped that his famous letter upon the condition of the South might more truly indicate the real state of his feelings and opinions toward the kukluxes than what they had termed his " unwarranted interference " with Mr. Johnson's purpose to make General Townsend Secretary of War in the place of Mr. Stanton, would seem to do.

Congress had passed a resolution authorizing the district military commander to remove from office all disloyal persons in Mississippi, and to fill the vacancies thus created with loyal men. Now that Grant was soon to take his seat, the enemy had made up their minds that " Mississippi will surely be reconstructed, but upon what basis cannot now be definitely stated," as the *Banner* announced. But still, as the *Banner* also further said, in the same issue, of that resolution of Congress, " it is for General Gillem to decide whether or not it is to be nugatory."

Just how General Gillem was to go to work to nullify the will of Congress, the *Banner* did not at that time venture to explain.

Shortly afterward, and when General Grant had been inaugurated and General Ames had been appointed to succeed General Gillem, the *Banner* did venture to comment as follows upon that fact:

" Grant is as bad as we said he was. He has not cared a pinch of dirt for the 'fair trial' which many Democratic papers so generously gave him."

But now " we all" Republicans had an organ. In its first issue the Yazoo *Republican,* among other things, said:

" We shall strive to forget the past, and, throwing our energies into the work, we shall endeavor to build up rather than destroy, and help to advance the interests of all. And to this end we shall advocate, among other things, impartial suffrage as the means, under our system, to secure impartial justice. We shall advocate a system of free public schools. We shall advocate the reconstruction of the State upon the Congressional plan."

But at this point, a little handful of Northern men in the State discovered that the Republican party had been " too proscriptive," and lacked " respectable leadership," and they very soon were known to be having lengthy consultations with members of that " Central Democratic Association." Whether upon their own motion or by invitation of the Democratic Association, I am not able to say. It was said at the time, and it was well known, that Mr. Ethel Barksdale, editor of the *Clarion,* was a chief counsellor and leader in this movement. It was also well known at the time that these very respectable Northern gentlemen professed to have "influence with Grant," and that they had succeeded in making Mr. Barksdale believe that they had such influence.

As the time approached, therefore, for the election, when our new constitution would be again submitted to a vote of the people by the aid of those Northern gentlemen that Central Democratic Association discovered that, after all, the new constitution was good enough for them, if only certain " proscriptive clauses " could be eliminated.

Whereupon, certain members of that association * met these very worthy and " highly respectable Republicans " in what was christened a " Conservative National Republican Convention."

The result of their efforts to give to the " Republican party of the State a respectable leadership," was the following ticket:

For Governor—Lewis Dent, " *carpet-bagger,*" and President Grant's brother-in-law.

* Otherwise called conspirators.

For Lieutenant-Governor—E. Jeffords, "*carpet-bagger*."

For Secretary of State—Tom Sinclair, an illiterate freedman of *Copiah County.*

For Auditor—A. W. Wills, "*carpet-bagger*."

For Treasurer—Jos. McCloy, "*carpet-bagger*."

For Attorney General—General Robert Lowry.

For Superintendent of Education—Thos. Gathright.

It was said that their nominee for governor resided in Coahoma County, Mississippi; but he was never a resident of the State, certainly not of that county, as the following certificate appears to show. It was distributed throughout the State during that campaign by the Republicans; I helped, of course:

"PROBATE CLERK'S OFFICE,
"FRIAR'S POINT, MISS., *Sept.* 18, 1869.

"MR. S. J. IRELAND:

"SIR: In answer to your inquiry as to whether Judge Lewis Dent is a resident or property holder in Coahoma County, Mississippi, I have to say that he is not a resident of this county, nor does his name or that of his wife, or any other person by the name of Dent, appear on the tax-rolls of this county, either as a landholder or a poll-tax payer.

" Very respectfully,

" GEO. R. ALCORN,

" *Clerk of the Probate Court, Coahoma County, Mississippi.*"

[Seal of my office.]

The only "high-toned, honorable gentleman" on the ticket was General Robert Lowry, an old citizen.* As their nominee for attorney-general, if elected. he would become the legal adviser of their government. The others, with only one exception, were all " new-comers" who, up to that time, had been known and described as carpet-baggers. Another peculiar feature of the ticket was " Tom Sinclair," nominee for Secretary of State. It was openly claimed for this ticket that it would have the hearty sympathy and support of the "illustrious " soldier, President Grant.

Our Republican convention met soon after, and it nominated the following ticket : For Governor, James L. Alcorn; for Lieutenant Governor, R. C. Powers ; for Secretary of State, James Lynch, colored ; for State Auditor, H. Mus-

* Present Governor of the State.

grove; for State Treasurer, W. H. Vasser; for Attorney
General, Joshua S. Morris; for Superintendent of Public
Education, H. R. Pease.

The following resolutions were adopted:

"1st. The Union first, last and forever.

"2d. Freedom of speech and of the press.

"3d. Universal suffrage and universal amnesty.

"4th. Free schools, presenting the benefit of education to every
child in the State.

"5th. Opposition to that unequal and unjust system of taxation
that discriminates against labor and bears unjustly upon the industrious class.

"6th. Revision of the code of laws of the State, so as to make it
conform with the conditions of free labor, with a view especially to a
more summary process for the recovery of debts.

"7th. Adherence to the 14th and 15th amendments to the Constitution of the United States.

"8th. The exercise of the whole political influence of the State with
Congress for the immediate removal, as provided, of all the disabil-
ities imposed by the 13th and 14th amendments.

"9th. The ratification of the 15th amendment to the Constitution
of the United States.

"10th. The new constitution of Mississippi, with the disfranchising and proscription clauses left out."

Our nominee for Governor was an old slaveholder—one
who had come into our camp. Mr. Vasser and Mr. Morris
were also old citizens and slaveholders who had joined our
side. Mr. Lynch was the most brilliant orator of his time in
Mississippi. The others were "carpet-baggers." Along with
those "proscriptive clauses," which the President decided to
submit to a separate vote, was section 5 of article 12, that
clause prohibiting the legislature of the State from loaning
the State's credit. It was understood that the supporters of
the Dent ticket had procured this action.

But this appears to have been about all they succeeded in
doing in the way of influencing President Grant, although
their candidate for Governor was his brother-in-law; for
while our convention was in session the commanding general
was invited to address it. General Ames replied as follows:

"Gentlemen, you have my sympathy and you shall have
my support."

It was not necessary that he should say more, yet, under the circumstances, he could hardly have said less, in justice to the President himself or to us. It was enough.

From that moment the Dent ticket began to lose confidence in itself; for, seeing that it had failed to capture President Grant, the conspirators themselves lost respect for it. Some of them made desperate efforts to rally their following to its support by openly proclaiming their purpose in nominating it. Among these was General William T. Martin, who made a speech, September 11th, 1869, to his Democratic friends at Natchez, in the course of which he said:

* * * "It matters not how much objection we may have to the Conservative Republican nominees, nor does it matter how odious the constitution may be to us, even as now submitted, I, for one, deem it expedient, in order to rid ourselves of Yankee-paid hireling office-holders, who are enemies to our people, to support the Conservative Republicans and vote for this constitution with all its enormities,* at the same time voting against the particularly objectionable clauses as submitted to a separate vote. By doing so we get our own officers† in power, and secure the control of the State government, then we can strip this odious constitution of every objectionable feature, and we can mould and form it to suit ourselves."

I shall not comment on this "movement." It speaks for itself.

* Did the General also object to section 22 of article 12?

† Let the reader turn back to pages 280 and 281 and again see who they were who were thus styled "our own officers" and who were the persons to be controlled.

CHAPTER XL.

A GENERAL BREAK-UP—"I TOLD YOU SO"—THE PRETTY PICKLE
OF THE ENEMY—DANGER SIGNALS.

THUS much about State politics was necessary to give the
reader an adequate idea of the situation in Yazoo.

Our party in the county had met in convention, pronounced
in favor of universal amnesty and also in favor of the reten-
tion of section 5, article 12, of the constitution. It had
also pronounced in favor of the "Alcorn ticket," as against
the "Dent ticket," and had nominated a full county ticket,
nearly half of whom were native white men.

The General and Captain Clark had been nominated for
the State House of Representatives. I had been nominated
for the State Senate. The convention also passed a resolution highly commendatory of the action of President Grant
and of General Ames.

I was not altogether satisfied with our ticket. But it was
the best we could do. Mr. Hillyard, our sheriff, and one
other, were the only persons from the class known as "best
citizens" whom we could induce, even with "fat offices," to
come out on our platform, which was the State platform,
heretofore quoted. Some insisted that Mr. Hillyard was
never one of Yazoo's best citizens, that he was originally
from the North, and, while it was true that he had been a
slaveholder, he had owned no more than half a dozen or so,

and was a " common sort of fellow." Now that he was on
our ticket he was in his true place—was a scalawag.

The other was a preacher. He had been owner of quite a
large "slave family." Parson Sivrup was a good man, they
all agreed. But he could never be coaxed into saying right
out in meeting that he was a Republican. He could say so
very freely in private, though, and this was something to be
thankful for.

The other ticket was called Republican too. But then it
was styled the "National Republican ticket," except when it
was called "the Conservative ticket." In the North, no Republican could have taken the least exception to that name.

With us it meant altogether more than its name implied.
It signified that its following were Republicans, with a
mental reservation; if they could at the same time be conservatives. In Mississippi, conservatism meant opposition to
change, and that meant opposition to any tampering with
Yazoo laws and customs, or interference with Yazoo practices; therefore, the conspirators become *National* Republicans.
It sounded well at the North, and, in Mississippi it was, after
all, but a name. And to cap the climax, even in Yazoo,
they nominated a "nigger" to go to the legislature and sit
alongside "de white gen'lemens and make de laws;" as their
candidate explained to his audiences.

When that fact was announced to "we all," I could not
help it, so I said—

"There, old fellow, I told you so."

"Told what?" inquired the General, for he had forgotten.

"Do you not remember me telling a company of Yankee
planters on a certain occasion, that the Johnnies would prefer
to vote for their old slaves rather "—

But now he remembered, and broke in on me thus—

"That was two years ago; I shall never be surprised at anything they may do, now that I know them better."

Their nominee for the State Senate was Major W. D. Gibbs.
He came of a very ancient and very distinguished family.

He was a very large planter, too, and supposed to be quite
wealthy. The "nigger" candidate had been this gentleman's
slave—also the slave of his father before him. He was still
living there on the same old home-place working "fur ole
mars jez' 'e same 'ez b'fo' de wah, no differn." His name
was Reuben Pope. They called—everybody called him
Reuben, except ole mars, who had always addressed him as
Rube—but neither in "slave time," nor since "freedom
came for all," had Rube ever been half the trouble to Major
Gibbs as now; for the Major had pledged himself to make
a thorough canvass of the county, and having been provided
with the necessary outfit, together these two, the Major and
Ruben, (master and slave), traveled up and down through
the "swamp" country chiefly—for there were more freedmen in the swamp than in the hills—holding meetings on
all the large plantations. Here is just where the Major
made a mistake. He should have "sont" Reuben. As it
was Reuben had waited on the Major so long that it had
become "second nature" to do so, and so could not help
waiting on him now, nor could he help calling the Major
"mastah."

Ever since our stronghold experience, our party had carried a flag along for use at our meetings. In this canvass, the
boys would have a drum and fife. Therefore, with "our
band" and our flag, we were able to make a most attractive
display. Seeing this and being determined to keep up with
"them d—n Yankees" for at least once in their lives, the
enemy undertook to get up a band too. Just here a new
difficulty presented itself to the enemy. They could neither
coax, buy nor drive the colored musicians to play for them.
The white musicians at first "swo' b'fo' God," they never
would play for the "niggers." But some of them yielded
after awhile, and a "sort of a band" was thus improvised.
But they had no flag, and had to send abroad for one. At
last they were ready and had everything arranged. But just
here the Major made a fatal blunder. Instead of carrying

the flag himself, or hiring a "po' white" to do so, he entrusted it to Reuben. This was the way they traveled. The
Major, with one of his chief supporters—very often it was
Captain Telsub, or Major Sweet, or Ben Wicks—rode on
ahead in their carriage. The band followed with Reuben and
the flag in the "band wagon."

This was too much. The patient, long-suffering freed people could not stand it any longer. So long as they had been
content to take Reuben along with them and to allow him to
assist in the care of their teams, to black their boots, and so
forth, the colored people had listened respectfully to them,
and also to Reuben when it came his turn to speak. They
had even gone so far as to treat Reuben decently in a social
way; would kill a chicken for him now and then, the same
as for old master, and would always give him a place to sleep
in. But Reuben, as standard-bearer for the *Democrats*, was
too much. It broke the back of the Major's camel. Poor
Reuben! It soon got so that no one had any chickens for
him, or any place for him to lay his head. The white folks
couldn't—just couldn't have him in their beds, nor at their
tables. Now they were in a pretty pickle. The Major and
his friends could not understand what it was possessed "our
nigros." Reuben was a negro like themselves, had been a
slave, had been a preacher, and was known throughout the
county. True, he had been a "so't of driver" for the Major's
father, but was always thought well of by his "own color"
until now. What could it mean?

I could have told them, but they did not ask me. Indeed,
they *knew* that I had no knowledge of the negro character.
At the same time I knew that they had no knowledge of the
free negro's character. They persisted that a "free nigger"
was a much worse sort of an animal than a "slave nigger."
I held that he was far better. Right there lay the gulf, between us, and there was great danger that it would grow
still broader and deeper.

Although Grant was President, and peace prevailed throughout the borders of Yazoo, during this memorable campaign the irreconcilables were still an element of discord, and on two occasions resorted to violence. They are worthy of a place here only because they illustrate the truth of what has gone before as respects the aggressive element in the ranks of the enemy. A few such "National Republicans" as Henry Dixon, Harry Baltimore, Ben Wicks, Captain Telsub, and Major Sweet, were sure to be present at each place of registration, at all political meetings, and at the polls afterward.

The first occurred at the place of registration.

As usual, Charles, though no longer a resident of the county, the General, and myself, were the target of the enemy, who taunted the freedmen with running after and supporting for office men who owned no real estate in the county. A blacksmith who owned no *taxable* property, being a freedman, ventured to respond to the taunt from a certain Dr. Pompous, by inquiring:

"Doctor, 'whar yo' tax 'ceipt?"

Of course a " freedman, free negro or mulatto" had no right to ask such a question. It was a misdemeanor by law, for, if not insulting in terms, it was doubtless so in "gestures largely, or acts," or "about" to become so. However, as the freedman had ventured he "was in for it," and stood up to it like a man, while his comrades began to gather close around him. They could anticipate the result, you see.

Dr. Pompous was not prepared for this. Why should he be? He had never had just such an experience before, probably.

But the doctor was equal to the emergency, and quickly and hotly exclaimed :

"Why, you d—d nigger ! Dare you insult me in that manner ! I'll teach you something, by G—d."

There was, however, another surprise in store for him. The blacksmith stood his ground and squared himself with great double fists for defense, as the doctor made a rush toward him. This so enraged the white man that he quite forgot the place and the occasion, and in great fury fairly leaped at the blacksmith. His passage, however, was barred by fully a dozen strong freedmen, who caught him some around the legs, some around his arms and body, while others pushed him back with their hands. Not a blow did they strike. Seeing the freedmen thus rally to the support of the blacksmith, the doctor's white neighbors and friends rallied in his behalf, and some of them out with their pistols.

At this critical juncture the registrar (who, under the law, was a *Federal* peace officer) sprang between them, and seizing the doctor ordered the freedmen to disperse.

" Ordered the freedmen to disperse ! Well, what did he do to the whites? "

"Nothing."

" Nothing ?"

" Well it amounted to that. He told them he was a Federal officer, sworn to keep the peace and to report all disturbances. He hoped they would see the necessity of keeping peace, at all hazards."

" Was that all ? "

" Yes." It had the effect to keep the peace for the balance of the day. You see it was a concession by the officer, that the white man had been insulted, and a compliment to him for his forbearance in not shooting " the nigger " instead of attempting to whip him, which had the effect of bringing about the best of feeling among the whites, who now rallied the doctor for having been obliged to compare tax receipts with a "nigger " or fight.

This was only understood by those of the crowd who knew that the doctor had paid no taxes since the war, and that the blacksmith had paid each year a poll tax of five dollars, a street tax of five dollars and other taxes, amounting to five dollars more.

The registrar himself told me of this occurrence, and added that, though he was a Federal peace officer, had he acted upon the fact that the whites were the aggressors, it would, to them, have been only "another illustration of the terrible nature of the tyranny under which they were groaning," and as their blood was up, the result might have been a bloody riot. As it was, perfect peace and good feeling had been restored.

The second one occurred at the hustings, and the reader will find the details of the incident as well as the result of it, in the succeeding chapter.

CHAPTER L.

YAZOO STUMP ORATORY—CAMPAIGN ARGUMENTS—THE LOGIC OF
EVENTS—A DEAD BULLDOZER—ONE TIME WHEN THE "NIG-
GERS" DID NOT RUN.

AS my reader has already inferred, "the enemy" hoped
to conquer "our nigros" by dividing them, and they
had been induced to put Reuben Pope upon their "Conservative National Republican" ticket for the legislature
with that object solely in view. In their political school,
the end had always justified the means, and although
Reuben was a very bitter pill, considering the end to
be gained, they could swallow him. They could go further. Under the spell of their anticipations, they could
wrap Reuben up in the grand old flag and swallow the whole
bundle; for, after all, it was a dose that could in nowise
take effect in any other quarter than upon "our nigros."
Indeed they were merely to pretend to swallow it. It was
the negroes who were to be cajoled by their sleight-of-hand
into making a square meal off of Reuben and the old flag.
Herein the enemy exhibited the same lack of correct knowledge of the *free* negro's character as formerly they had done;
for, while they reasoned that the freed people lacked dis-
cernment to enable them to see the hand of Esau in this
arrangement, the fact was that the colored people knew
old master so well they were on the lookout for just such
tricks. The only feature of this trick that appeared to sur-

prise them in the least was the old flag sugar-coating. The
"black folks" for so long had been witnesses of "old mars'"
contempt for the flag, that it had not occurred to them as
within the range of possible events that the "white folks"
could so far deceive themselves as to suppose for a moment
that its use for such a purpose would be accepted by any one
as evidence of real change of heart on the part of their former masters.   "Ole mar's 'low nigger got no sense 'kase he
ha' got no larnin'," Uncle Peter explained while "argufy-
ing " that feature of the campaign with some equally shrewd
companions. And Uncle Peter was right; for the old flag
had an opposite effect from what was intended. But the
enemy were not dismayed. They still boldly claimed that
Rube was gaining strength daily—making " the breach in the
colored vote of the county wider and wider every day,"
they said, and they weie boisterous in their offers to bet
that he would be elected. At first this feature of the canvass was not understood by any of us. Unkle Peter shook
his head and vowed, " Darz sholy sump'en g'wain ter drap,
sartin. Yo' jes' lis'en ter whar I'z a tellin' yo' all. Dem 'ar
white genl'menz has no mo' money ter trow 'way den we
all po' niggers, min' dat. I'z a talken now. Unkle Peter iz.
I tell yi' jes' you take car' yo'self. Dey is getten ready fur
some mo' mischuf, day iz; I knows um; can't fool me if I
iz a nigger and got no larnin'. I wor bornd wi' um, I wuz."

These sage observations of Uncle Peter were called forth
by the announcement that the enemy had challenged me to a
joint discussion of the issues of the day with Major Gibbs.
Anticipating this challenge and also the line of the Major's
argument, I had prepared myself with certain incontesta-
ble documentary evidence: ammunition that there had as
yet been no favorable opportunity for me to use, and I cheerfully accepted the enemy's proposal for a series of mass
meetings.

The first of these was at Dover Cross-Roads, in the southern part of the county, and in the neighborhood of the

Major's home   The arrangement was for my opponent to lead off with an hour; I was to follow with an hour and a half, and he to close with a half hour.

The audience was composed of about five hundred colored men, women, and children, and perhaps as many as forty or fifty whites assembled in the open yard about the front of the cross-road white folks' church, from the front of which was our speaker's stand.

There were not more than a half-dozen white Republicans present, most of whom were seated on the platform.   All the white Democrats—" National Republicans "—were upon the outskirts of the crowd, save only the Major, who, of course, had a seat with me upon the platform.   Of course there were no white ladies at all present.

The Major began by saying : " My colored feller citizens and friends," and then addressed his remarks altogether to the "feller citizens."   His tone and manner were as gentle and persuasive as a turtle-dove's, but notwithstanding that, before he was half through, considerable numbers of the colored folks had strayed off to the woods near by or to the corner store over the way.   As he had addressed himself altogether to the colored people I thought I might address my remarks to the white folks present, and so I did, for they were the sinners.

The Major had the advantage of me from the start, for he was able to say that they all knew him, knew his family. He was no stranger.   I could only say in reply to that part of his speech, that I had been for four years a resident of the county, and was already tolerably well known.   I hoped they would know me better after awhile.

The Major had said that he could appreciate their situation, their poverty, their distress.   If only they, the colored people, would " t'ar themselves away from their false leaders," and trust him, he not only could do, but truly would do a " heap mo' " for them than any stranger could.   Replying to this I begged the white people to allow me to say that the

Major's ability to keep any promise he might make must wholly depend upon the purposes and the temper of his party, and without wearying them with a recital of what the Major's party had done for the colored people, I proposed to show them what it had done for the white people of the State. Among the acts of the Major's party which I recalled to their memory was the following :

While under the control of the Major's party, the State legislature having chartered two banks, indorsed their bonds to the extent of several millions of dollars. These bonds the banks sold in Europe, and the proceeds they divided amongst their confederates in the swindle. Afterward the State repudiated its obligation as indorser, and left the creditors without any remedy at all. By this single act the Major's party had blotted out the name of the State from all the world's marts.

Then I reminded them how they had never had free schools, nor but few of any kind ; how the efforts of the nation to aid them in that direction by generous grants of land had been made abortive by converting the proceeds of those lands to private uses ; how, always, taxation had been laid upon the feebler industries, and only the great slave lords had shared in the benefits of the system. Only a very few years back this same party, under a different name, but the same party, had met together in a convention and passed the secession ordinance, refused to allow those whom they claimed to represent to pass upon their work, and thus without any vote of the people, even the white people, had dragged the State headlong into a long and bitter war. To be sure that was when slavery was in the saddle. But though slavery was in the saddle, and, as the war progressed, it appeared to be also in the balance, at that moment when the scales were even, this same party, under a different name, of course, but the Major's party all the same, passed a law which expressly provided that all who owned as many as " twenty negroes " should be exempt from conscription, exempt from fighting for slavery, and then provided their conscript officers with blood hounds to be used in hunting down the poor whites who refused to be conscripted, and who ran away rather than fight for the protection of the slave-holder's right to own twenty or more negroes. At last, when they had failed to break up the Union by the secession road, they had retreated back only to the very first "forks" and gone off pell-mell upon another, which, in my opinion, led to the same end as the former, though, as I had never travelled either one, of course I couldn't say positively, but would leave them to judge for themselves, and therefore I read from their own books the record of their proceedings and their acts. By these, I said, must the Major's party be judged. And judging from their record I would leave them to infer as to the Major's ability to carry out his promises, however sincere he himself might be. Then, without venturing to promise anything for myself, I begged them to consider whether it would be possible for me or for my party to do worse.

The Major had declared that nobody but Yankees had prejudice against the freed people on account of their color. This, he insisted, was true, because even Fred. Douglass, "the greatest black man that ever lived, and the man who made the radical party," had only a few days before been refused a seat at the table in a hotel up North; "the same place where Colonel Morgan, their god, came from." More than that, he said, they even hung colored folk to lamp-posts up North; "there where Horace Greeley, the worst abolitionist that ever was, lived and published a newspaper;" even in Massachusetts, "where all the abolitionists came from"—a State represented in Congress by a man "who believed white men ought to marry nigros—the colored ladies;" even there there was "heap mo' prejudice and hard feelings against colored folks than in the South." For one, he had no prejudice "No true Southerner had any prejudice against the color which God gave the nigros, and which they could no mo' help than they could fly." They all knew his black

mammy, Aunt Sally. Why! she had suckled him, and he loved
her to that day as much as his own dear mother, almost.*

I confessed my inability to make as satisfactory reply to
this as I could wish. But, while it was true that Yankees
were greatly prejudiced against color, I believed that the
fact was due in large part to the efforts of former slave-
owners, who were interested in making the negroes appear
to be naturally very offensive; to possess certain physical
characteristics which were repugnant to the tastes of refined,
sensitive persons. Knowing that Yankees were, as a class,
that sort of people, the slave-owner had taken advantage of
the fact to show that slavery was a sort of necessary evil by
making the victim appear naturally so offensive in color,
features and smell that they could not be tolerated in any
other sphere than one of menial service. They had, I regretted to say, been so far successful, that many Northerners
had been ashamed even to admit that they were fighting for
the freedom of the slave, whereas every one knew that they
were. It was natural, I continued, that there should still
remain much of this feeling in the North, for slavery had
died very hard, if indeed it was yet quite dead. But, I
said, the Major was hardly consistent; for if it were true that
Mr. Douglass made our party, it could hardly be that it was
prejudice against color.

However, it was well known that first impressions were
most enduring. The old slave masters had always taught
the Yankees that all negroes have and emit at all times a very
foul odor. I presumed there were many Republicans who
still believed that. The Major's story about Aunt Sally would
hardly be believed in the North, not because infants were not
put out to nurse there, but because it had always been represented to Northerners, by those who were supposed to know
the negro best, that *all* negroes, women included, had a bad
smell.. Yankees had been taught another thing by the old

* I have heard a great many native Southern men speaking to mixed assemblies of
colored and white men, and have never yet listened to one who did not make the
same claim to kindly consideration by the blacks.

slave-owners. They had been taught that the negro's color was so tenacious, there was something in it so subtle that no matter how white one might become, through the bleaching process of the old slave system, they were certain to "breed back," as the saying was, and become in a few generations again as black as ever.* I feared greatly, I said, that these inventions of slave-owners, for the purpose of better securing their property, would some day return to plague the inventors. I denied that either charge was true, and appealed to the Major to sustain me, which he did. Therefore, I said, it was clear that Northern prejudice was due to lack of correct information and to the misrepresentations of slave-owners. Happily, all that was now passed, and I hoped the time was near at hand when there would be no prejudice anywhere against *color*. Indeed, we should have no prejudices. The Major had also said that the Yankees never would have gone to war but for the tariff; that the Yankees wanted " we all Southerners " to pay them a bonus for making the machinery and goods which the South was compelled to have from the North. This the South had refused to do, and so the war came.

" Now," said he, " they are paying these carpet-baggers to work on you all agin us," and he had added threateningly, " It'll get yo' all into trouble, sho.'"

In reply to this part of the Major's speech, I insisted that the tariff was not an issue of our campaign. The only question pertained to the reconstruction of the State. When this should be finally settled, and we had a free government in the State, we could discuss the tariff question. The Major had declared that there was no difference between our platforms. To this I replied that apparently there was not, but in truth there was. Their platform had not one word to say in denunciation of the great wrongs the Major's party had inflicted upon the poor by their wicked system of taxation; not one word in condemnation of any part of the conduct of

*The Major winced under this, for it had been said that one of his ancestors was a black.

that party in the long years of its control. True, the platform favored a system of free schools, but my hearers must
remember that this was the same party that only four years
before had, in effect, by law prohibited the education of a
large majority of the people of the State.

In the course of his remarks, the Major had charged that
while our candidate for governor had been a large slave-
owner, and was known to have been one of the most cruel
slave masters in all the South, so cruel and inhuman that he
had once punished a slave by castrating him, their candidate *was General Grant's own dear brother-in-law.*

To this I replied that while it was true that our candidate
had been a very large owner of slaves, he had long ago re-
pented of that folly, and in proof of his sincerity had been
for years standing squarely upon our platform, and that not
only he but his former slaves and his neighbors all denied the
charges of inhumanity which were now, for the first time,
brought against him.

The Major had boastfully referred to the fact that they
had a colored man on their ticket; a plain, honest, hard-
working man, like themselves, and then, there was Reuben,
Reuben Pope, on their county ticket. They had known
Reuben—Mr.—Mr. Pope—it *was* difficult for the Major to say
Mr. in that presence and in that connection, but he did—
they had known Mr. Pope all their lives.

(All his hearers knew Reuben Pope well, for the meeting
was within but a very few miles of that candidate's home,
which was still the Major's home. But it had been better
for the Major, no doubt, had they not known Reuben. As
it was, they knew him too well. Although he was also a
preacher he had in some way not been able to make himself
popular with the freed people, and now that he had come out
openly on the side of the enemy his colored neighbors despised
him. But Reuben Pope was a live fact. There he was, a pure
African, so far as I could see, and the " high-toned, honora-

ble gentlemen of Yazoo " had placed him upon their "National
Republican " ticket alongside of a representative of one of
the "oldest and most distinguished families in the county."
He could neither read nor write, nor did he own any real
estate.)

Replying to this part of the Major's speech, I reminded
the people of the fact that less than two years before the
Major's party had unanimously refused to vote at all, solely
because the freed people had been allowed the same privilege.
I presumed there were many in my audience who had heard
many of the Major's party associates swear they would die
before they would go to the polls and " vote with a nigger."
My hearers must judge for themselves what had wrought so
great a change in the temper and purposes of the Major's
party. The Major had proudly declared that his party was
in favor of the constitution I favored; that the only reason
they had opposed it before was because it had disfranchised
the white people, and he was glad to say that many of his
colored friends had opposed it for that reason, and thus aided
their white friends to defeat it. Now, that those disfranchising clauses had been left out, everybody favored it.

To this I replied that the so-called disfranchising clauses
went no further than the Constitution and laws of the
United States, and. if it were true that the whites were
disfranchised by the laws of the nation, how was it possible
that those same disfranchised whites had been able to cast
enough votes to defeat the new constitution? The fact was,
I said, that only a year before the whites had refused to vote
on the question of calling a convention to frame a free constitution, because, as they themselves declared, the colored
people were allowed to vote too.

When the convention had been called in spite of them, and
by the aid of the votes of the freed people almost alone and
when that convention had performed its duty and the new
constitution was submitted to the people, black and white,
for their approval or rejection, finding that it was sure to be

approved unless they should vote, they had been able to get
enough votes in the boxes against it to defeat it. My hearers
knew by what means, and we need not open old sores by
referring to them. Now, however, after only one year had
passed, we found this same party not only willing to vote alongside of the colored people, but also to vote for one; not only
that, but actually favoring that constitution they had all the
while been denouncing as a "monstrosity," a "bundle of
enormities;" not only that, they were now anxious to have
for their governor the brother-in-law of the man they had
unanimously all the while denounced as a butcher and as a
tyrant, *solely because he was the relative* of President Grant.
My hearers must judge for themselves of the true character
of the "conversion." I would not say it was not sincere.
I hoped it was. But ordinary prudence suggested that we
leave them on probation for at least a year or two.

Comparing the two tickets as a whole, in proof that "our
people"—he was not willing to admit that the Southern men
upon our ticket any longer belonged to that class—that "our
people" had no objection to Northern men because they
were Northerners, the Major had boasted that a majority of
the men on their State ticket were from the North—"the
same place yo' god, Mawgin, come from," and were "just as
good friends of the nig—of the colored people" as Colonel
Morgan, and better, too.

For a reply I said yes, that was true. I had never supposed for a moment that the Major's party had any more
prejudice against Northerners than was wholesome and good
for all concerned, provided the Northerners were shrewd
enough to anticipate their wishes and willing to conform to
their ways. The pity was that in this case their candidates
had never been able to do this until after Grant became President, and it was a further great pity that, having roundly
abused those same candidates as Yankee-paid hirelings, they
should never have discovered their mistake until after Grant
became President and General Ames became military com-

mander. Much time— a whole year—and great expense, all the expenses of the Major's party of the year before, could have been saved, besides some lives and much bitterness of feeling, if the Major's party had only have nominated and supported this same ticket a year earlier.

During the Major's talk there had been but very infrequent manifestations of approval from the whites and none at all from the blacks ; but, although my remarks were argumentative and dry, the colored portion of the audience had increased in numbers and were pressing close about the stand.

Up to this time, while I had borne quite heavily upon the Major's party, I had made no attempt to reply to the more personal features of his speech. Indeed, it was quite difficult to make any reply to them. They were rather in the nature of innuendo then open reflection upon me, and I was somewhat at a loss how to meet them. I could see that he was thoroughly understood by both white and black, and, as the custom of the country would never admit of my wholly ignoring his criticisms of me personally, it became my duty to make some allusion to them. Indeed, were I not to do so he would be sure to call attention to the fact in his closing remarks, when, by the terms of our agreement as to order of speaking, there would be no chance for me to reply. He had been a little inconsistent in some of his statements. For example, he had said : " These men ain't down here for no good ; just stirring up strife, and getting yo' all " (meaning the freed people) " into trouble. Yo'll see."

He had savagely denounced our legislative ticket because of the number of Yankees on it. At the same time he had warmly approved their State ticket for the same reason, and had even boasted that there were more Yankees("old abolitionists ") on their State ticket than on ours, and he had charged and had dwelt at considerable length upon the fact that I owned no real estate in the county, and could not, therefore, represent the property interests of the people, and he had appealed to the "colored people " to exhibit a wise discretion on this first occasion of their "free exercise of the great privilege of voting for the officers of government," and prove their capacity by voting for old citizens, *gentlemen* whom they had known all their lives, and who, by reason of their being property owners, were identified with "the interests of the *South*," and would labor for the "welfare of we all."

About the moment I began my reply to this part of the Major's speech, a young country white man, a stranger to me, who had climbed upon the stand in rear of me, touched my elbow and whispering into my ear, inquired—

"Colonel, yo' got a pistol ?"

"Yes," said I, for I had that morning provided myself with one.

"Thar's g'wain to be trouble y'here to-day, Colonel, an' if yo'll gie it ter me I'll stan' by ye."

" I thanked the young man for his kindly offer, but thought I could defend myself, and so informing him, I resumed my talk."

As to the Major's references to myself, I declared that many of them knew when, where, how, and under what circumstances I had come amongst them ; of our struggle with Colonel Black and his allies and so forth. At this point the Major interrupted me, to explain that he had never sympathized with Colonel Black and his friends in that matter. For one, he was in favor of welcoming Northern *gentlemen*.

"Yes," I replied, "the Major had *privately* assured me of that fact several times, for which I felt obliged, of course. But the fact remained, nevertheless, that, now that General Grant "—here the colored people gave a shout and the whites growled—"now that General Grant was President, the Major and his friends had gone all the way to Washington, and taken the General's brother-in-law to be their candidate for governor. He was a man who did not reside in the State, and the only ground he had for claiming citizenship was the fact that his wife, a Southern lady, had once owned a plantation in the State. While they were doing this, and while they were

clamorous now for Northern immigration, they could not forget
that General Greenleaf, Captain Clark, my brother and myself,
were carpet-baggers. Not only had it been impossible to induce one of their number to be a candidate on our ticket,
they were so bitterly hostile to it that they had put up a man
against us who could neither read nor write, and were all going
to vote for him simply and solely because he was a colored
man, hoping thereby to be more certainly able to defeat us."

Here the colored portion of the audience cheered, and some
of them exclaimed : "That's right, Kunnel ! Now yo' is a
talkin' the trooth ! Can't fool us dat er way nohow! We
noes Reuben Pope, ya, ha, ha ! "

In other words, they had shown by their acts that a new-
comer's status among them depended entirely upon his political preferences. If, being Northern born, he affiliated with
them he might expect to be called a gentleman. But, if he
stood up for Republican principles and the common rights of
the colored people he was a carpet-bagger. Now, said I,
fellow-citizens, all, you must judge for yourselves as to the
meaning of this so-called National Republican ticket. Look
at it. Their State ticket is made up almost entirely of Northern men and carpet-baggers, so called. Have they offered
to put even one of that class upon their county ticket for the
legislature ? With the exception of Reuben Pope, they are
all of the same political party that tried to take the State
out of the Union, that passed the black code, and that have
always been opposed to Republican principles. Now, said I,
the Major's party has done the same thing in nearly every
other county, and that means that, should they be able to
elect their county ticket, they will have so large a majority
in the legislature that they will be able to work their will in
spite of the Governor and all the other State officers, for the
reason that those officers would be powerless with the legislature opposed to them. Then I challenged the Major to
point out any such inconsistencies in the record of our party
or in our present ticket. Whereupon some one of the whites
exclaimed :

" Yo' don't own no land."

I had heard similar exclamations before during my talk, and was now prepared to answer it.

" Do all your candidates own land ?"

It was agreed that Reuben did not, and I suggested that there were four on their State ticket who were believed not to own any land in the State, and, besides, there were at least two on their county ticket who did not. I had understood, I said, that my opponent for the Senate owned none in the State or elsewhere. This was laughed at. I begged them not to laugh, for, without wishing to be personal, I thought I could prove that the Major owned not an acre of land. Then I brought out my documents and read from the sworn statement of my opponent himself, made before a registrar in bankruptcy that the only property he *owned or controlled* was a horse, saddle and bridle, saddle-bags, double-barrelled shot-gun, and a navy Colt's revolver!

This announcement, authenticated by the seal of the court, produced a decided sensation, for my opponent resided upon a large and valuable plantation, which, however, shortly before going into bankruptcy, by some " hocus pocus " had become the property of his wife; in name.

I might have added that Mr. Mix, the tailor at Yazoo City, had informed me that the Major obtained credit of him for an elegant suit of clothes only a short time before taking the benefit of the bankrupt act, and included the amount in his schedule of indebtedness filed in that court, and had paid the bill by notice of his discharge by that court of all liability therefor.

Shortly after the interruption by the young countryman which I have mentioned, two men, strangers then to me, came out from the little group of the enemy which had collected at the front of the corner store just over the way, bringing with them a half drunken-fellow—judging by his manner—of whom they let go as they approached the mass of freed men and women in front of me.

This half-drunken fellow elbowed his way violently through the mass, pushing along with himself what appeared to be a half-witted or half-drunken black man that had come into view from a quarter unknown to me, until he reached a point directly in front and below me. His approach had been so violent that it had greatly disturbed the people along his way, and, having reached the point indicated, he commanded the negro to curse me.

"Tell 'im he's—hic-a-hic—liar; G—d d—n him."

His tone was one of suppressed anger, and, though resolved not to allow it to interrupt me, he repeated it so often that the portion of the audience about him were greatly disturbed by it, and became somewhat indignant when in reply to a polite request of one of the leading colored men present that he should keep still, he exclaimed "You're a d—d lyin' s— of a b—"

I had kept right on with my remarks, not regarding the offender further than to keep watch of him, and of the group of the enemy at the store front, amongst whom were some guns. But the colored man who had addressed him, now joined by two or three others, made a motion as if to take hold of his arm. At that instant the bulldozer "whipped out a pistol" and fired at the colored man, who would have fallen to the ground had he not been caught by a comrade.

Upon the instant I sprang from the platform amongst them, followed by two of the "white Unionists," and some from the group about the store rushed over toward us.

There were as many as ten, perhaps thirty, shots fired, on both sides, and when the battle was over, the women and children, most of whom ran at the first discharge, came back on the grounds from out of the bushes near by and from down the road beyond, about the moment that the Major and I had reached a conclusion that it would be just as well that I should agree to not finish my speech there on that day, if he would not claim his right to close, and I promised to let it be known from our side that he had done all he could to "stop the row."

The only man killed was the bulldozer, who had not retreated more than ten steps when he fell, and was dead before
the battle was over.

The man he had shot, however, became a cripple for life,
from the very bad wound just below the groin.

Mr. Foote had received but a "slight scratch," a woman
thought she had been hit, and I escaped without anything
more than the smell of fire upon my clothes. I had merely
stood my ground, and had not fired. It had ended almost as
soon as it began, and the "niggers" did not run, either. The
news of the battle reached town before we could, notwithstanding we drove pretty rapidly, and passed over the base
of Peak Tenariffe at least three hours earlier than Colonel
Black and I had done on a former occasion. Mr. Barksdale and certain other "law-abiding citizens" had already
held a hasty consultation, and recommended to the sheriff
the employment of a large number of extra deputies to enable him to put down the "insurrection already begun,"
p'edging him the aid of "every good Democrat" in the county
to keep the enemy quiet, if only he would "protect them
against the nigros," who, it was feared, having once tasted
the sweets of self-preservation, would fly into all sorts of
license unrestrained.

The sheriff to " humor them," solemnly promised to protect
them and the "white women and children from the cradle
up," and swore in some few extra deputies to that end.
But the "insurrection" ended where it began, with the bull-
dozer, and our joint discussion ended also, and that was thereafter the most peaceful, good-natured campaign ever held in
the county, and the election the most quiet, orderly, and fair
ever held before or since in Yazoo County. General Grant
was President and General Ames was *military* governor
then, and, though the vote was large, the new free constitution was ratified *unanimously*, and the Republican ticket was
elected by an overwhelming majority, and there was perfect
peace in Yazoo.

CHAPTER LI.

AN EXAMPLE OF "ŞUPERIAH STRATEGY"—A BRIEF RESUME—
THE LESSONS OF 1869—HAPPY POLECATS.

IN strict justice to that "National Republican party" of Yazoo I ought to add here that an effort was made to induce me to take sides with them in that canvass. The "chairman of the Democratic White Man's party" of 1867 and 1868 and Captain Telsub essayed the task, and I must confess they performed their duty in a most bungling manner. First came Captain Telsub, apologizing for his past rough treatment of me, and explaining how it was all due to the very natural feelings of "we all," who had been "fo'ced to give up everything," etc. He hoped I would forgive and forget, and now that everything had been settled by the election of Grant, who, he believed, would, after all, make a good President for the South, there was no longer any reason for keeping up the old feelings. I begged the Captain not to worry himself about anything that had occurred in the past. I hoped he and all the rest of them had forgiven me my shortcomings as fully as I had theirs. This he assured me he believed was the case—that in fact I was much better thought of by the high-toned people of the county than I was or could be aware of under the circumstances. The fact was my brother and I had been misunderstood by "our people;" there had been misunderstandings all around. But he would like me to have a talk with the chairman.

I assured him nothing would give me greater pleasure at
that time. Thereupon, the Captain withdrew, and within ten
minutes returned with the said chairman, who went over
pretty much the same ground as the Captain had. I was glad
to hear him express such sentiments, and so told him; adding
that I looked upon it as a most happy augury of the future.
Indeed, I had hoped that he would identify himself with our
party. I said I thought it the true policy of all the better
class of the white people. The Captain coughed at this point,
and the chairman turned red as he replied that it was impossible; for, while it was true that there was no longer any real
difference in the platforms and policies of the two parties,
yet " our people" had determined to support the " liberals "
as presenting the better ticket, and—well, it was more accept-
able to them; therefore he should go with his people, and
they were going to win, too, for Grant was sure to be their
friend in the movement. *He could* not oppose his own
brother-in-law; besides—well, they knew where Grant stood.
They had assured the President that the election should be
a peaceful one; that no one should be interfered with in his
right to vote. The only obstacle he declared in the way of
an overwhelming victory for their ticket was the " clannish-
ness of the nigros," who, having got used to following a certain set of leaders, would stick to them for fear of being put
back into slavery if they did not. He wished to see that sort
of thing broken up. Every good citizen should desire the
same thing. The policy of his party, he frankly admitted,
was to " divide the nigro vote." They could not do that
without the aid of those in whom they had for some unac
countable reason put their trust. There was not a man in the
State who had the confidence of the negroes to a greater extent than I, unless it was my brother. He and his associates
had been talking the matter over, and they had come to the
conclusion that if I could be satisfied that they meant to keep
their promises made to the negroes I could be induced to
take the lea ling place upon their ticket, and then there could

be no doubt of the result. I could take my choice. My acceptance would satisfy the best citizens that I intended to become one of them, and, thereafter there would be nothing in the way of my achieving any place in society or politics, to which I might aspire, and everybody knew I had a right to aspire for the highest. Then he stopped.

The chairman's serious demeanor and the very grave countenance of Captain Telsub, together with my feelings as the chairman advanced in the unfolding of the object of their visit, made the atmosphere of my room somewhat oppressive, and I arose and opened the door, which they had closed behind them on entering. This appeared to increase their embarrassment, and they both trembled with suppressed excitement during my reply, at the close of which they walked out, but no farther than the length of the gallery, when they halted and for a moment consulted together. Then the Captain, with face larger and redder than ever, returned, and walking close up to me, said: "Morgan, you all have sacrificed everything here in this county already. Yo' must know that ou' people never will submit to be governed by niggers. Sooner or later you'll see that I'm right. Now ther's a chance faw yo' to make youah peace with we all, and a stake, say $5,000——Besides"—— But the Captain did not wait to finish his sentence, and ever afterward hung his head whenever he met me.

We had all learned much that year, and all came to have a better knowledge of each other.

First, the enemy found out where Grant stood. They had not been able to deceive him again, nor were they able to deceive General Ames, nor had they been able to deceive the "garrison" of the late "stronghold of Yazoo." The trick of the enemy deceived none but their own followers, who, delighted at what they were quick to proclaim was a master stroke in diplomacy, were led to hold out "one campaign more." Of course it did not deceive the colored voters; for, while the enemy with a smile that was "childlike and

bland," held up Alcorn to be scorned by them because he had
been a " cruel slave-holder," and held up " General Grant's
own dear brother-in-law " for their Moses, the colored people hung their heads in very shame at the stupidity of their
old masters, and grew more suspicious of them and consequently more " unreliable " for old masters' purpose, than
before.

The conspirators had failed to divide the colored vote,
even though they nominated Judge Dent and a Yankee State
ticket, and even though in counties like Yazoo, where the
colored voters largely predominated, they had nominated at
least one such man as Reuben for the legislature, and boldly
declared that their ticket proved that they were just as good
friends of the freed people as the Republicans were or " dared
be." On that point they were answered by the colored men
themselves, who everywhere and on every occasion retorted
that they did not need to have any of their "own color" on
any ticket upon which I ran. This fact was in a measure
illustrated by their poor Reuben, who lost standing not only
with the brethren on the plantation, but with those on adjoining places, and in the church. While in the canvass, not
having been permitted to share any of the hospitalities extended to the other candidates, and being heartily scorned by
the family servants of those who entertained them, he had
fared very badly indeed. But his party had provided him
with an elegant new suit of clothes, fine silk hat and cane,
and some pocket money, and allowed him to carry the flag.
Toward the close of the race, it was rumored that the Major
had had him to eat at the same table with himself by way of
resenting the jeers of the colored people, who had often
asked Reuben if he intended to act as " ole marsa's body-
servant" after he should " take his seat " in the legislature,
as one of their law-makers. But all the devices of the enemy had failed, and when at last the votes were counted, the
result announced, and it was found that he had not been elected
by a large majority, that his own party had "scratched" him,

all Reuben's egotism, all his ambition to become a law-maker went out of him, and he returned with his "ole massa" to the old home, and afterward became a Republican.

We had been able to penetrate the " darkest holes " in the county, such as Sartartia, Deasonville and Dover, and had a Republican meeting on one of the plantations of Ben Wicks and that of Harry Baltimore, and had carried the grand old flag wherever we went. The enemy had learned from us, too, as we have already seen; they, too, carried the grand old flag about with them. We were content that they should. They had also *seen with their own eyes* that the " freedman, free negro and mulatto," dared shoot to kill. But now it was all over and the victory was ours. Of course we were happy The enemy were disconsolate.

At the beginning of the " Dent," "National Republican," " Conservative," " Liberal " movement the irreconcilables stoutly protested. They would not "stoop to beg votes of our nigros." Never! They insisted that the freed people had no more constitutional right to vote now than they had the year before, and they were unwilling to accept the election of Grant as settling the question of their status in the Government. They were too straightforward and honorable to resort to a subterfuge for the purpose of deceiving them into voting for their candidates. They would treat them as they had always done. Any other policy, they said, would but open the door for still further concessions to " that usurpation at Washington," and " end in the degradation and final subjection of the Caucasian to the African." They would " die first." But as the canvass progressed, they were gradually " whipped " into the "National Republican" traces, and at the last, actually took their places in line with the negroes *and waited their turn to vote.* What a picture! To them it was "nauseating." To us it was fun. The character of that " movement " was exposed by the fact that the conspirators took great care to place all responsibility of it upon the shoulders of the little handful of Northerners at its head, and refused in any way to commit their own party, as an organization, to their platform of principles.

But it afforded General Grant an opportunity to render "the South a great service," while at the same time helping a member of his own family into the United States Senate, which, it was understood, was to be Judge Dent's reward, and it could thereby be done without danger of subjecting the President to the criticism of his own party. The enemy hoped and confidently expected by the same trick to obtain a majority in the legislature, which after all was the seat of power.

Once enthroned there, they would be at liberty to pursue their old means of fraud and intimidation without restraint. Should they fail to win Grant, they could make a "still hunt" for Republican votes and palm off upon the "freedmen, free negroes and mulattoes," their ravenous wolf for a gentle ewe lamb. If, thereby, they could succeed in electing a bare majority and no more to the legislature, they would have an attorney-general upon whom they could rely for such construction of the new constitution as would protect them in any revolutionary proceeding they might see fit to adopt, and could "shape and mould" things to their liking.

But it all failed, and again illustrated how little they knew of the character of President Grant, or the character or capacity of the *free* negro, and how low was their estimate of both.

It was a *dernier ressort*, to be sure, and fitly illustrated the desperation of the enemy. Now that it was all over, the irreconcilables only said, "I told you so," and resumed their former occupation of cursing the "insolent, lazy, ungrateful nigros," and "bided their time." Hoping and believing that their nausea would be followed by symptoms indicating a change for the better, in the condition of the "sick man" of Yazoo, almost believing that our remedy would drive out the taint in the blood of the patient, we all went to work in the now enlarged field, and were happy.

CHAPTER LII.

HARRY BALTIMORE'S OPINION OF OUR FIRST "NIGGER CON-
STABLE"—MORE STRAW FOR BRICKS—A CASE IN POINT—
ADDITIONAL INDUCEMENTS TO A SOLID SOUTH—A TRUTHFUL
PICTURE OF SOUTHERN DOMESTIC LIFE—A LINE THAT WAS
NOT WIPED OUT AT APPOMATTOX, NOR EVER AFTERWARD.

MR. FOOTE, early in the administration of General Ames,
had been made a constable. One day one of Harry Baltimore's hands came to town and lodged complaint with our
Republican magistrate against that "high-toned, honorable
gentleman," for beating him, and for setting his dogs on him.
The magistrate issued his warrant for the arrest of General
Baltimore, and placed it in the hands of Mr. Foote for execution. Now, the magistrate and General Baltimore were
"white men." Foote was a negro—so called—but he executed
that warrant with such courage and discretion, that, during
his trial, General Harry Baltimore felt called upon to say, in
open court, that while the magistrate was "a d—d thief,"
Mr. Foote was a high-toned, honorable gentleman ; for he
could do no other way than "try to execute the d—d warrant."

Mr. Foote had another experience that year. A young
white man set out to "teach him a lesson," but he learned
one of Foote instead ; for Mr. Foote whipped him. This
was 1869.

We made great strides forward that year. Our varied contests with "the enemy" up to this time were likely to prove the best instructors. Some of the officers of election were young men who had been educated in the school taught in the little church we helped to build.

One day while I sat in my office—no longer next door to the livery stable—revolving in my mind projects for the further improvement of the situation, there came a gentle, timid knock at the door, and I heard faint cries of a child accompanied by a mother's hush-sh-sh-h. Opening, there stood a comely black girl, with a babe in her arms. I bade her come in. She was neatly but wretchedly clad. There was only a faded wrap upon the infant.

The mother's shy and expressive embarrassment while she tried vainly to soothe the babe, with her evident desire to say something to me, prompted the offer of a chair. This she took, with a surprised, grateful look and word of thanks.

"What can I do for you?"

"I comed y'here fur ter see de Kunnel—da lawyer. Beez yo' de gen'leman?"

"Yes; I am practising law—a little."

But the child had not been hushed, and the mother, pale from her agitation—yes, black women can turn pale, so can they blush; I have seen both—arose, and, pacing the floor with the child at her breast, thus soothed it. This action failed to calm the woman, however; for, as she began her story in response to my request, the hot tears came chasing each other down her cheeks to her breast, and the child drank them in with her milk.

Now, gentle reader, don't turn away; this is a life picture —hardly that. I cannot paint it in true colors. I could not turn away from the subject, but sat and listened patiently to the whole sad tale as it came from the trembling lips, drooping, sorrow-stricken eyes and brow of this poor child of *Our* Father. There she was, not over twenty, in her faded hat and feather, patched calico gown and bare feet. Scarcely

differing in any special degree in form, figure or speech from
thousands of others, there was, nevertheless, something about
her that won my profoundest respect.

Though her skin was black it was smooth, beautiful in
texture, and her forehead was high and broad, while her
eyes, large and soft, were very beautiful. Her teeth were
two regular rows of genuine white pearls, and her neck and
shoulders so delicate in size and moulding, a reigning Eugenie
would have envied her them. She was modest, bashful, and
wore a simple, honest countenance. Her agitation ended
with the story.

Then I said—

" How long have you lived on his plantation ?"

" I wor raised dah."

" But have you worked for him all the time since the surrender ?"

" Yaas, sah ; in der feel."*

" And he has never paid you anything ?"

" No, sah ; mo'n dis y'here what I got on' an' some little
things fur de chilluns."

" How many children did you say you have by him?"

" Nebber got no mo' n jes dis y'here one an' tudder one
yan with grannie by de quar'r."

" Can you prove that he is the father of both ?"

" Nebber had no sweetheart 'cept 'n him no how."

" But how can you prove that ?"

" Reckon da all 'low dat day is jes like 'im. Missus she
done said so, too."

" Who is your mistress ?"

" Mars own deah wife, I low."

" Does she know all about it ?"

" Yaas, indeed she do. She done tole 'im otenter do me
dat er way no how."

" You say he beat you. How did he do it ?"

" Done cut me with he raw*hide,* he did, an' he tuk an' put

* In the cotton and cornfield.

all my things outen da road, an' tole me nebber comed da no mo'.

" Why did he do that ?"

" I doan know."

" Had you said or done nothing to make him angry with you ?"

Then she hung her head very low.

" Come," I insisted, " if you wish me to take your case you must tell me all about it."

" Wul—he done gone an tuck up wi' dat gal Sarah, what got no chilluns, and 'low he didn't 'ten ter see me no mo'."

"Well, what did you do then ?"

" Nuthin'—cepu' I went down dar whar Sarah wor an' tole her"——

" What did you tell Sarah, my child ? Tell me all about it."

" I jes' lowed she wor a nasty, mean 'ooman ter tell lies on me dat er way."

" What did Sarah do then ?"

" She hit me wi' a eah a cohn."

" Then what did you do ?"

" I struck 'er back."

" Then you had a fight, did you ?"

" 'Specs hit wor."

" Go back to the place and tell your master that if he don't pay you whatever may be justly due you, I'll bring suit for you against him for seduction."

" Whor dat ?"

" For adultery; you may also tell him that you'll have him arrested for beating you."

" I done tole him dat afo."

" Well, tell him you have seen me, and that I advised you to do so, unless he will settle fairly with you."

She never returned to me, remained on the place, and her children became pupils in our Sabbath-school, in the little church on the hill we helped to build.

After every such occurrence I could not help taking a fresh survey of my field of labor.

Let us, I would say to myself, put ourselves in the negro's place. He is not a savage, however barbarous he may be. This is clear from the facts of his history on this continent. Even as a slave his highest model of man was the noblest gentleman. This aspiration amounted to a passion. The slave's ambition was to have a real gentleman for a master, a real lady for a mistress, and he could discriminate with wonderful accuracy.

The "savage is untamable," runs away from or fights "civilization" to the death. The negro runs toward, embraces, clings to it, and prefers slavery to the savage state. His color was his badge of servitude. This he could change but in one way—miscegenation.*

Throughout the world some form of caste has always existed, but in no other country, nor in any other time was the line, however defined, restricted to the indefinable region lying between races. Biologists racked their brains for the data to enable them to set up a theory by which to set bounds to it in our country, and physiologists and lawyers lay heads together in solemn conclave in quest of such an exposition of their theories as would satisfy the quickened consciences of a "Christian public."

From thence came rules, bearing the "great seals" of "sovereign States," called statutes, in arrogant defiance of God and of nature.

These statutes created an arbitrary line between the extremes of color, declaring what classes of persons should occupy one side of the line and who should "keep their places" upon the other side. These classes were termed the superior and the inferior. When slavery was "destroyed," the act no more wiped out that line than it changed the opinions of the slave-owners upon the origin of slavery. The divinity which had hedged about that institution also shielded

---

* Referring to this evil, one of Mississippi's most gifted writers and brilliant lawyers, uses the following language in a volume before me : "It" (slavery) "had still greater *private* evils, which grew, and in the progress of years sent their poison deep down into the heart of domestic life, and produced, in thousands of instances, not only the most degrading social vices, but unfailing fountains of tears."

the lines of caste, which had been drawn in defense of it. So, when the superiors came together to frame a new code of laws for the State, they perpetuated all the rules which lay at the base of the old; for, as by the old slave codes, all persons of "African descent" were set over on the inferior side of the line, and called either "slaves, free negroes, or mulattoes," so now, slavery only "having been" destroyed, the superiors graciously pasted a patch over the word "slaves," upon which they wrote "freedmen," and, thus altered, the new code read: "Acts to confer civil rights on freedmen, free negroes, and mulattoes."

The more securely to guard and defend the prerogatives of their *caste* in this new code, the words "citizen" or "citizens," "man" or "woman," "person" or "persons," as applicable to those upon the "inferior" side of the line, those of "African descent" were expressly and purposely omitted. It was but another of the "ways of the country," another of the disguises of slavery!

Under the old slave codes, the line between the races varied according to the whim, caprice, or interest of the slave-owner. In Mississippi it was several times changed. The last change fixed it where it proved, as was no doubt intended, most convenient for a large and by no means disreputable class of the best citizens of the State. It proved a great blessing, I am certain, to several of the most high-toned and honorable ladies and gentlemen of Yazoo.

This *was the law of suffrage* as set forth in the State revised code of 1857, which recognized as a "white" every free-born male inhabitant twenty-one years old, who had any less than "one-fourth of negro blood."

All this class were permitted to vote, hold office, own lands, houses, sue, be sued, and enjoy whatever position in the social circle their merits deserved, with or without property, or education. All others of the colored people were prohibited by *State policy* from exercising any legal, political, or civil rights, and were chattels owned by individuals or by the State. In the latter case called "free negroes or mulattoes."

This rule afforded the negro man and woman a too forceful temptation, and thousands yielded to it upon pressure from the " superior " ráce, which often was applied violently to compel acquiescence when glamour and bribes failed, and alas! in thousands, ay tens of thousands of cases, justified to the negro, resort to those arts in amorous intrigue for which the constituent elements of African slavery on this continent afforded a field of unsurpassed fertility. For did not the church warp to its defense the inspired writings? Did not tHe " superior " race everywhere, Sunday, Monday, every day, in winter and in summer, in times of jubilee and in seasons of sorrow, shield this river of evil with the mantle of Elijah? and thus this "peculiar institution became another temple of Eleusinian mysteries, whose hallowed precincts were never, at the peril of life, here and hereafter, to be profaned by any more of the light of reason. Every approach to its sacred portals was barricaded by a series of State and Federal legislative enactments and judicial decisions. Intolerance stood with a drawn sword, forbidding education to the negro, or the publication, utterance, or dissemination of any skepticism upon the subject of the ' divine origin ' of slavery."*

> " O'er all there hung a shadow and a fear,
> A sense of mystery the spirit daunted,
> And said as plain as whisper in the ear,
> This place is haunted.''

Yes, this was the stubble ground of slavery, grown rank in the planting of Andrew Johnson, while under the spell of "the enemy;" for under their new code, that Andrew Johnson code of 1865-'66. that " black code " of the Mississippi conspirators, the line between the races was left precisely where it had been located by the slave code of 1857, and, during the four years succeeding the war, the evils which it had inflicted upon the State during its existence in slavery, were augmented. The practice of concubinage may have

*Hon. J. S. Morris, Mississippi, in his Political Manual, published 1869.

been more general in slave times, doubtless was; for then a rebellious concubine was not permitted to run away. Then in addition to her personal attractions for her master, his sons, or guests, she was property.

If by reason of his relations with her, he recoiled from administering "proper punishment" with his own hand, he could send her to the local authorities, and, by paying the usual fee—one dollar—have the service performed for him.

If the mistress, as sometimes happened, disapproved of her husband's relations with her servant, or of his seléction, she could wreak vengeance on her rival by turning her over to the overseer, or sending her to the authorities to be whipped. In the case I have quoted, these "good old time" methods could not be made to apply. Grant was President. The free constitution had been ratified, and the black code had become, thereby, a dead letter.

This poor, down-trodden, oppressed and distressed " high-toned, honorable gentleman," really had no other remedy than the one he resorted to.

Poor thing! He could not help himself, being a " white " and on the " superior " side of the line, " bohn and bred," and his victim being a " black." Therefore, he " cut her a few licks " and bundled her, bag and baggage, almost naked, without a cent in payment of her years of toil and sacrifice for him *and his*, nor a morsel of food for herself and his children, into the highway. And when, after she had seen that "radical incendiary and miscegenationist Morgan," and come back to him with the law for her shield, no wonder he cursed " that black-and-tan convention;" that " radical rump Congress;" that " butcher Grant;" that " levelling monstrosity, miscalled a constitution;" that " imp of radicalism, Morgan," bewailed " the degeneracy of the times," and took her back to his shelter, if not to his bosom. Alas, poor thing! The shield of the law protected him no longer. He was powerless to prevent or even resent it; for, was not the " heel of the tyrant " upon his neck, and his face to the ground? Poor thing!

Such incidents as this and others of a similar character, all having their root in the fundamental axiom of the enemy, had forewarned me of the real nature of the contest upon which we were entering. It was an evil that no constitution or form of government, however rigidly enforced, could cure. More virulent now than formerly, it was a pustule in the heart of the social order, which could not be reached by the courts. The instrumentalities of the law would but break the lancet of the best known legal remedial agents, in efforts to penetrate the fibre surrounding it; for who among "the enemy" would dare to testify in court against a violator of any of the provisions of the new rules? And should any of those upon the "inferior" side of the old rule dare do so it would have been seized upon by the whites as a sufficient indication of another "rising" of the negroes for the purpose of killing "all the white men, women and children from the cradle up."

The evil, I foresaw, could be extirpated, if at all, in no other way than by example as well as by precept—by rearing a generation of colored *women* who could neither be purchased by the blandishments of a system which made household-pets of concubines and prostitutes, nor bulldozed into subjection to the libidinous demands of dissolute "masters, mistresses or employers," and by rearing a generation of colored *men*, whose manhood would as quickly resent all overtures for the possession, for such evil practices, of their mothers, wives, sisters, and sweethearts, as would the manhood of the " best white man that ever lived."

Already during the five years since the war, Mr. W. H. Foote, James Dixon, Houston Burrus, Frank Stewart, and scores more of Yazoo freedmen, were demanding the same courteous treatment on the streets, in the stores, and at their homes for their wives, as common decency exacted for other ladies from the public, the merchant and his clerks, or callers at their residences.

At first this was met with contempt and often drew out

acts of greater license from those white men who had always acted upon the privilege which their color gave them under the old rule, to enter a negro's house without knocking and stand or sit with hat on, and, when evil nature prompted, to suggest an intrigue with wife, mother, sister or daughter. The old rule permitted a white man to pinch or put an arm around a colored woman while shopping, or openly invite an intrigue, or when she was on the street to stare at, make remarks to or about her of an insulting character, or, as was sometimes the case, openly invite an intrigue, and, when resented by the lady, press it by some coarse speech or action

Mr. Foote was never known to allow his wife to be thus insulted without resenting it in such a manner as would forever deter the intruder from repeating it. He prided himself on the fact that he was a " Southern gentleman," and he acted upon the " Southern rule " of " an eye for an eye, and a tooth for a tooth" to the bitter end.

How to cure this evil was then and remains to this day *the* unsettled " Southern question."

It remains unsettled because the American people, who have striven for so many years to comprehend and settle the " Mormon question "—a much lesser evil—have utterly ignored, if they have not been wholly ignorant of, its character and magnitude. I foresaw that it would shortly become the mainspring—hidden, of course, under a " nigro rising " as its mask—of future hostility to the workings of the new rule.

All hostility to the agents at work in the planting of the provisions of that rule was repressed merely, not by the power of the rule nor of its agencies, nor yet of the great mass of freed people behind it, but by the respect which the rank and file of " the enemy " had for the Federal power in the hands of a President who was in sympathy with a loyal Congress and the heart-beats of the American nation. It was repressed only as the appetite of the wolf is while the lambs are within the fold and the shepherd on guard is awake.

Mr. Foote, Frank Stewart, James Dixon—no relative of the "human hornet"—and many others of the Yazoo freedmen were not lambs, but the mass were. Were they otherwise they had never been slaves. It was evident to me that Mr. Foote's policy would not cure the evil. It would, for a time, protect himself and his family from open insult so long as the dread of the Federal power remained a factor in repressing the instincts of the wolf, but not any longer. So I said then, so I say now, and so my patient reader will say when we shall separate.

Surveying the entire field, my only hope was in the *steady, unswerving power from without*. I trusted implicity in that power; for, had not the watchword been of our fathers, from the day when they threw overboard the tea in Boston Harbor, "Eternal vigilance is the price of liberty"?

Why should I doubt their fidelity to it? Why should I question their love for or faith in our cause? Why should I suspect them of faintheartedness now, of all times the most fructuous of happy results for the champions of universal liberty, a harvest season for mankind never yet equalled on the face of our modern earth? I could not doubt, I did not question, I would not faint, and bent my head lower still under the heavy yoke, while I set my plow for deeper and still deeper furrows in my new field.

CHAPTER LIII.

CHARLES wrote me from Washington County of their
complete victory there. He had been most heartily welcomed by "the best citizens" His only enemies were among
Northerners, the freed people, and a few "irreconcilables."
The season had been a good one. The crop was even larger
than the year preceding, and, better than all, the freed people were nearly all getting about a fair share for making it.
The year before they had purchased new clothing, new beds
and blankets, new cooking utensils, etc.; horses and mules,
and some shot-guns for hunting purposes. This year they
were beginning to buy—— land ! It all made things lively
in Yazoo City. The number of small traders was rapidly
increasing. Theretofore, a half hundred men had owned
the bulk of cultivated land in the county, and furnished
their laborers, as well as their plantations, by orders on their
factors in New Orleans, or at one or the other of three houses
in Yazoo City, of which Mr. Barksdale's was chief. Now,
however, the laborers were making their own purchases, and
they sought for the cheapest dealers.

Thus it came about that the business and commercial fabric was undergoing a reconstruction no less in its farreaching consequences than that worked out in "politics." All was transition, change, and the intelligent, cultivated young men, as well as their elders, looked out upon a future they were not competent to penetrate any distance at all, for their eyes had been trained in other and wholly different glasses than those required for the purpose.

Some of these young white men had already emigrated to Texas, or to the North, where they were always heartily welcomed, and others were preparing to follow them. There were others who, having brave hearts and strong hands, "felt a working" within themselves to dare the future, whatever it might have in store, and went to work. But there were others who "just could not work." It was "degrading." One of these, the son of an eminent physician, a young gentleman of twenty or twenty-one, who had been carefully trained and educated, mainly in Northern schools of learning, while one day standing upon the corner of Main street and the Benton plank road, with a Northerner, who soon after related the incident to me, somewhat excitedly exclaimed to him :

" See there, Dick ! See that nigro there on top that load a' cotton ?"

" Dick " saw a rather aged freedman seated on top of a wagon, upon which there were six or eight large bales of cotton. He also saw that the wagon was new (it was from Yankee land), that there were six or eight mules in the team, that it was an extra fine team, that the freedman was driving it, and that he appeared to know what he was about, and so he replied :

" Yes, I see it; what of it ? "

" Well, sir, by G—d, Dick, would you believe me ! That nigro owns that turnout, cotton and all."

" Well, what of that ? I expect he made it himself, didn't he ?"

"Reckon he did, of course ; but then, what are we all
coming to ?   At that rate, d—-d if they don't own the whole
country, sho'tly, now that they can buy land !"

Many of the old men evidently looked as far into the
future as this young man, and no farther ; and they "couldn't
understand it at all."   One thing was certain, if that state
of things should continue many years, the " African " *would*
own the country.   The only thing to prevent it, would be *a
fair competition with him for the right to own it.*

This meant honest effort, manly labor on the part of the
white man.

Would the white man prove himself to be the equal of
the negro ?   It was an interesting question to me.   It
was an entertaining one, also ; for, to "own this whole
country" meant to own a country surpassing the valley of the
Nile in extent and in richness.   It was a question I delighted
to study, and I felt grateful for the prospect that I was to
be a participant in the race, and a sharer in the harvest.

The evidences before me satisfied me that it would not
be a bad thing after all, in the progress of it, that I had the
affection, nay, the love, of almost every negro man, woman, and
child within the borders of Yazoo, several of whom had
already named their male babies "Colonel Morgan."

There were two "old established, reliable, and respectable
journals," both weeklies, published in Yazoo County, both at
Yazoo City.   One, *The Democrat*, was the organ of the
irreconcilables.   The other, *The Banner*, was the organ of
the "Conservatives," most of whom had been old line Whigs.
Its proprietor, a widow lady, and its editor, had been known
as staunch Unionists before the war.

Since the war they had been altogether "too respectable "
to admit of " such a disreputable thing " as the trailing of
their banner in the " cesspools of radical reconstruction," and
though moderate in tone, had been the most implacable
enemies of the " whole radical scheme " for " tyrannizing the
South into submission " to "the decrees of a rump Congress."

Our *Yazoo Republican* was, of course, a "carpet-bagger," possibly a "O'oophie" (dog), possibly a polecat." It represented "we all" Republicans, and favored the early construction of a railroad to Yazoo City.

Now that peace had come again, and we were in places of power; now that the curses, contempt and blows of "the enemy" had changed to smiles and caresses, young "white gentlemen" of Yazoo of my own age, and even older persons, acted as though they would like to be friendly and sociable, if only I would be complaisant. But so many had ways I could not tolerate—ways that were abhorrent to my notions of good breeding—I did not encourage these advances. I was no anchorite, either. During our bachelor life in Yazoo there had always been a very few "white gentlemen" and two or three white ladies who would recognize me on the street. But I felt myself so wholly ostracized that now, when all was changing, it was an extremely embarrassing subject for me; and I have no doubt, was equally so to "the enemy."

Our new "radical sheriff" was the first under the new regime to receive any sort of recognition from Yazoo City "society."

His family began to "elevate" themselves accordingly, for so it is, I am told, the wide world over. Then, how would I manage it should I come face to face at an entertainment of any kind where the "human hornet," Harry Baltimore, Ben Wicks, Bob Sweet, Joe Telsub, or any of the "Cyclopes" were the hosts or even guests. Our new sheriff, having kept himself and family out of active participation in the former contests, was less "objectionable," a less embarrassing subject, though he often complained to me of the outrageous slights, even insults, put upon himself and family because he had taken office of the radicals. His wife was a proud, haughty woman, and felt these things most keenly. The Northerner who had "surrendered" failed to cut the knot by marrying a most beautiful, accomplished, and worthy "Southern lady." Not only was *he* excluded from the Yazoo "upper

crust," and limited in his social status to the "stags," the
"ladies" of Yazoo refused longer to recognize her.   Yazoo
"society" knew full well that I would never approach their
charmed circles upon my knees, nor by the back-door route.
The "stags" knew that I had no pleasure in their vulgar
orgies, whether carried on in the stores of the merchants after
business hours, the back offices of the lawyers, the rear apartments of the numerous saloons and restaurants, or over the
"cave," "hole in the wall," or "banks."   Poor Rarety and
such as she in Yazoo were so often participants in these
gatherings, that whenever, out of hunger for some sort of
social companionship, I ventured upon the "ragged edge" of
the Yazoo social order, all my former teachings, my sacred
theories, my inborn principles got up such a rebellion within
my soul that I turned at the very threshold, and ran as far
away from the edge of this social precipice as my conscience
would carry me under the thump, thump, thump of my ach-
ing heart.

Now that Grant was President and in "sympathy with
fanaticism," now that the free constitution, including sections
22 of article 12, had been unanimously ratified, now that the
"trick" of the enemy had failed to prevent the "nigro rising," quite to the top, now that the "what is it," Foote, the
General, the ex-bureau agent, and myself, all "polecats,"
were the law-makers for Yazoo, now that the "freedman, free
negro, or mulatto" sat on the jury, that his poll-tax had
been reduced to two dollars, that he was no longer more liable
to arrest for failure to pay it than "ole mars," that the auction block for "runaways" had "been destroyed," that "our
nigros" could testify in court "against a white man," that
Uncles Peter, David, Jonathan, and the late "little garrison," not only had the right but were enjoying it, to buy and
carry arms, that they were already buying land, that rape of
a negro girl by a white man was a rape, that the white man's
"black sweetheart" began to "kick against the pricks," now

that all these things were no longer *in futuro* but *in
esse,* and now that all present danger that " our nigros "
were " about to rise," with intent to " kill all the white men,
women, and children, from the cradle up," had passed into
the limbo of the forgotten kukluxes, and the dead Dover
bulldozer, I deemed it high time that I should take a
wife.

CHAPTER LIV.

A VISIT TO MY BROTHER—MORE WAYS OF THE COUNTRY—REVE-
LATIONS.

CHARLES was not getting on with the colored people in Washington County as he had in Yazoo. He had been no more warmly received there by the whites than he had in Yazoo, but the circumstances were different. The colored people of Yazoo had been eye-witnesses of his courage and fidelity to correct principles, and he was more popular with them, after his defense of the "stronghold," and the badge incident, than any other man in the county. Prior to his arrival there, the people of Washington County had passed through precisely similar experiences to those in Yazoo, and Northern and colored men had endured the same series of hardships and dangers. I resolved to visit my brother, and see for myself just what the trouble was, for in our schemes for the development of the Yazoo Delta, Washington County was likely to become a most important factor. It lay on the opposite side of that Delta, and on the great "Father of Waters." After my arrival there I was not long in determining the cause of Charles' trouble. A different influence from that at the base of the Yazoo organization had taken root, and formed the base of the organization in that county.

This sprang from three causes:

First. The tendency of the " African Methodist Episcopal Church " to segregation. This church had directly and indirectly a considerable influence in Washington County. The Rev. Mr. ——* was quite popular there.

Second. The success in the previous campaigns in that county of the spirit which prompted the " purely Yankee ticket" in Yazoo, in the fall of 1867, allied with the element favoring segregation. They had united on a man for sheriff and tax collector for the county only hopelessly to divide upon the refusal of the commanding general to appoint him; and

Third. The appointment of my brother to the most important office in the county, a man who had no sympathy whatever with the principles or purposes of either faction, and who had not been tried as by fire in the Washington County crucible.

Then there was another cause. During their seasons of sore trial, since the war, the freed people, everywhere in that State, had come to suspect the fidelity of every man upon whom " ole marsta " smiled. Charles' reception by " the enemy " in that county had been too hearty. He was no politician ; he fairly loathed the arts of that class of professionals ; he had no thought of remaining in office any longer than during the transition period from the old to the new order of things. Then he would resume the development of his schemes for the improvement of the material foundations of the " New Empire."

He had already selected a site for a saw-mill, oil factory, and a store ; and, in company with others, was projecting, on paper, a plan for a railroad from Greenville to Vicksburgh on the south, and Memphis on the north ; another one east to Yazoo City, and beyond, to connect with the Great Northern,† and west to Little Rock, or some St. Louis connection. His face was a sufficient introduction for him.

* This was a " colored " divine who, in 1866-'7, had endeavored to plant the same seeds in Yazoo County. His failure there was doubtless due to the efforts being put forth by the Bureau for the education of the freed people.
† Now the Southern extension of the Illinois Central R. R.

He had no trouble in making the full amount of the bond required. Some of the wealthiest citizens of the county became his sureties, including Colonel Holland. He had never intended to attempt to dictate the policy of the Republican party of the county, nor to allow his office to become a " spoils agency" for that party's uses. Whatever influence he might have, he loyally purposed should be given in aid of a genuine reconstruction of the county. Had he been in office in Philadelphia, New York, or Chicago, he would have been considered an " impracticable reformer."

All his sympathies were with the freed people, in whose wretched condition he saw, as I did, a field of labor worthy the uninterrupted sacrifice of the money and the labor of every patriot and philanthropist in the land. But he felt that he was not suited to such work by training nor by temperament; therefore he would sustain by his example, and by his substantial contributions those who were fitted for it. But it cut him to the quick that the intelligent portion of the freed people of the county failed to appreciate his past services in behalf of their race, or his present purposes in the same direction. He " couldn't understand it at all."

" Why, my dear brother," said I, "it is a very simple matter."

" A simple matter ! Albert, how you talk ! It is not a simple matter; it is a very serious matter; for it satisfies me that the freed people haven't the capacity to recognize and properly appreciate their true friends."

" Whew ! Charles ! Now you have forgotten your dearest friends. You've forgotten your registered oath of kinship with negroes. Tell me what has wrought such a change in ' the polecat' of Yazoo ? "

Charles was staggered just a little by this home thrust; but rallying, he replied :

" The colored people of Yazoo differ as widely from these barbarians as the savages of that county do from the white people of this."

I could not restrain an outburst of hearty laughter at the absurdity of his speech, in the face of all the facts. This vexed Charles, who rather petulantly exclaimed :

"What are you laughing at ? I am sure I see nothing to laugh at. I tell you, Albert, this is a serious question. The idea, and after all I have done and sacrificed for these people! I don't intend to ask their votes; my only desire is to do them good, and they won't even come to my Sabbath-school."

Then I—

"Charles, do you remember a little talk you and I had in our room at Mrs.——, in 1865, the evening after your return to Vicksburg from your first visit to Colonel J. J. U. Black, agent in fact' of Mistress Charlotte Black, of Tokeba ? "

"Humph! Now what has that got to do with this question ? You're forever going back to Tokeba. I'm not ashamed of my judgment of Tokeba, as a business venture. Had it not been for those hyena rebels, we would have come out with a handsome profit on our investment, in spite of the failures of the first two years. You know that as well as I. Therefore, why will you rake up that old subject every time we try to talk over any plan for the future ? I don't like it."

"Nor do I like it, Charles, but I have found it profitable at times, since I came South, to go back over my tracks to the starting-point, if only for the purpose of testing 'my bearings.' I am sure I find no pleasure in such a retrospect. I reckon——"

"There it is again ! I do wish you'd leave that word out of your vocabulary in future ; I've heard it until I'm sick of it. Fact is you're imbibing altogether too many of the ways of this country for your own good. You not only talk like a Southerner—you are beginning to look and act like one. You need have no fears of me, my boy, you'll have grown to be a rebel before I shall be."

But I heeded not his raillery. The question was indeed a serious one to me, and was growing more and more serious every day of my life.

" But you're dodging the subject, Charles, let me hold you to it. Then you do recollect our talk on that occasion ?"

" Well, what of it ?"

" Do you not recall a certain incident in my personal experience that I then offered as likely to suggest a peculiar phase of life in this sunny Southland, one which might prove a serious obstacle to the success of your plans ?"

" I presume so; but what are you driving at ?"

" You recall the incident ? "

" Yes."

" What was it ? "

" O, pshaw ! "

" No, not pshaw, but Major——"

" You don't mean to say that your Major ——, the cowardly fellow who tried to entice you to meet him where he could safely have you hung to the limb of a tree by the roadside, is the same——"

" The very same fellow whom you introduced to me a bit ago. Yes, my brother, unless I am wofully mistaken. He perfectly resembles him and bears a similar name. His fellow assassins of that date called him Major "——

" It isn't possible. You must be mistaken. He had evidently never seen you before."

" That was more than five years ago; besides, circumstances are changed. How large a place is this ? "

" About eight or nine hundred. Your experience was at a river landing. Oh, he can't be the same man. He's one of the most courteous and hospitable gentlemen I've met here. I have taken dinner at his house twice, staid there all night not more than a month ago, and have a standing invitation to halt there whenever I'm passing, or come out at any time and stay as long as I'm pleased."

" You have ! Does he drink whisky ? "

" Not quite as liberally as old Black did. He likes it though. But I know he can't be the man. You are mistaken in your impressions. This is not the place at all."

"How large was this place in November, 1865 !"

"Well, there, I don't know. I've understood, though, that the town has grown up since the war."

"Exactly. Well, if this is not the place I landed at that pitch dark night, when I sought in vain for hotel accommodations, and got shelter of a freedwoman who kept a restaurant 'fur de white gen'lemens *tendin'* co't,' then it's the very next landing below here, I am sure, and if that fellow whom you introduced is not my Major he is that assassin's 'own deah brother,' or first cousin, and I know it."

"I wonder if it can be possible!" exclaimed my brother, in a mood of thorough disgust.

"Well, this is the county seat of Washington County, isn't it ?"

"Why, of course."

"Well, I know that I landed that night in Washington County. The plantation I came up to look at was in Washington County. They said they were having court in the 'barn-like structure,' which stood some distance to the north of the landing, and back from the river in what was then an open field. The assassins, you'll recollect, were in attendance on that court as litigants, or witnesses, or jurymen. All these facts are just as clear in my mind, my brother, as is my recollection of your enthusiasm on that night in Vicksburg, when you traced on your map for me the outlines of your newly-discovered empire—on your map, Charles, only on your map. How long ago was that ?"

Charles was silent. The old "vacant stare" did not return, but hot colors came and went in his cheeks, and seeing that my medicine was a-working, I concluded to let well enough alone, pulled out a cigar, lighted it and began making "curliques" of its smoke.

"There it is again! Do you know how many cigars you smoke in a day? Albert, why don't you quit that disgusting habit ? "

"My brother, do you know this cigar has saved me many a heartache ? "

"Many a heartache! I know it has poisoned your con-stitution already, and will kill you sooner or later if you don't stop it."

"Yes, many a heartache. It's my safety-valve, old boy; I had long since 'busted' into 'splithereens' but for this same *disgusting habit*. You 'don't understand it at all,' of course. But do you know whenever the blood comes and goes too rapidly through my veins, as just a moment since it was doing in yours, I light a cigar and let off steam. It soothes me. So if indeed and in truth it is a poison, you must charge my habit to the causes which suggest its use."

"What an argument! But it is worthy you, my brother, who smoke tobacco for a sedative. Well! did I ever think it would come to that! Strikes me you might employ your arts in support of a better cause."

"Name it!"

"Well tell me what earthly good can the fumes of that stuff do you now?"

"Soothes me, Charles, soothes me."

"Yes, old Black always took his whisky when cold to warm him, and to cool him when warm. Bah!"

But I continued to puff, all the same, for my indignation was getting the mastery over me in spite of the sedative. Finally, unable to restrain it any longer I exclaimed,— "Charles, what an ass you've made of yourself here, to be sure!"

"Ass of myself?"

"Yes. Now listen to me while I give you a piece of my mind."

He had always acted as though in some way my natural protector—as an elder brother is apt to do—and this unex-pected "rising" on my part was such a surprise to him that he stood mute, and listened in blank astonishment, while I scolded:

"It's less than four years since the high-toned, cultured ladies of Yazoo called your sister Mollie, who was worship-

ping God in the same house with them, a polecat; it's less
than four years ago now that a Federal officer, sent to
Yazoo City to protect the erection of a school-house for the
freed people, was so warmly welcomed by the high-toned
honorable gentlemen of that town, that he reported no need
of troops there.   It is but a little over three years ago, that as
Sheriff Finley's deputies drove our mules through the streets
of that town, to be sold in obedience to the behests of as bold
a robber as ever lived, those same *gentlemen* shouted ' hurrah for
Colonel Black, we'll get rid a them d—n Yankee s—of b—s
now !'   It is less than three years ago, my dear brother, that a
Federal troop in Yazoo was so heartily and hospitably entertained, by those same robbers, that, while their officer, driven
from the lap of Delilah, was drunk in the street, United
States soldiers fired upon you and into the dwelling of a
gracious lady, because you were the '*he* polecat' of Yazoo
County.   It's but little more than two years ago that these
same high-toned, honorable gentlemen locked you up in the
common jail—in the murderer's cell, my boy; the murderer's
cell—and would have hanged you by the light of the stars to
the China trees in front of it, had it not been for the fidelity
and courage of the negroes, and the bluff of the Bureau agent.
Yes, it was five—not quite five years ago, that these same
' high-toned, honorable gentlemen, by G—d sir,' who have
welcomed you so heartily, would have welcomed your brother
an utter stranger, only twenty-two, and purely on business
bent, with a grapevine tied to a tree by the roadside, because,
and solely because, he was a Yankee; and you have allowed
these banditti to blindfold you and start you on the dead-watch
to their camp.   For shame !   My dear brother, wake up, look
about you !"

"Nonsense !   Come, I've heard enough of that.   Let's take
a walk."

His look and manner had entirely changed during my
"fever," and, putting his arm through mine, as he remarked
that the air in the room was foul from my smoke, he said:

"The open air will do you more good than your tobacco. Let's change the subject ——. What an infernal country this is to be sure."

"Not so fast, Charles; not so fast," said I, rejoiced at the effect of my remedy—you see I had taken control of his case before the virus of slavery had reached the blood-currents in his system, and while he was still amenable to the light of reason—"not so bad, my dear boy; not so bad as it might have been had African slavery continued for another century upon this rich soil. The 'sick man of the South' is very sick indeed, but it is only a question of endurance, my brother. All that is required is time, a steady nerve and persistent cutting away of the pustules as rapidly as they appear upon the surface. Then with a wise and careful dieting, and skillfully applied tonics the patient may recover."

"A long time! a long time! Albert, I fear we made a mistake when we came to this country. Fact is, I've doubted the motives of these fellows here from the first. They've been altogether too kind, some of them, while those not in the lead have been a little slow in taking the cue, and their treatment of me has contrasted rather strangely with that I have received from the more prominent of the old citizens. But that don't worry me half so much as the —— well, not ingratitude exactly, but—the truth is a rascally set have got on top of our party here and if they ever get into full control of affairs they'll steal themselves rich and bankrupt the county."

"Tell me what evidence you have of that."

"What evidence? Why! just look at them. Have you ever seen a more scurvy set?"

"Say, Charles, when I arrived over from Jackson to see about getting you out of that 'murderer's cell' in the 'common' jail of Yazoo, how do you reckon you and General Greenleaf looked to me?"

"Nonsense! I know I never looked like any of this tribe here."

"How do you know?"

"Oh, well, let's change the subject."

"Wait a minute. That negro Dabney was in the convention with me. He is one of a number who requested me to draw a section for our new constitution that would assist to cure the greatest of all the evils of this country. He had had a wife or daughter, or sister—I forget now which—taken from him by force, and that, too, since the war, and prostituted to the vilest uses, and he had not known where to seek a remedy. In common with all the colored men in that convention he wanted so stringent a provision as would for all future time guarantee to a virtuous, high-minded negro woman immunity from such outrages, or place in the hands of her natural or lawful protector the legal means to that end. He is temperate, sober, and, as I have good reason to believe, honest. Then there is Major Jones. He was also in the convention with me. He came to this county in 1865, about the same time we came to Yazoo, and rented a plantation here. He was one of the staunchest men in that body and is a very respectable gentleman."

"Charles, you should get acquainted with *Republicans* here, even at the risk of making enemies of Major —— and his fellows."

"O, well, let's change the subject. I see you've been kicking up a breeze in the Senate. Tell me about it."

"There's nothing at all in it."

"Well, the papers are all talking about it, and giving you great credit."

"Democratic papers you mean. Of course, all that's taffy."

"But what have you been doing? It seems to take with the 'assassins,' as you call them."

"Not assassins, Charles. 'The enemy,' you mean. The next batch that reaches your 'berg' here will doubtless curse me as bitterly as the last batch the steamers brought you praised me."

"Been doing something more, eh? Well, what was all

this other about? I can't make out from the newspaper accounts."

"I found myself on the 'other side' of the House, upon an important question, sprung upon the Senate. There had been no canvassing upon it, and it was full in the face of every safeguard experience has adopted for the preservation of our liberties—the liberties of the people. It was an ill-advised, hastily constructed measure, and as the Republican blood was up, it was likely to pass. It could not have relieved the Government's embarrassment in the case, and would have stood a lasting reproach to our party, had it not been opposed. So I attacked it, and, after quite a bitter struggle, in which many of my old friends denounced me as an apostate, deserter, and all that sort of thing, it was 'postponed.' That killed it."

"Let's see, that was the Yerger case."

"Yes, of course everybody knew that I had no sympathy with Yerger, the assassin of Colonel Crane. The great fuss the enemy have made over it but illustrates one of their methods of making converts to their cause. Our fellows were as ashamed of it afterward as while in the heat of their passion over the release of Yerger they were mad at me."

"But let's talk of something else. Isn't it about time you began to think of taking a wife?"

"Humph! well that is something else sure enough. But Yankee fashion, I guess I'll answer your question by asking another. When are you to be married?"

"Soon after the legislature adjourns."

Then Charles stopped short in the dirt road over which we were walking through the plowed fields,* and turning upon me a most doleful countenance, exclaimed:

"Look here! are you going to marry that rebel woman?"

* Greenville at that date was surrounded on the west by the Mississippi River, and on all its other sides by open fields that stretched away a level plain to the dense forests of gum and cypress, out of which they had been wrought, in those "good old days before the war," when there was no need of retail merchants in those parts, for the New Orleans, St. Louis, Louisville, and Cincinnati packets took orders from the planters along the river on their factors abroad, and delivered to them their plantation supplies regularly on yearly contracts.

It was my brother's turn to scold now, so he appeared to think, at least, and he seized his opportunity with a zest that showed me how deep was his interest in any step I might take, so vital to my future happiness as my marriage.

" Why ! " I exclaimed. "Charles, what's the matter with you ?"

" Matter enough, I should think, from all I can hear."

" Well, what have you heard ?"

" Why ! all this talk about your engagement to Miss——, what's her name ?"

" So—you've—heard—that—too, have you? Pray, who told you?"

" Several have mentioned it to me. It was only last week that Colonel Withers, the biggest old reb in this county, on his return from a trip down the river told me he had heard that you were engaged to her."

" Well, what did he have to say about it ?"

" Oh, he thought it an excellent idea; good way to close up the bloody chasm, you know, and all that sort of nonsense. He actually congratulated me upon it. Pretty fellow, you, to talk to me about allowing these assassins to blindfold me! For my part I'd much rather submit to that operation by a man than any woman I ever saw."

" Ha, ha, ha! had you ?"

" Better look sharp, boy."

" Charles, my dear, big brother, will you promise not to go back on me ?"

" Well you're my brother, of course, but then why haven't you said something to me about it before ?"

"Ah! I see. You mean your consent. Well, I ask you now. Have I your consent to marry the only girl in this wide world that I care a 'tinker's baubee' for, as Colonel Black used to say ? "

" What an old hyena he is ! "

" But you're off the subject, Charles."

" My consent ? Why, you're of age, man. As you make your bed, you must lie, you know."

" Yes, I've heard that remark before, and shall doubtless often hear it again. But you promise not to disown me, do you ?"

" Y-e-a-s. Yes, I'll promise, but—"

" Look me in the eye, old polecat. I am anxious to see how you take it—there, steady now! You are *mistaken*, my brother! God willing I am going to marry a 'nigger' school-marm."

CHAPTER LV.

MORE REVELATIONS AND MORE STRAW FOR BRICKS—VIRTUE BY
CONTRAST—CROSSING THE RUBICON.

MY brother's eyes did not droop at my announcement.
They did search my very soul. He must have been
content with what he saw at the bottom, for, taking my arm
in his, in that affectionate, brotherly way, which was all the
more precious to me because it was not often he did it—
Charles was not very demonstrative in his affections—he
pulled me around, and we resumed our walk.

"Your cigar has gone out, I see."

"Yes ; let me re-light it ; do you know I'm awfully glad
you don't appear to need the sedative."

"I should think you would."

"Only it's gratitude, not disgust, that has excited my nerves,
old fellow ; I'll throw it away, shortly ; fact is, I've promised
Carrie to quit it altogether before our wedding day."

"Well that's a good beginning, anyhow."

"Good ; now tell me about yourself, Charles ; why don't
you get married ?"

"You haven't told me who it is yet that is to take the place
of your cigar."

"Oh, do you recollect a certain Sabbath-school you visited
with me while in Jackson last fall ? "

"The one that had so many unrecognized children of ' first
citizens of Mississippi' in it ?"

"The same; by the way, I had not learned all about her day-school then; the truth is, my dear brother, there are children of Governors, United States Senators, members of Congress, of the 'High Court of Errors and Appeals,'* of the Legislature, and of sheriffs, justices of the peace, doctors, lawyers, ministers, merchants, planters, school teachers, blacksmiths, carpenters, and general laborers, in that school. Would you believe it?"

"Yes, I don't doubt it; it's just so here; only the parents are less distinguished; being at the ancient, political and social centre of the great State of Mississippi—the arch-traitor's home—I am not surprised at it at all. But it must be a very large school to accommodate all the classes and grades you've mentioned."

"The first time I visited it there were seventy odd pupils, by actual count."

"Is it possible! and but one teacher?"

"Only my girl."

"I wonder how she manages them all?"

"Do you recollect a remark you made of her as we left the Sabbath-school that day?"

"I don't know that I do; I remember that I thought her a most heroic girl"——

"And said she'd make a better member of the legislature than any of those you saw in that august body."

"Ha, ha! Yes, I recollect."

"Well, I'm going to make her my wife."

"Mollie told me you were very much in love with a Miss ——, at Fox Lake."

"You know I was a boy then. Perhaps had she waited for me, I might have fallen in love with her after I got back from the war."

"Were you and she not engaged?"

"Oh, no. You know how it was at the old home. I used to see her home from church, attend Good Templars Lodge,

* Now styled the Supreme Court.

and little parties with her—as her escort. We were not engaged, and when my three years were up and I didn't come back, I suppose she thought 't'wouldn't pay to wait. I hear she has an excellent husband, and they love each other well. I saw them when I was home last."

"What a humdrum place Fox Lake is getting to be."

"Yes, the railroad killed it. But it'll wake up by-and-by."

"What a difference between the people there and here!"

"Don't let's talk about that. I get homesick whenever I think of it. Why don't you tell me *why you don't get a wife?* You always have managed to put me off, but now I've told you, you shall tell me."

"You haven't told me where she is from yet."

"You've forgotten I told you all about that when we left her school that day."

"Then you said nothing of your intention to marry her."

"She's from Syracuse, New York."

"Good place to come from, by George!"

"I see you are determined to have the whole story. Her mother has been a widow several years; had a large family on her hands; lost her eldest boy and main support in one of the last skirmishes about Petersburg. Ever since 1864 they've all been teaching—mother and four children—in the South. They live together—the mother and two daughters—at Jackson. Carrie is the most—perhaps I ought not to say most successful, where all have done so nobly—but certainly the most popular teacher there, unless I except one or two most estimable Quaker ladies. Certain it is that she has not only won the love of all the freed people, she has also won the profound respect of even 'the enemy,' who treat her with great deference, notwithstanding her calling. Mr. Barksdale, Judge Potter, and many of the solid men of the capital city have manifested their appreciation of her tact, skill, ability and devotion in many ways. She is as tireless in her work as she is skillful. Think of it, she not only manages that large day school—sometimes numbering a hundred—but she attends to

her religious duties, superintends—at least leads—the Sabbath-school, runs a temperance society, and has put in execution various other plans for the social elevation of the freed
people."

"I don't see how she stands such a strain."

"My dear boy, the cause in which she is engaged—the
cause. Just think of it; there are not half teachers enough
for those hungry, starving children. Then too she is a wonderful creature, that girl of mine; never has been sick a day
in her life! Never has taken a dose of any kind of medicine!
Her breath is as pure and sweet as if it came from off a bed
of spring violets."

"Ha, ha, ha! haw, haw, haw! You forget yourself, my
boy. That should be a secret."

"Don't care, we're engaged; guess a fellow can kiss his
girl after they've been engaged as long as we have."

"How long is that?"

"'Bout a year."

"Well, I guess you do love her. Where did you first meet
her?"

"The first time I saw Carrie I lost my head, banged if I
didn't. It happened this way: I was at Jackson on some
business or other connected with the election. General
Copeland invited me to visit that school with him; said he
had something to show me better for the eyes than fine
gold; ay, than many pearls. We were detained, and so
were late. As we approached the building, I heard a multi-
tude of voices singing 'Your Mission;' and strong and clear
above the tones of the children those of another. There was
something in that voice that won my heart for the singer
even before I saw her; I can't describe it. It was not pathos.
I think it was will-power. Whatever it was, it gave her
tones a sort of magnetism, or what you please; only, it
caught hold of me, and I halted to listen, restraining the
General, who was anxious to reach the building before the
exercises closed. Then they sang 'John Brown's Body;'

and then some little thing about rising—'We are rising as a people' and so forth. When they began that I was as anxious to get among them as the General. We found a girl, simply, but as I thought, exquisitely dressed, at the head of what seemed to be an army of children, varying in color from the pale, blue-eyed, flaxen-haired Caucasian type, to the pure-blooded African. Advancing down the aisle to greet us, with the simple grace of an honest, blushing country girl, yet with all the dignity of a veritable queen, as I fancied, she welcomed us with a smile, and said : ' We are always glad to have such distinguished gentlemen visit our school ; it encourages the children.' 'Encourages the children !' Just think of it ! She was apparently but eighteen herself; of slender figure, and many of her 'children' were not only much larger, they were also older than she. I thought I detected a mischievous twinkle in her eye as she said it; and quickly led the way to the front, where some of the children had already placed seats for us, just as if they understood it, and then she resumed her place. After giv ing us a few illustrations of the progress of the school, displaying her masterful discipline over the herd, and giving the *children* a chance to show how much they loved their teacher—and they fairly worshipped her, old boy, no mis-take—she turned the entire school over to us, with permission to talk to them or catechise them, as we saw fit. Oh, well, it's a long story, Charles, I'll cut it short by just saying that after the General had catechised them, and I had praised them, and she had turned them loose, as we walked with her on her route homeward, I learned that she had been over two years similarly engaged. Well, I fell head over heels in love with her, and ever since that the thick clouds over the old stubble-ground of Yazoo have been drifting away, until now I can see the sun, and hear faint sounds of melody from the happy songs of a *risen people.*"

" Well, there; hadn't you better get down off that horse and remain with us below, yet awhile ? "

"Reckon, perhaps, I might as well, since my story is told."

"Albert, have you considered all the obstacles in the way of such a step?"

My brother all at once became very grave and awfully solemn, which was heightened, if possible, by my reply, for I retorted thus:

"Obstacles! What obstacles, pray? Ought there to be any obstacles in the way of my marriage to such a girl?"

"There should not be, but in Ohio it is a penitentiary offense for a white man to marry a woman of African descent. And now that I think of it, I apprehend that you'll find it quite difficult to escape the same penalty here in Mississippi, unless by some hocus-pocus you can prove yourself to be of the same blood. Considering your complexion and features, particularly your nose, that would be as difficult an undertaking as the former, in my opinion, and——"

All Charles' serious aspect had now vanished, and I could see that he was preparing to retaliate on me for having on a certain occasion called him a jail-bird. Anticipating which I interrupted him:

"My dear brother, you're a long way behind the times."

"Behind the times! Well, I judge that you at least mean to keep ahead."

"There may be less glory, but there certainly is more honor on the picket line than with the reserves. I wish I were able to keep up with the outposts. As it is, I am, after all, but a laggard, for the truth is, the only obstacle in the way of my marriage is my inborn timidity, bashfulness."

"Now that's rich!"

"But it is true, Charles, old boy; the battle was fought in this country when the rebellion collapsed at Appomattox. Garrison, Phillips, Lucretia Mott, Gerrit Smith, Sumner, and a small army of heroic souls have won all the honors. There is now no law in Mississippi standing between my betrothed and me. There are none now to forbid the banns. African slavery on this continent is dead."

"Are you sure there is no law ?"

"More than a month ago I introduced into the Senate a bill repealing all the laws upon that subject, and five days afterward that bill, having passed both houses, was approved by the Governor."

"Is it possible! I haven't heard a word about it."

"It is a fact."

"You must have had a pretty hard fight; I don't understand it at all ; how is it that the Democratic papers have kept so still about it ? "

"There was no opposition to its passage."

"You surprise me! Now, don't tell me that the Democrats voted for it."

"Some did, both in the Senate and in the House ; there were none who objected."

"Well! well! what next ?"

"This next : The leaven of liberty is working here, even here upon this old stubble-ground of African slavery and hot-bed of miscegenation.. I have another surprise for you. Read this." Saying which, I handed my brother a copy of the following :

"AN ACT* declaring and making legitimate certain illegitimate children of James Anderson, residing in Holmes County, State of Mississippi, as therein specified in said act.

"Whereas, James Anderson has, by petition to the Legislature of the State of Mississippi, prayed for the removal of all illegitimacy from certain of his children, and given reasons therefor in said petition, which are just and humane in their character ; therefore,

"SECTION 1. *Be it enacted by the Legislature of the State of Mississippi,* That Sheppard Anderson, born August 31st, 1854, and begotten of Catharine Lee ; Richard Anderson, born March 5th, 1859, and begotten of Jane Anderson ; Lewis Anderson, born May 1st, 1860, and begotten of Nellie Ellis; Caleb Anderson. born September 12th, 1863, begotten of Jensey Hunnicut; Edward Anderson, born July 8th, 1864, and begotten of Alice Courtney ; and Jane Anderson, born October 7th, 1858, begotten by Margaret Fisher ; and all of which said children are the illegitimate issue of said women by said James Anderson, a citizen residing in Holmes County, State of Mississippi, be, and the same are

*See Laws of Mississippi, 1870, pp. 567-'8.

hereby, declared and made the legitimate children of the said James Anderson, for all purposes in law or otherwise.

"SEC. 2. *Be it further enacted,* That this act shall take effect on and after its passage, and all laws inconsistent therewith be, and the same are hereby, repealed.

" Passed the House of Representatives, June 8th, 1870.

" F. E. FRANKLIN,
" *Speaker of the House of Representatives.*

" Passed the Senate June 11th, 1870.

" R. C. POWERS,
" *President of the Senate.*

"STATE OF MISSISSIPPI,
" OFFICE OF SECRETARY OF STATE,
" JACKSON, MISSISSIPPI.

" I, James Lynch, Secretary of State of the State of Mississippi, do hereby certify that the above and foregoing act, entitled ' An act declaring and making legitimate certain illegitimate children of James Anderson, residing in Holmes County, State of Mississippi,' was duly passed by both houses of the legislature, at the dates above specified, by the respective presiding officers thereof, and remained in the hands of the governor, and was not returned by him within five days (Sunday excepted) after it was presented to him, and that in the meantime no adjournment of the legislature occurred to prevent its return, whereby said act became a law of said State by operation of the constitution thereof.

" Given under my hand and the great seal of the State of Mississippi, hereunto affixed, this 27th day of June, A. D. 1870.

[L. S.]   " JAMES LYNCH,
" *Secretary of State.*"

" Well, Albert, there is but one thing about this that surprises me," said Charles, after concluding the reading of the foregoing, " and that is that such a man should apply for such legislation."

" Nothing surprising in that fact, my brother, when you shall have reflected a moment. Deep down in the heart of all men is a sense of the *law* of right and of love. Heretofore in the South that principle has been repressed by statutes, and even men of the courage and of the wealth of this Holmes County repentant rebel, have not been able to throw off allegiance to such barbarous restrictions upon simple right and justice. Now, the way having been opened for them by a *power from without*, they are relieved of the bur-then; besides, in this case, the father of those seven children by six different slave women is growing old and wishes before the final day to prepare himself for Judgment. He owns several thousand acres of land, was formerly owner of many slaves, and, without some such provision, I presume that he feared his otherwise only lawful heirs would refuse to do any-thing for *the negro*."

"Let us change the subject, I am disgusted with this one."

"What an outrage to compare this woman I love with those old slave-lords, or any of their 'lawful or unlawful heirs!' By the laws of Ohio, she hardly could have done so, but by that old Mississippi slave code, she doubtless would have ranked as a white woman. So much for the difference—when they lay alongside of each other, an l are commercially re-lated—between slave and free institutions as they affect our preju lices. Under the circumstances, and here in Missis-sippi, Carrie ranks as a colored woman. She was born in lawful wedlock, in a State of freedom, and is descended by blood—you know I believe in blood—from the best stock of old England on one, of Holland on another, and of Africa or Madagascar, I don't care which, on the other. She is the grandest woman living, my brother."

"Don't your conscience trouble you just a little for having enticed such a teacher from such a field?"

"Well, no. I believe the normal state of women is that of *true* marriage. Besides, her mother said—well, she said Carrie was old enough and sensible enough to choose for herself, and as she appeared to be willing to change her field of labor for a new one, it hadn't troubled me any that way yet. No, sir."

"I too believe that the normal condition of *man* and woman is marriage, Albert, and I expect to leave this hole next week never to return until I bring with me my wife. I should doubtless have been married three years ago, but for our troubles at Tokeba."

"Thank you, Charles—I mean God bless you, old polecat. Now I can understand that awful vacant stare of yours."

"What's that about vacant stare?"

"That awful vacant stare of yours during the last year of Tokeba, and while you and the General were hemmed up in our little Yankee stronghold."

"Pshaw! I don't know what you mean, I am sure."

"Of course you don't, Charles; I've no idea you can at all understand it; it's like some other mysteries. But do you know those awful spells of yours, when you'd sit for hours looking into the fire, or at the blank cold walls of the little stronghold; when it seemed that your face grew longer and your cheeks hollower and your eyes larger every time, used to make me feel miserable indeed."

"Nonsense."

"No nonsense about it. Wouldn't wonder if you should yet deny there ever was such a thing as a stronghold in Yazoo, or a kuklux, or a jail, or a murderer's cell, or a Colonel ——."

"There, there; come, you haven't told me the foundation for that story about you and Miss —— yet. How about it?"

"Well, you know——"

"No, I don't know."

"Nothing but this, then. Of late the old enemy have sort'o been——"

"Sort'o been!"

"—— Been getting very kind of sweet on me. They were slower getting to it in Yazoo than at certain other points— where Miss —— lives, for example. The lady in question is one of the most brilliant and accomplished I ever met, a splendid woman, no mistake about that; but then—oh, well, they ar'n't of our kind by a long shot. That's all there is to it, and when I saw that my visits to her father's house were being misconstrued by the public, I got Carrie to accompany me to the House of Representatives one day during a recess of the Senate, and caused announcement to be made of our intended marriage. You know if a fellow is seen here in public with a girl as many as three or four times, or calls on her that number of times, the legitimate inference is that they are engaged. But tell me now about your girl."

" An old classmate of mine. I'll bring her over when we get back."

" Going to have a wedding tour ?"

" No more than a short trip to the lake. She lives not a great way from Cleveland. Then we shall come directly here."

" Carrie and I shall marry in Jackson and take the cars at once for a wedding trip. We shall spend a few weeks amongst her friends in New York."

CHAPTER LVI.

A WEDDING—AN "OUTCAST'S" HOME—OUR FIRST SOCIAL EXPERI-
ENCE—THE ENEMY CATCHING AT STRAWS—THE PROMISES OF
THE TRUTH ARE CERTAIN—A TEMPERANCE CAMPAIGN IN YAZOO
—A SOCIAL REVOLUTION.

SHORTLY after the conversation between Charles and
myself, reported in the last chapter, he came to Jackson,
accompanied with his wife. I was satisfied, I am sure. I
never saw so contented a look on his face before. He was
too young yet to manifest any feeling of triumph, and too
old to act foolish about it. It was easy enough to be seen,
though, that he was very happy.

Soon afterward the records of the Circuit Court of Hinds,
the capital county of Mississippi, bore the fact of my marriage to Miss Carrie V. Highgate, on August 3d, 1870. The
bond required was about the same as that exacted of my
brother, a failure to give which had resulted in his incarceration in a murderer's cell in that Yazoo common jail. But
now that Grant, instead of Johnson, was President, and the
new constitution had been ratified unanimously, and the
black code had been repealed, and the "nigros" had "done
riz," I had no trouble at all to give it.

Within one week from the day we began keeping house
in Yazoo, wife and I—how strangely that contrasts with
"Yankee stronghold"—and while I was not at home, two

colored "ladies," of the same sort as Rarety, dressed in the height of fashion, bonnets, silks, jewels, kids, etc., etc., etc., called to pay their "respects" to "Mrs. Senator Morgan," and to " welcome " her to " 'Azoo."

Mrs. Morgan had lived South long enough to know how to meet the emergency, so she had two chairs placed on the porch, and bade them be seated. She told me afterwards that she welcomed them kindly, but they promptly lifted their skirts and indignantly withdrew.

In less than forty-eight hours the details of this " social incident," exaggerated out of all semblance of truth, were known throughout the county and traveled abroad. Some of the observations of the enemy, as reported to us, were most amusing. Yazoo society was racked to its foundations, both on the recognized and on the unrecognized side.

" How dare she!" exclaimed Mrs. Colonel and Mrs. Major and Mrs. Captain and Mrs. Judge and Mrs. Flunky, to their colored servants.

" She's no better than the balance of ye. Hi! We always did believe you all would find out some day that yo' god Mawgin was no mo' friend to you all than we all always wor. Now you'll see faw yo' own self. Pity he hadn't done got her b'fo' gettin' on top we all, by you alls votes an' done stole himself rich. Reckon he'll be buildin' a grand house to put her in now, if he can get you all to tote the bricks. Heap mo' mischief in sto' fur ye, mind, onless yo' drive um out a y'here."

Colonel Black, the " human hornet," the " Cyclops," all the irreconcilables, were in the happiest of moods.

" That settles it!" some said; " Got 'im now!" said some; " Thank God, the tyrant's dethroned !" said others. And they all agreed that " Next time we'll vote 'im out with nigro votes, by G—d."

But there had been many changes in Yazoo within three years, and the more conservative and practical of " the enemy " said :

"What you all making such a fuss about ?   You'll find yo'r mistake.   The nigros are free now; they're not d—d fools.   High time you all knew that," and so forth.

Mrs. Stockdale, Mrs. Snodgrass and others of the most respectable and accomplished "white ladies" of Yazoo, all of the first or next to the "first families," said :

"Served them right; glad to see that Mrs. Morgan is not a coward, nor her husband a demagogue."

When I heard that I said to Carrie, "Life in the old land yet, wife."

We afterward learned that certain "white ladies" of Yazoo had prompted the women to call, and furnished a large share of the "finery" for the purpose.   This incident still further illustrated :

First. The lamentable ignorance of the irreconclables respecting the character of the free negro.

Second. The tenacity with which they clung to the hope that, by hook or by crook, they would sooner or later regain control of the county government.

Third. That they were "politicians," all, male and female, old and young.

Fourth. Their readiness to seize upon every incident, in the private, no less unscrupulously than in the public life of their opponents, without regard to their feelings, and make use of it for the accomplishment of their purposes.

Fifth—and perhaps this embraces all the others—their general "cussedness."

During my residence in that county I had not said or done anything, publicly or privately, that could by any fair means, be construed as indicating on my part the possession of agrarian convictions or sentiments, or that I wished to see any of the *legitimate* distinctions in the social order destroyed or changed.   There was not in the county a man, woman, or child who had ever seen me intoxicated, or tipple.   Not one who had ever seen me gamble, race horses, attend cock-fights, or who had heard me use profane or vulgar language.   Not one who could say that I had ever shot, shot at, struck, struck at, or wronged any human being in their goods, their lands, their houses, or their persons, or in any way. The incident was not due to *caste* prejudice, for although I was an open advocate of the political and civil equality of all men, I had often declared publicly—I had never taught the contrary privately, by precept nor by example—that there could never be social equality except among equals. I had drawn, reported to the constitutional convention, advocated, and voted for the clause relating to concubinage and adultery in our new constitution, and in my public speeches, in the county and elsewhere, I had summoned all virtuous men and women to make war upon these odious and destructive practices, as being more dangerous to the peace and happiness of the people of the State than the yellow fever and cholera scourges, the liquor scourge, or the old slave scourge, *because*, they were *between* "*two races*," one of which had always maintained its " superiority " *by force, and had perpetuated a " separation " of the two in all those affairs of life which tend to develop the moral nature of man, and perpetuated their contact in all those affairs of life which tend to develop man's lower nature.* It could not have been due to anything my wife had said or done, because they knew nothing about her. The incident was due to the inborn purpose of the lighter to rule over the darker-skinned man. It was due to the instincts of a race, once civilized, but now reduced by the inherent concupiscence of African slavery, to lecherous savages.

But it was " simply a question of endurance," and with such a woman by my side as my wife, I could endure all things. Wife and I tried to act just as though no such incident had ever happened. In this a little diplomacy was necessary; but while we were " wise as serpents " I am sure we were " harmless as doves." We not only refused to make any apology, we did not attempt to deny the act which had given such offense to the " nigro," and which had raised such bright anticipations in the minds of the enemy, either by any

sort of public or private notice of it or its consequences. All
we did or tried to do was to *stand erect,* and that we did to
our own satisfaction.   Therefore, it "shortly" came about
that as all their former tactics had done, this trick of " the
enemy" also reacted upon themselves, one of the first consequences of which was that the new social distinctions which
the General and his family, the ex-bureau agent and his
family, other Northerners with their families, and Charles
and myself had endeavored in vain to establish amongst the
freed people began to take root.   Theretofore, in the churches,
the schools, and all social gatherings among them, the colored
concubines of white men had been able to maintain their
supremacy.   These ranked according to the rank of their
white "sweethearts."   Think of it, sweetheart applied to
such an object in the *white* social world!

While " Liz" was the concubine of a wealthy planter she
stood at the head of colored " 'ciety ;" when she became the
concubine of a merchant or a lawyer she stepped down one
point, and when she had dropped down another peg and was
the concubine of a "po' clerk," she took her place in the
ranks of that "social set," and thus she continued to descend
in the social scale until she became the wife of a "po' no
'count nigger."   Meanwhile her daughters were following her
example, *often in her very tracks,* and close upon her heels down
the long descending scale—unless, as was often the case, the
concubine had too much pride and self-respect to rear daughters for such a purpose—in which case she destroyed herself
to prevent it, or killed them.   Indeed this system had been
the source of unfailing fountains of tears—all unavailing.
But the thick clouds had lifted from off the old stubble-
ground of Yazoo, and the rays of the risen new sun were so
bright that they dazzled the eyes of "the enemy" and of
even the members of the former little garrison of the Yankee
stronghold, so that some of them, too, for quite a little time
could not see.

Had Carrie and I been alone in this struggle, the result

would have been different. We were not alone. We had on our side, not only a little handful of noble spirits in Yazoo, and in the State outside that county, we also had Elijah's bones, for the secret recesses of the hearts of the enemy swelled and expanded under the pressure of the light of life remaining hidden therein, and forced from them profoundly respectful demeanor toward Mrs. Morgan and toward myself. Then, too, in addition to such aids, there were warm and true-hearted friends abroad, who wrote us kindly cheering words, words of succor and of comfort. Of this class the reader will forgive me for quoting the following letter, which I shall give entire:

"PETERBORO', *Nov.* 15, 1880.

"*Colonel Morgan:*

"MY DEAR SIR: In the midst of my preparations for going in the morning to the National Historical Society Convention at Syracuse, I received your deeply interesting and thrice welcome letter. I must not only acknowledge the receipt of it, though it will be only in brief lines that I can do so. God be praised for bringing your enemies to be at peace with you! I am rejoiced to learn that kindness is shown you where you expected to have to encounter hatred. You chose a sweet, loving-hearted girl for your wife, and she chose you for her husband. The result is a happy pair. But this is not the most important result. The most is its contributing largely to break down the unnatural and unchristian barriers between races. You and your dear wife have in this respect set a useful example before the world. I am happy to learn through you that your wife is 'as well as usual.' Mrs. Smith joins me in my kind regards to you. Your friend,

"GERRIT SMITH.

"P. S.—The *Star* (thanks to yourself) comes regularly to me."

The promises of the truth are certain.

During this season "we all Yankees," "nigros," and "scalawags" in Yazoo, gathered the first fruits of all our planting in that county during the reconstruction period, and with high hopes for the future, prepared the ground for other seed, and prayed for the blessed showers of love from on high to quicken them.

There were not quite two thousand souls in Yazoo City. There were forty-one places where intoxicating liquors were

kept for sale at retail, and every wholesale and retail dry goods,
grocery and general supply store in the town, with two exceptions, both Yankees, sold them—when they did not give them
away to attract custom. There were also seven different
houses of worship, and three regular besides several irregular gambling houses.*

Notwithstanding his terrible front, the Yazoo temperance
association prepared to attack this monster, too—how fearless
lack of worldly wisdom will make good men and women·
Under the "local option law," passed by our "radical legislature," all women above the age of eighteen were granted
an equal voice with men upon the question of license or no
license for the sale of intoxicants. Of course, this included
the colored ladies of Yazoo. For a long time the "white'·
temperance associations of the State had labored in vain for
this opportunity. Now that they found the "nigros" rallying
to their support, they suspected the effect of the law (which
they had themselves drafted and supported) and began to
fall away from the movement. The "white" churches of
Yazoo City were quite active on their side of the "line," and
the "colored" on theirs.

When the campaign closed in Yazoo City more than two-
thirds of the colored men and women within the corporation,
of the requisite age, had signed in good faith a petition
requesting the proper authorities not to renew the licenses of
those who had been licensed or to grant new license to any
one for the sale of intoxicating liquors. In the "white"
churches the pastors had utterly failed to get two-thirds
of even the ladies forming their membership, and the
petition was "lost" or "strayed" or "stolen" while in
the hands of the devoted pastor of the "white" Presbyterian
Church, who had worked long, faithfully, and most devotedly
in the good cause. Thus the movement in Yazoo failed.

I had taken no active part, nor had my wife, in this cam-

* Gambling was carried on extensively in the private houses of the "best citizens."
I knew of no houses of "ill-fame" in Yazoo. They are not a "necessary evil" in the
South.

paign, more than to give it a silent moral support by example and good wishes for its promoters.

Previous to the inauguration of the campaign I had on several occasions, in the little church we helped to build, and at public gatherings, strenuously advocated reform in this direction, but as a leader in the political field I did not deem it prudent to enter into such a canvass, and so contented myself and satisfied my political supporters by allowing this work to be done by those who were not directly responsible for "higher trusts." Yet the whisky-dealers and the "whisky-guzzlers" and their friends not only traced the movement directly to my door, they also held me responsible for it. This, of course, was not all they laid at my door during this period.

Another outrage was perpetrated upon the high-toned, honorable, down trodden, oppressed and distressed white citizens of Yazoo. So long as the concubines could remain at the head of the Mississippi social order on the " inferior side of the line " they appeared tolerably content and took advantage of the new constitution only for the purpose of enforcing their rights as heirs in cases where there were none having a prior right. Now that the concubine's position as a social leader of the colored people was not only in danger, but several of them in Yazoo had been " turned out of church " because they were "living in adultery" in the sight of man as well as of God, many of that class began to inquire whether there was any legal inhibition upon their marriage with " white sweethearts." Finding there was none they not only kicked against the pricks, they actually began to wear armor against them. Of course this could never be made by the whites a pretext for another "nigro rising," never ! It would endanger their standing in the " civilized world." Grant and not Johnson being President, the new constitution having been ratified—unanimously, the "young one " and his " imps " being already "on top," the enemy were now thoroughly besieged and in a most sorry plight.

One began the erection of an elegant new residence just south of our home—how strangely that contrasts with stronghold—and allowed it to be given out that it was for his concubine—a relative of Lizzie's ; another gave money to his; another secretly married his ; another satisfied his with promises ; some surrendered all " claims " on theirs, while the great mass " bided their time." These last were harassed nigh unto death by the " insolence " of their concubines, who, perceiving their advantage, became stronger supporters than ever of Republican principles and of that " miscegenationist, Mawgin," while the great mass of the colored men came to look upon me as in deed and in truth a Moses, because they were now permitted, in addition to all the other blessings that had come to them with their freedom, to call their firesides their own, and to erect within their homes a sacred family altar without imminent peril of desecration and pollution from the unholy touch of " superior " white men.

CHAPTER LVII.

MARVELOUS PROGRESS OF THE FREED PEOPLE IN THE ART OF
SELF-GOVERNMENT—REAL CARPET-BAGGERS—HOW THEY CAME
TO YAZOO, AND WHAT BECAME OF THEM—ANOTHER STRAW FOR
BRICKS—YAZOO ELECTIONS, 1867 TO 1875—A DENT TICKET
FULL-GROWN.

BUT that which seems to me the most gratifying feature of
the period of which I am now writing, is the marvelous
progress made by the freed people in the art of self-government. I presume that many of my readers—if indeed I shall
have many—will smile incredulously at this point; they
have often done so before in the course of this story. That
cannot be helped. All have my free consent to smile, to
laugh, or to cry whenever the mood shall prompt them. This
is said to be a free country, and I believe in its fundamental
institutions. But I am digressing, and am reminded that I
have left only space for facts.

About the close of our political campaign of 1869, and from
that on, there were frequent arrivals at Yazoo of persons
from the North and from adjoining States, all of whom
brought with them a universal panacea for all the woes of the
people, "both black and white." Some came "highly recommended" to some one or more of the State official digni-
taries, others came bearing no other testimonials than the
merits of the political nostrums they had to introduce. This

class were of both races, and of all shades of politics, complexion, calling and employment, or profession. Some openly espoused the cause of " the people," and became "good citizens ; " in other words, Democrats. Others as openly espoused the cause of " the people," and became " scum "— carpet-baggers ; in other words, Republicans. There were a few who espoused the cause of " ou' color," and at once began to find fault with both Democrats and Republicans. One of these was a quite intelligent colored man, whose parents had passed through the color crucible at the North and still felt the pain of the burn. By way of illustrating the fact that he had inherited their remembrance of Yankee prejudices and their secret contempt of the Yankee character, he began, almost immediately upon his arrival at Yazoo, an effort to gather the freed people into a separate political organization. To accomplish this purpose, he gravely assured them that their liberties did not depend upon the leadership of any man or set of men, but upon themselves; that they were under no obligations whatever to any person, or to any party for their freedom, because freedom was the natural state of man, and their emancipation was evidence merely that the country had come to the point of recognizing the fact. The obligation, therefore, was all on the other side, and could not be discharged until the white man, who had always lived upon the negro's toil, went a step farther and made some sort of restitution. According to his philosophy, the fact that the freedom and citizenship of the negro had been put into the Constitution and laws of the country, was ample guarantee of its permanence, and, as the colored people of Yazoo were largely in the majority, two to one, they ought, therefore, to rule. Had he stopped here he might have made some headway amongst " ou' color " in Yazoo. But he did not, and continued to advance in the unfolding of his scheme, until he had openly denounced me as a fraud, and not a true friend to the colored people. Then he found it to his interest quite suddenly to leave the county, which he did, and, returning North, spread the news amongst "ou' color" that the carpet-baggers at the South were not only deluding the poor freed people to their ruin, but were an intolerable nuisance to the State. In proof of this he cited his own case, and declared that I had incited the "poor, ignorant freed people,"—my dupes—to drive him away, because I feared the presence in the county of "intelligent gentlemen of color."

Now, the truth is I knew nothing of the affair until long afterwards. Then I was able to recollect that about that date I had been frequently inquired of concerning colored men, strangers, who were holding meetings in the county. As they had kept entirely away from me, and as my only information of them came from the freed people, I could only say that I knew nothing at all about them. If this had enraged my friends to such a pitch that they had taken the matter into their own hands, I am sure it was not my fault, and I declare that I knew nothing at all of the intentions nor of the conduct of those friends until, as I have said, long afterward. There were other aspiring colored young men from the North, more wise than those of the class to which the one I have mentioned belonged. These came seeking honorable employment, or waited until they became acquainted with the people before they attempted to lead. Several of this class became useful citizens, engaged in merchandizing, planting or school teaching, and thus grew to be real helps in the work of clearing the old ground and in cultivating and harvesting the crops that grew upon it. These were recog_ nized and preferred by the people according to their merits At this time, Mississippi and other Southern States enjoying free governments, offered a tempting field for ambitious and worthy young colored men at the North, where nearly all the doors to the trades and higher employments, in private as well as in public life, were closed against them. I was not at all surprised that they came flocking to Mississippi and Yazoo. For one I was glad to have them come. If their

purposes were good, they were not only likely to become helps
in our good work, but would be able to achieve any position,
in public life at least, to which their merits might entitle
them.   Equally with the free schools for demonstrating the
capacity of the negro, we also needed, as I believed, examples.
And it seemed to me likely that these examples would more
readily be found from among the class who had had some
chance in life, however pinched and narrow, as for a long
time it was in the North, than from among the freed people
in the South.   Here, where there was free scope for their
powers, they could grow into a broader manhood and, as I
sincerely believed, into a broader citizenship.

Nor was I surprised that some should yield to the temptation such a field offered, to attain personal advancement
through the strength of mere numbers, rather than by the
sympathy and support of the best.   This tendency was increased by the sullen, stubborn refusal of the old slaveholding class to recognize any of the colored people, male or
female, as other than natural inferiors; and in some counties
it became a very great curse, not only to the freed men but
also to the whites.

But in Yazoo, colored men from the North found a match
for themselves in many of the freed people, whose sterling
good sense and practical knowledge of affairs in some measure
made up for their lack of school training.   Our local elections afforded ample means for testing these qualities, and
for bringing out the comparative merits of the two.   Northern colored men, even in Yazoo, had to contend with the
prejudices of the freed people, which often were as bitter as
the prejudices of the native whites against "we all Yankees."   So that unless the Northern colored man could make
his race argument or reasoning in favor of segregation do
service for him, the freedman who aspired for leadership was
likely to carry off the prize.   These contests were no less a
school for me; for they afforded rare opportunities for
the study of human nature, especially that side of it which
is the result of the long centuries of race conflict.

From the first I strove by precept and by example to create lines of competition upon a higher plane, and the affection of the freed people, which I enjoyed to the fullest extent, enabled me to keep down any serious divisions in our own ranks growing out of such contests, or from other causes. One incident alone will illustrate this truth:

Some Northern colored men, aided secretly by two or three disaffected white Republicans, succeeded in gathering together some three hundred freed people, in what was termed a mass convention. It was no doubt designed to build up an organized opposition to me, and may have been inspired by the enemy, or possibly, by jealous rivals outside of the county. I had given the meeting no attention whatever, was not present, nor had I prompted any one to represent me. Yet, at the moment when the conspirators thought they were in full possession of the meeting, an old colored farmer— planter is the word used there—got up and, remarking that he had not seen me in that convention, said he would like to know how many "Morgan men" there were in the house, anyway, and at once moved that all Morgan men come over on to the right side and stand up, and all others stand upon the left side. Friends of mine present at the time, afterward told me that it appeared as though the whole house arose as one man, and crossing over stood upon the right side. The same fact is also illustrated in another and perhaps a better way. In 1867 my *majority* in a total registered vote of 8,830, of which in round numbers but 1,800 were cast, was 1,200. That year " the enemy " not only refused to vote at all, but also kept from voting as many of the freed people as they could, and the reader will remember, there was no Republican organization in the county. In 1868, in a total vote cast of 3,306, my majority was 300.

That was the kuklux year, when the enemy not only voted their own entire strength, but also voted as many of the freed people as they could bribe, coax, or drive to vote their ticket, and kept from the polls as many as they could by the same means induce to remain away.

In 1869, in a total vote cast of 3,457, my majority was 1,700.

That was the first year of Grant's administration, and when the enemy resorted to the trick of nominating " General Grant's own deah brother-in-law," and " Rube " for the purpose of deceiving " our nigros " into voting with their old masters for their " National Republican " ticket.

In 1871* I was not a candidate. The term for which I had been elected to the Senate would not expire until 1873. But the ticket known as the Morgan ticket, was chosen by a majority of 1,969, in a total vote cast of 3,963.

In 1872 Grant and Greeley were the candidates.

It went somewhat against the grain to vote against Horace Greeley, but considering the company in which he was, the Republicans could not help comparing that "movement " with our " Dent movement." Indeed, there were those who profanely declared that the Greeley movement was our Mississippi Dent movement full grown.

Therefore the Grant ticket in Yazoo, like our Republican tickets of preceding years, was known also as the Morgan ticket.

In a total vote of 3,300, Grant's majority was 1,500.

In 1873, in a total vote of 3,100, my majority over my opponent was 1,900.

There was no general election in Mississippi in 1874.

*There was no general election in 1870.

CHAPTER LVIII.

FURTHER ILLUSTRATIONS OF THE POLITICAL PROGRESS OF THE
NEGRO—THE ENEMY SEE A SIGN—MAKING A SHERIFF'S BOND
—DO ELECTIONS ELECT—RESULTS THAT "OLD BILL ALLEN"
WHEN HE "ROSE UP" COULD HARDLY HAVE FORESEEN—
MEETING AN OLD ACQUAINTANCE—ANOTHER "NIGRO RISING"
—MORGAN IS SHERIFF—DEATH OF MR. HILLIARD.

THE election of 1873 was in a certain sense the climax in
our State of "radical rule," so called by the enemy. It
was the year when the varied progressive influences converging from different and often widely separate centers of
thought, interest and action, converging upon Mississippi,
with none other than weapons of truth, met and for a third
time overcame "the enemy" upon ground of his own choosing. Up to this time Mr. Hilliard had held the most lucrative office in the county—that of sheriff and ex-officio tax
collector—uninterruptedly, or for a period beginning in 1869,
and continuing more than four years.

Notwithstanding our disagreement upon the school and
certain other questions, I had given him a hearty and unfaltering support. I had done this not because of any especial
personal regard for him, or that he entertained for me, nor
because I was under any obligations whatever to him, but
solely because I desired to lay the foundations of our party
upon a broader basis than mere race lines (which would have

restricted its membership to the colored people, led by a
handful of "Yankees "), and believed that an exhibition of
unfaltering political friendship for Mr. Hilliard would at least
be accepted by the native whites as evidence of the sincerity
of my professions in that regard.   I had given five years to
the cause of reconstruction in Yazoo and in the State without other reward than the consciousness of having done well;
and the empty honors of an office that, while entailing the
gravest responsibilities upon me and the hardest kind of
work, did not afford me a personal support.   My creditors
were clamorous for their money, and every one called me a
fool for giving to others the fruits of my toil and trials instead
of preserving at least some share for myself.

The same kind relatives who could not at all understand
why we had failed on Tobeka, now could not understand
why I was not yet able to pay my debts.   They read in the
papers that the carpet-baggers were all getting rich, and was
I not one of that class?   Besides, the old "guard" had
become dissatisfied with Mr. Hilliard.   So had nearly all the
freed people, who blamed him for not taking a more active
part in behalf of free schools.   Mrs. Hilliard and her
daughters had become leading members in the leading white
folks' church, and in Yazoo society.   It was said that the
sheriff was rich ; that he had saved "nigh on to fifty thousand dollars."

But be that as it may, the time had come when I had
expected, from the very outset, to ask for my reward.   The State
was reconstructed in all the departments of government, and
peace and quiet prevailed.

But my friends among the white Unionists, the Northerners,
and especially the old "guard," together with the great body
of the freed people, anticipating what would be my wishes in
the premises, were already using my name as Mr. Hilliard's successor, and when the convention met I was placed
in nomination for that office by acclamation.   It was the
most intelligent body of Republicans ever assembled in the

county. The contrast between it and the first Republican convention held in the county was indeed striking. Every one of the delegates had been chosen at numerously attended primaries, and nearly all of them could read, and a large majority could both read and write.

There were at least three colored men of the number who were worth, in real estate and live stock, not less than ten thousand dollars each, all of which they had made at planting.

There was also quite a "sprinkling" of native whites, among them planters, merchants, and one lawyer, all of whom had been slave-holders. I could not but felicitate myself on the fact, that every one of these was my hearty supporter and friend, notwithstanding I owned no land yet, nor any houses.

My term had expired in the Senate. I enjoyed no means or facilities whatever for influencing either those delegates, or the masses who had sent them there, to vote for me, other than my name and the memory among them of my services.

Without money or patronage at my disposal, and with convictions of duty respecting party leadership which forbade my making promises of reward contingent upon my election, at the close of my four years' term in the Senate, I was as powerless to reward friends or to punish foes within our party as my baby boy, then two years old.

But though Mr. Foote was a warm advocate of Mr. Hilliard's re-election, he, together with the official membership of the A. M. E. Church which had got a foothold in Yazoo too,* had been for weeks engaged in canvassing the county in Mr. Hilliard's interest, supplied, as was at the time openly proclaimed and well known, with " ample funds " for all manner of expenses, it all failed, and, as the denizens of Yazoo City will remember to this day, the shout that went up from the convention upon the vote nominating me, " nearly lifted the roof from the court-house," as everybody said.

*Upon the close of the campaign of 1869, the irreconcilables suddenly became especial admirers of Mr. Foote, often contrasted him with "them low down Yankees," and always to the disparagement of the Yankees. This, with the prejudices he already possessed, together with the tendency of his church to segregation had great influence upon him, and by 1873, he was an avowed advocate of a party that should be made up of "Southerners and nigros," to the exclusion of "Northerners."

And it gives me pleasure to record here that it did not cost me any promises nor any money at all, except the personal expenses of myself while travelling to and fro to attend the primaries. It also gives me pleasure to add that although my share of the expenses of the campaign from first to last for tickets, for travelling and all other expenses, did not exceed one hundred dollars ; although I made no canvass at all among the people, and but one speech during the campaign which followed the nomination ; although upon the day of the election and for several days before I had been ill in bed and under the care of a physician, and although " the enemy " made Mr. Hilliard their candidate and placed upon their ticket with him for *all* the county offices and many of the district offices *none but* colored men, my *majority* over him was nearly two thousand in a vote of thirty-one hundred.

The truth is that the irreconcilables had all along intended to use Mr. Hilliard for my overthrow. To this purpose was due the social eminence to which his family so suddenly attained, and the hearty support of their organ, the *Democrat.*

The result made them very mad indeed ; for they now had to carry a double dose of "nigro rule. " The first was at Dover, when they saw with their own eyes that the freedman, free negro and mulatto dared shoot to kill. The next was now, when they realized that I had not misjudged the negro, and that he was capable of not only feeling but also of expressing gratitude.

But all of a sudden, certain of them professed to have had a revelation. It was in the election news from Ohio. "Old Bill Allen " had " done riz up," and Ohio had gone Democratic! Seeking for the cause of this change, they discovered that in June, 1873, a new departure in politics was taken when the *Democratic* convention in Allen County, of that State, passed resolutions declaring that corruption in political parties had become chronic, and that " both political parties have demonstrated that they are powerless to check or control the existing tendency toward the utter demoralization of the politics of the country," also that a convention had been held at Columbus and participated in by both Democrats and Liberals. It had—

" *Resolved*, That we insist upon a strict adherence by the General Government to the constitutional limitations of its power, and we demand home government in all local affairs."

Also, that a Democratic State convention followed, which nominated William Allen for governor, and—

"*Resolved*, That the Democratic party seeks to revive no dead issues, but stands by its principles, which are suited to all times and circumstances. * * *

" It defends the reserved rights of the States and of the people, and opposes the centralization that would impair or destroy them."

Mr. Allen's majority was but about 800. Under ordinary circumstances, the fact could have had no particular significance in the South. But the circumstances were extraordinary. The convention in Allen County where the "Ohio movement" originated, was a *Democratic departure*. The excuse for it and for the Liberal convention which followed, sprang from a wide-spread disgust of the corrupt practices, apparent in *both* the great political parties *at the North*. The "bloody shirts" of Georgia, Alabama, Tennessee, Lou siana, and other Southern States, had frequently been unfurled and made to do service in Northern elections for the Republicans, until thousands of the most conscientious and enlightened members of the party thought they saw in every one of them —of those " bloody shirts "—a trick by thieves for the perpetuation of their opportunity to rob the country through the channels of politics. The investigations which had followed in New York and other cities, in States and in Congress, had uncovered to the country the fact that corruption did prevail to an alarming extent in both parties. Some traced the cause to the war, others traced it back to "Federal interference" in States at the South, while there were those who declared that the root of the matter was in the extension of the suffrage, so as to include the negro. Taking advantage of this feeling, a man of undoubted personal and political sincerity and integrity, was brought to the front in Ohio and placed upon a platform, which, while it embraced a plank covering the grievances of Republicans, also embraced planks which met the demands of extreme and irreconcilable Democrats everywhere, South as well as North.

The fact was, that many voted for the man, without regard to the platform upon which he stood, as a protest against the corrupt tendencies of the times. That elected him. This result was accepted by the irreconcilables in Yazoo as proof that the day of their deliverance from what *they* still called a "carpet-bag negro usurpation" was at hand. For was not Ohio a "hot-bed of abolitionism," the "home of Giddings," the very "backbone of radical power" at the North ?

So they talked to each other while they shook hands and congratulated themselves ; so they talked to the freed people, while felicitating themselves on the prospect that after all the time was not a great way off when they should be again able to "whip a nigger;" so some of them jocularly said to me while good humoredly inviting me to "read the hand-writing on the wall." I insisted that they were mistaken ; that the result was a protest against corruption, not against our Mississippi nor our Yazoo government; at which they would remind me of that resolution of the Liberals favoring "home government" and protesting against Federal usurpations of power. But, pointing to our majorities, I would always reply, "what is ours but home government— the rule of the majority ?" Notwithstanding all the progress we had made, all the examples we had afforded of the capacity of the negro for self-government, their response to this was always a kind of grin accompanied with a look which said, "Morgan, you may be honest, but you're green," and a final word, which was rarely more than "yo'll see."

Notwithstanding the fact that my candidacy for the sheriff's office meant an increase of taxes for school purposes, largely increased facilities for the education of the children of the

freed people, and was a rebuke to Mr. Hilliard and his supporters for their neglect of this cause, out of a total registered
' white vote" of more than fifteen hundred and of a total
vote cast of thirty-one hundred and thirty-seven, he received
but four hundred and thirty-one, while I received twenty-three
hundred and sixty-five. The fact is I received nearly, if not
quite, as large a number of white votes as he.* The Grange
organization in the county was at that time in the zenith of
its power and I know that the head of that organization and
many of its members voted for me. The bond which the sheriff
was by law required to make was in the sum of $20,000; that
which I was required to make as tax collector ran the amount
up to $105,000.

It was understood that none but owners of real estate
property could lawfully qualify on that bond. Before the
election I had received every assurance that I should have no
trouble on that score. So, as soon as the election was over, I
set out to make it. But from the very outset I met the secret
and sometimes open hostility of the leading irreconcilables,
who often made personal appeals to such as were disposed to
become my sureties not to do so, and succeeded in some
instances in persuading others who had already qualified as
sureties to withdraw. But there was another surprise in
store for " the enemy."

Learning of these difficulties freedmen owning real estate
promptly signed, qualified and became my sureties. The
result was very gratifying to me, for it discovered to all the
fact that the freed people of Yazoo were indeed making substantial progress. Had I wished to have done so I could have
made the entire amount of the bond with perfectly solvent
colored men for sureties. But that was contrary to my ideas
of good policy. There were perfectly solvent white men,
merchants and planters, already on it for considerable sums,
and for many reasons I preferred they should remain.

When the bond was complete and the time provided by

* There were some three hundred scattering votes.

law for me to qualify and enter upon the duties of my office
had arrived, I appeared before the proper officer, took the
oath of office required by law and made the usual personal
notice to Mr. Hilliard. He then for the first time informed
me that he had resolved not to surrender the office to me.

The only court then in session in the county was our board
of supervisors. That body held its sessions in the court-house,
and had, by law, absolute control of the county buildings. The
room in which the sheriff had his office was also in the court-
house. It was the duty of the sheriff, either in person or by
deputy, to attend all sessions of the board. Mr. Hillard was
then in attendance upon the board. Prepared with the certificate of the proper officers, showing my election to the
office by the people,* showing also the record of my bonds
and of my oath of office, and that the day had arrived when
by law the term of the incumbent, Mr. Hillard, should expire,
and when I should become the lawful sheriff, and, showing
that I was the lawful sheriff, I went before that body and
demanded to be recognized by them as sheriff in fact. It
was at this juncture that Mr. Hillard appeared with counsel,
and asked that I be not recognized. Upon the hearing before
the board, it was legally established that Mr. Hillard, had given
me no notice whatever of his intention to contest my right
to the office; that he had not filed in any court any notice
whatever of contest ; that he did not deny my election, and
that the only ground upon which he attempted to defend his
refusal to turn over to me the keys of the office room, was the
fact that a legal question was pending in the Supreme Court
of the State, involving the legality of the election.

* Following is a true copy of that certificate :
" *To all whom it may concern :*
    We, the undersigned, registrars of Yazoo County, Mississippi, duly appointed by the
commissioners thereof, certify that at an election held in said county, in accordance
with the provisions of the general election law of 1871, two thousand seven hundred
and ninety-six (2,796) votes were cast for the office of sheriff, of which
A. T. Morgan received... 2,365
F. P. Hillard received..   431
                                                                    ———
Making a majority in favor of A. T. Morgan of.................................. 1,934
And we therefore declare him to be elected to that office.
                                                        R. W. LEWIS,
                                                        GEO. M. POWELL,
                                                                Registrars.

YAZOO CITY, *November* 7, 1873.

Mr. Hilliard, his counsel, and the board at the time well knew that the question pending in the Supreme Court involved only the legality of the election for State officers, and had no relation whatever to county officers. Mr. Hilliard and all the rest knew that by the Constitution and laws his term was for but two years, and that that term expired that very day. So the board decided, and therefore declared that I was the sheriff, in law and in fact, and they commanded me to attend them at their sessions, thus dismissing Mr. Hilliard.*

One of the arguments presented by his counsel at that hearing fairly illustrates the animus of their entire proceeding. That counsel stated that certain rumors had come to his ears to the effect that I had threatened, if Mr. Hilliard should refuse to turn over the keys of his office to me, to send to the country for the colored people—even he called them colored people now—to come to town, when I would use them for an assault upon the building. And then he begged the board to consider what might be the consequences of such an act. "For," as he declared, " our people are not yet prepared to tolerate that method of asserting one's right to an office," and the result might be a bloody conflict—" a war of races."

Now, four years had passed since that alarm was last heard in Yazoo. Its revival, considering all the circumstances, awakened some laughter. But Mr. Hilliard and his coun-

---

* That order was as follows :

* * *

Minutes of the Board of Supervisors.

TUESDAY, *January* 6, 1874.

A. T. Morgan presented to the board his certificate of election as sheriff of Yazoo County, Mississippi, also the certificate of the clerk of the chancery court of the county, that said Morgan's bonds, as sheriff and tax collector, were duly filed in his office, examined, and approved by him on the 5th day of January, instant, and that he did, on said day, administer to said Morgan the oath of office, as prescribed by law ; whereupon it was—

Ordered, That this board do recognize the said A. T. Morgan as the only person legally entitled to exercise the functions and perform the duties of the office of sheriff of Yazoo County, and that said sheriff (Morgan) is hereby ordered and required to attend this and all future meetings of this board, and to execute and obey all its orders and decrees.

Ordered, That the board be adjourned until to-morrow morning at 9 o'clock.

S. G. BEDWELL, *President.*

J. M. DICKSON, *Clerk.*
By J. T. RUSSELL, *Deputy Clerk.*

sel treated the "rumor" as a very serious matter, indeed, and Mr. Hilliard was called upon to relate what he knew about the threats. When he had finished, it appeared that all he knew about it was what some one else had told him of what some colored man had been heard to say would happen, in the event that an effort should be made to keep me out of the office to which everybody knew I had been legally and in fact elected.

Being permitted to do so, I stated to the board that not only had I not made any threats, but that I had taken legal advice as to the means I ought to employ in the event of Mr. Hilliard's refusal to turn over to me, and my counsel was present. I did not deem it necessary to say that I should not resort to the means suggested, but, if any doubt remained in the minds of Mr. Hilliard and his counsel, I would assure them all that I should not do so.

This "rumor" of "threats" awakened in me and in at least one member of the board memories of an almost forgotten era. And I found myself recalling the fact that this counsel of Mr. Hilliard was the same who had appeared for "Mars' Si," the same who had been "counsel for the State" when Charles was tried on a certain memorable occasion, and who then was one of the Grand Cyclops of Yazoo. During the five years that had passed since Grant's election, we had often met, and on friendly terms. He had on at least two occasions not been able to withhold his meed of praise for duty well performed by me. But—

Well, I must be brief. Mr. Hilliard promptly yielded to the order of the board so far as to "withdraw," and I was at once installed in his place. That evening when he left his office room and went home, he placed three men on guard inside it. Under the law he was a trespasser, and I had undoubted authority to arrest him and hold him as such.

Had he made any formal contest, no matter how absurd the grounds of it might have been, it would have been different. He had made no contest at all formal, or otherwise, except to appear before the board as I have related.

I appointed some deputies and continued all the next day to act as sheriff for the board (whose sessions would continue for some days, it being a regular stated meeting) and for the county. That night a friend of Mr. Hilliard brought me direct from him an offer of $5,000 to allow him to remain in the office thirty days longer. This was in amount the same as the offer of Captain Telsub on a former occasion.

Considering the fact that in 1869 I had declined the office and secured his appointment to it ; that I had warmly supported him for a re-election to it ; that I had shared in none of the proceeds of it ; that he had achieved financial independence by it; that I owned no land yet nor houses ; that he knew thoroughly my feelings and my views respecting the uses for which party advantages should be employed ; and thoroughly well knew that I meant to be honest with the colored people, to whose fidelity mainly I owed my election, and also knew that I was pledged by inclination, by my record and by the issues of our preliminary canvass, to use the patronage of the office for the encouragement of a more liberal policy toward the freed people ; considering the fact that my acceptance of such an offer at such a time would have at once demonstrated to the colored people that I had been false to them, and to every body, that indeed and in truth I was a " fool or a knave;" considering such an offer from him to me; considering this outrage, I became exasperated. It was impossible for me to sleep that night, only by " fits and starts." All night long I kept revolving in my mind what had I done to cause this man to have so low an opinion of my judgment, as for a moment to suppose that I would fail to see that my acceptance of his offer would not only deprive me of the office forever, but also would forever blast my name ; or that he should for a moment suppose that seeing this I could be such a dastard as to accept such a fate for such a consideration. I had accepted the jeers, the scorn, the blows of the enemy during the reign of the kuklux. But that was in behalf of a cause that had made Mr. Hilliard

sheriff and, as everybody said, a rich man; that was when
Mr. Hilliard, "the poor Unionist" came by the back yard to
our "stronghold" to sympathize with its "little garrison."
This was now, when Mr. Hilliard, after having enjoyed the
flesh-pots from our planting until he was fat, and after having
been fawned upon by the enemy until his family had grown
vain and proud, and he had lost his head, had become a tool
for their uses, to the overthrow of Morgan, the destruction
of our party, and the ruin of our cause. I bore in my heart
no malice toward Mr. Hilliard, not one whit. The thing
about it which most tried me was the illustration it afforded
of the effect of the enemy's superior means for regaining the
control in affairs which they had so reluctantly surrendered
in 1869.

My wakefulness greatly worried my poor wife, who
"couldn't understand it at all." I had taken the liberty,
which so many husbands take, to keep the worst of the bad
news from her. What could it mean? What had happened?
Was I not the sheriff? Had I not been installed in office by
the only court then in session in the county? Was there to
be any further trouble? I explained as best I could, and
yet, though she is a rather quick-witted woman, she still
failed to see. The only thing about it was that Mr. Hilliard
still kept the keys of the sheriff's office and had men on
guard over the room.

I couldn't tell her all the particulars. It would take too
long, and I meant to get a little sleep if I could. But she
persisted in her desire to know what was the matter.

"Were there any questions remaining unsettled?"

"No, none."

"Well, then, what is the matter?"

"Nothing, only Mr. Hilliard still holds the keys of the
sheriff's office and has guards over the room."

"How can he do that?"

"He does it."

"Does he dispute your election?"

"No."

" Well, then, what is the matter ? "

And so every attempt to solve the mystery left us at the point where she began.

Our baby girl was not well that night and so what with the office and the child neither of us felt very much refreshed when daylight came. Carrie had proved a true wife and was worthy of my fullest confidence. But it seemed that I could not tell her everything.

That morning I went to the court-house earlier than usual, and went to the sheriff's room. The door was open and no one in except a young man, Mr. Hilliard's nephew. Walking in I informed him that I was the sheriff of the county and should remain in the office. He might, if he pleased bear my message to Mr. Hilliard, to come and get any personal effects he might have there. Without making any resistance at all the young man withdrew, and left the building.

Less than two hours afterward Mr. Hilliard was a corpse, and one of my deputies so badly wounded, that fears were entertained for a long time that he would not recover. But he did.

CHAPTER LIX.

THE MANNER OF IT—HALTING TO PAY TRIBUTE TO HEROIC NEGROES BEFORE THE DEAD ARE BURIED—1868 COME AGAIN—THE PART THE HUMAN HORNET TOOK IN IT—THAT YAZOO JAIL IN 1874.

THE death of Mr. Hilliard occurred in this manner: He was at home when informed that I had entered, and with my deputies was in full possession of the sheriff's office room. It was said that he became very much excited and ran down town to the office of his attorney, with whom he held a hasty consultation. Meantime quite a number of his personal and political followers gathered upon the street near by. From these and from others who were summoned by him a crowd, estimated by some to number twenty and by others twenty-five, was hastily formed for the avowed purpose of " recapturing " the room. During this time Mr. Foote, still a strong partisan of Mr. Hilliard, came to the office. Finding me and my deputies in quiet possession, he became very greatly excited and cursed some of my men, so that to avoid him, the office door was closed against him. Then he rang the court-house bell and went away.

The point where Mr. Hilliard formed his men was two squares distant and around a corner, so that the first knowledge I had of their purpose was his appearance at the head of the street upon which was the court-house, in front of his followers, hurrying toward us and presenting a most violent array. Seeing this some of the citizens scampered away. Others remained. There was no time for consultation, even for thinking, for in a moment they would be at the court-house. My first impulse sprang from a desire to preserve the peace and to save my brother William and my friends and deputies who remained, numbering six persons all told, from violence. Instantly acting upon it, I ordered them all within the room, to close and bolt the door from the inside, and to remain there, no matter what happened.

Then I started alone to meet the crowd, and meeting them half way, calling Mr. Hilliard by name, in a loud voice, I warned him that I was the sheriff; that I had possession of the office; that I had left my deputies in charge of it, and that he should halt. Mr. Hilliard not only saw me, but he must have heard me, for I was almost in front of him. But he refused to halt, and hastening his speed kept on. Then I made the same announcement to his followers, some of whom also heard me, for they hesitated. But Mr. Hilliard turned and shouted to them to follow him, which they did. While thus endeavoring to halt the crowd, they all passed by me. It was now impossible for me to regain the court-house ahead of them, so I followed, hoping that when they should reach the office, finding it closed against them, they would wait for me. But they did not, and Mr. Hilliard and some of his friends violently forced open the door, breaking the pannel, and one of them fired into the room. The shot was returned from the inside. At that moment I reached the steps leading into the main hall of the building (the same steps over which Hilliard and his party had passed an instant before), saw him reeling away from the now open office door, and was met with a blinding flash and crushing noise.* But the " ball " had opened, and when it ended, which could not have been more than five minutes afterward (it did not seem more than

*Made more so from the fact that the shots were fired from within the building.

one), I had cleared the court-house and yard of the last one of them, except my former friend, who lay bleeding and senseless upon the floor of the hall, near the front door, where he fell.

Right here, and before stopping to grieve over the fate of Mr. Hilliard, even before we stop to mark the grave of civil peace, which is worth more than human life, because human liberty cannot be without it, I gladly tarry to do an act of simple justice to the negro. Three of the men in that room when I left it were negroes. I had not gone ten steps on my way to meet the angrily advancing crowd, when I was followed by one of these who, as I was afterward told by others in the room, could not be restrained from following me, and declared that I should not go alone to meet them. That " nigro " followed me all the way and was close at my side throughout the conflict. My deputy on the inside who was wounded and who, in spite of it stood up like a man to the last, was also a " nigro." The only one of Mr. Hilliard's friends who stood by him with fidelity and who was the last man to leave the court-house, was " that nigro Foote." The last one of Mr. Hilliard's bourbon allies ran almost at the first fire; some of them in their haste cleared the high iron picket fence of the yard at one bound. When it was over, my first thought was for Mr. Hilliard and my wounded deputy, and I promptly dispatched a messenger for surgical aid. But before this duty had been accomplished I was notified that a complaint of some sort had been made against me before the mayor. I promptly inquired of that officer what the nature of the complaint was, and was informed that it was murder.

Now the mayor, a Southerner and ex-slaveholder, had been an avowed Republican for but about three years. He had been elected by Republicans ; he had all along been my friend. He knew as every lawyer and man of intelligence in the town well knew, that such a charge could not be sustained against me unless it could be shown that I was not

sheriff, and they all equally well knew that instead of arraign-
ing me on such a charge, the persons who inspired Mr. Hilliard, while not denying my election, to hold on to that room,
and after I was in peaceable possession, to make the attack,
and also those who accompanied him were the guilty persons.
They also knew that it would be my duty to arrest all of them.
But at the moment of receiving this information, I was
informed that certain irreconcilables, members of the bar and
others, were "in consultation." Profound quiet prevailed,
however. The angry crowd of Hilliard's followers seemed
to have wholly disappeared.

There were very few colored men astir, none at all from
the country, more than on any other day, and so far as I could
see or hear, while remaining at the office of the mayor
engaged in preparing for my answer to this charge of murder, there were no signs of further violence.

During the period witnesses to the assault by the Hilliard
party made formal complaint before the mayor against leading members of that party, and very soon thereafter, several
of the most violent of the irreconcilables of the surrounding
country made their appearance upon the streets and at the
mayor's office, and rumors were soon spread about of their
purpose to lynch me. During the period of this delay at
the mayor's office, I retained two of the most prominent
members of our bar, together with our Republican State
Senators for my defense. My relations with these gentlemen
had never been other than friendly.

As to the Senator, I had advocated his nomination and
election to be my successor in the State Senate against a
Northerner of certainly equal abilities and merits, thereby bringing upon my own head the wrath of that Northerner and of all his friends within and without the county.
But he had also been one of my heartiest supporters against
Mr. Hilliard in the same political canvass; had rendered me
valuable aid in the preparation of my bonds as sheriff and
tax collector, and had, up to that moment, been my friend

and confidant in all my plans relative to obtaining possession of the office. Therefore, I could have no reason to doubt his fidelity to me.

He and the other two were native citizens of the South, old residents of the county and ex-slaveholders. There were no other reasons known to me why I should not give them the fullest confidence as my counsel. I could not doubt them because they were Southerners, and had been slave-holders. To have done so would have betrayed a want of confidence in the political policy which I had always advocated that I did not in fact feel. I know that at least two of my counsel had opposed Mr. Hilliard's election. They all knew that my election, so nearly unanimous, had been supported by a large and respectable portion of the property class as well as by the freed people almost *en masse.* None of them had any doubts as to my legal rights in the premises nor as to my legal status.

Yet these my three counsellors unanimously agreed that mine should be the first case tried, advised that I should waive a hearing before the mayor and, standing committed as of course, at once apply for a writ of *habeas corpus* returnable before the chancellor, who would be present in a day or two to hold his court, and let the case go there. This struck me as being very peculiar advice, under the circumstances, and I inquired what reasons they had for not preferring that the cases of the assaulting party be first tried, especially as the questions involved were the same in all the cases so far as they related to my official status. The only reply I received to this was, that reports were spread that I " deliberately and wantonly shot down Mr. Hilliard while he was powerless to defend himself," and these reports were creating great excitement among Mr. Hilliard's friends.

To undertake to arrest and try them first might result in a further breach of the peace, whereas, on the other hand, should I promptly respond to the charge against me, and submit to a public trial, where all the facts would be brought out, the effect could be hardly otherwise than to allay excitement, prevent any further violence, and result in securing justice to all concerned.

It might occasion some inconvenience to myself, but that would doubtless be only temporary.

Of course I desired, above all, to preserve the peace, and while the course they advised was no less than a surrender of my case, because it was yielding to the mob-spirit at the bottom of the whole proceeding upon the part of the Hilliard party, I could not fail to see that no matter what my *rights* and my *privileges* might be, I could not hope to maintain the peace and secure justice for myself, nor to others, without the support of the law-abiding portion of the community, of whom my counsel on the part of the whites were fair representatives. Therefore, without suspecting either the sincerity or the fidelity of my counsel, I submitted myself to their advice.

Then there followed such a revival of the scenes witnessed by the little Yankee garrison of Yazoo in 1868 and 1869, as speedily transformed the peaceful town of Yazoo City into a seething caldron of warring political forces.

The appetite of the irreconcilables for office and power, sharpened by more than four years of enforced abstinence, overcame their discretion, made them blind to all the proprieties of the occasion, arrayed them in open defiance of all law, and obliterated in their bosoms all sense of justice.

It would be a day or two before the chancellor arrived. During this waiting all manner of rumors were set afloat, all calculated to inflame public sentiment against me. The charge that I had wantonly shot down Mr. Hilliard without giving him any " show for his life,"* was added to until it took on this form :

" While *Sheriff* Hilliard was off his guard Morgan stole into his office and shot him down like a dog."

Also this other form :

" Hilliard was first shot by one of Morgan's nigros. Then,

*A common phrase in Yazoo.

while endeavoring in his almost helpless condition to escape
from the court-house, he was met at the door by Morgan who
deliberately placed his pistol at the *sheriff's* head and fired
three shots into him."

"Shot down in his own office!" some proclaimed. "Betrayed and butchered by the man he had befriended," some
said. "First drawn into a trap set by Morgan and then shot
down without any mercy," some said. "A foul, wanton
murder!" said all of the irreconcilables.

The *Democrat* gave wildly exaggerated accounts of it and
proved its charge of murder against me by brief statements
"from eye-witnesses." Then, as if all this was not enough,
wild rumors were started that the negroes were "about to
rise," followed by "information just received" that they
were "coming in to burn the town."

It then became apparent to me that the leaders among the
irreconcilables had resolved on taking possession of the county
government, and were sanguine of their ability to use the
chancellor in the accomplishment of that purpose. Just how
they would proceed was not yet quite clear. Neither our Senator nor either of my counsel appeared to anticipate any such
purpose, and the Senator was strong in his belief that it
could be easily thwarted if it should be found to exist.

But the result proved the correctness of my judgment. The
irreconcilables kept their own counsels. The first step to
their goal lay over Hilliard's dead body. His bitterest enemies were chief among the mourners at his funeral, and they
overlooked on that occasion none of the devices known to
Southern political conspirators for stirring the hearts of "our
people." There was not in all the county a sincerer mourner
than I. The occasion was full of bitterness and sorrow to
me. I could not reproach myself for anything I had done,
yet it did not seem to me appropriate that I should attend
the funeral and make a display of my grief. I could not do
that.

No one had doubted that I would remain and stand my

"trial," and so the committing magistrate—the mayor—had instructed that I be not confined, but allowed to remain at my home until the hearing before the chancellor should occur. But no sooner had the ceremonies at the grave been concluded than there arose a demand for my close confinement. Major Sweet, Captain Telsub, and the human hornet were foremost in giving voice to that demand, and their leaders avowed that the example of leaving me " at large," while under the charge of so foul a murder, would prove most pernicious. Then there were those who declared that I was in open defiance of the laws; that my manner under the charge was full of bravado; that I was consorting and conspiring with the negroes, and when the rumor was noised about that the negroes were coming in to burn the town, there were those who professed to have certain knowledge that I would lead them in the work of destruction. So, for the sake of peace, and that I might not appear to any one to show want of respect for the laws, I voluntarily informed the mayor that he need not hesitate to lock me up in the jail from any feeling of regard for me. My counsel heartily approved my action, and advised the mayor to have me confined. This was done, but it failed to allay the "excitement" of the enemy, who demanded that my deputies, and all who were in the office-room, holding it for me when the Hilliard party attacked it, should also be arrested and sent to jail; and so my deputies were confined in jail with me.

I had not been shut up in a cell but was allowed the freedom of the jailor's apartments. Upon discovering this the irreconcilables found in the fact new cause of complaint against our Republican officials and insisted that I be locked up in a cell. This was done, and very soon afterward the discovery was made by the irreconcilables that I was not in the murderer's cell but in one of the common cells.

All the concessions that had been made to the mob spirit up to this moment had but inflamed the zeal of its leaders, and confirmed their followers in the justice of their demands, which were often of such a nature as greatly to alarm my friends for my safety, and so intimidated the chancellor that he appeared to do their will as fully as if he had been one of their number.

During the progress of the " trial " the most violent characters in all that region hung about the streets of the town, insulting Republicans and my witnesses, and making all manner of threats against them, against me and against the chancellor should he " dare refuse to do his duty." The result of it all was that the chancellor refused bail and returned me to the jail. Then he came to my cell and frankly informed me that he had done it to save my life, declaring that I would have been killed by the mob had he released me.

But he and all the rest were soon to know for a certainty that the " excitement " was not due to the "indignation of the people " at the death of Mr. Hilliard but to an entirely different cause; for no sooner had the decision been rendered than there arose a demand for a sheriff, and the chancellor was appealed to to declare that office vacant and appoint one.

In Mississippi the chancellor has jurisdiction only in " all matters of equity, and of divorce and alimony, in matters testamentary and of administration in minor's business, and allotment of dower, and in cases of idiocy, lunacy and persons *non compos mentis.* He could sit as an examining or committing magistrate in a criminal cause; but was not a law court. The circuit judge had jurisdiction in all matters involving title to a public office; and in all such matters the chancellor had no jurisdiction whatever. Under the circumstances, the true sheriff being in jail, the law made it the duty of the coroner to act; but this obstacle was speedily removed. This chancellor promptly granted an order declaring the coroner's bonds insufficient. Then, under the authority conferred upon him by law to appoint an officer to execute the process of his court, and to attend its sessions, this same chancellor assumed that he not only had the authority to do so, but that it was his duty to appoint a sheriff and tax collector for *the county*. A strange coincidence was the fact that at the moment the chancellor made that discovery there appeared before him a man whom the leaders of the irreconcilables recommended as in every way worthy of the place. In proof of his ability to make the bonds required of that officer for the faithful performance of his duties, a bond, *already prepared* with "good and ample" sureties, was presented to the court.

Now, this applicant, thus recommended and here ready in court to assume the robes of office so soon after my "incarceration," was none other than the former chairman of the County Democratic Committee, one of the irreconcilables; a man in whom the enemy put such trust that, when called on to name a member of the board of registrars for the registration of voters and for the holding of elections in the county, they had chosen him.* He was the same who had signed and delivered to me my certificate of election to the office, Geo. M. Powell. Having at the beginning yielded to the mob spirit, the chancellor was now a slave to the mob; so, notwithstanding the Republicans of the county outnumbered the Democrats as two to one, this chancellor appointed a trusted leader of the Democrats.

* Under the law passed by our free State government, both parties were entitled to representation on that board, which was composed of three members. In Yazoo "we all" Republicans had always freely accorded to our opponents the privilege of choosing for themselves who should represent them on the board.

CHAPTER LX.

A NEGRO " RISING " THAT TOOK EFFECT—WHY THE " YOUNG ONE "
WAS NOT PUT INTO A MURDERER'S CELL—HEROIC CONDUCT OF
" OUR NIGROS "—A SECOND " TRIAL "—A RIGHTEOUS JUDGE—
THE DECISION—A SPECIMEN BRICK FROM THE YAZOO DEMOCRAT
—PEACE RESTORED—FAWNING IRRECONCILABLES.

UP to the moment of Mr. Powell's appointment by the
chancellor, there had been no " rising" of the negroes.
But now they came pouring into town in large numbers, and
presented a most defiant attitude.

The demand of the mob for the appointment of a new
jailor was immediately complied with by the chancellor's
new sheriff. But the negroes planted themselves across the
street just above the jail, and openly and fearlessly proclaimed that the new jailor should not act. Taught by their
experiences in 1867, 1868 and 1869, the negroes believed that
all these proceedings pointed directly to the death of myself
and deputies at the hands of the mob. They had been most
orderly and patient under all the outrages that led up to
this, the culminating point; because they had been committed
under the forms of law. I had all the time been in communication with them, and had warned them to do no violence.
But the removal of the jailor, who was friendly to me, and
the appointment of a successor whom every Republican knew
to be capable of doing anything that the enemy might re-

quire of him, not only led the colored people to believe, but also convinced me that the ultimate purpose of the irreconcilables was to lynch us. By the action of the colored people at this juncture the situation became extremely critical. They were armed only with their hard-wood sticks, excepting only a few who had pistols, but the enemy could see that they were not only very numerous, but also very determined. The chancellor's new sheriff could have summoned his following and speedily cleared the streets, because they had or could quickly procure arms for the purpose. But he hesitated to do this. The new State government, with Ames at its head, was already installed in power.

The new legislature, having a large Republican majority, was in session at Jackson, and the friends I had made during my service in the constitutional convention and in the State senate were devising means to check the "insurrection in Yazoo." The human hornet and his friends were anxious for leave to "clear the streets of the nigros," but the chancellor's sheriff, having assumed the duties of that office under color of his appointment, was responsible for the peace. He hesitated to attack these negroes, and two whole days were spent in efforts to "pacify them." But they could neither be purchased nor cajoled. They firmly refused to allow the new jailor to act, and thus again, as often before, my life was saved by the fidelity and courage of negroes. The enemy finding that the colored people could not be moved from their purpose, began negotiations looking to my transfer from our Yazoo jail to that of some other county. This was finally effected and I was secretly taken from the jail and conveyed to that of Hinds County, at the capital, which was my own selection. Now the State authorities began to act. The chancellor had been appointed to fill a vacancy caused by the death of his predecessor. The appointment was withdrawn or revoked and another appointed in his place The chancellor's sheriff was promptly removed, and the governor appointed my brother William to the place, "to continue during the disability of the lawful sheriff," myself. The chancellor's sheriff for a time resisted, and the human hornet and his aids fumed and raved terribly at this new " outrage " put upon them, but all to no purpose; for at the expiration of two months I was again in full possession of my office. My deputies had been released from jail and perfect peace reigned throughout Yazoo. A faithful account of the proceedings instituted by the State authorities for the overthrow of the conspiracy in Yazoo, by which the irreconcilables hoped to regain complete control of the county government,* would make "mighty interesting reading," I have no doubt, but the limits of this narrative will not admit of such an account here. I ought, however, not to fail to state here that, though Governor Ames' treatment of the case was heroic it was justified at all points by the facts and by the law. Also, that I obtained other legal counsel and at the conclusion of another hearing the chancellor, Hon. Thomas Walton, delivered in writing his opinion upon the law and the facts in the case, which, after a brief statement of the law, was in the words following:

* * * One of the first points to be settled is, Was Morgan sheriff? It is shown that he had been legally elected and had his certificate of election ; that he had given bond as sheriff and collector of State and county taxes, and that these bonds had been approved by the proper officer. * * * He had also taken the oath of office and he was *de jure* the sheriff of the county. But there is another important circumstance. He had been installed in office as the sheriff and officer of the only court sitting in the county since his term commenced : the board of supervisors. That board is one of our courts. The statute makes it the sheriff's duty to attend the sittings and declares him to be its officer, and thus acting under the authority of the law, this court had refused to recognize the deceased as its sheriff and officer, and had placed the prisoner in that position. He was, therefore, recognized as sheriff of the county by the only judicial tribunal sitting in the county and competent to act in the premises. Manifestly, if there was any sheriff *de facto*, it must have been the prisoner, and I cannot consider that this character was wanting to him in consequence of his being locked out of the room where the sheriff's records

* The conspirators did not stop at their possession of my office, but began proceedings looking to the ouster of all the principal officers of the county.

were kept, and illegally deprived of their custody. This room is in popular language ordinarily called the sheriff's office, but the possession of this room by no means carries with it the possession of the sheriff's office. The sheriff, it is true, has the right to such possession, and it is his duty to take possession of such room. Morgan did so in this case. Whether he did so by lawful or unlawful means it is not necessary to decide. * * * I must, therefore, consider the prisoner not only as the sheriff *de jure*, but as duly sworn, duly bonded, duly installed in office as the officer of the only court in session, and as in possession of the records and sheriff's room; a possession which whether properly obtained or not, was bound to continue. He was, in short, the sheriff *de facto* as well as *de jure*. As such he was bound to preserve the peace and keep off intruders from the court-house and prevent trespasses upon it.

After he had thus established himself in his office, the deceased took the advice of counsel as to how he should recover the room. He was advised to collect a body of citizens, to go and remonstrate with the prisoner for taking possession of the office, and demand its restoration to the deceased. If Morgan refused to give it up, Hilliard was advised then to adopt legal proceedings for its recovery. He did collect some fifteen or twenty persons. But, instead of taking the advice given him by counsel, he made an attack on the court-house, and broke open the sheriff's door. He was met, with his attendants, some fifty yards from the court-house, by Morgan, who proclaimed to the crowd that he was sheriff, that he was in possession of the sheriff's office, and that they must keep away from the court-house. This the prisoner was required to do by the peremptory terms of the statute. His injunctions were disregarded. The throng hurried by him, the deceased crying out to them to follow him, and rushing rapidly toward the court-house, without regard to the advice he had received only a f ew moments before from his counsel, to remonstrate with the prisoner. At this point it is well to remember that the deceased had been negotiating with the prisoner, and offering him money to be allowed to hold the office for thirty days. The deceased, it is testified, confessed that he knew the law was against him in his contest for the office; but he was negotiating and offering to pay for time. Morgan must have felt, in view of this state of things, that the deceased was actuated by an unlawful purpose. Knowing this, he saw him with a large crowd rushing upon the court-house in an hour of great excitement, and in utter disregard of the true sheriff's injunctions to keep away from that building. Morgan turned and followed this crowd to the court-house * * * * Morgan was an officer of the peace; he had commanded it; bound to keep off intruders from the court-house; he had warned them off; bound to suppress affrays; here was a most violent affray for him to suppress, and the statutes are now, as the common law has always been, that the sheriff may even justify killing, if necessary for suppressing an affray. The same is the law of riot, and here was undoubtedly a riotous attack upon the court-house. Hilliard was the ringleader. With his own hands he had just broken the door—his attendants had opened fire. He was advancing on Morgan—one of his attendants was still firing; how should Morgan know whether this advance of Hilliard was not a hostile advance? How should he know that Hilliard, as witnesses state, was seeking to escape? There were two other escapes equally convenient, one behind the stairway, and one through the other end of the hall. If he came upon Morgan, instead of choosing these other escapes, while Foote, his companion, was still firing, how should Morgan know that this advance was peaceable? It is said Hilliard did not fire. But he led this movement, which was undoubtedly a violent breach of the peace. He had Foote with him in that unlawful movement, and Foote was firing all the time; and Hilliard being engaged in the act, Morgan must have been in great difficulty to distinguish nicely at which of these men, both engaged in this violent act, to strike. It would be a hard case to hold a sheriff for murder, even though he killed a man under these circumstances, when the law makes it his duty to act, and to act with promptness and determination. Nor does the law put so severe a construction upon the conduct of its officers whom it charges with the duty of compelling men to keep the peace. It is the settled doctrine that, though an officer in striving to suppress an affray or riot, should exceed the bounds of propriety, and kill a man unlawfully, the law is slow to impute to him that malice which constitutes the crime of murder. A sheriff may no doubt be guilty of murder in suppressing an affray, but the law in such a case requires clear proof of malice, and does not rest in the presumption that the killing was malicious, and was therefore murder. There certainly was no such proof in this case, and I am satisfied that in no event could the prisoner be held for any crime greater than manslaughter. In the entire absence of any evidence of malice on the prisoner's part, it is impossible to suppose that when Hilliard, in the midst of this terrific combat, made his advance on the position where Morgan stood. Morgan could have shot him with the belief in his mind that Hillliard was at that moment non-combatant. Acting as an officer, without evidence of malice, it is incredible that he should thus slay a recognized fugitive. Yet, if he had done so, it would not always be murder ; for if in the heat of such violence the officer kills, even after resistance ceases, it has been adjudged to be only manslaughter, in the absence of proof of malice; the law, in order to preserve the public peace, being compelled to indulge every presumption in favor of an officer striving to suppress violence.

I must, therefore, bail the prisoner. I have deemed it proper to put this opinion in writing, because Judge Drennan's conclusions were different. It is proper to add, however, that new witnesses, not examined before him, have testified before me, as I am informed by counsel.*

During this troubled period, many well-meaning and very worthy persons, in the county and outside of it, who knew me only by reputation, and some who knew me personally, were drawn into an attitude of open hostility to me through the gross misrepresentations of the *Democrat*, and of those irreconcilables who expected to profit by my overthrow.

Throughout the State the criticisms of the press and of prominent irreconcilables upon my conduct and upon the conduct of the governor, in the measures taken by him for the restoration of order in the county, had been most severe and reckless.

Chancellor Walton had been for years at the head of the law department of Oxford University. His reputation for integrity and superior legal qualifications was equal to that of any lawyer in the State. Up to this moment he had enjoyed the esteem and confidence of the "best citizens" of Mississippi. He was a courageous, just man; but by this act, releasing me from jail, he at once became a target for the malice of the irreconcilables.

Ames being governor, and the important offices of the county having been by his firm policy removed from the reach of the starving sleuth-hounds of slavery, there was no longer anything to tempt the irreconcilables of Yazoo to violence ; and therefore, Chancellor Walton had been able to conduct the examination in an orderly and lawful manner, by which the testimony taken upon the hearing was submitted to writing, and was subsequently published. Then there came a revolution in public feeling toward me, the governor, and the chancellor; which also found expression through the press.

The following, from the Jackson *Clarion*, (Democratic,) a paper edited and published then as now by Mr. Ethel Barks-

*For this decision in full, see report of Select Committee of the United States Senate, on Mississippi Election of 1875, vol. 2, pp. 1779, 1780 and 1781.

dale, present member in Congress from that district, will
serve to illustrate the extent as well as the character of this
change:

"Having read the testimony and the statements of both sides, we
have never been able to reach the conclusion that Morgan was not
entitled to bail, even if he did the killing, about which there seemed
to be some doubt."

Also, the following from the *Liberty Herald* (Democratic):

" A great hue and cry has been raised against Walton on account of
his decision to admit Morgan to bail, but after a careful investigation
of the testimony we cannot see how Walton could well have decided
otherwise."

As illustrating the methods employed by the irreconcilables
to obstruct the course of justice in Yazoo at all times, the
following is but one of many specimens: A young man of
the town named Massey swore that he saw Mr. Hilliard
endeavoring to escape by the front door of the building after
the firing commenced, and that he appeared to be non-combatant. At that instant, he said, I deliberately placed my
pistol at Mr. Hilliard's head and fired. Our county assessor,
Mr. Morrin, swore that he was upon the street in front of the
court-house, where he saw the commencement of the assault
by the Hilliard party, and, that at the first fire Massey ran
in such haste that he jumped over the high fence at a point
which made it impossible for him afterward to have seen what
was going on at the court-house door. The very next issue
of the Yazoo City *Democrat* contained the following:

"T. D. MORRIN COMES INTO COURT.

" This fellow, whose name should not blot our paper, but for his tall
swearing against a gentleman, testified yesterday, under oath, that
Mr. E. K. Massey had not told the truth in his testimony before
Judge Walton. We cannot expect Mr. Massey to notice such a contemptible cur. How can he notice a man who allows his face to be
spit upon without resentment? As Mr. M. cannot meet him, WE
mark him *one*, that he may be known of all men. Bear this brand on
your face, COWARD. Bear this on your collar, DOG, beneath the notice of this community,* unworthy of notice by a respectable court."

*Still, in 1874, as previously in 1865, 1867 and 1868, when uttered by a Southern white,
the terms " our peeple" and " this community " were intended to include none but
such as were in the ranks of " the enemy."

During the canvass for the office, notwithstanding the fact that I was the only Republican candidate against him, the irreconcilables had been unable thoroughly to unite upon Mr. Hilliard. This was due in a large measure to the same feelings as prevented them uniting in 1869 for Dent (Grant's "own deah brother-in-law), against Alcorn, or for Greeley against Grant in 1872. The element opposed to Mr. Hilliard based their opposition upon principle. They no more objected to his "nigro ticket" than they did to him. Both were equally offensive to them. They would neither handle, taste, nor touch the unclean thing, and all who had been in any way identified with the Republican party, to them were forevermore unclean.

Of the more than four thousand registered voters in the county, we have seen that but four hundred and thirty-one voted for Mr. Hilliard. It would be fair to say that of that number at least fifty were colored men. Therefore, of the more than fifteen hundred registered white voters there were less than four hundred who voted for Mr. Hilliard. All the remainder had either abstained from voting or had voted for me or for Mr. Mangum, who stood as an independent, and received some two hundred votes.

The element that supported Mr. Hilliard had stooped to conquer. Their brethren, too proud to stoop, had refused to vote for either of us, and had not voted at all, or had voted for the independent. But now there was no need to stoop. The way was open which led to power and dominion in Yazoo. Mr. Hilliard was dead, and I was in jail, charged with murder. It would only be necessary to march in and occupy. So the enemy appeared to think and so they did act; for immediately upon the death of Mr. Hilliard and my submission to the advice of my counsel, all the elements among the irreconcilables appeared suddenly to unite, and to have a common purpose. Men who had been in hiding for five years, "biding their time," once more appeared in town and took part in the raid on the county government by add-

ing their voices to the hue and cry of the irreconcilables
against me. But the body of the whites stood aloof and
would have nothing to do with it. They, however, lacked
the manly independence to come out and take an open part
against the usurpations of the irreconcilables. They had
always *followed.* That attitude had become a habit with them.
In the five years of peace we had enjoyed in Yazoo,
they had ventured to act and vote for themselves. But in
the presence of the violent demonstrations of the irreconcilables they were cowed, and, therefore, silent.

But no sooner had I resumed the duties of my office than
some of the most violent of the irreconcilables became fawning suitors after favors. The rough characters again disappeared, and the open, manly irreconcilables again went in
hiding and "bided their time." Peace had come again to
Yazoo, and I resumed my planting in the old stubble-ground.

CHAPTER LXI.

AN ACCOUNT OF MY STEWARDSHIP, 1869 TO 1875—A SURVEY
OF THE FIELD.

THE smallest political subdivision in Mississippi is the
county government. " Town meetings" are unknown
there. There are township territorial subdivisions, but no
township governments. For this reason the county officers
and the county " rings" are the most powerful factors in State
politics. The leading spirit in the county government is likely
to be also a leading member of the central or State government, and, per consequence, of the State " ring." In old times,
therefore, it had not been a difficult thing for a handful of
leaders, like Mr. Jefferson Davis, to take the State along with
themselves to perdition. There were no town meetings to
protest against it. In the reorganization of our new State
government, the old subdivisions had been preserved. In
our State convention a proposal to change the system, and
to introduce township government was opposed by nearly
every member of the class known as old citizens, and by
most of the colored members.

The former opposed the change mainly on the ground that
it would prove to be a dangerous " innovation." The people
were opposed to innovations. The colored members opposed it
chiefly because of the lack of proper material in our party out
of which to form the township governments—a weakness
which the enemy would be quick to take advantage of.

By the old constitution, during the slave regime, the county board was styled the Board of County "Police;" by our new constitution the county board was styled the Board of County "Supervisors." The change was in name merely. The supervisors had no more nor any less powers of government under the new than under the old system. In fact, the law relating to the powers, and the duties of the board of police was continued in full force as to the board of supervisors.

' By this law the board not only had such powers of government as usually belongs to such bodies in free States, but also all those powers usually attaching in free States to the township government.

Thus the board of supervisors would be the most important position in our new government. I resolved to guard that position myself, and, having asked for it, I was appointed supervisor for "Beat No. 3"—the Yazoo City beat—by General Ames, and was made president of the board by the voice of my colleagues. This was 1869.

My pay as such member would not exceed ninety dollars per year. I therefore was not likely to get rich off of that office unless I should steal the revenues it would be my duty to levy. If my assumption of the robes of so important an office in the county administration was an "audacious imposition" upon the property class, what was it that made it so? Two years before I was quietly pursuing on Tokeba my private business, and had come to the front in county politics not from choice, but from an imperious necessity. Had Major Snodgrass possessed courage equal to his convictions, he could have done away with any such necessity, and would doubtless have enjoyed the sympathy and support of a majority of the inhabitants of the county as fully as now, in 1869, I did. But he lacked the courage, and Judge Isam Major Sweet, Colonel Black, and all the rest, really acted as though it was their duty to oppose, even with violence, the principles and policy which had brought me to the front. Having crossed the Rubicon in the political contest (this, it must be borne in mind was two years and more prior to my crossing of the Rubicon in the social war then in progress), and the "ball" having opened, there was no way of retreat, had I even desired to run away from the heavy responsibilities which leadership in Yazoo County affairs would impose upon me. I had now no desire to run. To have done so at that juncture ought to have entailed eternal ignominy upon my name. So I felt then, and so I feel now. My place was at the head and I took it. In this step I had the active sympathy and support of three-fourths of the men, women and children then living within the county limits, and of thousands outside.

I remained in that place, and continued to have the warmest sympathy and support of *three-fourths* of the people of the county, with only individual exceptions now and then, from the first to the last. The "first" was the day before our election for delegates to the State convention, in 1867, when I received fifteen hundred votes to three hundred for the purely Yankee ticket, and the three votes that were cast against "convention." The "last" was in 1875, when I received but two votes and "the enemy" more than four thousand. The former was when "that tailor" Johnson was President, and there was a two-thirds *Republican* majority in Congress. The latter was when "that butcher" Grant was President, and there was a two-thirds *Democratic* majority in *only* the lower House of Congress. Between the two epochs lay Credit Mobilier, Pacific Mail, Sanborn Contracts and Henry Ward Beecher.

Considering the ground I have been over up to this time, I think the reader will agree with me that I have not had very much to say of myself as leader and "dictator" in Yazoo. But we have now reached a point where I must give some account of my stewardship, and tell the reader what I, backed by the loyal and true of our brave crew, did in Yazoo, during the period of my trust. I shall be brief, and I shall begin with our party's management of the county finances.

At the beginning of our term of office, the board discovered that nót only was there no money in the treasury,
but that the total indebtedness of the county could not be
ascertained for lack of proper records. We were able to
know, beyond a doubt, that it amounted to quite ten thousand
dollars. It might be thirty thousand. It was in the shape
of county warrants, which, up to that moment, had sold
down as low as forty-five, and rarely went higher than sixty-
five cents on the dollar. But a small patch of the county
poor farm was being cultivated. The county poorhouse was
a hovel, into which only the most wretched of the crippled
and diseased poor could be induced to enter, and where vice
was at a premium. The courts were being held in a little,
old hall.* The only protection for the valuable county
records were the brick walls of this hall, and a watchman.
The highways had been neglected; some of them were impassable. The bridges were nearly all old, and sadly in need of
repair. Populous settlements were deprived of access to the
county site for several months in the year for want of
bridges, unless men could spare from their business the time
requisite for a tedious, circuitous, and expensive journey,
partly by private teams, and partly by irregular river packets.
The county jail was a rickety old brick contrivance, with a
board fence, half rotted down, and toppling over in places.
There was but one cell in it that could be made secure against
the escape of a prisoner.† It was, indeed, a common jail.
There was not a free public school-house in the county.
Mississippi was an old State when Nebraska was peopled only by
Indians and hunters, but in 1869 there was hardly an organized county in what is now the State of Nebraska that had
not a better free school building than any house used for
school purposes in Yazoo County in 1869, and it was among the
first counties organized in the State—a center of population,
of wealth, and of commerce. The only school-houses in
use were such as had been erected for private schools,

*Over a store-room.
† The one in which they had placed my brother but little more than a year before.

and some that had been erected with so much of the proceeds of the sixteenth-section school lands, as had not been stolen by Yazoo slave lords.

The report of the superintendent of public education of the State for the year ending December 31, 1871, is a most interesting study. Upon page 146 and thence to 208, will be found a series of tables entitled "Statement showing the condition of school funds, arising from sale and rental of school lands in each county." The table for Yazoo County will be found upon pages 199 to 208. From that table it appears that during the administration of that fund by the enemy, seventy-six "loans" out of it had been made, for which the only record preserved of the fact, was the name of the borrower; fifty-seven had been made upon notes, without any security whatever. In the cases of seventeen "loans," the unpaid interest was found to equal and in a majority of that number largely exceed the amount of the principal. Of the whole number, only fifteen were secured by "trust deed." In ten cases there appears to have been some security, but the nature of it is not mentioned. The loans vary in sums from $26.00 to $6,390. Of those of which there was record, all except nine were due and payable prior to the appointment of our Republican board of supervisors, and a large part of them all were due prior to the war. Yet up to 1869 no effort had been made to collect them.

Judge Isam, Judge Syam, Major Sweet and Mrs. Black are among the borrowers, as are also a considerable number of the "smaller fry" of the kuklux organization, including the author of that "piece" in the *Banner* entitled "Kukluxes." A feature of that table which will specially interest my reader and illumine this page, is the following :

"Loan"—name of school commissioner and by whom the loan was made, "W. D. Gibbs;"* to whom the loan was made, "W. D. Gibbs;" when due "March 1, 1867;" amount, one of "$611.20;" one of "$1,150"—total, $1,761.20; amount

---

* The reader will recognize him as my opponent for the Senate in 1869.

of interest unpaid, " $846.14;" total principal and interest, $2,607.34, "not secured."

The total of loans of which there was a record was, $56,-061.14. The total of unpaid interest, $24,262.21. Of this fund in his report for that year, our county superintendent said:

" The fund derived from the rental of the sixteenth sections has been greatly diminished, and is almost a total loss. * * * Claims for leases and loans, including the interest thereon, amounting to the large sum of $86,568.96 have come into possession of the officers authorized by law to receipt for and have the custody of the same. Of this large sum only $26,690.15 was deemed, some nine months since, on a critical examination, to be good ; $30,250.15 have been put in suit, while only $8,782.06 have, so far, been collected, which, under the law, is to be invested in State or United States bonds.''

Of the pauper fund it was discovered that several of the "first families" had been, for months at a time, furnished with provisions, on the ground that they were for old and indigent freedmen, free negroes, or mulattoes, and I wondered how much of the allowance to Colonel Black, Uncle Primous and his old, old mother on Tokeba had received. The reader should keep in mind that there were no township levies, collections or funds.

During the four years that had passed since the surrender, large sums had been collected from the people of the county in various ways by our predecessors, yet there had been no effort made in the direction of a new court-house and but little for the improvement of the roads, bridges, or for the poor, and nothing at all had been done for schools.

CHAPTER LXII.

ACCOUNT OF MY STEWARDSHIP CONTINUED—A SECOND CROP OFF THE OLD STUBBLE-GROUND OF YAZOO.

HAD the county finances been in good shape, there were obstacles enough in the way of a successful establishment of the new government to make it a doubtful experiment. With the county heavily in debt, its paper so greatly depreciated that only those inside the county ring would deal in it, and extensive immediate outlays absolutely necessary for the proper security of the county records, the dispatch of the business of the county, especially of the courts, the construction of bridges, etc., etc., to work at the same time for the establishment of free schools appeared to many of the Unionists a "suicidal undertaking," to some of the Northerners, a hopeless task, and to the enemy an outrage, for which the people of the county "without regard to color" would hold the perpetrators responsible to the full extent of the law and outraged public sentiment.

Many well-meaning friends said "we must not attempt to do all at once." Among these was our new sheriff, nearly all the Unionists, and some Northerners.

"Well, gentlemen, I said, which of these pressing demands would you postpone?"

Some said the free schools, some the new court-house, some the new bridges, some favored the funding of the county debt in long bonds, while others said postpone none, but carry them all along together ; only establish but few schools just enough to satisfy the freed people; pay the debt gradually ; build only the most important bridges, rent suitable buildings for county purposes, and protect against fire by hiring watchmen.

To all these protests and arguments, I offered the following :

In my opinion, the success of our efforts to establish a free government here, and to introduce a new and better civilization, absolutely depends upon our ability to open at once a free school in every principal neighborhood ; and to make the schools successful for the purpose, the very best teachers that can be obtained should be employed. We can put up with cheap houses, but we must have the very best teachers. All this will cost money, of course.

The enemy profess to believe that the negro is incapable of learning to read and write. We must demonstrate *at once* the falsity of this assumption, and the purpose of it. Therefore the free schools cannot be postponed.

The commerce of Yazoo City is every year largely diverted from us for want of repair of county highways and bridges, and the people are put to great annoyance and inconvenience on account of it. By reason of all which their tax-paying power is reduced.

We can postpone the payment of the debt, but will it be wise to do so ? Should we attempt to run the government on a credit basis, we put ourselves at once into the noose of the county speculators, and thereby nearly double the expenses.

We can postpone the building of a new court-house, but would that be good policy ? The expenditures for rent and for watchmen would annually equal a reasonable interest on the amount required for the purpose.

"Gentlemen, let us shoulder the load at once, and carry it all."

"Why, man, you're crazy ! It can't be done," said the Unionists.

"It's a mistake," said the Northerners.

"It's an outrage, and the people, without regard to color, won't submit to it," said the enemy.

"Let's reason together," I said; "if we pay as we go we can do it."

"But you've got no money and no credit, *how* can you do it?" said they all.

"Increase the taxes," I responded.

"The people won't submit to an increase sufficient for the purpose," replied the Unionists.

"That won't work," the Northerners.

"We won't pay it," replied the enemy.

"The people of the county are as well able to pay annually, two per cent. of the value of their property and incomes now as formerly they were able to pay one per cent," I replied.

"Man, you're wild," said the Unionists.

"How's that?" said the Northerners.

"You're a fool" said the enemy, "or a knave."

"When the war broke out" I replied, "nearly one-half of the planters and merchants of this county were in debt to the full amount of the cash value of their property in lands and slaves. Is that not so?"

"Well, that may be true—what of it?"

"One-half of the remainder were in debt to fully one-half the value of their said property."

"Well, what has that to do with this question?"

"This; this indebtedness was somewhat increased during the war, and at its close, the legislature passed a stay law, postponing the collection of all debts. At this juncture the Northern creditors of our merchants, planters and others, came forward with offers to settle, some on a basis of one-half, some one-quarter. In some instances they forgave all. Is that not so?"

"Well, as a rule, yes," said they all.

"My understanding of it is, that the principal merchants here in Yazoo City and others in the county settled at one-quarter, while some paid nothing. Well, in addition to this and afterwards the United States Congress amended the national bankrupt law so that fully three-fourths of the principal debtors of this county have been able to pay off all their debts contracted since the war, and at the same time keep their lands and much other property. So that now many of them are better off than ever before in their lives."

" Hain't thought a that afo'," said the Unionists.

"By George, that's so!" exclaimed the Northerners.

" You all stole our nigros, and bankrupted we all," said the enemy.

" But the same negroes are here to this day, and you all agree that while they own no land, they work just as faithfully as before they were free, and in the last campaign you all told them, and insisted upon it, that, after all, being the laboring, producing class, they would have to pay the taxes. In proof of which, you cited Mill and other standard authorities."

Now the Unionists said nothing. The Northerners whispered in my ear, " bully for you, Morgan, give it to 'em.'

The enemy with one voice said, " damn it," and when we came to consult the " freedmen, free negroes and mulattoes," they with one voice said, " stan' yo' groun', Kunnel, we'll stan' by ye, nebber did low't 'ole mars had no sense, no how."

The truth is, that while the assessed value of the property of the county, from 1865 to 1869, was in round numbers, four and a half millions, it could not have been purchased of its owners for less than twenty millions of dollars.

By way of illustration, Tokeba, for which we paid seven dollars per acre rent, in 1866 and 1867, and would have continued to pay the same sum through 1868, but for the deter. mination of Colonel Black and the enemy to " get rid a'them d—d Yankee s— of b——s now," was assessed at one dollar per acre for some, and none at a higher rate than eight dollars per acre.

The Payne plantations, perhaps the most valuable in the county, with two great gin-houses on them that could not have cost less than forty thousand dollars each, with almost new board and rail fences, extensive "quarters" and fine "mansion" houses, were assessed at from one to ten dollars per acre.

My recollection is that there was not an acre assessed at so high a figure as twelve dollars. Yet the Northerners who rented them in 1866 and 1867, paid ten dollars per acre annual rental for the cultivated lands. The total of the individual indebtedness of the county, which had been forgiven, amounted to as much as a million and a half dollars, and the total indebtedness from which individuals had been relieved by the bankrupt courts, amounted to at least three millions more. It may have been ten millions. It will be impossible ever to know the exact sum, because so many applicants scheduled the amounts of their indebtedness as "unknown."

At the close of the war cotton was worth from thirty-five to ninety cents per pound, instead of from five to eight or ten cents, the price before the war; and while the price had rapidly declined, yet, in 1869, it was still going at from fifteen to twenty-five cents per pound, while the average hire of a laborer to make the crop was fifteen dollars per month. The years of 1868 and 1869 had been exceptionally good ones, and both "white" and "black" were beginning to indulge in luxuries. So I concluded that, taking everything into consideration, it was probable that the four succeeding years would certainly be as favorable as 1866-'67-'68-'69. Besides, father used to say that the time for making hay was when we had sunshine. We were having good hay-making weather in Mississippi, now that Grant was President, and I could not help feeling that possibly something might happen, such as a sudden storm of wind or rain, before we should complete our task, unless we made all the haste possible. Therefore, I proposed that we revise and correct the inequalities in the present assessment rolls and make a slight increase in the total valuation while doing so.

This was done. Plantations like Tokeba were increased in

value upon the roll to two, eight and twelve dollars per acre; those like the Paynes to two, ten, and fifteen dollars per acre, according to the land and improvements; while those that had been assessed at too high a rate correspondingly, were reduced in value upon the assessment roll. The result was an increase of the total valuation of the real and personal property of the county in round numbers to five millions.

Upon this valuation it was the duty of the State government to make its levy for the purposes of a State revenue. After which, taking the State levy for a basis, and, to some extent, a guide, it became the duty of the county supervisors to make the levy for a revenue for county purposes.

It was too late to think of doing anything toward establishing our school system that year. The most we could do would be to make some provision for a revenue for the purpose, which we did, and the total levy for the year, for all purposes, was fixed at fifteen mills upon the valuation mentioned. This amount embraced the State levy, and our levy for meeting all the expenses of the county, such as for courts, paupers, roads, bridges, to create a fund for a new courthouse and to pay the county debt.

The enemy employed legal counsel and fought these innovations, as they were termed, step by step, but in vain. I had anticipated this opposition and, in the selection of members for this vital point in our loyal government, had procured the appointment of two colored men, who, with myself, constituted a majority of the board. It may be regarded as a little singular that I should have been willing to entrust so sacred an interest to the chance of an alliance between two "ignorant nigros," as they were called by the enemy, and the old ex-slaveholder on the board. A little reflection, however, will satisfy the reader that I acted from correct principles. It is true that, as a rule, Southern men, whether Unionists, Conservatives or irreconcilables, have always maintained that the negro is unreliable when placed in charge of an important trust.

Most of such people maintain, even to this day, that he is not only unreliable, but incapable.

But here were two freedmen—men who had been slaves until the war freed them—one of whom could barely read, who could not sign his name, the other of whom could write only about as well as he could read, and that was very poorly, and yet I trusted them implicitly. In the first place, I knew that the freed people were in truth craving an opportunity to educate their children. I believed that these men, in such a position, would wish to represent faithfully the known wishes of their "own color."

I also believed that the great mass of freed people did in truth appreciate their freedom, and would be as prompt to condemn wastefulness or extravagance on the part of their representatives as the whites, *if not more so.* And, although the color of one was "light," and his eyes gray, the color of the other black, with black eyes, I felt that I could trust them. They both had worked hard since the war, and saved their money, and upon the very first opportunity had purchased land.

The result proved the wisdom of my choice, for while the Northerner on the board "wavered" several times during the contest, and while the ex-slaveholder often got very hot, indignant, and "outraged," the voices of the two colored men were always on the side of the right.

First "the enemy" attempted to coax, then to bribe, and then to drive them from me, but, without a particle of coaxing, or of "convincing," or of bulldozing, from me, or any of my friends, these men stood firm as a rock, upon the naked line of duty, swerving neither to the right nor to the left, and I here testify that they discharged their duties faithfully, ably, and most creditably to themselves and the county.

The fact is, they were *men*, with the instincts common to good, well-meaning men. They were also *citizens*, and they appreciated the fact. They were *public officers* in charge of a sacred trust. They were *representatives*, and they under-

stood that fact, and they bowed loyally to the known will of
their constituents. Under this administration the rate of
tax for all purposes at no time exceeded twenty-five mills
upon the assessed value of the property of the county, and
this increase was made necessary by reason of the reduction
of the poll-tax to two dollars, the repeal of the tax on the
" privileges " heretofore referred to, and the demands of the
schools and the courts.

The largely increased litigation between the whites result-
ing from the war, formed but a small part of the total increase
in the expenses of the courts. Formerly the master was a
law unto himself in all matters between himself and his slaves.

To be sure, there were laws upon the statute books regulating the relations between master and slave, but they were
rarely appealed to.

If a slave committed any offence of a lower grade than a
felony, his master tried and punished him. If the offence
amounted to a felony, it was often the case that the master
put himself in the stead of the courts, and called out his blood-
hounds or his neighbors to assist him in cases which he could
not manage alone.

The amount of business before the courts brought by the
masters against their slaves, or by slaves against their masters,
and that between the slaves formed but a most insignificant
part of the whole.

If the population of the county in " slave times " was
twenty thousand—there being two slaves to every " white "—
it followed from the causes I have mentioned, that only one-
third of the whole, or about seven thousand, were likely to
have business in the courts.

By the change in these conditions produced by the ratification of our new constitution, the whole population had
access to the courts.

The extent of the increase from this cause may be illustrated if not supplemented, by the fact, that the former wholesale methods, so to speak, of doing business, was being trans-

formed into those of a retail business, which embraced the details of affairs, and consequently resulted in new complications.

The sudden increase of the illiterate class, already fifty-seven in every one hundred of whites in the State, by the addition of the freed people as active competitors in life, was another cause of this increase; so that the legitimate expenses of the courts, civil and criminal, became three times as great as before. It should also be borne in mind that this was not a virgin soil, like the prairies and forests of the great West, where the germs of civilization needed only to be dropped and a few scarecrows erected to keep off the gophers, blackbirds and wild pigeons, to insure a rich harvest; but it was the *old stubble-ground of slavery,* where every seed of the new civilization we were planting must needs be protected against swarms of wild geese, sand-hill cranes, foxes, hyenas and wolves; creatures of prey that could not be frightened by men of straw, but must be met face to face, both night and day, by a watchfulness, physical courage, and purity and strength of purpose, that should demonstrate the better quality of the new husbandmen, as well as of the new seed.

Nothing daunted by this opposing array, the remnant of the garrison of the little Yankee stronghold of Yazoo, backed by the little church we helped to build, the agencies of Northern philanthropic societies, the mass of freedmen, free negroes and mulattoes, protected by the broad shield of that grand old flag, which we still carried as representative of the then settled purpose and convictions of the free North land, we planted, cultivated and went forward in the harvesting of the second crop of freedom ever grown on Yazoo soil.

CHAPTER LXIII.

ACCOUNT OF MY STEWARDSHIP CONTINUED—RESULTS—OF WHAT
THE SECOND CROP CONSISTED—OUR NEW COURT-HOUSE—THE
POOR-HOUSE—THE JAIL—NEW BRIDGES—IMPROVED HIGH-
WAYS—IMPROVEMENTS IN YAZOO CITY—A NEW FIRE-ENGINE
—EFFORTS IN BEHALF OF A RAILROAD—FREE SCHOOLS—TAXA-
TION.

THE reader has already seen what was accomplished by
"the enemy" during the years of its control prior to
the war, and in the four years which followed that event, in
the way of county public improvements. In this chapter I
shall endeavor to faithfully set down what was accomplished
by "we all radicals," in the six years of my "dictatorship."
By the beginning of the year 1875, the requisite repairs upon
the county highways and bridges had been completed, and
new bridges built, so that in that respect the county had
never before enjoyed equal facilities. Improvements upon
the poor-farm buildings had been made, the farm put in
cultivation, system and order enforced in its management
and among its inmates, and the institution had become
nearly self-sustaining.

The capacity and security of the jail had been enlarged by
the addition of safe, iron cells.

A new court-house, costing quite seventy thousand dollars,
had been erected and paid for as the work progressed, and

had been " accepted " by a committee of the oldest and best members of our Yazoo bar association. Everybody said it was a credit to the county.

The county indebtedness had at no time exceeded the annual levy for current expenses. The finances had been managed in such a way that within the first year of our control, county warrants went up to par, and remained there during the entire period, with only short exceptional occasions. At the close of 1873 there were outstanding obligations amounting to quite thirty thousand dollars, but nearly if not quite the entire sum would be absorbed by the tax-levy of that year, the collection of which had been interfered with by the " insurrection."

Yazoo City was an incorporated town, its government was under the control of the Republicans, who were in a majority. As in the county so it was here; extensive improvements had been wrought; new side-walks, pavements, and gutters, had been made, and, above all, perhaps, a new steam fire-engine had been provided. Our Yankee postmaster, aided by a few public-spirited fellow-citizens, was foremost in all these good works.

We had failed, it is true, to get a railroad to our town, but that was by no fault of " we all Yankees." Three lines had been chartered, and at one time the prospect was very bright indeed that we would have one. But the great panic spreading throughout the North had interfered with our plans. Mississippi hardly felt the great shock, it is true, but as we were depending largely upon Northern capital for our road, and as the panic wrecked for a season all such prospects, our proposed railroad withered and shrank so far away that it had not yet reached Yazoo City, nor even Mississippi.

On all these improvements our party leaders had been practically a unit, and the great body of the freed people had stood squarely by us. I am sorry to say that there was not the same harmony among " we all Republicans " upon the school question.

By the annual message of Governor James L. Alcorn for
1871 it appears that there were schools open in Yazoo County
from 1865 to 1870 as follows:

1865—For white pupils, 6; for colored, 3.
1866—   "   "   "   8; "   "   5.
1867—   "   "   "   8; "   "   2.
1868—   "   "   "   12; "   "   3.
1869—   "   "   "   14; "   "   6.
1870—   "   "   "   14; "   "   6.

None of these were free public schools, and those for the
colored people were organized and supported entirely by the
bureau, or by Northerners or by the freed people themselves,
with the exception of the " Democratic school" of 1868.

At this point I deem it to be due to my reader to quote,
relative to the progress of our free system from the reports of
the State superintendents.

From the report for 1871:

"No feature of the new system of government met with more
determined opposition at the outset than the school system. A
majority of the wealthy and intelligent classes, unable to divest themselves of the irrational prejudices and passions, the outgrowth of
slavery, clinging with a tenacity worthy of a better cause, to its con-
comitant social, political, and educational theories, they contested
the introduction of the people's schools with a determination that
seemed at times would overwhelm and destroy them. This antago-
nism was inspired by a class of idle politicians, and an unscrupulous
press, whose acme of ambition seemed to be to thwart every measure
and effort looking to the development and prosperity of the State;
preferring darkness to light—ignorance to intelligence.

"This partisan hostility at length culminated in open violence,
particularly in the eastern portion of the State. I have deemed it a
matter of duty, unpleasant and painful as it is, to report some of the
most flagrant cases of incendiarism and violence towards teachers
and school officers which have occurred since the inauguration of the
free school system."

From the same for 1872:

"In submitting this my second annual report, it affords me much
pleasure to be able to say, that the results of the educational work of
the past year are of the most encouraging character. Our free public schools are rapidly gaining favor among all classes of the people,

and the cause of education throughout the State is steadily advancing. Irrational prejudices and passions are gradually giving way to reason and an enlightened conservatism. The masses of the people, including a large proportion of the wealthy and intelligent classes are beginning to demand a conformation to the great fundamental changes in our State and national policy, particularly with reference to popular education."

From the same for 1873:

" As the people become familiar with the workings and results of our system of schools, they are convinced not only of its practical utility as a means of educating their children, but that universal education secured by a system of public instruction is necessary to the very existence of a government like ours.

" The growth of our educational institutions is indeed marvellous when we consider that our system of public education has been in practical operation only about three years."

From same for 1874 :

"Steadily the system of popular education is growing into favor with the people of our State. The former obstacles which prevented the growth of our public schools are rapidly diminishing, and they are now receiving almost unanimous support from the people. * * * Considering the great opposition which the system has had to encounter from a vast majority of the intelligent portion of our inhabitants, and the great breadth of its operations, we have every reason to congratulate ourselves."

There was no violent opposition to the establishment of the system in Yazoo County. The difficulty was of another kind. The school board of the county was composed of very worthy and capable men, Unionists and Northerners, and one colored man. At its head was the county superintendent, a Yankee who had been a bank president, was a large real estate owner in the county, and a gentleman of considerable culture and of very superior abilities, but he possessed the same failing as most Northerners who settle there sooner or later seem bound to discover. He was conscientious in the discharge of his duties, but was extremely desirous of having the good opinion of " Southerners."* He was also anxious to have the good opinion of the colored people, and I have no doubt meant to do for their best good in his

*He afterward married a most estimable lady of that State.

management of that branch of our county government, but the white Southerners associated with him, were extremely timid. They went forward with their work as though their first duty was to consult the enemies of the system, and although our board of supervisors repeatedly assured the school board of their willingness to levy for whatever amount they could wisely use, their three first annual estimates were far below what they should have been. In addition to this, while the number of educable children in the county, according to the assessors' returns in 1872 was: Whites, 2,180; colored, 4,183. Up to and including 1872 this board had established but twenty-five schools for the colored, and had given forty-one to the white children.* And as if to cap the climax, in 1873, they actually proposed a reduction of the tax-levy for school purposes.

The colored people were beginning to clamor against this partiality, and the politicians among the enemy were taking advantage of what apparently was our neglect of the colored people, and, as I was at the head in the management of affairs, were holding me responsible for it.

To have attempted to set up a system which "mixed" the races in the schools, nearly everybody said would lead to a "war of races," so "separate" schools had been provided for by State law. The colored people did not complain of this, but they did demand equal school facilities. In justice to them they should have had the forty-one, and the whites have been content with the twenty-five schools; if no more than sixty-six could be provided. There was no reason at all, nor had there been, for this slow progress in that vital work.

But at best, the system at first was only tolerated by the whites, because they could not help themselves. The question now was, whether they should be allowed to strangle it while we had it in charge. I resolved to take the responsibility of saying no. Therefore when the superintendent's term expired I recommended and procured the appointment of my brother in his place.

*See State School Report for 1872.

Now this was not my brother, the "jail-bird," but another one.

Soon after Charles' transfer to Washington County, the ex-bureau agent was also transferred to a field where his services were likely to be more helpful to our cause than in Yazoo, where, it was said, we had more than our share of good material.

Shortly afterward, however, General Greenleaf and our "Republican magistrate" died, and went straight to Heaven, I believe.

All these transfers so reduced the little garrison that Mr. Foote, the old "guard" and myself were left the sole survivors, in the county

During this period my brother William came down to visit me. Things had grown to be so much brighter-hued in Yazoo, that I had little difficulty to induce him to remain and to unite his fortunes with me in my new home. It was this brother whom I got appointed superintendent.*

The result was a marked change in the conduct and growth of the free-school system.

It had always been difficult to procure competent native white teachers for the colored schools. Native white ladies, even as late as 1874, would "starve" before they would teach "a nigger school." The former superintendent complained bitterly of this lack of teachers; but neither he nor his associates upon the board took the right steps to get them. My brother's heart was in the good work as thoroughly as my own. He sent North for teachers. Under the new management there were no steps backward. On the contrary, in 1875, the close of my brother's term, according to the official reports, there were in the county free schools as follows: White, 45; colored, 63; total 108; of teachers employed, there were: White, 79; colored, 23; of school-houses and rooms, there were 109. Sixty of these houses had been erected and paid for during the period. There had not been a day from 1869 to 1875 when the holder of a

* The same who succeeded Powell in the sheriff's office.

warrant on the school fund could not demand and receive in lawful money of the United States the full amount expressed upon its face.

The proceedings instituted by the school board for the recovery of the school funds squandered by the enemy during their long control in Yazoo, were so far successful, that in 1875 there was in the county treasury belonging to the various school funds more than twenty-seven thousand dollars, the bulk of which was in United States bonds.

At the outset the free-school idea met the determined hostility of the irreconcilables, the faint acquiescence of the conservatives in the ranks of the enemy, the lukewarm adherence of the Unionists, the sympathy and active co-operation of the Northerners and the unanimous and greedy support of the " freedmen, free negroes and mulattoes."

But in spite of all the obstacles in the way of its growth, in 1875 the system in Yazoo was a complete success, a fact acknowledged by all except possibly a handful of the most violent of the irreconcilables.

It had become so popular that old and wealthy planters often came personally to the superintendent or members of the board, and pleaded for a school on their own plantations, declaring that they not only wished it as a means of improving the freed people, but also, because they had observed that the laborers on other plantations where schools were, or who were in the neighborhood of schools, were more contented and worked better.

It was found impossible to supply the demand. To have done so at once would have so greatly increased the taxes that it would have been burdensome to the government.

It is with a feeling of no little pride and gratification that I am able to add here, at the close of this account of my stewardship, that the tax-levy at no time during the entire period exceeded two and one-half per cent, and in 1875, was but two and one-fifth per cent for all purposes.

CHAPTER LXIV.

A SURRENDER—NOT OURS BUT THE ENEMY'S.

"THE enemy," while we planted looked on in amazement and gradually descended through all the stages from bitter, implacable foes, blunt frenzy, helpless indifference and enmity, to placid acquiescence, to secret, and finally, before the election of 1875, to open support. Members of the Yazoo bar, even Mrs. Black's attorney, confessed that the business of the courts had never been more ably or more satisfactorily conducted; that the laws had never been more faithfully or more justly executed; that the county had never before enjoyed greater peace, and the planters and the rank and file of the enemy all agreed that the county had never been more prosperous.

There were, however, a few exceptions to this universal voice, viz.: Colonel Black, the human hornet, Ben Wicks, Major Sweet *et al.* But we had shouldered the load and carried it in triumph. Not only were the grown-up men and women apparently reconstructed, the little boys and girls appeared to be equally so. I frequently had occasion to visit remote parts of the county, often traveling in an open buggy or on horseback, the usual mode of travel there, and was, as a rule, hospitably received wherever I went. On one occasion I well recollect, I was detained to a very late hour in the night, and, being in a sparsely-settled neighborhood, I solicited (of a colored man) shelter from an approaching storm.

He was a large planter. In the three years that had passed
since the bars had been removed to his right to purchase land
he had acquired quite two thousand acres, a great part of
which was good corn and cotton land, and under cultivation.
He insisted upon my remaining all night, had a chicken killed
and served for me with other substantial food, and a quite
lavish supply of delicacies. His "spare" bed was a model
of neatness and comfort ; his wife a model cook and house-
keeper. I rested sweetly, and arose as refreshed and com-
forted as though my host had been a white man and his wife
a white lady, and doubtless got a much earlier start in the
morning. I had not been at this home, however, more than
long enough for the storm to subside and to eat the excellent
supper spread for me, when I was notified that about a hundred of my constituents had assembled in the broad ground
about the house, expressly to pay their respects, and they
would accept no excuses. I had to submit to a hand-shake
from all, old and young, men, women and children, and also
to make a speech. It was quite eleven o'clock, but I talked
to them for a half hour at least, praised them for their loyalty, frugality, and orderly conduct, and—for there were some
who needed it—scolded them for their intemperance in the
use of liquors, bad treatment of their wives, indifference
to the means for social elevation, extravagance in dress,
besought them to save their money, while the sun was shining
to buy lands, and referred to my present host to give point to
my appeal as well as to my criticisms.

Shortly after my return to town, I received a message from
my host's former master, regretting that I had spent the
entire night in his neighborhood without partaking of his
hospitality—if no more than a breakfast. I afterward learned
through a personal friend in the neighborhood that the Colonel was piqued and felt himself slighted. Such instances as
this were of frequent occurrence during 1872 and 1873. So
many of the " solid" colored men of the county had acquired
lands, were living in good houses and possessed all the com-

forts of a civilized home I often enjoyed making such trips to the country. The teacher of the colored school usually made such a home his boarding place, and in the neighborhood of such colored planters there were always to be found several bright, intelligent "freedmen, free negroes or mulattoes," male and female, who would seek me out for counsel and advice in their plans. It was wonderful the progress they were making, in acquiring an education and in all the arts of peace. There were several of this class of colored planters who kept open house, so to speak, and many a "high-toned, honorable gentleman," belated on his journey, was glad to partake of their hospitality.

The difference between them and myself, however, was always in this: These men made a convenience of such homes, while I made the fact an opportunity for solid enjoyment on my own part, by the instruction I was able to give, and the lessons I could always learn. It was a rule with me, too, to visit each neighborhood as often as once or twice a year, and talk to the people—all without regard to race or social position being invited. Such meetings were always feasts for me, and I have great reason to believe of great benefit to the freed people themselves.

I took up but a small part of the time with my own "talks," and always managed to draw out "speeches" from my hearers. This had the effect of developing considerable native talent.

Among the speakers thus brought out was a small black negro, who came to be known as the "little giant." "High-toned, honorable gentlemen" often attended these meetings, just to hear him. He could barely read, and could not write at all. He was a common plantation laborer.

But his tongue, as often tipped with fire as with honey, lashed all evil-doers with a mercilessness I have never seen matched. His appeals to dear "ole marsta," for justice for "my people" were irresistible, and I have seen our whilom "Chairman of the Yazoo White Man's Democratic Commit-

tee " as often wipe from his eyes tears of sorrow as of laughter in the course of one of these speeches. I well recollect
one occasion when, after having by a series of witty passages,
peculiarly descriptive of local times and incidents, got his
audience into full sympathy with himself, in a manner that
would have been mistaken for drollery by those who had
never been privileged to look into the secret places in a Mississippi free negro's heart, but which was really an awkward
expression of his hopes, or of his fears, for the future of
himself and his race, suddenly pointing at the object of his
criticism, this orator exclaimed; " Thar he is now, my dear
ole' marstah. We wor rais togedder. Doan' ye ' member,
mars Henry, when I was a chile—jez a little picaninny, runin'
aroun' in my shirt on de play groun' dah by de fo'ks ob de
ole road, how ef yo' ' lowed to hit me I alwuz hit yer back,
an' how yer deah ole father, kind, good ole marstah, now
gone yan'ter to glory, never would ' low ye ter 'poze on *me*
no how, an' ter dis day, gran, she say how my own deah
mother, gone yan'ter glory 'long a ole marstah, jez' tho't
der same o' ye as o' me—kase bof on us call her mammy, an'
kase she allus 'low ter gi'e yo' yer din' jez er same ez me;
no diffunt—sos't we wor hongry. Den doan' ye 'member
by'n by how ye went away dar up ter de Norf, whar de
kunnel comed frum, and got yo' edecation and comed back
y'here agin' real hansome an' peert, an' marry ole mars
Langford's daughter *Sayrah.* Den ole marstah, yo' father,
how proud he wor ! An' he gi'e yo' er big plantation jinin'
on ter owrn, an' dah yo' iz a libben' ter dis blessed day.
An' eber senz I wor growed lerge'nuff fur to pick up taters,
toat wah'r'r fur de fiel' hans', foller de plow, huz de coh'n
an' pick de cotting, I'z been a doin' on it jez er sam'z 'do I
wor boh'n dar; and senz de s'render no' d'ffern.

  " Y'here all my ole feller servanz, da knows dat iz de troof.

  " My dear bre'r'en and sister'e'n, white no mo'n de black,
none on ye eber y'hearn me blamin' ole marstah kase we wor
his'n, dat day ter dis, no mo'n now we isn't. Day bull-whip

an' day blood-houn's gone. Come agin no mo'. An' I 'low no
us't ter talk 'bout um no mo.' Ole marstah 'low he praise
de Lord kase dey is. He 'low, an' young mars Henry he
'low, day duz, day cotting growin jez er same ez b'fo de
wah, no differn.

" Marstah, he sen' young mars Henry yan'ter de Norf fur
ter git *he* edecatin' jez er same ez ole marstah Henry done
sont young mars Henry 'fo de wah; no differn'. An' we iz
all happy an' prospus, jez er same ez 'fo de wah; no differn—
cep'n we iz free now an' got no lan' yit; kase young marstah
Henry an' mars Henry 'peers like dey gwain to keep dair'n
fur young mars Henry comin'."

While thus delivering himself the young giant's colored
hearers expressed their sympathy and approval by low, half
suppressed moanings.

His master's face was a study. He could not take offense,
for the orator's tones were so pathetic that they covered the
terrific arraignment which the words presented.

At times he bowed his head as if in grief and sorrow. At
other times he would raise his face toward the speaker only
to display the changing colors which his anger, pity or grief,
according to the tenor of the words to which he was listening, forced to the surface.

The little giant never closed one of these speeches without
some reference to General Greenleaf, my brother Charles, or
myself. On this occasion he walked to where I was sitting
and, placing his hand affectionately upon my shoulder, in a
voice so full of gratitude and of love that I shall carry the
word's through life's journey as a most precious token, he
said: " Y'heres my own deah brother. See dar, brer'er'en
de Kunnel doan' 'ject ter dat! He's mo'n dat. He's ou'
father. De Kunnel doan 'ject ter dat neether! De Kunnel's
ou' saviour.*

" Brer'er'en, 'member de time when he wor in de firy furnace for we all po' niggers. Never furgit dat day. De

*Neither this orator nor any of the colored people of that county ever appeared to
think there was any profanity in calling me their saviour.

Lor'-God-A'mighty leading of 'im den, an' 'twel yit; no differn. He never wor ashame' we all. 'Member how de-
Kunnel allus hold up he head; nebber s'render. Captain
Telsub could'n make 'm do dat; nur mars Dixon, nur mars
Baltimo, nur Kunnel Black, nur day kuklux. De Captain,
he jez like de Kunnel, too. Marstah Henry heself 'low white
folks had no sense treat de Kunnel an' de General an' de
Captain dat er way. An' marstah, peers like he think nigh
on ter same ob de Kunnel now ez we all duz. Peers like
day is all jealous kase we po' niggers loves de Kunnel so.
Brer'er'en de ole so's a healen up, sho! Bress de Lord !"

By the time our orator had reached this point, his colored
auditors were wrought up to such a fever that they began
shouting in the old camp-meeting style, and stamping the
floor, effectually drowning the speaker's voice. " Ole marstah" appeared to enjoy it too, and at the close congratulated
me heartily. He acknowledged that he was jealous of the
love of his old slaves, and appeared to sincerely regret the
" foolishness "—even he called it by that name now—of himself and his associates in opposing the reconstruction of the
State upon the Congressional plan.

The attempt of the irreconcilables, upon the death of Mr.
Hilliard, to capture the county government, interrupted
these pleasant relations but for a brief spell, for when all
the facts became known, I was as fully exonerated from all
blame by the great body of the whites as I had been by the
courts.* So far as I could see the irreconcilables were my
only enemies. I had not despaired of their conversion, yet I
knew it must be a great way off. The reader already knows
what their attitude toward me was in 1867 and 1868. Even
after the election of Grant, in 1868, and down to the death
of Mr. Hilliard, that attitude on the part of the human hornet, Harry Baltimore and Ben Wicks, had undergone no
appreciable change. The human hornet's hostility to me had

*Very soon after my release from jail the Grand Jury fully investigated the circum-
stances of the killing of Mr. Hilliard, and reported to the court that they could find
no grounds for an indictment against me.

been intensified by my appearance against him in 1872, as attorney for the State upon his trial for the killing of one of his hands, a negro. I never had been called upon to perform that service against Ben Wicks, and his hostility was solely due to political antagonisms, so too was Harry Baltimore's, and so too was that of all who agreed with those persons. Ben Wicks never sat down to table in Dave Cottonridge's restaurant when I was present that he did not offer me some personal affront before either of us went out; often he would come to my table, no matter who might happen to be with me, or present in the dining-room, and, placing his hands upon a chair opposite, would lean over toward me with his well-known bravado, and stare at me a full minute, often accompanying the act with some foul observation upon the Yankees, or the negroes. For a long time the human hornet, Captain Telsub, Major Sweet, Colonel Black, Harry Baltimore, and others of their set, imitated the example thus set them, but in 1874, in less than ninety days after my release from jail, there was an appreciable change in the conduct of all those persons towards me. Major Sweet had changed so far as to manifest a desire to get acquainted with me. I had had an opportunity to extend a courtesy to the human hornet, and the coals of fire thus heaped on his head extorted from him warm thanks. Countrymen having business with the sheriff often went away to hunt up some friend of mine that they might make known their "surprise" at finding me to be "a gentleman." I recollect one real old man, who never came to the courthouse oftener than once a year, and who had never seen me before. He remained for some time staring at me before he made known his business, and then informed my office deputy that he wished to see me. On being informed that he had been looking at me, the old man blushed, stammered an apology, and, in a half-dazed sort of way made known his business. When it was concluded, he walked out into the hall and to the first person he met exclaimed,

" humph ! I 'lowd Morgin wor a nigger." Then, after waiting about for some time, during which he returned several times to stare at me, he walked away, saying to himself, " but I'm d—d ef he ain't a real gentleman."

It was about this time that my brother William one day came smiling into my office and informed me that he had some very important news to impart. Ben Wicks had surrendered! Now such an announcement required some sort of explanation. When that had been given I somewhat doubted Mr. Wick's sincerity. He was about to lose a considerable number of his most trusty " nigros " because there was no school in his neighborhood. This would have been a serious loss to him. Therefore it was that he had first petitioned and then come in person to ask that " a nigger school " might be " started " on his plantation. But it was cause for congratulation nevertheless. Once started on that road, if we could keep it open there was a chance that he, even Ben Wicks, might experience a real change of heart. Mr. Foote and the leaders in the A. M. E. Church had seen and experienced enough during the " insurrection " which followed the death of Mr. Hilliard, to raise doubts in their minds as to the wisdom of their hostility to Yankees. They had supported Mr. Hilliard because they had faith in him, and could see no danger in the fact that his chief counsellors and supporters were among the leaders of the irreconcilables. The suddenness and the vigor of the attack made upon the county government, together with the appointment of Mr. Powell to be sheriff, had alarmed them, and from this time on they were among my most stalwart supporters.

CHAPTER LXV.

A GROWING SEASON IN YAZOO—MORE STRAW FOR BRICKS—BRICK
WITHOUT STRAW—AS COVERING FOR A PURE HEART AND AN
ENLIGHTENED MIND WHICH IS MOST BEAUTIFUL, A DARK OR
A LIGHT SKIN ?

THE period from 1869 to 1875 in Yazoo was one of substantial, and as I now look back upon it, of wonderful progress. When once we had fairly entered on our work and the
incrustations of slavery surrounding the hearts and the minds
of the people, " both black and white," began to yield under
the fructifying power of liberty—liberty restrained by just
and equal laws—there seemed almost no limit to their expansion. The school rooms provided were filled full, the capacity of the teachers taxed to the uttermost, the kinks wrought
in the mental fibres of the people by the most—by African
slavery, were rapidly untangling, and the infections which
that foul leper had scattered abroad in the social and political
body were being rapidly expelled. Men and women who,
born into a world that forbade them to aspire, to hope or to
die, had never realized a picture, began to make them.
What if the result was a daub ! In the sight of Him who
made us all it was beautiful, nay it was perfect. It was
more than a prayer. It was Peter on the water before he
began to sink. In Yazoo, under our planting, the daub took
on form and beauty until all said it was a picture. The irre-

concilables were not pleased with it. It was a rebuke to
them, and how dare "our nigros" presume to do that! It
was more, it was a menace, a perpetual menace. It menaced
the hoary and time-honored privilege of a "white" to be
the superior of a "black!" But Grant was still President,
and there still remained a Republican majority in Congress.
Therefore, rave ever so madly, we had no fear that any rebel
would be allowed to thrust his fist through our picture, nor to
cut it, nor to use it for a target, while at pistol practice. So
the negroes, men and women, held up their heads, walked
upon the side-walk, when they were in town, even dared to
sue at law a white and take away a coat or gown, "sassed
back," and often "struck back," and I never knew one to
refuse to employ a white man or woman to do their drudgery
for them solely because of their complexion. Still more
wonderful and incredible was the conduct of Aunt Sophia—
Mrs. Sophia Waters, I should have said; for times had
indeed changed in Yazoo. Mrs. Waters was no longer Aunt
Sophia. But I am approaching dangerous ground now, and
out of respect to the feelings of some of my readers shall
tread lightly. Mrs. Waters was a colored lady; she had been
the slave of old Judge Fox, up to the time of the arrival of
the "Bureau" at Yazoo. Since that event she had accumulated some property. She at one time had money laid by,
but the Freedman's Bank swallowed that—for a season at
least. She also had a daughter, a real beauty, quite advanced
in her studies and a very sensible girl. Judge Fox's son
Dick fell in love with Josephine, Mrs. Waters' daughter, and
"wanted" her, but neither the girl nor the mother would
receive him upon any other terms than as a suitor for her
hand in marriage. Now Judge Fox was rich, so everybody
said, and both he and Mrs. Fox loved Dick dearly. Dick
became almost distracted and begged his mother for her consent. The plan was to marry and sail away to some land
where a woman was a woman for aye that, and aye that.
The mother at last consented, but the father, old, and near

death's door, raved and protested until she withdrew it. Then a conspiracy was formed to obtain the girl for Dick according to the prevailing custom in that region when the high-contracting parties are on opposite sides of the *caste* line. Whether they accomplished their purpose or not, I cannot now say, but it would seem that they did, for, shortly afterward, Dick consented to take a white girl to be his wife; of course the white girl consented too.

Alas! the fathers of the Congressional plan of reconstruction, had they been able to have anticipated such things, could never have framed a law to meet such a case, nor such as the following. The papers never mentioned it. They could not, one of the prerequisites to its fitness for the columns of the *Democrat* or of our *Banner*, was still wanting in 1875. Zealous efforts had been put forth by "high-toned, honorable gentlemen" and ladies all along the family tree, even to the very roots, of the persons who were directly concerned; a white man and his white wife. These efforts failed to discover any trace whatever, even by that "surest of all tests," the finger nails, of negro blood in the family of either, yet—well, everybody said the child was a mulatto. It was a high-toned family. Being such, and there being no trace of negro blood anywhere to be found in any of its ancestors, it could not be said to have "breed back on the nigro." It could only be a "freak of nature." That settled it—*i. e.* nature settled it, and the husband joyfully recognized his own.* Of all the bright, quick-witted, modest and aspiring young girls in the Sabbath-school Charles and the General organized in the little church on the hill we helped to build, Susie Poindexter was first. Her ability to memorize was something marvelous. She rarely recited her lesson without reciting also an entire chapter, which she had herself selected. Susie was a good girl; but eight years old when she began, in the winter of 1867–'8, now, in 1874, she was fourteen. Her parents had taken a just pride in her develop-

*He sent the boy North to be brought up

ment, and we all hoped that she would be able to acquire a
sufficiently thorough education to fit her for excellent service as a school teacher. We had no fears for her morals.
She was a strong, high-minded girl, but just at the point
where the "brook and river meet," I lost sight for a time
of Susie. When finally I met her it was upon the street.
Her former pleasure at meeting me thus, and her grateful
smile and courtesy were lacking. She appeared anxious to
avoid me, and had a guilty look upon her face. At once
realizing the truth, I set on foot inquiries which resulted in
informing me that a "high-toned, honorable gentleman," one
of Yazoo's "best citizens," was revelling in the "personal
satisfaction" of having entangled upon his hook, while fish-
ing upon the "inferior side of the line," one of "Morgan's
black pets." When next I met Susie I held out my hand to
her and greeted her with all the affection I had formerly
manifested toward her. Then she began to cry, Still holding on to her hand, I asked her to come and see my wife,
and talk it over with her. At this she cried all the more,
and replying through her sobs: "Oh, Colonel Morgan, it
ain't no use for me to try, I'm nothing but a nigger anyway."
She withdrew her hand and ran away. Susie Poindexter was
but one of the number who began with such bright prospects, only to fall away. Some met ruin in their own home.
The Sabbath-school and the day school were the only places
where they could stand without besmearing themselves with
pitch. If perchance it was not within the dwelling of their
parents, it was likely to be in that of their mistress or
employer, and almost always upon the streets, or in the fields
where, during a large part of the year, they were required to
work. At all times liable to the grossest vulgarities and
obscenities from white youth and men, and from black, too,
the wonder is that many more were not defiled than there
were. The fact is, the aspiring young colored girl, black or
light complexioned, has always had to contend with such a
multitude of obstacles that those who have conquered them

are entitled to wear a crown in this world, as well as in the next.

Had we any such in Yazoo ?

Yes, more than a few. The Emancipation Proclamation of Mr. Lincoln wiped out forever all stains upon the characters of colored women that affected their reputation for chastity and womanly purity. In the eye of all the civilized world it was to them a new birth, and every colored woman who realized the fact, and entered purposely into the battle of life by the new path, ought to have been and should hereafter be recognized by every true American woman or man, as the equal of the noblest in the land. Thus I believed and taught during my " dictatorship " in Yazoo, and thus I still believe, and mean to continue to teach. The result in Yazoo was to inspire colored women with the belief that the new path led out of Egypt to the promised land, where a pure heart, and an enlightened mind possibly might so light up a dark covering that it would be merely a question of taste which, the light or the dark skin, was most beautiful

CHAPTER LXVI.

ABOUT NIGRO RISINGS—THE WOLF AND THE LAMB—SIGNS OF THE
END—WAS IT A RACE CONFLICT—PREACHING STATE SOVER-
EIGNTY AND PRACTICING THE OPPOSITE—SPECIMENS OF SUPE-
RIAH STRATEGY AND STATESMANSHIP— COONS IN THE CANE
BRAKES—A HUNDRED SCALPS—A PEACE-MEETING—RESOLU-
TIONS.

EIGHTEEN hundred and seventy-four was a memorable
year in Yazoo politics. The " Ohio idea," respecting
" local self-government " and local sovereignty *vs.* the sovereignty of the individual, so aptly illustrated in that State in
the person of Governor Allen, was bearing rich fruitage in
Mississippi, where it was most happily illustrated in the persons of the human hornet, Colonel Black, Judge Isam,
Captain Telsub and George M. Powell,

The Republican idea represented in Mississippi in the person
of Governor Ames, had done battle with the Ohio idea on
its chosen field in Mississippi, our Yazoo stubble-ground, and
overcame it. Peace had come again in Yazoo. But just
outside our borders, on the south, in the county of Warren,
the Ohio idea, and certain other ideas, appeared to stay.
They were to have a charter election in the city of Vicksburg, Warren County, and for months in advance of it the
irreconcilables there had been preparing for the " war of
races," which they assumed was " about " to occur. Now

those irreconcilables in Vicksburg, like their brethren in Yazoo, professed to believe in local self-government, and all the time protested against outside interference. But while openly doing that they were secretly making provision for as much aid for their cause from the outside as they should need for their purposes. All sorts of false reports of "nigro risings," "nigros threatening to burn the city," and so forth, were manufactured by them and published throughout the State, in their newspapers, and by special couriers. As a result of these measures, about the first of August reports came to me that there were three " independent military companies " being organized in the southern part of the county, and that they were " patrolling " their respective neighborhoods, disarming colored men whenever they were found with any kind of weapon, arresting some, and terrorizing all. To ascertain the truth about those reports, I sent out two deputies, both white men and ex-confederate officers, and a colored man, into the neighborhood of these "companies " with instructions to quietly travel about among the people and ascertain the truth. One of the deputies reported to me that he had found a " company " of white men under arms and drilling. He knew the " captain " well, and was informed by him that the organization was not for service in Yazoo County, but in response to calls for help from the white citizens of Vicksburg, who were hourly expecting an attack by a "mob of infuriated nigros," who were " threatening to burn the town." This deputy obtained from that " commander " the oath which each member had sworn and signed his name to, which I have preserved, and which is as follows:

" AUGUST 4, 1874.

" We, the undersigned citizens of Yazoo County, Mississippi, hereby pledge our word and honor that we will support and protect each other and families through this present condition of excitement and danger; and that we further pledge our honor to send our aid and assistance to any part of the State that may be suffering from such danger; and we firmly declare that we do not assemble in arms for the purpose of violating any of the laws of the United States or of the State of M'ssissippi, but for the purpose of protecting our homes from the hands of ruthless bands of armed men that have been reported to us as assembling in this county and adjoining counties, contrary to the laws of the United States and the State of Mississippi.

W. T. BAIN.	J. KITCHUM.
T. B. BROWN.	S. J. WILLIAMS
T. J. HARRELL.	J. P. GRAY.
J. M. CHILDERS.	T. J. H. JACKSON.
F. S. DIXON.	C. R. KASE.
R. F. GALDEN.	R. T. NEELEY.
T. C. WHITE.	W. ATKINSON.
W. R. SMITH,	T. F. LOUIS.
R. E. GARRY.	J. W. CASTLYS.
M. W. WHALEN.	F. B. JOHNSON.
J. MCMACKMASTER.	L. L. WETHERFORD.
B. Y. BROWN.	J. C. GRAY.
R. W. BAIN.	R. HOPE.
M. M. LANGFORD.	W. F. GALDEN.
S. A. CLUNAN.	F. FULCHER.
D. H. SAULTER.	J. P. BAILEY.
S. K. HERRING.	M. R. BROWN.
J. R. CAULY.	F. O. COLTON.
H. CARLY.	

The reader will note that the "oath" which this "military company" swore and subscribed to, did not designate the color of the "ruthless bands of armed men." Nor did it designate precisely the neighborhood where such bands were to be found, nor say that there were any such bands. On the contrary all the subscribers seemed to know of such "assembling" was what had been reported to them. My deputy reported that after talking with them a few moments they appeared to be ashamed of themselves, and shortly afterward separated to their homes. Among the number were some of the worst as well as the best young white men of the county. F. S. Dixon was a brother of the human hornet.

The man sent to Dover made a similar report, as to the Dover company, except that its members appeared not to be at all ashamed of what they were doing, and gloried in it. The oath which they had sworn and subscribed and the object of their organization, was similar to that of the former company.

The third organization, nearer to Vicksburg than the other two, was "out on a scout" with their Warren County brethren, and could not be got at.

Now every member of those companies, and their aiders and abettors, knew that I was the sheriff and chief peace-officer of the county, yet not a word had reached my ears of the cause of their complaint, from any one of their number, until I sought for it as I have related. My first information of their organizations came from a colored man living near Dover, who had had his squirrel gun taken from him by members of the company.

Reports of "negro insurrection" again became common throughout the State. One was reported in Tunica County, about the centre of the swamp region, and General Chalmers, in command of an army, recruited largely from Memphis and other parts of Tennessee, and which was variously estimated in the public prints at from two to ten thousand white men, crowded on steamers chartered at Memphis for the purpose, hurried to the scene, creating terror and consternation among the negroes wherever they appeared. Democratic newspapers throughout the State, and the South, contained vivid accounts of the "ravages of the negroes," and of the courage and chivalric conduct of General Chalmers and his brave men, thus rushing to the rescue of the "white men and women from the cradle up," of far away Tunica. We employed different means for suppressing the "rising" about to occur in Yazoo at this juncture.

The *Democrat* appeared with a "blood in the eye" editorial on the affidavit of one Simon Battaile, which it published, and which exposed what Simon said he knew of a "deep-laid, dark and damnable plot" on the part of the negroes to "rise" and so forth, and the *Democrat*, and also the *Banner*, called on "our people" to arm and prepare for it.

Now it so happened that Simon was one I had for several

days been searching for with a warrant for his arrest on a charge of grand larceny. But here he was now, " exposing " this so-called " nigro rising." In less than twenty-four hours I had Simon in jail, where he confessed to me that he knew nothing of any " rising " more than he had heard that the colored people were planning for a celebration* of some sort to be held at Yazoo City. He had done this thing in order to secure the aid and sympathy of the " best citizens " to help him out of his own trouble.† The prompt exposure of Simon's part in the conspiracy of the irreconcilables to compel " our nigros to rise," which was made in the columns of our Yazoo *Republican*, postponed the rising, however. During this time the excitement prevailing at other points in the State, which had been created by the efforts of the irreconcilables " to send their aid and assistance " to their brethren at Vicksburg, who were engaged in a " last ditch struggle " for the " supremacy of the white race, and the preservation of Southern civilization and honah, by G—d, sir," was not general in Yazoo. It was made so, however, by the arrival at Yazoo City, one morning, of a steamboat from Vicksburg, which brought an appeal from " our people " there, for arms. It continued on up the river, stopping at all the principal landings, spreading the appeal and gathering up all the double-barrelled shot-guns and rifles that were offered for the purpose. Upon its return I went on board and saw the captain, who informed me that he was gathering the weapons for the use of himself and crew, for defense against a " mob of nigros gathered upon the river's bank " below Sartartia, for the purpose of " capturing " his boat when it should return to Vicksburg. I placed a deputy, an ex-confederate officer, on the boat, with instructions to accompany it to the county line, and to arrest all persons who might appear with arms to do violence against it, or any one on board. He did so, got off at the line and returned by land. He reported that he had not been able to find any negroes with arms. On

---

*A frequent annual gathering upon the close of the summer's work, and before cotton picking commences.

†The sequel proved their fidelity to him, for he escaped the legal penalty for his crime of grand larceny.

the contrary, they all appeared to be in distress at the violent proceedings of some of the whites, who were leaving that part of the county with their arms for the purpose of giving aid to their brethren at Vicksburg.

All the proceedings I have mentioned occurred about the same time. I was able to preserve the peace of the county and protect the colored people only by ceaseless watchfulness and tireless effort, day and night. I employed at my own expense a number of special deputies, through whom I was able to keep myself informed of the plans and purposes of the enemy. One of the armed "companies" had already separated to their homes. To the "captain" of the Dover "company" I wrote the following:

"YAZOO CITY, *August* 6, 1874.

"DEAR SIR: I have information, by me deemed reliable, establishing the following points :

"1st. There are three companies of armed white men in that portion of the county lying south of the Yazoo City, Vaughan's station road. W. T. Bain is captain of one, Dr. Robinson, J. R. Bell and others, officers in another. I have not yet ascertained the name of the officers of the other company.

"2d. These companies are organized with the *public* purpose of protecting their wives and families, their property and homes, against armed bands of colored men ' reported ' as organized against law in the county, and they ' furthermore pledge our honor to send our aid and assistance *to any part of the State* that may be suffering from such danger." * * *

"My deputies have traveled over the entire portion of the country infested by the ' white ' organizations referred to, and are unable to find out the existence of any armed bands of colored men. Had the citizens of that portion good reasons to apprehend danger to their person and property from the colored people, it was their duty to have reported their fears to me. It is my duty to execute the laws and preserve the peace in my county. I shall endeavor to do my duty.

"These armed bands of men, for whatever purpose organized, are unlawful. When the executive power of the county, as established by law, shall have been found unable to preserve the peace, such organizations may be necessary and justifiable; until then they are unnecessary, unlawful, unjustifiable, and in contempt of authority, and it is my sworn duty to suppress them. Every portion of the county except that mentioned above is now enjoying profound peace and quiet. I regret to find that the peace and quiet of any portion of the county should be disturbed; more especially do I regret it when I consider the character and standing of the farmers who are being drawn into the organizations referred to. If necessary, I shall send a sufficient number of deputies into your neighborhood to preserve the peace. I feel sure that your companies of armed white men will promptly disband, and that the bearer hereof, Mr. J. R. Redding, one of my deputies, will have no trouble in preventing ' night-patrolmen ' from doing further violence to the laws, or to the rights of colored citizens to travel the highways of the county unmolested. Mr. Redding has full and specific instructions from me. * * *

" A. T. MORGAN,

" J. R. Bell, Esq.   " Sheriff."

The night-riding and interference with peaceable colored people suddenly ceased, but the result was due, doubtless, not so much to the respect of this "captain" or of his followers, for my authority, as to the fact that the election at Vicksburg had passed, the irreconcilables there had triumphed, and "assistance" was no longer needed. But their victory cost them dear, for it was at the time said that fully one hundred colored people were killed before they surrendered to "the superiah strategy and statesmanship" of their former masters.*

In Yazoo my efforts were seconded by all the colored people and by nearly all the whites who were not of the irreconcilables, or of the sleuth-hound class.

A largely-attended "peace-meeting" was held in the town, at which our Senator, our postmaster, the pastors of the colored churches, Mr. Foote, our "little old orator" and myself, were speakers. The following resolutions were unanimously adopted:

From the Yazoo City *Herald*, Republican:

" Whereas, owing to recent occurrences of violence and bloodshed in many parts af the country, especially in Tennessee, Louisiana, and more recently in Mississippi, at Austin, in Tunica County, and to other causes not necessary to mention here, the minds of the people of Yazoo County have become greatly disturbed and excited, so much that two of our local newspapers, one in an extra and the other in a cool and well-matured article in its columns, advise the white people to organize and arm for ' self protection;' and

---

*The following was wired by one of the victors at that election to the chairman of the Yazoo Democratic Committee, which may explain the kind of assistance required there. The word "coon" signifies negro.

" Coons in the kanebrakes. We have taken a hundred scalps, and are masters of the situation.   " R. O. LEARY, *Mayor*."

" Whereas certain white citizens of this county, prior to and on the day of the election lately held in Vicksburg, were armed and organized and ready to march at a moment's warning; and

" Whereas the necessity of this arming and organizing is based upon the pretense that the freedmen of the county are engaged in plotting violence against the white people of the county, and are organizing in leagues and societies of a secret character and are arming; and

" Whereas we believe the banding together of white men, or colored men, in military organizations, in secret societies, or companies, in times of domestic peace, when the courts are in full possession of all their powers, and the chosen officers to execute the laws in the full and perfect possession and enjoyment of all the powers and functions of office, is revolutionary and wicked, and calculated by its usurpation of authority and disregard of the Constitution and laws of the country, to lead to anarchy, the destruction of liberty, and the ruin of the State; and

" Whereas certain newspapers published in this and other States, notably in Vicksburg, advocate the arrangement of political parties on grounds of color or race distinctions, assuming that this Government of ours ' was created by white men, and to be ruled by white men'—

" *Resolved*, That we regret the violent conflicts that have occurred between the white and colored people of our own and sister States, and denounce the originators of these acts of violence as enemies to good government.

" *Resolved*, That we know of no secret or other organizations among the colored people of this county, which have for their object the organization of military bands, or the procuring of arms for any object or purpose whatever, and that we believe the colored people are entirely without arms or ammunition, suitable for aggressive or defensive warfare, and that we know of no purpose or intention on the part of any of the freedmen of this county, either to organize, arm, or in any manner assume an attitude toward their white fellow-citizens other than one of peace and good-will. * * *

" *Resolved*, That we denounce the attempt made at Vicksburg, and contemplated at other points of the State, to organize political parties upon grounds of race or color, rather than upon measures of public policy or the ability, character, or virtues of men, whether such attempts be made or contemplated by one race or the other, as pernicious, wicked, and destructive of all the principles upon which our Government is founded, and we pledge ourselves, each to the other, to oppose all such attempts, by whomsoever made, with all our influence and our votes.

" *Resolved*, That our form of government was created by the people and for the people, and, by the grace of God and the inherent virtues of all the people, shall not perish from off the face of the earth."

CHAPTER LXVII.

NEGRO LAND-OWNERS—OLE MARSTAH'S CARRIAGE RECONSTRUCTED
—A BLACK CLOUD—CAPTAIN CRAPO'S SOLUTION OF THE RACE
PROBLEM—A BETTER ONE THAN CRAPO'S—MAJOR SNODGRASS'
SOLUTION OF THE SAME—DID MASSACHUSETTS SOLVE IT—A
TIDAL WAVE—MASSACHUSETTS DEMOCRATIC—EXULTANT TEARS
—JUBILANT JOHNNIE REBS—WHAT MAJOR GIBBS SAID ABOUT
IT—"PEACEABLY IF WE CAN, FO'CIBLY IF WE MUST"—
"SIXTEEN HUNDRED ARMY GUNS" AND OTHER GUNS—A "NIGRO
RISING."

ACCORDING to estimates made by myself in the fall of
1874, there were at that time three hundred colored men
owning real estate in Yazoo County. These holdings varied
from a small house and lot in town, to more than two thousand acre tracts of cotton and corn land.

Several of the colored planters were in quite independent
circumstances. Their wives and their daughters no longer
worked in the cotton and corn fields. Each one owned a
carriage, not always of the best pattern, to be sure, but ample
for the family and sufficiently elegant in appointments for
country uses. In some instances it was "ole marstah's"
family carriage reconstructed. Many more colored men
owned live stock; horses, mules, cows, sheep, hogs, and chickens innumerable. The total real value of the property of

the colored people of Yazoo at that date, was not less than a million and a half dollars. They were in truth rising. Indeed there was danger that "our nigros" would, before long, "own the whole country."

Besides, the overthrow of free government in the surrounding States, particularly in Alabama and Tennessee, was forcing the more enterprising colored families into Mississippi, where, under our Republican government, there was better security for persons, and more certain returns for their toil. This negro immigration was styled by the irreconcilables, a "black cloud threatening the supremacy of the white race." The marvelous fecundity of that race, their physical strength and powers of endurance, their wonderful progress in the science of politics, and their boundless ambition, as fully recognized by the leading minds among the enemy as by myself, and much more than by the people of the Northland, had completely changed the aspect of the *free* negro question from one of doubt and sincere apprehension of his ability to survive, to one of the white man's ability to do so while in the presence of the negro and while the conditions of existence were equal. The greatest minds in the State, on the "superior side of the line," were gravely debating the question, which would be the wiser policy for the white man, emigration and the abandonment of the State to the negro, or a general arming of the white race with the purpose of checking by force the "threatened supremacy" of the negro race. To such persons these were the only alternatives.

Trained in the schools of slavery—African slavery at that—they could not bring themselves to contemplate the possibility of an equal race with equal burdens, between the dwellers upon the two sides of the arbitrary *caste* line, which the existence of that system of slavery had made essential to its perpetuity.

Miscegenationists in practice, as the complexion of more than half the negro population amply attested, they pretended to abhor amalgamation because it was an unnatural and therefore unhealthful relation of the races. This pretense was as hypocritical and insincere as were their professions of loyalty to the Constitution of the United States, and of the State, in their provisions guaranteeing the civil and political equality of the negro. Their conduct upon these questions was prompted by their desire to preserve and perpetuate the *caste* line, well knowing that its destruction meant the destruction of the white man's time-honored privilege of ruling the negro, and the desire sprang from their lusts.

Now no one advocated amalgamation as a solution of the " race problem." The Republicans of Yazoo advocated equality ; not the equality of unequals ; that would be impracticable; but the equality of all in public burdens and public privileges. If that should result in the overthrow of privileges the result would be none other than just. And if the final result should be amalgamation ? Why should that question concern " we all Yankees " in Yazoo ? The first time a " white" looked upon a " black " did he ask himself, the black or any of the bystanders whether he must marry one ?

When the first cargo of African slaves were landed upon our soil, was that question asked or considered ? The union of the States with slavery was intolerable, impossible. When Mr. Lincoln issued his Emancipation Proclamation, and, when the amendments to the Constitution confirming that proclamation were ratified, was the question whether a white should be forced to marry a black allowed to have weight against the policy or justice of those acts ?

For one, I did not have time to stop and consider the question. There were weightier subjects claiming my attention. Captain Crapo, a leading merchant of Yazoo and one of our " best citizens," was my next-door neighbor. His children by his lawful wife, and those by his favorite concubine, a quite numerous and interesting family as a whole, at play, altogether, just like any other " happy family," were the "social superiors" of my two toddlers—a boy and girl—because their " paw" was a "white gentleman" and I was only a "mean, low-down Yankee." *Everybody* said mine were the prettiest, and all that, yet, those children and my children never got closer together than when they peeped at each other between the pickets on the fence which divided our yards, except once when some member of the " happy family " had removed one of the pickets, and a seven-year-old " white " member of that family was caught, by our nurse, holding in her lap and fondling, just as any other " little mother " would do, our boy, Albert T. Morgan, Jr., whose massy golden curls were her especial delight. The excellent wife of a very "prominent citizen," having stood it as long as she could, considering the close proximity of Mrs. Morgan, and the example of her husband, one day worked herself into such a rage over it that she took matters into her own hand, and literally drove her husband's concubine, bag and baggage, out of the house. Of course it was all charged to me; all such things were as well as the poor crops, the " insolence of our nigros " and so forth. So in view of all these things—those happy families, those angry wives, those insolent negroes, poor crops and so forth—I was in great concern for the future of the human race, and every day found me asking myself what must be the end of such a vile system! And yet what could I, what was I going to do about it? My only hope was in our schools, in the little church we helped to build, and that other one, (which was doing equal if not better service in reforming this evil) the A. M. E. Church, and in the continuation of the "rising " then in progress. It was " simply a question of endurance," if we could hold the fort for a few years longer.

Now all these questions had been in abeyance for five years; that is, it had been agreed not to discuss them publicly. But the negro was rising. That fact forced these questions again to the front. During 1874 they formed the absorbing topic of discussion, some among the enemy openly advocated the application of force in the solution of the question. With his superior intellect and with vastly superior means at hand, it would not be difficult for the white race to "put down" the negro, if the attempt was not too long delayed.

Easy-going, well-meaning "Christian" men like Major Snodgrass, reasoned about it thus: The well-being of society requires a privileged class to act in the mechanism of the social structure as a sort of balance wheel. That the negro is inferior is evident from his history. That the white man is the superior of the negro is not questioned. Should we undertake to build up our balance-wheel of both black and white material the quantity of white matter displaced will equal the bulk of black matter absorbed. That degrades the white man. Now degraded white men and negroes are equals. What if the two should suddenly unite? In such an event unless the privileged class outnumbered the degraded class, the balance-wheel might fly off and the machine go to pieces.

Thus Major Snodgrass reasoned, and thereupon concluded that it were better to preserve the old line, and maintain the superiority of all white men at whatever cost.

The *Banner* was a conservative paper. Yet, it just could not help giving expression to its feelings thus:

"North Carolina and Tennessee have gone Conservative by increased majorities. 'Oh, how these victories make us of Yazoo feel humiliation! * * * How long shall this state of things be allowed? Would not death be preferable? If so, then what?"

And both in the *Banner* and in the *Democrat* regularly appeared "communications" and quotations suggestive of force as the true race solvent. While the questions were being thus discussed, the enemy had another revelation. This time I was able to read the handwriting on the wall, but I shut my eyes and stubbornly refused to do so.

Massachusetts gone Democratic? Surely that was a lying dispatch. I would never believe it. But the next morning it was not a lie. It was the solemn truth. Ah! how it hurt. All day the news came worse and worse, and the hurt grew worse. The irreconcilables could not believe their eyes. The enemy said it was too good to be true. The next day there was more of the same sort. Then reading through their tears of exultation, the irreconcilables began to crow, and all the enemy to cackle. My! reading through my tears, how they did burn. But that would never do. I was captain of the ship—" dictator." It would not do to whine. Already Uncles Peter and Jonathan and Pomp and the pastor of the little church we helped to ;build, and the " guard " and all the rest were asking me what it all meant. What should I say ? What ought I to say ? Putting on a bold front I said it meant that the enemy had captured our magazine, but we still held the fort. Therefore it meant nothing.

The " tidal wave " not only engulfed Massachusetts, it swallowed up the House of Representatives in Congress.

Friends, colored men, came from " way below Sartartia, 'jinin' on to Warren County," from Dover, from Silver Creek, from Bentonia, and from " way yan in Homes County," to learn from me what the matter was.

" Ole boss "—it was boss and no longer " mars," with many colored men in 1874—" Ole boss actin' very queer 'bout some thing or other "* some said.

" The Captain boun' to say they has got we all now," others said, " kase de Yankees gone back on us." Mr. Foote, Mr. Burrus, Mr. Dickson, Elder Jackson, Rev. Mr. Gibbs, sister Rachel, and most of the solid colored people looked very grave and anxious. They not only read the news for themselves, they also interpreted it.

The enemy had not only read, they were " jubilating." They came from everywhere, on horseback, by " companies," in carriages, and on foot. Their leaders interpreted the news to them while speaking from the balconies, dry goods

---

*In Yazoo colored men had also improved very greatly in their manner of pornouncing English words.

boxes, and from wagons, in the light of huge bonfires, far into the night. MASSACHUSETTS had " wheeled into line !" had " repudiated the carpet-bagger! " had " put its protest on record against nigro- rule !" The " carpet-baggers and scalawags would have to go now !" Less than two weeks before, the most brilliant orator of that occasion, in a private conversation with me, had confessed the superiority of Northern civilization over that of the South, expressed regret for the past conduct of himself and Southern leaders, and led me to hope that he would at an early day declare himself a Republican, but it was all over now.

Not long afterward and near midnight, just as the last one of the crowd of tax-payers that had filled my office since early morning, had been waited on, and I had put away in the strong vault the day's cash receipts, two large planters from near Dover, who had been belated, entered and wished to settle their taxes. It was " the last day," and of course I obliged them. One was my opponent for the Senate in 1869. We had been on none other than friendly terms ever since that event. The other was an equally large planter, and gentleman of prominence. Of course we were soon " talking politics." In the course of which, the major, my aforesaid opponent, had the goodness to inform me that everybody believed I was an honest man, and meant to do for the best; that my course as leader and " dictator " in Yazoo had been upright and wise; that Yazoo's exemption from the multi-tude of evils that " nigro rule " had inflicted upon some other localities in the State, was due to me; that I had made a good Senator, and was making a better record as sheriff and tax collector; that " our people " were especially pleased at the thoroughness with which I was enforcing the collec-tion of " delinquent taxes " especially of " the nigros" (*he* no longer said " *our* nigros "); that he had no especial com-plaint to make against our local government. The taxes had been rather heavy, but then, we had given them some-thing in return; and, after all, the " nigros " paid the taxes.

Personally he regarded me very highly, and would like to see me prosper. But, as my friend, he would say, I should have to quit my party. It had been repudiated at the North, even by Massachusetts, its mother, because it had grown to be so corrupt that no honest man could longer stay with it and look his neighbor in the eye. I had passed many trials and dangers in Mississippi, and was entitled to some reward. " Our people made fools of themselves at the beginning and your party took advantage of we all's folly to perpetuate its power. We have learned wisdom. No one objects to the nigros votin' now. But the white man objects to *nigro rule*, and won't submit to it any longer. It's time for yo' to quit yo'r ship. It is sinking mighty fast, and it'll keep on till it reaches bottom. With yo'r suppo't we could carry the county without any trouble at all. But, with or without it, we have made up ou' minds that we can, and by the Eternal, we will carry the county next time."

" Whew! Major, how'll you do it? Recollect, my majority was 1,934 only two years ago, and your party was then ' hopelessly' divided."

" Thar's been a mighty change since then. The whole country is tired of free-love Beecher, Credit Mobilier, and radical corruption. We won't harm you all unless yo' get in ou' way."

" Who do you mean by you all ?"

" Why! yo' all Yankees and nigros—yo' party."

" But you forget that full as many of you all voted for me at last election as for my opponent."

" That was a choice of evils, and things have changed. Do yo' reckon we all's gwain to 'low ou' people to split up so long as the nigros remain solid faw yo'r party ? That's just what's been the matter all the while yo'all's been in powah. We all couldn't help ou'selves. But now you'll see."

" Our party was never more united than now. When you Democrats have succeeded in overcoming our two thousand majority, I hope I may still be here to see."

"I hope yo'll stand from under. It'll save we all a heapo' trouble. I tell yo' we all white people have made up ou' minds that we can, and we are going to carry this county next time. Peaceably, if we can, but fo'cibly if we must."

Not very long afterward the *Banner* published the following correspondence, with comments calculated to stir the hearts of the people:

"DEMOPOLIS, *August* 18, 1875.

"DEAR SIR: I inclose to you the two letters, which are genuine, written by two negroes, Eddins and Sanders, who removed from this neighborhood last year to Yazoo City, in your State. These letters were in one envelope and addressed to a negro here named John Thompson. They may furnish the people of that portion of your State with timely warning to take steps for their safety, and I send them to you to use as your judgment may dictate.

"W. E. CLARKE.

"HERNANDO MONEY, ESQ.,
          "*Winona, Miss.*"

Then follows the letter here given *verbatim et literatim:*

"YAZOO CITY, *July* 31, 1875.

"Mr. Thompson My Dear

friend, it is with Pleasure I write you this to inform u of some Politocal newse. They are preparing for the Election very fast & also for riots. They is a little place just 15 miles Below hear by the name of Starttia the colored people are buyin amonnition in Yazoo City. The colored folks have got 1600 Army guns All prepared for Bussness. I wish you were out hear you must Be sure and come out this fall if you please. Be sure and send me all the new e and other Papers and that Rosgam off of the Pine Trees. I am still your wife.

"BENJAMIN FRANKLIN EDDIN.

We have no more to say at present But you must cum and liv with us next year if we liv But I still and so close James Remain

Your Thrue friends,
BENJAMIN FRANKLIN
EDDIN
and JAMES RED SANDS.'"

CHAPTER LXVIII.

A PROPHECY FULFILLED—WHY GOVERNOR AMES FAILED TO OR-
GANIZE THE MILITIA—TRUSTING FREEDMEN AND WHAT BE-
CAME OF THEM—THE WOLF AND THE LAMB—GRANT'S " PROM-
ISE "—METHODS OF THE CONSPIRATORS—THE NIGHT BEFORE
THE BATTLE—" HE'S A THIEF "—A SHOT HEARD ROUND YAZOO
—WHAT WAS IT—"READ, READ, READ !"—SPECIMENS OF NEWS-
PAPER ENTERPRISE IN YAZOO—HOW DICK MITCHELL FORFEITED
HIS LIFE.

"BENJAMIN FRANKLIN EDDIN and James Red
Sands," whose letter closes the last chapter, were
mighty factors in the Mississippi election of 1875. But
before my readers will be able to understand the significance
to Mississippians of that communication it will be necessary
to retrace my steps a little way.

Remembering how bitterly they had been deceived in
1867, when the same State gave an overwhelming majority
against negro suffrage, many leading men and a great part
of the enemy saw nothing in the election of " Old Bill
Allen " in Ohio to excite any hope of relief from that quarter against " Federal interference in Southern elections." So
this class continued steadfast in their policy of cajolery and
bribery of negroes and white Republicans, as the surer way
to final control.

To be sure they had made little progress, as was amply
illustrated in Yazoo. This fact enabled irreconcilables who
had the courage to act upon their judgment respecting the
significance of Mr. Allen's election, to press home with some
effect their arguments favoring the reconstruction of parties
upon strictly race lines. In Vicksburg, particularly in Warren County, there had been Republican maladministration

Therefore the irreconcilables succeeded in carrying the whites
almost *en masse* into a contest which they openly and boastfully proclaimed was one for the " supremacy of the white
race," and so styled their organization the " white man's
party." The result there was accepted by the irreconcilables,
and by many others, throughout the State, as evidence of
the greater efficacy of such an organization for the overthrow
of the Republican power in Mississippi. " Independent military companies," in Yazoo, as we have seen, made their first
appearance August, 1874, and in that portion of the county
which was nearest to Vicksburg. We have also seen that
their professed object was to send " aid " to their brethren
at Vicksburg.

In the town of Yazoo City, where the vote had always
been close, the Democrats that year succeeded in electing
their ticket. The irreconcilables claimed the result as a triumph of the " Vicksburg color line policy." But the mass
of the whites denied that it was, and manifested considerable
hostility to that policy. We have also seen what was the
immediate effect upon Yazoo, of the " tidal wave " that
engulfed Massachusetts.

But no sooner had the crowd of " Johnnie rebs " dispersed to
their homes than our Yazoo world resumed its normal state.
On the surface all was peace and good-will. But it was my
duty to know what was going on underneath the surface.
I knew that the men who as often as once a week quietly
rode out of town to the fair grounds, or to the flats below
Peak Tenariffe, or, to those above town, were a secret military organization, and were engaged at target practice. I
also knew that every effort possible was being put forth to
persuade quiet, law-abiding young white men in the town to
join this company ; that in the country, similar organizations were being formed, and the very best young white men
were being induced, upon one pretext or another, to join
them ; that white women were foremost in the work of re-
cruiting for those companies, and that the changes taking place

in the official membership of the county grange, were proof of a design to make use of the machinery of that organization for the promotion of a movement for a reorganization of parties upon the race, or "color-line."

One day, during this period, a friend placed in my hand a book which he said was being secretly circulated throughout the State. Many of our young white men had already read it. The author signed herself "Your Sister Sallie." The book was called "Sister Sallie." Sister Sallie was able to *prove* that the "land of Nod" was so called because its inhabitants were all lazy, sleepy, nodding negroes, who had been cast out of God's presence and made to dwell separate and apart from the whites, and she boldly and bravely declared that all the woes with which the South had been afflicted during the twenty years' war which the Yankees had waged against them, were directly traceable to the unnatural and wicked relations which had previously existed between the white men of the South, her brethren, and their female slaves. The war, and "the great woe" of negro suffrage, were God's judgments, sent upon her brethren for their rebellion against Him in that particular. Then she warned them that there was but one step remaining to complete their degradation to the level of the negroes, and that was the "*marriage* of their sister—their own, dear sister Sallie, to a buck negro." Proceeding to contrast special characteristics of the women of the two races, she proved conclusively, as she no doubt sincerely believed, "that white ladies" possessed many and varied charms that were lacking in " negro women," and, that white was in every particular superior to black, since the whites were human beings, "God's own people," and the blacks were but "animals," who should never have been brought from their native country, the land of Nod.

This remarkable woman closed this remarkable production with a heart-rending appeal to the chivalry of the State to save herself and her sisters from the terrible doom impend-

ing over them by the presence of the negroes in their midst.
I read this book, and then, in conformity with my solemn
promise, returned it to my friend. I have not since been
able to procure a copy.* At the North such a book could
have had no effect. Not so in Mississippi. There old and
young read it with avidity, and renewed their oaths of allegiance to Sister Sallie and to King Cotton's "Table-round."

It was impossible for me not to see in all these preparations a settled purpose on the part of the irreconcilables to
take possession of the government by force if necessary. And
although it was my duty as captain of the ship to maintain
a confident exterior, I knew that Major Gibbs was speaking the truth when he warned me, on the occasion I have
mentioned, that such was not only their intention, but that
they also believed in their ability to accomplish their purpose; for as the major, and others like him during that period,
often declared, "we all hold the strings to Uncle Sam's
money-bag, at Washington, now."

I visited the capital and stated to the Governor the facts I
have here related, and was not at all surprised to learn from
him that he was constantly in receipt of similar information
from other Republican strongholds. The signs all pointed
one way. There could be no mistaking them. I attended
a caucus of the Republican members of the legislature, called
to consider the situation, and made use of my knowledge of
the plans and purposes of the enemy in behalf of a measure
which the Governor had suggested for organizing and arming
the militia of the State, so that in case of riot or insurrection, he would have the means with which to defend his
own authority, and execute the laws. Two-thirds of the
members of that caucus were personally known to me, and
had been witnesses to my faithful services in behalf of the
establishment of our free State government. Many of them
were my warm, personal friends. They believed everything I said respecting the situation in Yazoo, and what was

*It was at the time understood that the author of the book lived in Hinds County,
Mississippi, and was a well-known minister of the Gospel of the lowly Nazarene.

made known as to other localities. Yet nearly every colored member, who spoke upon the subject, opposed arming the militia. The two principal reasons assigned by them for opposition were:

First. It would tend to arouse race antagonisms.

Second. They had faith in General Grant, and believed that he would come to their aid should they be attacked.

Besides these, there were good, well-meaning colored members, who refused to believe that "ole marstah" would resort to violence to accomplish his political ends. There were a goodly number of old masters in the legislature, and they were all as gentle and harmless, outwardly, as cooing doves. It was not an unusual thing during that session to see these old masters and those good, trusting negroes, arm in arm, upon the public streets, exchanging courtesies in the committee rooms, at restaurants and at saloons, upon the most familiar terms.

Perfect peace reigned throughout Mississippi, and the warning voice of the governor, and others, found an echo only in the laughter, derision, or curses of the Barksdales, the Georges, the Singletons, Lamars *et als.*, who meekly, everywhere and at all times, declared that they never would consent to obtain power through such means as they were most foully and wickedly charged with preparing to use. But no sooner had the legislature adjourned, than affairs took on a different aspect. The gentle, cooing Democratic doves ruffled their feathers and cawed like hungry cariron crows.

The following from the Raymond *Gazette*, a paper published in the capital county and copied generally by the press of the State, is a fair specimen of their "racket:"

"There are those who think that the leaders of the radical party have carried this system of fraud and falsehood just far enough in Hinds County, and that the time has come when it should be stopped —peaceably if possible, forcibly if necessary. And to this end it is proposed that whenever a radical pow-wow is to be held, the nearest anti-radical club appoint a committee of ten discreet, intelligent, and reputable citizens, fully identified with the interests of the neighborhood, and well known as men of veracity, to attend as representatives of the tax-payers of the neighborhood and county, and true friends of the negroes assembled, and that whenever the radical speakers proceed to mislead the negroes, and open with falsehoods, and deceptions, and misrepresentations, the committee stop them right then and there, and compel them to tell the truth or quit the stand."

The " good, trusting negroes," who had refused to believe that old masters could do such things, were the very first to cry for help against the general arming of the whites, which was being rapidly pushed.

But the color-line movement made less rapid progress in Yazoo. At a numerously attended convention of the enemy the report of the committee on platform was amended by striking out the resolution favoring the Vicksburg " color line." policy. There was a bitter struggle, and the amendment was adopted by but one majority. Yet that majority was Mr. Fountain Barksdale, the same who had so gallantly fallen in line with " our nigros" and rescued my brother Charles on a certain occasion from a " murderer's cell " in that " common jail," and from that kuklux band. When I heard that, I was tempted to go straight to Mr. Barksdale, and resign my " dictatorship " in his favor. But, while that would have brought relief to me, and to my anxious wife, it would have been a betrayal of my party associates; desertion in the face of the enemy. It sprang from gratitude to him and my joy that, after all, my planting had taken deep root, and might continue to thrive even though I should be destroyed. It lasted for only a brief moment, and henceforward I saw only the martyr's crown.

The changed manner of the enemy throughout the State so alarmed Republicans that a hasty consultation was held at the capital and a committee dispatched to visit the President, lay all the facts before him, and learn what would be his course in the event of a general insurrection against the constituted authorities. Returning, this committee reported, and their words were passed from one to another of the local leaders, that the President had assured them of his full sympathy and had promised to protect our government and the right of Republicans to vote, to the utmost of his authority. But he had also said that the people of the North had grown tired of these appeals for help from the South. It would therefore be necessary that it should be clearly such a case as, under the Constitution, would justify his exercise of the Federal power in our behalf. To make such a case it must be made clearly to appear that the enemy were actually using force, not merely threatening to do so, and, that, its application was so widespread and violent that the State authorities were powerless to control it.

This report was perfectly satisfactory to " we all " Republicans. There were few cowards in our ranks. Resting secure in " Grant's promise," for so the President's assurances were regarded, they prepared to meet the enemy, feeling, that should they be killed, their death would not have been in vain.

In Yazoo, our party had never before been so united. The conduct of the irreconcilables after the death of Mr. Hilliard and especially that of those who had won victory at Vicksburg upon the color-line, had greatly alarmed the members of the A. M. E. Church, and they were now among my staunchest supporters. So far as I knew I was the unanimous choice of our party for re-election.

No Republican meetings had yet been held in the county preparatory to the approaching election, when all the county officials, members of the legislature, a State treasurer and members of Congress were to be chosen. So, as preliminary thereto a meeting of our county committee was called. At that meeting the preparations being made by the irreconcilables for carrying the election by force, were freely commented on by all.

The publication in the *Banner* of that production of Eddin and Sands, was viewed with some alarm. The *Banner* had

not been a sensational paper. No one present knew or had
ever heard of either of the persons. All knew that the
statements about arms were false, and believed it was a for-
gery.

A telegram had been already sent to the State authorities
to that effect, and the human hornet had called its author
to "personal account" for his "presumption."

All knew of the organization of white independent military companies, and of the very extensive arming that had
been going on. Some had seen whole boxes of Winchester
rifles and shot-guns, brought into the county for distribution
to these companies. Mr. James M. Dickson and Mr. Houston Burrus mentioned an effort made by the human hornet,
by tumbling before them as they walked down Main street
a pile of dry-goods boxes, to compel them to quit the sidewalk, and walk in the street, or fight. It was 1868 come
again, but our party was stronger now than then. One of
the members of that committee was an ex-confederate captain ;
another, our Senator, and the colored men upon it could
read and write. All the important officers of the county
were in the hands of our party. Ames was governor, Grant
was still President, and we had his promise. So these brave
and loyal committeemen unanimously agreed upon the following:

"*Resolved*, By the Republican Executive Committee of Yazoo
County, this August 30, 1875, that a delegate convention be, and is
hereby, called to assemble at Wilson's Hall, in Yazoo City, on Wednesday, September 22, 1875, and to that end it is hereby ordered that
a convention be called in each of the several beats of the county on
the days and places, to wit." * * *

There had never been in the county a more harmonious
meeting, and the strongest feeling of fidelity to each other
and of devotion to our cause prevailed throughout its session. The Yazoo City Republican Club would hold a meeting at Wilson's Hall on the night of September 1st, and I
was requested to be present and make a speech indicative of
the policy of the party in the forthcoming campaign. This

I promised to do, and due announcement of the fact was made.

Now let the reader turn back, again read the correspondence at the close of the preceding chapter, and, if he has not already done so, compare the spelling of such difficult words for beginners as "preparing" and "sure" and others all correctly spelled, with "u" for you, "newse" for news, "cum" for come, "liv" for live, and "thrue" for true. Also, note that the words " Yazoo City, July " are not only correctly spelled, but also, that the punctuation and style of the whole, words, and figures following, is perfect.

I made diligent inquiry for both Eddin and Sands, but could find no such persons. There were not only not sixteen hundred army guns in the entire county, there were not sixteen, in the possession of colored people. There were no armed military or other companies or organizations amongst them. The colored people of Yazoo were wholly without arms except now and then an old pistol or squirrel-gun.

Many good people at the North have blamed them for that, as though it was an evidence of their incapacity for self-government. These friends forget. They forget that when the war closed General Howard and other Federal officers having authority in the South advised the freed people not to purchase guns, because it might offend their old masters, and get them into all sorts of trouble; that every missionary sent among them advised the same course, and, that General Grant, and all of us did. These friends also further forget that every one giving such advice accompanied it with an assurance that the Government at Washington would protect them against violence from the rebels."

Notwithstanding these facts have passed into history, and, notwithstanding the white people of Yazoo knew that the colored people were wholly unarmed, the *Democrat* published that fraudulent communication and commented upon it as follows:*

*I have lost or mislaid the comments of the *Banner*, which were of similar purport.

"THE NEGROES ARMED—THEY EXPECT TO HAVE A FIGHT, AND ARE
PREPARED FOR IT—FOREWARNED IS FOREARMED.

"We clip the following article from the Winona *Advance*; it speaks
for itself. It has been our opinion all along that the negroes were
all armed or arming. * * * We call upon the young men of this
city to form a company* for the protection of their homes and fami-
lies†. For we truly believe it must come sooner or later, and at the
first fire let these political leeches that pass as whites be the first to
fall. They urge on the negro, and they should suffer."

Did the *Democrat* believe that " the negroes were all armed
or arming ?"

" No."

"How do I know ?"

" Because if it were so the *Democrat* would have made the
discovery in a different way, and from a different source than
Alabama."

Four-fifths of the colored population were living constantly,
day and night, under the eye of white employers, or white
overseers. It would be impossible for them to have brought
sixteen hundred, or even one hundred, army guns into the
county without discovery.

The *Democrat* knew that.

The *Herald*, Democratic, published the same correspondence, *six days after its appearance in the Banner*, and after
ample time had elapsed for its editor to have ascertained
whether the statements made were true, and commented as
follows :

" SIXTEEN HUNDRED ARMY GUNS—THE NEGROES OF YAZOO 'PRE-
PARING FOR THE ELECTION AND ALSO FOR RIOTS '—THE ' COL-
ORED PEOPLE OF STARTTIA ' PREPARING TO TAKE THE WAR-PATH
—READ! READ! READ!

"The letter published below was sent to a friend of ours by a prominent lawyer and most worthy citizen of Demopolis, Ala., who vouches
for the genuineness of the document. One would infer by reading it
that the colored voters of Yazoo are ' preparing for the election very
fast and also for riots;' and further that they are ' buying ammunition in Yazoo City,' ' have 1,600 army guns,' and are ' prepared
for business.' The purchasing of army guns and ammunition and

*That company had already been formed.
†This meant only their white families, of course.

preparing for riots is a lovely way, indeed, to get ready for elections. But as the dapper little son-in-law of the national spoon-thief, Ben Butler, religiously believes that the death of twenty-five negroes is really necessary to the success of the radical party in the present canvass, perhaps it is his emissaries who are putting mischief in the heads of these black people, in the hope that radicalism would in the end be benefitted thereby. The original of the letter published below is in our possession, also the letter of the gentleman into whose hands it fell, and who promptly forwarded it to Colonel Money,* of the Winona *Advance*."

Shortly afterward, a colored man was found living on the human hornet's plantation who was said to have confessed that he wrote that letter. But as he could hardly write, and could scarcely spell at all, no one believed him.

But I am content to let the sequel show the object of that production. I well knew the place where the irreconcilables met in "consultation." It was there a well-known leading church member, chairman of the white man's committee, made his memorable declaration: "The only way to get rid of Morgan is to kill him. We've tried coaxing and bribery. We've tried to drive him. Meanwhile his hold is growing stronger and stronger. He must be killed."

I had lately several times seen the human hornet coming from there, and once, just before the day of our meeting, we met and passed each other on the street. His face was so white and pale, his lips so clinched and livid, his gait so nervous and meteoric that I shall never forget the shock he gave me, nor the sulphuric odor in his trail. From that moment I believed that he had been chosen to kill me when the opportunity should arrive, and I also believed that the fraudulent correspondence was intended as a cover for the crime. It had already been published throughout the State and telegraphed North. On the day of the meeting, the pastor of the A. M. E. Church, of the church on the hill we helped to build, and other leading colored men, came to me with further evidence of the purpose of the enemy to attack our meeting that night, and many craved my consent for the

*A Democratic candidate for Congress.

Republicans to go armed. This I not only refused to give, but forbade them to do so, and I expressly advised them to carry their Bibles instead.

They saw as clearly as I that the storm was at hand, but they could not know as I did its extent and power. It was my duty to shield them and preserve the peace. At the same time, as a citizen and a candidate for re-election, it was my duty to attend the meeting and to make the speech.

" Why not postpone it ?"

" Because that would have been a surrender, and would have encouraged the enemy to further aggressions. Besides, we had promise of aid from the Executive of the nation, upon the express condition that we went forward with our canvass, and were attacked with such violence as the State government would be powerless to suppress or control."

Similar meetings would be held in other parts of the State, about the same time. Our only escape from the issue was in a cowardly surrender.

" We all" Republicans in Yazoo would die if necessary for our cause.

Would the enemy attack us ?

I believed they would, in some manner, that night. But we had often before passed through similar trials by the exercise of patience, forbearance, and self-control. I believed I should be able to exercise those virtues on this occasion as fully as I had done so many times before. But would *all* the others ? I had urged them to do so, as the only means of escape from actual violence. There had been many tests of their ability to do so. I believed that they would. There was some consolation for me in the fact that my wife and children were absent at our summer home at Holly Springs,* and knew nothing of my peril.

On my way to the meeting the human hornet crossed my path, and there was the same sulphuric odor in his trail that I had the last time before observed. The hall was lighted

*This was a frequent resort for persons unable to go any farther North, and w o wished to escape the summer epidemic of the swamps.

by small tallow dips. Except upon the speaker's platform, where there was a lamp and several candles, the light was dim.

There were present our Senator, the ex-confederate captain, and several more "native white Republicans," perhaps a hundred colored men, the mass of whom were in the raised seats in front of the platform, and one of my deputies, an ex-confederate officer.

I had just commenced my speech when there filed into the hall, in regular order, as if by preconcert and arrangement, some seven or eight of the most substantial white men of the town, and took their seats all together immediately in front of me.

This recalled to my mind the recommendation of the Raymond *Gazette*, for a "committee of ten discreet, intelligent and reputable citizens" and so forth. Following this "committee" came the human hornet, Fritz Halder and others of the violent class, who lounged about inside the doorway. Almost from the first the former began interrupting me, and sometimes to dispute my statements. This was politely objected to by some one in the audience. But I suggested that they be allowed to ask questions, and I promised to try and answer. At this point the human hornet withdrew, and almost immediately returned, bringing with him a reckless, worthless colored man, whose property had been levied on by the delinquent tax collector,[*] for unpaid taxes.

This colored man found his way to near the middle of the audience, and then began a bitter denunciation of me. He was requested to sit down, whereupon the human hornet rushed to his side, and while in the attitude of drawing his pistol, proclaimed the right of the fellow to go on, and his purpose to protect him in it. Even this did not disturb the Republicans in the audience, all of whom preserved a calm and orderly exterior, however great their indignation, and I felt so confident of their ability to maintain this attitude,

* R. B. Mitchell, the ex-confederate captain, then present in the hall.

that I was encouraged by.it to persevere in the policy of submission to the insults and wrongs of the enemy, as Charles
and the General had so successfully done in 1867 and 1868,
particularly in their Sabbath-school.

I felt sure that it was all done to provoke some of us to
resistance, when, as during the reign of the kuklux, they
would seize upon it as a sufficient pretext for any violence
they might choose to inflict. Therefore I proceeded in what
I had to say with great caution. As a careful surgeon seeking among the vital organs of the human frame for some
murderous bullet will exercise his greatest skill and caution
to not cut them, and will take care lest he cause needless
pain, I endeavored with all the skill and tenderness of which
I was capable, to get hold of the heart-strings of the enemy
without shocking them, and thus find my way to their intellects. But, as one walking from shore to shore upon a rope
spanning Niagara's chasm must realize how slender indeed is
the line between him and the river of death below, I could
not help feeling that all our planting on that old stubble-
ground hung, as my life did, by a single thread, and so
whenever there was an interruption, or the enemy appeared
ruffled, I would cease speaking until the surface at least was
calmed. Thus I hoped to pass safely through. But should
I reach the other shore ?

The result showed that I had miscalculated the extent of
the enemy's trust in their majority in the House of Representatives at Washington.

I had not believed that they would dare to kill unless
some sort cf violent resistance to their methods was offered
by some one. There was the weak point in my armor, and
it was at that point they surprised me. For after the battle
of *nerve* had proceeded for perhaps half an hour, certain of
the " committee " appeared to get restless, the hornet became
exasperated, and upon my mentioning the name of the chair-

man of our board of supervisors,* he exclaimed in accents
of fire: "He's a thief! he's a thief!"

Some person sitting at the right of the platform, and full
twenty-five feet from the hornet, replied, "Oh! no! no!"†
rapidly.

Instantly the hornet, with the rapidity of a meteor,
and with pistol in hand rushed toward the person. Then
there was a shot, and then a volley, all within an instant of time. The lights on that side the hall went out;
those upon the platform burned brightly.

There are those who refuse to believe in special provi-
dences.

What was this?

At that moment, as from the first, I believed that I stood
for the best thought, the highest purpose and the noblest
impulses of American freemen. I also believed that " committee," as a whole, together with the hornet, and the
sleuth-hounds in attendance, at the same time stood as from
the first they, too, had done, the loyal representatives of the
same thought, purpose, and impulse, that had made an armed
camp of the South in defense of secession, slavery, and miscegenation, and, when the former was overthrown and the
camps disbanded, had pursued their main object, first in the
guise of kuklux, later in disguise as National Republicans,
and now, again, because Ohio and Massachusetts had gone
Democratic, and they held the purse-strings at Washington,
were once more openly in arms in defense of that object.‡

I did not run. On the contrary, observing the violent
movement of the hornet, I turned toward him and commanded peace. At that instant the first shot was fired, and
before I could take two steps toward them, the volley. I
stood, fronting them, in the full glare of the lights upon the

---

*This man was the most popular Republican with the enemy there was in the
county.
†Afterwards the enemy said that the words were " it's a lie."
‡The spokesman, or leading member of that " committee," was the very person who
ruined poor Susie Poindexter, and who afterward boasted of his skill in capturing
" Morgan's black pets."

platform, when that volley was fired, and the hornet and his
aids were not more than twenty feet distant.

That volley was fired directly at me, and each bullet was
aimed to kill.

What was it ?

The end piece of the little plain, pine board table,* at
which I was standing when the first shot was fired, afterward contained three bullet holes. The window facing and
wall at the back of the platform was "literally peppered"
with bullet marks. The day following, when asked by his
admiring associates, "why in h—l he allowed Morgan to
escape," the hornet, puzzled and confused by his failure to
kill me, declared:

"I stood just so"—describing his position at the front and
right of the platform, which put him directly in my front as
I turned and commanded the peace, and was not twenty feet
distant from me—"and emptied every barrel of my two
navies at the ——"

He stood in the dim light, while I stood upon the platform in the bright light.

What was it ?

Eight days afterward the *Banner*, commenting on the
situation in Yazoo, and upon my supposed whereabouts, said:

" He abruptly disappeared from public life on Wednesday night,
September 1, while delivering a peace-lecture on the color-line, and
as has been discovered, he took refuge in the negro church at the
foot of the hill until last Friday morning, when he hastened to Cassius Ames, to whom he cries to help him ere he sinks. Cassius can't
do much for him, and he is sinking pretty rapidly himself."

From Yazoo *Banner*, September 2, 1875 :

"A RIOT IN YAZOO CITY—THE NATURAL RESULT OF RADICAL
TEACHING.

*   *   *   *   *   *   *

" Many shots were fired, perhaps more than forty.

" When the smoke of battle cleared off, there laid on the floor Dick
Mitchell, who died in a few hours, and W. H. Foote, the circuit

*This end piece was about eight inches wide and three feet in length.

clerk, supposed to be badly shot. We regret the death of Dick Mitchell. He was a brave man, but forfeited his life by joining Morgan and our enemies, and drawing his sword in their defense.

"The shooting ended at Wilson's Hall; the fire bells were rung and the city picketed. At 11 P. M. all was quiet. Morgan and Everett left the city.

" The citizens met to-day (Thursday) with Colonel Garnett Andrews commanding—with a full staff—and two full companies are organized, which will keep the peace of the city. All business is suspended.

"LATER.

"11 O'CLOCK, A. M.—Taylor's cavalry, one hundred strong, reached the city about 10 o'clock. Other companies are reported on the road. Stay at home, gentlemen, we have two full companies organized here, well officered and equipped, and will hold in check all enemies, foreign or domestic.

" All is quiet now."

———

" FROM YAZOO COUNTY—STILL PREPARED FOR EMERGENCIES—THE RADICAL LEADERS NON EST—MORE TROUBLE ANTICIPATED.

"*Special to the Vicksburg Herald, September 4:*

"YAZOO CITY, *Sept.* 3, 1875.

'' The city keeps up its warlike appearance. Taylor's scouts were out through the county yesterday, and report things quiet. Dr. B. R. Holmes brought in a company of men last night and reported ready for duty. There is hardly a negro to be seen on the streets The two Morgans and Everett, and all the white negro leaders have not been seen. The only hope is that they have left the county for the county's good. It has been reported that negro meetings were held in different portions of the county last night. Trouble is looked for, but we are ready to meet it. Morgan's hiding place remains unknown. No business doing.   C. KNARF."

From the Yazoo City *Democrat*, September 7, 1875:

" On last Wednesday, September 1, it was freely circulated on the streets that A. T. Morgan would make a speech that night having for his subject the " Color-Line." From what we learned, every one of both parties was invited to attend.

'' As the shades of night set in, beating of drums was heard for the purpose of rallying negroes to hear the speech of their lord and master, A. T. Morgan. The crowd gathered at Wilson's Hall and the speech began. The crowd was largely negro, with some ten or fifteen of our leading and most law-abiding citizens. At the beginning of Morgan's address he invi ed all present who disbelieved any thing he might say, to rise and answer him. During his speech, a negro by the name of Robinson, a Democrat, rose, to answer Morgan when the negroes began to yell, 'put him out! put him out! he is a Democrat!' Two or three gentlemen present then rose and said Robinson shall speak, and we dare anybody to try to put him out. There was some excitement over it, and pistols were drawn, but finally things were quieted. Morgan then resumed his speech, and spoke in loud praise of the board of supervisors, when one of the gentlemen present answered that the board was no account, or something to that effect. Morgan then said, 'Why, there is Captain Bedwell (one of the board), you can have no objection to him.' Mr. Dixon then replied, 'Bedwell is a thief.' When a negro said 'That's a lie.' Mr. Dixon then stepped forward and said, 'Show me the man that said that.' and continued walking towards the place the voice came from. When he neared the spot a negro, Jim Clark, drew his pistol and fired, the ball striking the floor. A general firing then began, which resulted in the shooting of R. B. Mitchell, a white Republican, who died at 3 o'clock that morning, and the shooting of W. H. Foote, the negro circuit clerk, who is still suffering from the wound. The firing caused some few to turn pale, and the rapid motion of many legs. The negroes were panic-stricken, some few going down the steps head first, while the greater portion, with the Morgan Bros. to set the example, went out of the windows.''

From Yazoo City *Herald* (Democratic), September 10, 1875:

" WHAT IMPUDENCE.

"Our dapper little Governor Ames comes to the front with a proc-lamation ordering the disbandment of all the military companies now organized in the State. If he has brains enough to know his right hand from his left, he ought to know that no more attention will be paid to his proclamation than the moon is popularly supposed to pay to the baying of a sheep-killing dog.''

From same :

" DISBAND.

"Ames emerged from his hole the other day and staid out long enough to say to the companies in Yazoo and other counties, 'dis-band.' But at the present writing they are not disbanding worth a cent nor do they have any idea of doing such a thing.''

CHAPTER LXIX.

AFTER THE BATTLE—WEARY WAITING—MY NEW STRONGHOLD—
WHAT WAS IT—LET FRED ANSWER—GRANT'S UNFULFILLED
"PROMISE"—MORE "SUPERIAH STRATEGY" A REWARD FOR
MORGAN, DEAD OR ALIVE—THE ENEMY IN POSSESSION—FAITH-
FUL FRIENDS—A RIDE FOR LIFE—"PROFOUND PEACE" IN MIS-
SISSIPPI—WHERE THOSE "SIXTEEN HUNDRED ARMY GUNS"
WERE—WHAT MIGHT HAVE BEEN—A BLOODY GROUND—THE
PART ALABAMA TOOK IN IT—THE PART SENATORS GEORGE AND
LAMAR AND MR. BARKSDALE TOOK IN IT—MISSISSIPPI CAM-
PAIGN LIES EQUALLED ONLY BY CAMPAIGN MURDERS—A DEMI-
GOD—THE BRAVEST OF THE BRAVE.

DID I shoot? Yes, twice; but while standing thus in the
bright light upon the platform the light in which the
hornet and his party were went out.

It was said that the enemy put out the lights. I am inclined to think, however, that the dim light of the few tallow dips upon that side of the hall was obscured by the dense
smoke from the rapid discharge of the enemy's pistols. At
all events, it became so dark there that I could see no one.
Then it was that I got out of range of their pistols by way
of the window at the back of the platform, to a ladder
which reached from it over a narrow court to the roof of
the hotel adjoining. This ladder gave way under me and I

fell to the pavement, full twelve feet below. Shocked and dazed for a moment, I quickly recovered and climbed back into the hall. While doing so I heard the market-house bell striking. It was unlike the fire signal, or any other that I had ever heard upon it.

The hall was not yet entirely empty. Men were still hurrying from it by the rear stair-way, and Mr. Mitchell lay at full length upon the floor. I spoke to Dick (every one called him Dick), and it would seem that he recognized my voice, for he raised his eyes to mine.

It was a murderous bullet. Entering the neck from the rear, it ranged downward, touching the spine in its course. The pistol from which it was fired had been placed so close to the neck, that the flame from the powder ignited his coat-collar, and powder was burned into the skin.

It was said that at the moment the hornet started toward the man who had presumed to question his charge against Mr. Bedwell, Dick and Fritz Halder were seated together upon a dry-goods box. Afterward, as many still remember, Halder went from store front to store front along Main street, boasting, "I killed Dick Mitchell, I killed Dick Mitchell."

Mr. Foote was badly wounded in the side, but had made his escape. There were others wounded, but Dick was the only one killed. Our Senator and all the other white Republicans had left the hall. My deputy, Mr. Redding, remained in care of Dick. He at once informed me that the hornet and his party left the hall by the front way so soon as I escaped through the window. I had not been two minutes here when some colored men, who were searching for me, came and informed me that the main street was full of armed white men, and that they were searching for me. On the street at the rear of the hall were quite a large number of my colored friends who remained, to "die by you, Colonel." They were not armed; some few may have had pistols. But what could we do against that mob of whites, some of whom I could see, with guns in their hands, hurrying toward the market-house.

These friends of mine did not fail to comprehend the meaning of it all. They meant what they said. They would have followed me in an effort to arrest the hornet and his aids, but that I would not attempt to do.

Finding my way home, I had not been there five minutes when the house was thronged with colored friends, some of whom had stood by our little garrison in its darkest hours, and among them the pastor of that other church. All were anxious that I should make a stand and fight the mob. But to their prayers and entreaties I held firmly to my resolve, and advised them all to go home, go to bed, advise every colored man they could see or could get word to, to do the same, and, upon no pretext whatever to come to town.

" What yo' goin' to do, sheriff?"

" Stay right here in my own house."

" Day'll be y'here and kill yo' sure."

" Never mind me, you all go home, as I tell you."

" Never 'low to leave the Colonel that way—never! Die first!"

Then I reasoned with them, pointed out to them the folly of fighting those well-armed companies, and reminded them that every one of our white friends had vanished. After reason and persuasion failed, I commanded them. Then they departed; some cursing, some crying. The last one had but just disappeared through the back yard, when tramp tramp, tramp, sounded the tread of the hornet's company, upon the pavement, approaching my house. This was my castle. Fortunately, only a few days before, I had purchased a fresh supply of cartridges for my Spencer rifle, and with this, and other weapons ready to hand (the very same we had armed our ancient stronghold with), I would be able to make at least a show of resistance. Now they were upon the gallery and banging against the door. My hostler, Frederick Harris, opened it and they entered.

" Whar's Colonel Mawgin ?"

" Doa'n know, Mar's Dixon, 'deed I don't, Kunnel hav'n bin y'here senz de meetin' I 'low."

Evidently they believed him, for, after spying about upon the first floor a moment, they went away regularly as they came, tramp, tramp, tramp, keeping step for all the world just like a company of trained soldiers.

What was it?

Let Fred answer.

Scarcely had they departed when I heard his soft step upon the narrow stairway leading to my stronghold. In an instant his black face appeared, his eyes shining through his grateful tears like two stars, and his words, just above a whisper, low and solemn:

" Praise de Lord, Kunnel! praise de Lord! I jes prayed an' prayed, an' He answered my prar, an' comed an' stood 'afo' me dar, an' put de words in my mouth, and done sont Dixon away."

But all night long I heard every little while the tramp of squads of men marching.

The next day, looking out from the window of my stronghold, I could see them. They were as well armed, and under as perfect discipline, apparently, as any troops of our late armies were. Including the cavalry company from the country, there were not less than three hundred armed white men in the town. Their weapons were Winchester rifles, needle-guns, double barrelled shot-guns and pistols.

There were no armed colored men anywhere that I could see, or hear of, and scarcely any at all to be seen upon the streets. This was a great relief to me, for it showed their faith in me, and took away the only pretext there was for the presence of armed whites, whose numbers, nevertheless, were constantly increasing. The enemy promptly caused a warrant to be issued, charging me with attempting to murder Dixon, placed it in the hands of the hornet and his aids, offered a large reward for me, dead or alive, visited the capital of the State, Holly Springs, and other points where I possibly might be found, in search of me, marched to the court-house and took possession of it and of my office—upon the ground that the sheriff was a fugitive from justice—assembled the board of aldermen of the town and caused an appropriation of a thousand dollars to be made for pay of the soldiers, established a cordon of pickets around the town, with instructions to allow no colored man without a pass to enter or depart from it, and by such, and various and sundry other means, usurped full and complete authority. Still " our nigros " refused to " rise."

The details of this insurrection would, doubtless, make " mighty interesting reading " for the general public. They would fill a volume. I have not space for them.

Trusting in the President's "promise," I had remained in the town because, when the United States troops should come, it would be essential to the success of their mission that some semblance of lawful government remained. I believed that the presence of no more than two United States soldiers, with authority from the President to act for the preservation of peace, and for the protection of the lawful government, would be sufficient to cause the enemy to disperse to their hiding places, when I could once more resume the functions and duties of my office, Republicans might once more return to their homes, and we could proceed with our canvass. Once it was rumored about that the troops were coming. The effect of this rumor was enough to induce the hornet and his company to quit the court house, and abandon my office; but it was a false report. Immediately afterward the town resumed its " war-like appearance," and the enemy's methods were resumed with renewed vigor.

From my hiding place I could see the rows of bright, shining army-guns near the market-house, stacked, and with sentries on guard over them, precisely as I have so often seen them in our old army camps, and on our marches against the rebels, in those other war days.

I could also see armed bodies of mounted men riding out on their " scouting " expeditions to the country for the purpose of suppressing " nigro risings " that were " about to occur." These parties usually went " armed to the teeth,', and carrying ropes at their saddles.

During all these long and weary days of waiting and
watching, my friends in the town remained true to me.
Some were in the ranks of the enemy, and rode with the
hornet on his raids. They knew my hiding place, and,
whenever the enemy came too near, drew them upon some
other trail. But this could not always last.

On the eleventh day, the leaders of the enemy became
convinced that I was still in the town, and arrangements
were making for a final search. This time they would invade
my stronghold. They had kept a vigilant watch upon it for
several days, and the four corners of that square were guarded
with extra pickets; but my friends were keen and watchful.
That night just before the hour for posting the pickets, I
was to endeavor to escape from town. The plan was for
Fred to have my sorrel mare saddled and ready with the
stable door open, and nothing left for me to do but mount
and ride away. Friends were stationed on each corner
between my stronghold and the stable, with pre-arranged
signals in case of detection or immediate danger.

So, disguised in some old clothes, at that hour when the
shadows of our long Yazoo twilight cover the old town with
a mask, I walked from my brother's house full two squares
to the stable, found faithful sorrel, just as faithful Fred had
promised she should be, mounted her and rode away. People whom I knew were passing to and fro. But none knew
me, until just as I began the ascent by the plank road of the
long hill back of the town, just opposite the little church we
helped to build, where a sentry with musket at a "right shoulder
shift," one of the enemy, startled perhaps by my mare out of
his listless, drowsy gait, recognized me.

What was it ?

As though he had received a direct revelation, this " white,"
armed with a Winchester rifle, turned on his heel and ran
away as rapidly as his legs could carry him towards headquarters, the market-house.

Now I was free, for sorrel was a fleet-footed beast.

Nine miles out I passed some friends, colored people, who

were having a prayer-meeting at the church near by. They warned me that Bentonia was guarded in the same way as Yazoo City, by a white company, and one of their number volunteered to guide me by a circuitous route, through the fields, to a point beyond the town, thus enabling me to escape that danger.* Before 10 A. M., the next day, I was at the capital. Here I found our Senator, and also found refugees from all parts of the State. The State was one vast camp of armed white leaguers. In Hinds County† as many as one hundred Republicans, it was said, had been killed. The Governor's office was thronged with men who had come to him for help. Yet only the day before General J. Z. George, then chairman of the State Democratic Executive Committee, now a United States Senator, sent the following message. I give it with editorial comments, just as it appeared in the Vicksburg *Herald*.

From Vicksburg *Herald*, September:

.'' STRIKE, BUT HEAR!

' Referring to the lying dispatch which Ames, the murderer,‡ induced Harney, the negro sheriff of Hinds County, to send to Washington, General J. Z. George, the chairman of the executive committee of the Democratic party of Mississippi, dispatched the following:

'' JACKSON, MISS, *Sept*. 11.

'' *To Hon. Edward Pierrepont, Attorney General United States America.*
' *Washington, D. C.:*

*   *   *   *   *

'' The people of Mississippi claim the right of American citizens to be heard before they are condemned. I reassert that perfect peace prevails throughout the State, and that there is no danger of disturbance unless invited by the State authorities, which I hope they will not do.   '' J. Z. GEORGE,

'' *Chairman Dem. State Ex. Com.*''

From Yazoo City *Democrat*, September 14, 1875:

''Let unanimity of sentiment pervade the minds of men. Let invincible determination be depicted on every countenance. Send forth from our deliberate assembly of the 18th, the soul-stirring an-

---

*I afterward learned that I had not been gone from that "nigro church" twenty minutes when a body of mounted cavalry from Bentonia rode up and inquired for me.
†The capital county.
‡ Meaning Governor Ames.

nouncement that Mississippians shall rule Mississippi, though the
heavens fall. Then will woe, irretrievable woe, betide the radical
tatterdemalions. Hit them hip and thigh, everywhere and at all
times. Carry the election peaceably if we can, forcibly if we must.''

From same:

"God speed the day when Mississippians shall rule Mississippi,
and the Alonzo Phelps and Murrels of radicalism shall find their
fate in a 'stout rope' and a short shrift. Then will 'peace reign in
Warsaw.'

" The time for begging colored men to vote with us has passed.

" A. T. Morgan has turned up in Jackson. The *Pilot* says he slipped out at night, and we think it was a d—d good thing for Morgan.''

From Yazoo City *Banner*, September 16, 1875:

'' Morgan, the murderer, by the aid of some of his white radicals
here, skipped out of town last Monday night.

" Young man, your actions of last Monday night was noticed. Better keep your optics well open. A word to the wise, etc., etc. ''*

From same, September 23, 1875:

" Creswell, of Piney, was in town again on last Tuesday, but has
failed to join our club. Our correspondent ' M.' has one eye on him.†

" Morgan, the murderer; Bedwell, the little man in search of
health; Everett, the man who it is supposed shot twice in Wilson's
Hall, are all yet—to use the *Democrat's* phrase—still 'rusticating.'

" We see by the last *Democrat*, a journal published in Yazoo City,
that a colored gentleman of African ways and means was found hung
some three miles below here. *Hung by his own color, 'tis said.*''

From same:

" LATEST NEWS.

" Buck political negroes gone off with Morgan—wenches wedded to
carpet-baggers, and can't work out—young negroes ain't worth a d—n.
No cotton pickers to be found for the big crop. Ain't we in a hell of
a fix ?''

Special to Vicksburg *Herald:*

"JACKSON, *September* 25.

'' The following message was this day telegraphed to Attorney General Pierrepont:

* This was meant for Charles Fawn, a " Yankee," who was killed a few days later.
He assisted me to escape.
† Creswell was a Southern Republican who would not join the Democratic " Club."

" HEADQUARTERS EXECUTIVE COMMITTE OF
" DEMOCRATIC PARTY OF MISSISSIPPI,
" JACKSON, *Sept.* 25, 1875.

" *To Attorney General Pierrepont, Washington, D. C.:*

* * * * *

" The undersigned members of the Democratic State Convention,
assembled here to-day, from every part of the State, take pleasure in
assuring you that everywhere throughout the State, the most profound peace and good order prevails.

(Signed)   JAMES Z. GEORGE, *Chairman,*
       H. H. CHALMERS.
       EDWARD C. WALTHALL.
       JNO. A. P. CAMPBELL.
       THOMAS B. SYKES.
       JNO. A. BINFORD.
       UPTON M. YOUNG.
       J. B. CHRISMAN.
       H. M. STREET."

Not only was Mississippi one vast armed camp of white
leaguers, all the surrounding States were ready to " send
their aid " to their brethren in Mississippi.   On this subject
the Mobile *Register* said:

" If the tocsin of war is sounded by Ames he will find men, money
and arms trooping across our border to defend our kinsmen and our
trade.   This is no vain and idle threat.   The moment Ames organizes
his militia let the Democratic and Conservative young men organize
bands of minute•men in every county.*   Let them stand by their
arms."

The Governor's intention to send two companies of militia
into Yazoo was abandoned because of the greatly superior
force of the enemy, some idea of which will be gained from
the following:

From the Yazoo City *Democrat*, October 9, 1875:

" A SPECK OF WAR—PROMPT ACTION OF OUR PEOPLE.

" Last Monday evening the startling announcement flashed over
the wires to this place from Jackson that A. T. Morgan would leave
that city by special train for Vaughn's Station, with a white and
negro militia company, for the purpose of invading Yazoo County
and reinstating himself as sheriff.

*These " bands " were already organized, already standing by their arms, and ready,
all along the Alabama border, to "move at the click of the wire."   Some could not be
restrained, and actually marched into Mississippi.

" A county meeting was immediately called to take such steps as were necessary to meet the emergency. The meeting was held at eight o'clock Tuesday morning in the spacious cotton-shed at the landing. Of its proceedings it is unnecessary to speak. The determination depicted upon every countenance showed, conclusively, the one sentiment of our people.

"At 11 o'clock on that day a company of thirty-five men left our city, commanded by the intrepid Captain Henry M. Dixon. (The company was greatly augmented after it left.)

" This company was joined at Benton by Captain H. L. Taylor and his gallant boys; Dr. B. R. Holmes' Dover and neighborhood company; Captain Jessie E. Bell's Sartartia company, commanded by Captain Johnson; Captain Samuel Griffin's Piney and Tcheva Creek company ; Captains Smith's and Stubblefield's Benton companies, and Captain Mitchell's Deasonville—as brave a regiment as ever met an enemy—all under the command of that gallant and experienced soldier, Captain H. L. Taylor.

"The companies were distributed as follows: Captain Dixon's command, then numbering 50, was ordered immediately to Vaughn's Station as an advance guard, and reached their destination about twilight. They were reinforced early on Wednesday morning by Dr. Holmes' company, fifty men.

"Captain Mitchell's company was stationed at Deasonville.

" The balance of the command halted at Benton, the whole numbering between eight and nine hundred men, all mounted and variously armed.

" Headquarters were established at Deasonville, with couriers at proper stations.

"Drs. J. P. McCormick and J. D. Burch, surgeon of this city, were at the station with Captain Dixon's company, Dr. R. C. Henderson at Deasonville, and Dr. W. C. Smith at Benton.

"Never was a command more properly distributed, under better control, and more eager for the fray, than these brave and gallant men last Tuesday night and Wednesday. And we venture the opinion that had Morgan and his invaders attempted a landing in our county, Vaughn's Station would have been known in the future annals of Mississippi as the Bloody Ground.

" The command remained until it was ascertained that the county would not be invaded, when they quietly returned to their homes.

" All honor is due to Commodore Birmingham and Captain Mitchell, of the station, who threw open their houses and stables, and fed both man and beast, for which they would not receive a dime.

" In the meantime the people of Yazoo City were not idle. On Tuesday four companies were organized and commanded by Colonel Andrews, Captain C. V. Gwin, Captain E. Scharfer, and Captain Owen Brown, with Colonel W. H. Luse as battalion commander.''

Two of every four of the officers of those companies, including the regimental " field and staff," were practical miscegenationists, polygamous, unrepentant rebels. The same is true of one-half of the rank and file. They were in armed rebellion against the State government. Their brethren in Alabama, represented by the Mobile *Register*, were not only standing by their arms, ready to move at the click of the wire, but had chartered trains to convey them to the " scene of conflict."

Others like them and like those in Yazoo were ready in Warren, Madison, Hinds, Holmes, and other counties to do the same thing. In the face of this array the Governor's two companies of militia, one " white," the other " black," could not contend. It was certainly not the fault of the colored company that they did not try.

My old friend, Charles Caldwell, was its captain. They were at all times ready to go.

Up to the day I left the county there had been but one person killed, so far as I could learn.

The colored people had remained perfectly passive, and the independent armed companies had all their own way.

What follows relating to the doings of the enemy in Yazoo, I shall have to state upon hearsay. I shall, however, set down nothing but that which came to me from perfectly reliable friends, from official sources, and through the press.

Shortly after I left, as I have described, it would seem that the colored men became somewhat restless. It was reported that some were lying in wait below the town to shoot the hornet. The following day " Captain " Taylor's company of cavalry rode through that neighborhood. Next day the body of a Republican was found hanging to a tree. Here is the way the *Democrat* noticed it :

" A colored man, named Horace Hammond, was found hung some three miles below here on Thursday. Whether he committed suicide or not is a mooted question, but the following verdict of the coroner's jury settles the business:

"We, the jury, find that Horace Hammond came to his death by hanging by parties unknown.

W. A. SHERARD, *Foreman*,
MICAJAH PARKER,
ELISHA PARKER,
GEORGE MOORE,
WILLIAM SHORTRIDGE,
HENRY WEATHERS, *Jurors*."

Such scenes soon became of frequent occurrence, until leading Republicans had been killed in every supervisor's district of the county. Colored men were forced to assist at some of them, as in the case of Horace Hammond, where some of the jury were colored men. In one instance the coroner's jury was made up from the number who did the hanging. Their verdict, however, was the same as in the case of Hammond: "Came to his death by hanging by parties unknown."

The hanging of Patterson has attracted some notice beyond the borders of Yazoo. He was my friend, an intelligent, cultivated, orderly, peace-loving man. He was one of the three members from our county in the State House of Representatives. I knew him personally and well. I never heard him use profane or vulgar language. His habits were exceptionally good. I never knew or heard that he used intoxicating liquors. It is said that as chairman of the Republican club in his neighborhood in former campaigns, he had made arrangements, regardless of the threats of the enemy, for a Republican meeting. The fact was noised abroad. The result was reported to Mr. Ethel Barksdale's paper as follows.

From the *Clarion*, October 20, 1875:

"MURDER IN YAZOO COUNTY—PATTERSON, A NEGRO MEMBER OF THE LEGISLATURE, KILLS ANOTHER NEGRO IN HIS BED.

"YAZOO CITY, *October* 19.

"*Editors Clarion:*

"A horrible murder was committed on Silver Creek last night. Patterson, a member of the legislature, shot and killed another negro while in bed. They quarreled the day before, and exchanged shots. Patterson ran, but afterwards killed his antagonist in a most cowardly manner. His friends swore he should not be arrested. The negroes being numerous, it was thought best to send to this city for assistance, and a company left here this morning to arrest the assassin. In all probability they will do it. DEMOCRAT."

Next day the *Clarion* contained the following:

" YAZOO COUNTY—A DEMOCRATIC COLORED MAN SHOT AND THE MAN WHO INSTIGATED THE DEED LOST IN THE WOODS—A VIOLENT BLACK-LINER OF THE INFAMOUS LEGISLATURE OF 1875 MEETS HIS REWARD.

" YAZOO CITY, *October* 20.

" *To the Clarion:*

" The deputy sheriff and posse who left here yesterday to arrest Patterson, who, it is supposed, murdered a negro on Silver Creek because he was a Democrat, have just returned. They report that they captured Patterson and another negro who is implicated in the murder. Patterson paid this negro fifty dollars to do the deed.

" The deputy and posse were returning to this city with their prisoners, when they were met by an armed body and Patterson taken from them. They report him lost in the swamp. The other prisoner was brought to this city and placed in the county jail.

" CAMPBELL."

Still later, and after it was all over, December 3, 1875, this same paper contained the following:

" THE LYNCHING OF PATTERSON BY COLORED MEN.

" A loud wail goes up from the radical organs over the lynching of Patterson, in Yazoo, but they forget to say anything about the unfortunate colored man whom he caused to be murdered. It turns out that it was all the work of colored people. Patterson and his accomplice were colored. and he was tried, condemned, and executed by colored men—two-thirds of whom were, no doubt, Republicans. The Yazoo *Herald* says:

" On being captured, the murderer confessed everything; and upon his testimony Patterson was arrested and adjudged guilty by the large number of negroes living on the place where the bloody deed was committed the night before. They were terribly excited against him. His body, when next seen, was in a state of suspension. The negro who acted as Patterson's proxy, upon the bloody occasion in question is now in jail, and it is only a question of time when he too, will take a swing at the expense of the county.'"*

This is the way an eye-witness, one of the hornet's company, described it:

" We just took him out there and got him on top of a mule and put

* I have been informed that he was afterward released.

a rope around his neck and tied it to the limb of a pecan tree, and drove the mule out from under him, and in driving the mule out from under him it pretty near killed him, and to keep him from dying there, with his feet on the ground, we took hold of the other end of the rope and pulled him up; before we could get the knot untied he died—it was tied in such a bungling way."*

That is the way and such the spirit in which my friend was hung by those "high-toned, honorable, Southern gentlemen!" So I believed then, so I still believe, and so my reader will, as I believe, when the story shall be finished.

Among other horrors of that campaign are the following:

From the Yazoo City *Herald* (Democratic), October 15, 1875:

"As our long-absent Senator Everett was engaged in assisting his brother at his gin-house the other morning, he chanced to discover from the gin-room a certain company, which was moving toward Big Black on a reconnoitering expedition, and since the world was made, no man of woman born ever mounted the roof of a horse sooner, or fled with more precipitation than was done by him on that exciting occasion. When last seen he was going toward the mountains of Hepsidam, where the lion roareth and the whangdoodle mourneth for its first-born."

From the *Democrat*:

"There is no radical ticket in the field, and it is more than likely there will be none, for the leaders are not in the city, and dare not press their claims in this county."

From the Yazoo City *Herald*:

"Captain Taylor† is putting forth all his energies in the present canvass, and if he does not keep his end of the line up it will be from no lack of exertion."

From the *Democrat*:

"The negroes are anxious to form a Democratic club in this place but are afraid. Let a committee from the white Democratic club be appointed to organize them, and assure their protection.

"The proceedings of the first colored club Democratic in faith formed in this county, we give in this issue of the *Democrat*. It numbers some seventy odd men. Colored people let the good work go bravely on."

---

* That his fate might be a warning to all other Republicans, his body was left hanging there until the buzzards came and picked it.
† Captain of the cavalry company.

I suggested a plan by which it was hoped a few votes might be secured in opposition to the ticket of the enemy, but it was met with the same hostility that had been manifested toward me.

The *Banner* met it thus:

" It is no longer ' renounce tne devil and his pomp,' but forswear his twin brother radicalism, with his manifold machinations and chicanery; then you, with your county, will be safe. Take a little advice, ye imps of radicalism hereabouts."

The " Conservative " suggested for the office of sheriff and tax-collector on that ticket, responded as follows: " Any other ticket in the field than that nominated by the Democratic party, through its accredited representatives, on the 2d instant, is Morgan's ticket. and must be so regarded."

Every leading white Republican remaining in the county surrendered and published the fact over his own signature, and then sent word to me that they had done so in the hope of preventing further bloodshed, and of saving their own property and lives.

One organized a company, and took his place in line with the white leaguers, " to kill niggers when necessary," and to aid in suppressing the " risings," which were " about to occur."

The chairman of the county Democratic committee entered the United States post-office and caused all communications addressed to leading Republicans relating to the canvass and to the approaching election, to be destroyed—burned.*

At last, when election day arrived and the result was announced, the ticket of the enemy had received (so it was declared) 4,044 votes. There were two votes for me, but as was announced at the time, these were cast by the hornet, who explained that it would " not do to be too d—d unanimous." Perhaps this was the real reason for the three votes cast by the enemy in 1867.

*See Report of United States Senate Select Committee on Mississippi election of 1875, pp. 1658 and 1659, testimony of the Postmaster.

The enemy's rejoicings over this result were as extrava
gant as their jubilations over the result of the election in
Massachusetts the year previous, or, as their violent efforts
to win it. The hornet was elevated into a sort of demigod,
and all sounded his praises. A movement was set on foot
to raise a fund with which to purchase a suitable testimonial
of their appreciation of his services. In order that all might
share in that pleasure, it was arranged that no one should
be allowed to contribute more than ten cents—except the
head of a family, who might contribute ten cents for each of
his or her children. This fund was quickly raised, and upon
the testimonial—a massive silver pitcher—was engraved the
following :

" To
The Bravest of the Brave,
Captain HENRY M. DIXON.

"Presented to him by his Democratic fellow-citizens of Yazoo
County, as an humble testimonial of their high appreciation of his
brilliant services in the redemption of the county from radical rule
in 1875."

The *Banner* said :

" Let no man dare say that a nobler man ever lived."

Then a great county gathering was held, at which were
present Ethel Barksdale and Otho R. Singleton, both now
in the House of Representatives at Washington, and L. Q.
C. Lamar and J. Z. George, present United States Senators
from that State. Before these distinguished persons, the
hornet and his company were paraded, dressed and armed
as when on their hanging expeditions, and there in the presence of the vast throng, over whom waved our grand old flag,
received, fresh from the lips of these, their true and tried
captains and leaders, Barksdale, Singleton, George, Lamar,
the thanks of "the people" of the county, " the people " of
the State, and, of "our people" everywhere, for their
" glorious services " in behalf of " our sacred cause."*

So far as I have been able to learn no trace has ever been

---

* It was here and by those distinguished statesmen (?) that Yazoo was christened the
Banner county of the State.

found by the hornet, by Taylor, nor by any of the armed
organizations, of those "sixteen hundred army guns" of
Benjamin Franklin Eddin and James Red Sands, or of either
of those characters. Their names are not among the dead
of that canvass. Indeed, after the campaign had opened in
right good earnest on the part of the enemy, nothing was
said or done about that matter. It appears to have been lost
sight of.

Throughout that period the Republicans were as helpless
as babes. There was never any resistance at all by them to
the violence of the enemy.

That campaign in Yazoo has been called "the coronation
of the Mississippi plan." So it was; for in twenty-six other
counties of the State that year the enemy were less humane.
In some of that number Republicans resisted by violence the
aggressions of the enemy, and were massacred in crowds of
ten, twenty, fifty, and, in one county, it was said quite one
hundred were killed. But in Yazoo, instead of summoning
the unarmed colored men against the disciplined and fully
equipped ranks of the white league, the Republican leaders
made their fight upon the picket-line, trusting to the reserves
at the North to fill their places when they should be all
killed, captured, or in retreat. Therefore, only leaders were
killed in Yazoo, and only so many of them as was necessary
to convince Republicans that their opponents would kill if
necessary, that they had the power to kill, and that there were
none to forbid it, or to punish them for it afterward. Therefore the mass of the Republicans remained silent and passive.
Ohio and Massachusetts had gone Democratic. Had I summoned a posse of colored men and resisted, of course there
would have been a general massacre in Yazoo, too. That
I would not do. Therefore the hornet and all his aids were
entitled to the thanks of mankind! The hornet received the
thanks of "our people" on the occasion mentioned. His
reward came later.

By such means as I have here but faintly detailed Yazoo
and Mississippi were "redeemed."

By such means Major W. D. Gibbs, my opponent in 1869, recovered his own without the aid of Reuben, and took his place in the State Senate; the attorney for Mars' Si, who was also for the State against Charles, and for Mr. Hilliard against me, was elected to the House, and Captain Taylor of the cavalry company, was elected to be sheriff and tax-collector.

Within twenty-four hours after their new government was installed in the places of "we all" Republicans, the county treasury was entered and every dollar of the school fund carried off.*   To this day, it is said that the robbery was by "persons unknown."

Then their grand jury, selected by the same means as were Gibbs, Taylor, and Mars' Si's attorney, on their solemn oaths, presented to the court "a true bill" for murder against me.

*About twenty-eight thousand dollars.

CHAPTER LXX.

VIEWS OF SOUTHERN STATESMEN UPON "OUR PEOPLE" AND "OUR
SACRED CAUSE"—DEATH OF THE HORNET.

"Conscious that they themselves* were animated by devotion to
constitutional liberty, and that the brightest pages of history are
replete with evidences of the depth and sincerity of that devotion,
they can but cherish the recollections of sacrifices endured, the battles fought and the victories won in defense of their hapless cause."
—*From L. Q. C. Lamar's Eulogium on Mr. Sumner, in the National
House of Representatives, April* 27, 1874.

THE events mentioned in the last chapter occurred eight
   years ago. All the chief conspirators are still living;
Barksdale, George and Lamar. They are all in the Congress of the United States.

Their dupes, Captain Telsub, the hornet, and Halder are
dead; all died by violence. The death of each was most
pitiful, tragic. The former was killed in Texas; a private
quarrel, it was said. It was also said that upon his body were
found some of the missing school funds of Yazoo County.
The hornet died a martyr to free speech, and while defending the negro's right to life, liberty and the pursuit of happiness.

For four years there had been but one political party in
the county. The irreconcilables dominated that party absolutely, and they called it the Democratic party. By their
admirers throughout the State they were called the " Banner
Democracy of the Banner County." That year, 1879, the
hornet became the leader of the " disaffected," and champion

* The slave-holding rebels

of a movement designed to build up an opposition party. He had the encouragement and support of many of Yazoo's "best citizens." "Our nigros" were quick to seize upon that movement as opening a way out of the political slavery in which they were groaning, and rallied to that standard almost *en masse.*

The banner Democracy found in that fact proof, "strong as holy writ," that the colored people were again "about to rise," and promptly set on foot precisely the same means as had been employed for the overthrow of our free State government. Rumors of "nigro risings" became once more frequent. The result was a large gathering of the armed "independent companies" at Yazoo City, July 25, 1879, when a formal demand was made upon the hornet that he should withdraw from his candidacy for the sheriff's office. To this demand he made the following response, which was published in the Yazoo City *Herald* (extra):

" *To the Public:*

"For the sake of the peace and harmony of the country, and the affection I bear for my family and friends, I agree to withdraw from the political canvass or race issue in the future, provided I will be protected in my rights as any other citizen; and my friend, R. A. Flannagan, is to be unmolested in his rights, etc.

"H. M. DIXON.

"YAZOO CITY, *July* 25, 1879."

Commenting on this the *Herald's* editor said that the reason assigned for the withdrawal, the "race issue," was not "satisfactory to the great assembly of earnest, determined men. He finally, however, consented to quit the canvass now and forever, * * * so the political canvass in this county may be considered at an end. The Democratic flag now waves over the glorious old county, uncontaminated and unchallenged, and long may it wave."

A challenge was to come, however. For immediately after "the great assembly of earnest, determined men" had dispersed, Mr. Dixon announced that his withdrawal had been procured by force, and while he was *in duress,* therefore it was null and void.

But the banner Democracy were equal to this emergency. Another meeting was called.

I have a souvenir of this event. It is a printed document, from which I extract the following headlines and so forth:

" PUBLISHED BY AUTHORITY OF THE DEMOCRATIC PARTY OF YAZOO COUNTY—PROCEEDINGS OF THE DEMOCRATIC MASS MEETING HELD IN YAZOO CITY, MISS., AUGUST 15, '79.

" Pursuant to a call a meeting of fully one thousand Democrats was held in Yazoo City on Friday, the 15th instant.'

" Dr. P. J. McCormick was selected to preside over the meeting, and on motion Mr. John T. Posey was requested to act as secretary.'"*

This " meeting " adopted the following declaration of prinples :

* * * " We declare as our belief that he has sought and is now seeking by all the devilish devices of a low, corrupt intriguer in politics to array the colored people of the county against the whites--to stir up a race prejudice and a race conflict—and to bring strife and confusion throughout our borders, and all this because he wants the fees and perquisites of the sheriff's office and sees no other way of getting them. For these reasons we say that the man H. M. Dixon is not fit to be sheriff of our county, and we here deny that he has a right to be allowed to run for such office, or for any office in this county on the issues thus made up by him.

* * * "To sum up in brief our opinion and estimate of the character of the man Dixon, we declare as our deliberate opinion that he is a murderer, a gambler, a bully, a thief, a man of violence, of blood, of lies, a man who will pack juries, a low, unprincipled demagogue in politics, and an infidel in religion. He unites in himself every quality required to make him the detestable monster that he is, and he wants every qualification necessary to make him the gentleman that he is not. For these reasons we say that we detest the man H. M. Dixon, and we say further that he is not fit in any sense to hold any office of honor, profit or trust known to our laws ; and we furthermore declare and say that he shall not hold any such office in our county if in our power to prevent it ; and as evidence of our sincerity in this declaration we do hereby further declare that we ratify and confirm the acts and doings of our fellow Democrats at Yazoo City on the 25th of July last, and that we will stand to and abide by their actions and the actions of this meeting at every hazard, and to the last extremity."

* * * " We further declare as our belief that the man Dixon appropriated to his own use some ($1,500 or $1,600) fifteen hundred or

* This secretary will be heard from again.

sixteen hundred dollars in money, warrants and notes, which was
taken from the body of the negro Patterson, who was hung on Silver
Creek in 1875.* It can be proved that Dixon took this money, and
that when he was asked in Yazoo City, a few days after the hanging,
what he had done or proposed to do with the money, he replied :
(waving his hand to the iron safe of Messrs. Nathan & Hirsh), ' It is
there, and I intend that the boys shall have a good time on it.' The
person who put the question replied : ' As one of the boys, I want no
good time out of that money.' A highly respectable gentleman (now
in this city) was requested by Patterson to take charge of his money
and send it to Patterson's relatives in Ohio. This gentleman will
prove that he saw this money put into Dixon's hands, and although
he urged that the wish of the negro should be strictly complied with,
he has reason to believe and does believe that the relatives of Patterson never received one cent of this money.''

It would seem that this declaration was adopted unanimously.

This souvenir was promptly inclosed in an envelope, post-
marked Yazoo City, August 18, and was addressed to me in
the well-known hand of Fritz Halder, who also wrote his
"compliments" in the upper left hand corner. I presumed at
the time that this was intended by Halder as a hint that he
was now ready to shake hands with me "over the bloody
chasm." But up to the present moment I have not been
able to see any cause for congratulation in the proceedings
of that meeting, for, before the souvenir reached me, indeed,
the very next time the hornet appeared upon the main street,
a man with a double-barrelled shot-gun in his hands killed him.
The man's name is Barksdale. He is, I believe, a nephew of
Congressman Barksdale, who is, I am informed, a brother of
the late William Barksdale, who was in Congress when Mississippi's Congressmen, with Jefferson Davis at their head,
seceded from that body.

Some of the "best citizens" of Yazoo saw nothing but
shame in it. Of the number was Mars Si's attorney for
the State against Charles and for Hilliard against me ; the
very same who was elected in 1875, when Yazoo was "redeemed" by the means I have but so faintly set forth, to

---

* Our Republican legislator.

Pat*erson's vacant seat in the State legislature. From a letter written and published by him just after Mr. Dixon's death
I extract the following:

"When is bull-dozing and intimidation to end? When are we to
have a free, unawed aspiration for office, canvass and election? When
is our mother district to be unstained with the blood of the citizens,
and when shall the graves cease to be filled with the dead on election
years and occasions? When are the wails and cries of the bereft
widows and orphans to be unheard in party organizations and elections? Why the continued threats and intimidation against those
who may see fit to organize the colored voters to vote any particular
ticket, when there are no tickets but what are almost exclusively
composed of old and tried white citizens of Yazoo County? They
know and we know that there has been bull-dozing, and even worse."

As may be inferred from the *Herald's* comments, the movement for an opposition party in Yazoo died with Mr. Henry
M. Dixon. Nevertheless, the public was at once informed
through the Associated Press and otherwise, that the killing
was the result of a private quarrel between Mr. Dixon and
Barksdale.

One of the last acts of this man's life was the publication
of the following card, which appeared in the *Herald* as an
advertisement:

* * * "I again say that the supposed Patterson money was used
to defray current expenses for the eventful campaign of 1875.

"I further state $3,000 was used as a bribe to have the ballot-boxes
stuffed, if necessary, and to issue certificates of election to Democratic candidates; that Dr. P. J. McCormick was chairman of the
Democratic Executive Committee at the time, and was party to the
contract. I have in my possession the necessary receipt to show who
received the $3,000; also the false key to the ballot-box

"I consider that my conduct throughout the canvass of 1875 was
indorsed by all Democratic citizens, and I do not fear that my character will suffer by any cowardly attack made for a political purpose.

"Respectfully, H. M. DIXON."

CHAPTER LXXI.

IN THE HANDS OF THE LORD.

"For in the hand of the Lord there is a cup, and the wine is red; it is full of mixture, and He poureth out of the same : but the dregs thereof, all the wicked of the earth shall wring them out, and drink them."—*Psalms lxxv; 8.*

FOUR years later, it was Christmas eve, 1882, a "high-toned honorable gentleman " named Posey, John T. Posey, " son of General Carnot Posey, of Confederate fame," attended a "negro ball " in Yazoo City.   There he met and had a "personal altercation " with one John James, " a nigger."   It is said that the quarrel was the result of a rivalry between Posey and James for the smiles of one of the "belles of the ball."   Posey insulted James and James struck Posey.   James was arrested, but Posey refused to prosecute.   That is, Posey refused to publish the cause of the quarrel.   He was a "gentleman," and James was only " a nigger."   Besides, the " belle" was only " a nigro wench."

During these long years of woe, during these years of "white supremacy" in Yazoo, a spark of Federal authority remained. Mr. Bedwell, who had married a " Southern lady," was still postmaster, and Mr. Foote had been a deputy collector of internal revenue.   Now " our best citizens " could tolerate Bedwell, but that " nigro Foote " was all the while a thorn in their side.   His office as well as his person was concentrated incendiarism, a perpetual menace.   How could " our nigros" be made to "keep thar places" with Foote in a place which, by divine right, belonged to a "white?" The situation was made more tragic by the fact that Foote dared, upon occasion, to shoot at a "white." Foote was allowed no peace in that office. He was frequently warned of plots by the "best citizens," to "get rid of that d—d nigger revenue collector." "The little Yankee garrison" had already been got rid of. The old "guard" had all been killed or had died, or "gone off" to Kansas, or had surrendered. The "what is it" alone remained. He had stood squarely by Mr. Dixon in his last raid. His friends were Southerners, and he had come to have an abiding hatred of the Yankees, whose failure in 1875 to come to the succor of our government, in its final struggle with the old slave oligarchs, had eliminated from his breast not only all hope of succor from the North, but also all respect for Northerners. Thus matters stood a year later, Christmas eve, 1883.

That evening John T. Posey set out, at the head of some congenial spirits from the "superiah" side of the line, to "whip a nigger." Naturally enough John James at that moment stood most in need of a thrashing. But James was employed at the meat market by one Lynch, "the butcher," a "po' white."

Learning of the intentions of Posey and his party James, with the full consent of his employer, and by his command, took refuge in the butcher shop.

Nothing daunted by this interference of a "po', no-count white man," Posey, at the head of his followers, went away and procured weapons.

Meanwhile several of James' friends, colored men, came to his succor. Posey and his friends returned. At that moment the "po' white," the employer of James, was standing in front of his shop. As the Posey party approached he walked out into the street, "held up his hands," and said :

"You can't one of you go in my house. I ain't a-going to have any row in there."*

*From the testimony of Posey's business partner, Thomas Williams, white Democrat, upon the "trial" which followed.

At this juncture Mr. Foote approached the Posey group. It would seem that he was alone. The handful of Posey's friends had grown into a crowd. At this moment an employee of Posey's appeared upon the scene. In his examination upon the trial which followed, this employee, John Link, a white and a Democrat, swore:

"I went out into the middle of the road toward Lynch's and with John Posey, who said that James was in that back room with a crowd of negroes, and that James had to be whipped. * * * Posey then started right towards Lynch's corner with the crowd, and remarked: 'Don't let Foote get behind me.'"

Then it was said, Foote and a "Yankee,"* who was one of the Posey crowd, had an "altercation." Then Foote was knocked down; then the firing began.

Upon the "trial" it was said that some colored men had said before the firing, that if it should begin, it would not end as it did in 1875. It was said that Mr. Foote had said this. If so, Mr. Foote spoke more truly than he knew. It did not end as in 1875. It began with the death of John T. Posey, Carnot Posey, John's brother, a young man named Nichols, and Fritz Halder. The Yankee was wounded. All were white.

Who did the killing?

John Link, above-mentioned witness, further testified upon that trial:

"Posey rushed right up to the front door of Lynch's butcher-shop. Mr. Halder arrested him on the sidewalk, almost immediately at Lynch's door. Posey told him to turn him loose, that he had no right to stop him."

At this point the recollection of all the "high-toned" witnesses, so far as I have been able to learn, becomes confused except in the case of one, who said that after Foote was struck, and while falling, he fired his pistol.

Did these whites kill each other or were they killed by Foote or by James and his friends who were "in that back room?"

---

* This Yankee was doubtless trying to prove that he was as "good a friend to the South" as any one else.

The next day it appears to have been believed by some that " our nigros " did it.

Foote was present, at all events. He did not run away. He trusted in his cause and in his white Southern friends. James ran away, was pursued, and shot to death; " riddled with bullets." His employer, that " po' white," Foote, and some ten more colored men, were charged with murder, arrested and locked up in that Yazoo jail.

And this is the way it ended. I quote from a special dispatch to the St. Louis *Globe-Democrat*, dated Yazoo City, December 29, 1883, from which all the foregoing extracts from the testimony at the "trial" have been taken :

" Five o'clock, the hour set by some of the most active for moving on the jail, came and passed. It was very quiet, and some of the leading citizens claimed that there would be no trouble to-night. It was only a calm before a storm.

"Half a dozen mounted men galloped into town over the highway leading up the Yazoo Valley. Then came a delegation from Bentonia. Then others. At 6.10, just after dark, a squad of men, armed with shot-guns, made their appearance on the lower part of Main street. They moved up toward Jefferson, and as they marched others joined them. The column grew at every step. They turned up Jefferson and went a block; then they stopped. An old gentleman spoke to them and said :

"' Boys, are you organized ? Aren't you too early ?'

'· Somebody replied : ' We tried to hold them back, but they would start.'

"Half a block north there was another halt. Some of the more prudent counseled delay. A great chorus of 'noes' greeted this. ' Go ahead, go ahead ; they'll get them all out if we don't hurry.' This last shout caught the popular sentiment. There was a great shout of ' Go on, go on,' then a cheer, which rang through the city. The crowd, grown to fully 200, pressed ahead at a rapid walk toward the jail. There was no masking, and not the slightest attempt at conceal. ment. Men recognized each other by name and shook hands while they waited for the committee inside to bring out the prisoners. There was some delay after passing the first door to the jail proper.

"Just at this juncture Mr. James A. Barksdale, a member of the legislature,* entered the jail, and, addressing several of those standing at the door, inquired for ex-Sheriff Taylor.† The latter could not be found. It was evidently Mr. Barksdale's intention to get Mr·

---

* The same who shot Mr. Dixon.
† Captain Taylor, of the cavalry company.

Taylor, who is one of the most influential men of the county, to join him in a final appeal to the crowd to let the law have its course.

" After ten minutes' work the cell in which was Robert Swayze was opened, and he was led into the hall. He made no fight whatever, but stood erect while the noose at the end of a long rope was put about his neck. Then his hands were tied behind him. Two or three conflicting commands were given—one was for a squad to go down town and get more rope. Somebody shouted ' Shoot 'em.' This was yelled down, ' No, no; hang 'em to one limb.' This last suggestion was accepted.

" ' Throw the end of the rope over the fence. We'll string him right up here.'

" The end was thrown over the fence, and a dozen inside caught hold and began pulling. Swayze was raised up to his tip-toes, and then the rope caught in a crack and stuck fast.

" ' This is cruel; why didn't you go to a tree ?' somebody exclaimed. An active fellow mounted another man's shoulders, caught the top of the fence and tugged at the rope, while the one on the outside held Swayze up. It seemed an hour. It was perhaps only a minute, until the rope was loosened again. Then it was pulled until Swayze was swung six inches off the ground. It caught again, but those outside said it was high enough, and the men inside stopped pulling.

" ' Hurry up with that rope. Ain't he dead yet ?' came from the door of the jail.

" ' It will take all night at this rate.'

" ' Put a bullet through him,' somebody said, but this was shouted down.

" ' Bring out that Internal Revenue Collector, we want him next,' came from the yard.

" It was not necessary, for the committee had already commenced on the doors where W. H. Foote was confined. Foote walked over and t ok a drink from a bucket of water, then placed himself with his left side against the wall and stood facing the spot where, as the door swung back, he would meet the first man who entered. Suddenly the door swung open. As it let in the crowd Foote raised his right hand with a missile in it and struck out. The first man went to the floor under the blow. Half a dozen were in before another blow could be given. Foote fought like a tiger.

" There was a shot, then another, and three more in quick succession. The light had gone out in the midst of the struggle, and as the shots were fired they illuminated the room a single second, and showed confused struggling. Then all was quiet. The man who entered first and received Foote's blow was a young farmer named A. Fatheree,* from Free Run, in this county, in the melee one of the bullets had struck him in the instep of the foot, making a very ugly wound.

*My recollection is that this is the same young man who in 1869 assayed to whip Foote, and got a whipping himself instead.

As soon as a light was brought in and Fatheree had been carried out Foote was examined. There were some signs of life. Six shots were fired with steady aim, and those who cared to entered the room and satisfied themselves that the negro was dead. His forehead was shot away, and blood and brain covered a space of the floor a yard square. Nearly all the bullets had been sent into his head. He was so mutilated as to be scarcely recognizable. Foote undoubtedly made the fight to provoke the shooting, that he might die that way rather than be hung.

"Ten feet away hung the lifeless body of Swayze, a dark outline against the high white fence. Close by was the iron gate through which the avengers passed back and forth. Occasionally somebody lighted a match and held it up in front of Swayze's head and face for a better view.

"Meanwhile the workers inside had reached a point where they were baffled. The iron cage from St. Louis proved as hard to get into as it is to get out of. A half hour slipped away, and those outside murmured at the delay.

"When those deputed to bring out the prisoners found that it would be impossible to get at Gibbs they told his fellow-prisoners that they must hold Gibbs up to the grating or all of them were likely to be shot in the effort to kill the one wanted. They took hold of him, but he said: 'I know I've got to die; I'm ready,' and faced the grating with little support from his companions. A lamp was brought and held. A bullet was fired through the negro's heart. He dropped, and another bullet was fired into him. Then the end of the rope was passed in over the top of the grating and Gibbs' cell-mates, two negroes, fastened the noose about his neck. He was then drawn up by those outside as high as the height of the cell would permit and the rope tied. There he was left. Three parts of the programme were finished.

"In a cell on the upper floor Micajah Parker was found. The little darkey, black as midnight, came out trembling. There was no rope. Swayze was taken down from the fence and dragged inside the yard. The rope was taken off and passed into the jail. It took but a moment to adjust the noose to Parker's neck, and then he was dropped over an inside balcony and the end made fast. Ten minutes were allowed for strangulation to do its work. Those outside who felt the curiosity went in to see the disposition made of Parker and Gibbs. A brief halt was made at the corner of the yard, and then the column marched down the street toward the business centre, growing smaller and smaller all the way. When it reached lower Main street it was reduced to the out-of-town detachments, and in a few minutes they were riding homeward.

The next day. From the same :

"Close by Parker's body was the door opening into the cell where

Foote made his desperate fight and forced those in front to shoot him. In daylight the remains seemed even more ghastly than they did last night. There were bullet holes in the face and forehead and chest, eight or ten of them. The left side of the head was shot away and the right side of the throat was cut. His hands were tightly clinched. They had stiffened in death as he had last used them. When the crowd was heard coming toward the jail an officer went to the door and said :

"'Foote, I expect your time is coming. You hear them ? Take it as easy as you can.'

"There was just the slightest tremor in his voice as he replied : 'Yes I hear them; I'll try to take it quietly.'

"Then he quietly put out the light and waited.

"But in the yard, just to the right of the walk leading up from the iron gate in the high fence, lay the body of Robert Swayze. It had lain there all night in the rain. The face was upturned and the head twisted, revealing two gashes in the side of the neck. Somebody had attempted to complete or shorten the work of strangulation by the use of the knife, but the wounds were not deep. The blood seemed to be still trickling from them. The hanging of Swayze was done on a sudden impulse as to place and was a bungling job at best. The end of the rope was thrown over the fence and he was hauled off the ground, but not altogether. The rope had caught once or twice and delayed the work. With a view of hastening matters, and to shorten the negro's misery, somebody climbed up and stood on Swayze's shoulders, holding to the top of the fence, and thus bringing a double weight upon the neck of the dying black.

THE INQUEST.

"About 9 o'clock this morning Coroner Rosenthal entered the jail yard with his jury, and as they stood around the body of Swayze, he read with uncovered head the law pertaining to inquests. In a similar manner the jury looked upon Foote, Parker and Gibbs. The jury stepped into the jail office and consulted about five minutes, then the coroner came to the door and said :

"'Mr. Sheriff, you can turn the bodies over to the relatives, or if uncalled for they will be buried by the county.'

"The jurors marched out, hoisted their umbrellas and walked downtown to the magistrate's office, where they consulted again. In about half an hour they were discovered, having agreed on the following verdict :

VERDICT RENDERED.

"We, the jury, duly impannelled and sworn, after proper and full investigation of the occurrence of last night, render our verdict as follows : 'That on the night of December 29, 1883, at the jail of Yazoo County, between the hours of 7 and 8 o'clock, a body of unknown men, armed and fully equipped, did take possession of said jail and the bodies of W. H. Foote, Micajah Parker, Robert Swayze and Richard Gibbs, and killed them as follows:

"1. W. H. Foote came to his death by gunshot wounds; the party doing the shooting unknown.

"2. Robert Swayze came to his death by being hung, and also by being cut in the neck with some kind of instrument unknown to the jury.

"3. Micajah Parker came to his death by being hung.

"4. Richard Gibbs came to his death by gunshot wounds. All the parties concerned being unknown to the jurors.

A. D. REDDING.

L. S. SCHWARZ.

R. J. BELL.

WM. RICHARDSON.

J. E. GUYNNER.

R. B. NESMITH.

"The word unknown wherever it occurs is underscored, as is also the final sentence."

So the sheriff was present at the coroner's inquest. Where was he the night before? Where were all of Foote's Southern friends? By the dispatch from which I have quoted, it would seem that the only persons who attempted to interfere were Barksdale and a good priest, Rev. Father Wise.

When news of these deeds reached me I began the task of writing this book. Then I promised myself to not " wave the bloody shirt." Nor have I. Let others do that. But if not for the living something remains for the dead. It is from a letter to my wife, written by one of her former pupils. I cannot trust the public with her name; the reasons why I cannot should be apparent. I quote as follows:

"YAZOO CITY, *January* 23, 1884.

* * * "It made me happy to know that you thought of me in my troubles. Yes; my darling husband is dead. He died the 29th of December. He had been sick four months. He was on the porch when the white men were shooting John James. He told me to put him to bed. That was Tuesday, and he died Saturday morning. I think the excitement killed him. My happiness is all over; I am broken-hearted. His grave is here, and I can't bear to leave it. * * *

"It commenced to rain the night Mr. Foote was killed, and has been raining ever since. It looks like the sun has refused to shine on Yazoo." * * *

CHAPTER LXXII.

THEN AND NOW—HAVE PATIENCE—WAIT—THE FORTY YEARS
IN THE WILDERNESS ARE PASSING AWAY.

" We must not fold our hands in slumber, nor abide content with
the past. To each generation is committed its peculiar task ; nor
does the heart which responds to the call of duty find rest except in
the grave."—*Mr. Sumner.*

IN 1870 a young man, and unschooled in the arts of Southern
politicians, I was thought by them to be a fit subject for
their practice. I was in the State Senate. It was known that
I had served on the Union side throughout the war. It was
known that I was not in full sympathy with my party on
certain questions then before our legislature. The " National Republican Conservative, Democratic, Home-folks,
Dent party " journals were talking about me quite approvingly. One of these opened its columns for an expression of
my views, and so forth. It was the Vicksburg *Herald.* It
was then, and is now, the leading commercial newspaper of
that State.

Replying to my letter, the *Herald* said :

"COMMENTS UPON COMMUNICATION OF ' JUSTICE.' "

" This morning we present a communication from a prominent
radical in this State—a man whom we respect as a man—one whom
we know, or at least believe, to be as near conscientious in his political convictions as any sane man, who is a member of the radical
party, can be. As his article, strange to say, is couched in respectful
terms, we readily and willingly discuss with him. We say, ' strange
to say,' from the fact that the radical cause is so hard to sustain in
discussion, that its defenders are almost invariably driven into a
species of ' billingsgate ' and personality, into which no journalist,
who possesses any pride whatever, can descend."

And then, " strange to say," itself plunges headlong into " billingsgate," as follows :

* * * " Negro suffrage was never sustained by the radical party through any love for the negro, or from any sense of duty. It originated from a two-fold cause. Greatest of these causes was a miserable, cowardly hatred of the South and people, by a class of men who had never been in the army, but who, to create political capital at the North, became " twelfth hour vaporers ; " men who proposed to perform prodigies of valor after the enemy had been conquered, captured and was bound—men who had skulked behind civil position and ' bumb proofs ' of various kinds until the enemy was manacled, and then with reckless hardihood and unparalleled bravery, jumped with both heels into his face and punished him in the severest manner. These were the men who originated negro suffrage, and it was originated because it was thought to be an engine of torture for the South and her people, and never through any love for the negro. *. * * Another reason why negro suffrage secured supporters from among the more respectable and decent portion of the radical party was, that in the negro as a voter it was thought there was an element of strength to the radical party, whose corruption it was plain to be seen was rapidly killing it among decent white men, as it will ere long kill it with all classes. But their valiant radical Congressmen pounding and belaboring in the most heroic style the bound South, never imagined that this thing of negro suffrage could ever become a two-edged sword, and while cutting and slashing the South would leave a gash here and there in the North."

I say, " strange to say." At that time it appeared strange. Now it does not appear at all strange to me.

Our Yazoo *Democrat* welcomed the new order of things thus :

* * * " We have only this much to say to our own folk The Constitution and laws are no longer what they were. They, too have been revolutionized and changed. But we must abide by them patiently, because they *are* law—bad, indeed, but still *the law.* Time will come when we can remould them. * * *

" Then, D emocrats, stand to your principles like a knight to his honor, never faltering. *There* is the key to success ; beware of bribery in any shape ; be not tempted to sacrifice your virtue for the fleshpots of office.

" In the meantime, let us get along as best we can. If we must for awhile have carpet-bag and scalawag rulers, let us prefer those who can do us the greatest good. Often, by using the balance of power when rival politicians of the other side cause division in their own ranks, and, by aiding the best, we can make a friend and beat a rascal."

After Credit Mobilier, Pacific Mail, Sanborn Contracts
and Henry Ward Beecher had wrought their fatal spell
upon the country—only five years later—our *Democrat* copied
the following from that same *Herald.*

From Yazoo City *Democrat,* June 1, 1875 :

"HAVE PATIENCE—WAIT.

"Time makes all things even. The South has been burdened and
insulted until it has sometimes seemed to the coolest and most candid
mind as if the intention was to enslave our people. 'Reconstruction'
was a cloak for robbers ; every new law passed by Congress to affect
the South had a poisoned sting somewhere concealed; the Southern
States were looked upon as the legitimate harvest-field of the rascal
and the thief. These things were, but time has worked some changes
and will work others. Chandler, Butler, Carpenter, Pomeroy and the
others whose hate of the South secured their election from constitu-
encies even more insanely biased, have gone to their political graves,
and they have no friends among the people. The honest men of the
North, no matter how they vote, repudiate the carpet-baggers. The
people of the whole Union cry out against any further attempts at
reconstruction. The officials placed in office by Grant's bayonets
have no friends outside of the White House. There is a popular feeling in every neighborhood from Maine to Texas, against the South
being further burdened and robbed and insulted. Northern journals
who were our bitter enemies one year ago, are now our friends and
well-wishers. This current of feeling is growing wider and deeper
every day and no matter what the President's feeling toward us, he
cannot stand before the popular and general demand that the South
shall be left to pursue her way in peace.

"We say to our people—have patience—wait. The long, dark night
is passing away. Be industrious, be economical, be content. It is
plain to all that peace and prosperity, such as has not been known for
a decade, will soon dawn upon us.—*Vicksburg Herald.*"

This was only six months after the news was received in
Mississippi that Massachusetts had gone Democratic.

"Our people" had but six months more to "wait." January following a government of their own choosing was
installed in power throughout the State, and L. Q. C. Lamar
was chosen United States Senator. We know by what means
and at what cost. My friend Patterson's life and money were
but a very small fraction of the whole.

The *Herald's* forecast was correct. What with corruption

that had " become chronic in both the great political parties "
at the North, the tales " of outrage and wrong" perpetrated
upon " our stricken brethren at the South," by " carpet-baggers and nigros," together with frequently recurring " nigro
insurrections," our brave and generous friends at the North
grew " tired." The President dared not keep his " promise."
The United States bayonets did not reach Mississippi. I did
not reach the other shore. A robber, liar, and murderer—the
Mississippi bull-dozer—stood in the way, and from that day
to this he has pursued his trade with most " superiah strategy
and statesmanship."

Some of the survivors of the campaign of 1875 the bull-
dozer has silenced by cajolery, some he has bribed to silence,
some he has silenced by threats and some he has killed. But
such as he could neither cajole, bribe, intimidate, nor kill, he
has pursued with a malice, a cunning, and a persistency that
has driven them from their homes and scattered them to the
four corners of the earth.

Chisholm refused to surrender or run, and the bull-dozer
killed his daughter that he might make surer work with him.
Gilmer refused, and he " filled him full of lead." Charles
Caldwell refused, and he " shot him all to pieces," and wantonly slew his half-witted brother. Page refused and he fired
his home and slew him and all his children, from the elder
son to the baby in the cradle. But why continue the list ?
I could add a hundred names more to it.

Ever since that day when Lamar, Barksdale, George, and
Singleton *et als.*, met with " our people " in Yazoo, and publicly thanked Mr. Dixon and his " company " for their " services " in the " redemption " of that State, and Yazoo was
declared the banner county, colored men there have been
whipped, hunted by hounds, and killed, and their mothers,
wives, daughters and sweethearts have been reviled, seduced,
raped, while Yazoo law gave them no redress.

At last the survivors, like bleeding stags at bay, turned
upon their pursuers and rended them. Then " our people "
turned to fiendish brutes, glutted themselves with deeds, the

story of which makes the heart sick. It was then, when all the light went out in Yazoo that I began to write this book and announced the fact in the press and by printed circulars. Then that same Vicksburg *Herald* published the following:

[From the Vicksburg Herald, March 19, 1884]

" WASHINGTON, March 13, 1884.—Some years ago, ' *we*,' the *Herald* and ' One of the People," held some slight converse with some of our State officials of that period, and together arrayed such strong lines of truth that carpet-baggery and knavery moved away. No lives were taken, no blood was shed, but ever ⌐ince that glorious disappearance nearly every one of that set have termed themselves ' refugees from home.' Now, what a farce this is, nay, what a cold-blooded swindle it is, for such fellows as truth and justice peaceably drove away from Mississippi to claim to be ' refugees from home.' *   *   *   *

" Now, inclosed you will find conclusive evidence of an audacity as unlimited as it is unscrupulous, unfounded, and unjust. Here is a circular headed, ' Yazoo; or, On the Picket Line of Freedom,' a new book by the late sheriff of Yazoo County, Miss.

" And all this from a man whose name can never be remembered in Mississippi save with disgust. Here he is, a ' refugee from home.' Driven away by his own sins, his own disgrace, with not one single hand uplifted to do him personal violence or wrong, he turns back upon the people he has wronged, after nearly ten years of secretive silence, and poisons and pollutes the atmosphere of public opinion by the most atrocious slanders. This is a secret circular, I believe.

*   *   *   *   *   *   *   *   *

" The object I have in view of inclosing this to you is that our people may be forewarned and forearmed against this additional scheme of ' outrage.' The forthcoming volume indicated by this circular is designed and intended as a campaign document to inflame the minds and arouse the anger of the people of the North. Its name, its title page, shows what a hollow, false pretense it is, claiming to be the work, the history of a suffering. Union-loving patriot, yet, at the same time, is one of the basest works of one of the basest of his kind. Like the man who secretes this horrid and horrible *menu* of infamy and falsehood, this book should be stamped indellibly with a mark like that set on Cain, that all the world might know that here is a cold-blooded, fratricidal murder! Here is an attempted, an assassin-like murder of all the good men of Mississippi; for what is the destruction of our good names, reputation, and honor, save the worst kind of murder? Here is a cold-blooded, atrocious wretch, who left Mississippi ten years ago, and who found a ' home ' and a salary, too, in one of the departments here, who has remained silent during the whole of that long period, now wants to come out as the chieftain of all our enemies, that he may fatten again on the damnable wrongs he has done to an honored people.

" The *Herald* has its host of friends and correspondents throughout the State. Let them draw the fangs from the reptile. Let them present the true history of this slanderer to the *Herald* that the *Herald* may give the whole truth in advance of this book to the country.

"Our gallant and able Senators and Representatives in Congress are fighting our battles manfully and nobly, and they need assistance in the contest. Let our people not only show themselves conservatives, but let us be able to put down slander by truth.

*   *   *   *   *

"The war of the bloody shirt has commenced, and there is only one way to defend ourselves, and that is by the truth. So far, thank God, the truth has won, and just so sure as the sun shines just so sure will it continue to be victorious. ONE OF THE PEOPLE."

As I have said, after the white leagues broke up our meeting, September 1, 1875, a warrant charging me with an attempt to murder him, was placed in the hands of Mr. Dixon, and a large reward was offered for me, dead or alive. I went about openly at the capital, and at Holly Springs, where my family were, and back and forth frequently, yet no attempt was made to arrest me. It is my belief that the warrant was not intended for any such purpose, but that it was intended as a means of excusing my assassination.

When, finally, I had arrived in Washington, and a Senate committee was engaged in investigating the Mississippi election, a Yazoo grand jury, as heretofore mentioned, indicted me for murder. That was in 1876. Since that date I have travelled in Virginia, West Virginia, Maryland and Missouri, of the Southern States, and in New England, all of the Middle, and most of the Western States. During all that time my place of residence has been the District of Columbia.

Fritz Halder knew this when he addressed to me that souvenir. I have been in regular correspondence with officials and others, Democrats and Republicans, at Yazoo City during the entire time. I have made no effort whatever to conceal myself. On the contrary, I have frequently written for the press, and always over my own name.

In 1876 I appeared before the Senate committee, in obedi-

ence to its summons, and freely and fully told that committee
what I knew of the means employed by the enemy in Yazoo
County, in 1875, for the overthrow of our free State government. At that time I " grossly insulted " the enemy, when,
while under oath, I said :

"I have been in public affairs in Mississippi since the organization of the party in that State. With all my experience
there I have never expended a dollar to buy or influence the
support of the colored men in my behalf. I have never expended a dollar for whisky, cigars, liquors, or treats of any
kind or in any way to secure the favor of the colored people.
I have no general sort of affiliation or association with them,
nor do I recollect ever having resorted to any means used
by demagogues in politics to secure their favor. I reluctantly
accepted office and was never beaten. I believe the colored
people gave me their support because, from the outset, I exhibited a sincere desire to see them educated and made good
citizens; and I believe that they appreciated that desire.
We have never had a color line in Yazoo politics, except when
it was raised by the Democrats, and colored men have never
clamored for office ; we have never had any difficulty in securing a fair division of the offices among all classes. And of
the county offices the native whites have always held the larger
share. We have had few Northern men in office in that
county, less than of the Southern whites; nor do I believe colored men are cowardly. They are unused to guerrilla warfare.
I know they are not cowards. They are cautious and too
intelligent to be drawn into a conflict in which they must
necessarily be the only sufferers. I am speaking from an
experience of years. I have seen them tried. They will
fight for their rights and liberties, if they have anything to
fight with." I here solemnly repeat that testimony.

Major W. D. Gibbs, Judge W. S. Epperson, the editor of
the *Herald* and many more of the " best citizens " of Yazoo
were before that committee at the same time, or subsequently, and if it had been possible for any of them to have
produced any evidence at all against me, they would have

done it then and there. Every one of them under oath denied that force had been resorted to to carry that election, and defended the character and standing of Mr. Dixon.

Senator Bayard, of Delaware, was present on that occasion, and in the course of his examination of me, referred to that indictment as though he would make it appear that the cause of the enemy's hostility to me was their belief that I had wantonly killed Mr. Hilliard.

I have not failed from the day the first shot was fired in the campaign of 1875, both in Mississippi, at Washington, and wherever I have travelled, to tell the truth about the methods of the enemy in Mississippi elections, and when I could with propriety, have sought the privilege of doing so. If this be " secretive silence," then the enemy are at liberty to make the most of it.

Notwithstanding this "secretive silence," and notwithstanding the fact that this *Herald* letter was published three months ago, if, before or since that time any order or requisition has been issued for my arrest, by anybody, I have not been informed of it. Perhaps the conspirators are waiting for the book before drawing the fangs.

General Greenleaf, our Republican magistrate, Mr. Foote, and Charles are dead. The reader knows already how all, except Charles, died. The only one who died by violence was Mr. Foote. Charles could not get away from that " wonerful country." Having withdrawn from leadership in politics, he was permitted to pursue, in Washington County, his " designs upon the country" in peace. When the great fever epidemic that devastated Greenville first appeared in the State, he was absorbed with the managament of his lucrative business. He had passed safely through previous fever epidemics; he believed he could withstand this one. At all events he would not run away. So, while his wife and all the children had the fever and recovered, he died there. Sister Myra wrote me all the terrible details. One ray of comfort remained.

The enemy at last became reconciled to him, and on the
last terrible night (so sister Myra wrote), all night long the
voices of the colored people gathered at the little "nigro
church" he helped to build there, were raised to God in
prayer for him. The first I knew of it I read his name in the
long list of the dead which, so soon as communication could
be opened with the town, was published in the New York
Herald.

Wife! There are those who do not know the meaning of
the word. She who wins the love of one brave, honest man,
and marries him, in this country ought to be, and of right,
is, a royal consort, a queen, the equal of a sovereign, free
man.

"But the American people are not yet prepared to approve
of the intermarriage of blacks and whites."

I submit that the American people are always prepared
to do right when once it clearly appears. I speak plainly,
as it is my right and my duty to do. I have made the subject a special study for years, and I state as the result of my
observation and experience that I firmly believe the institution of concubinage universally prevailing at the South has
already so corrupted their physical bodies, so dwarfed their
intellects, and so dulled the moral perceptions of the
people that it is matter of very grave doubt with me
whether the social body has not already become so infected
with this form of miscegenation as to exclude all hope of its
ability to expel the virus without prompt and skillful aid from
without. I also firmly believe that this condition is due to
that policy which perpetuates *by force* the subjection of every
individual, male and female, of the weaker race, to the will
of the stronger; a policy which creates such a temptation to
prey upon the weaker, male and female, as the stronger is
unable to resist.

And, as to amalgamation: were there neither law nor
custom against it, not one in ten thousand of the present gen-

eration, of either race, would intermarry with the other. But the undisputed right to do so by such as might desire to would remove not only the fact but the badge of inferiority as between those two, and would elevate womanhood, whether covered by a light or a dark skin, unto more perfect self-control and, per consequence, into the realm of accountability.

" Would you have me marry my daughter to a negro ? "

What a silly question! How unworthy a thinking, practical Yankee! No! I would not have you do any such thing. But, since you have asked the question, I will venture to say that I would greatly prefer that you should marry your daughter to a negro than that you should consent that she be the mistress of one.

How dare I talk that way? How dare you consent, as you have been doing for two centuries, that every woman of African blood shall not hope for a higher life? How dare you consent, as you have been doing for two centuries, that while your daughter may not marry a " nigger," nor yet be the mistress of one, your *son* may make my daughter his concubine, though he shall not marry her?

I have never denied nor been ashamed of the fact that my wife and my children have in their veins negro blood; " nigro taint " is the enemy's phrase. The only thing about it which grieves me, is the fact that so many of our good girls and boys can see no difference between miscegenation as practiced at the South, and amalgamation through honorable marriage, or, seeing the true distinction, nevertheless prefer and honor the miscegenationist above the amalgamationist.

Wife and I have been married fourteen years; we have six children. During all the dreary years that have passed since the enemy, by force and murder, took possession of my new field, stole our grand old flag from us, and occupied our temples, this woman and these children have been my refuge.

The world moves, though Yazoo may remain a dead sea. History has changed the meaning of fame. Formerly it was a report, now it is a judgment. It will not always be true that " the heart which responds to the call of duty finds no rest except in the grave." Have patience—wait. The forty years in the wilderness are passing away.

Some day the telegraph, the telephone and the printing press will assemble the world in one congregation, and teachers will appear to instruct all in the language and justice of truth.